THE HISTORY AND CONQUESTS OF
ANCIENT ROME

THE HISTORY AND CONQUESTS OF
ANCIENT ROME

NIGEL RODGERS
CONSULTANT: Dr Hazel Dodge FSA

H
HERMES
HOUSE

For my father

This edition is published by Hermes House, an imprint of Anness Publishing Ltd,
Blaby Road, Wigston, Leicestershire LE18 4SE
Email: info@anness.com
Web: www.hermeshouse.com; www.annesspublishing.com

Anness Publishing has a new picture agency outlet for images for publishing,
promotions or advertising. Please visit our website www.practicalpictures.com
for more information.

Publisher: Joanna Lorenz
Managing Editor: Linda Fraser
Editor: Joy Wotton
Designer: Nigel Partridge
Cover Designer: Adelle Morris
Illustrator: Peter Bull Art Studio
Production Controller: Wendy Lawson

ETHICAL TRADING POLICY

Because of our ongoing ecological investment programme, you, as our customer, can
have the pleasure and reassurance of knowing that a tree is being cultivated on your
behalf to naturally replace the materials used to make the book you are holding.
For further information about this scheme, go to www.annesspublishing.com/trees

PUBLISHER'S NOTE

Although the advice and information in this book are believed to be accurate and true
at the time of going to press, neither the authors nor the publisher can accept any legal
responsibility or liability for any errors or omissions that may be made.

CONTENTS

THE ARCHETYPAL EMPIRE

Above: Rome's influence was as much cultural as political. The Deir, a temple-tomb at Petra, Jordan, was built in the 1st century AD in Roman-influenced style before Rome annexed Petra itself in AD106.

Below: The ceremonial Via Sacra (Sacred Way) runs through the Forum Romanum, which itself was the centre of Roman life. The Arch of Titus is visible in the background.

Rome remains the archetypal empire, the object of admiration, fascination and at times of repulsion. How a small settlement of farmers grew into an empire that ruled so much of the then known world is one of the greatest tales in history. The ruins left by Roman might – aqueducts, bridges, basilicas, arches, baths and temples, many still standing, a few still in use 2,000 years on – have cast a spell on subsequent generations. Rome's empire was not only large – it stretched from Scotland to Egypt – but it lasted a very long time. For six centuries, Rome was mistress of the Mediterranean and western Europe, its sphere of influence reaching even further. If Rome could fall, observers have wondered, how secure is our civilization? Greater than Rome's physical legacy, however, has been its influence on culture and institutions.

This book is written in the Roman (or Latin) alphabet. Nearly two-thirds of the words in the English language derive directly or indirectly from Latin, the Roman language. Spanish, French,

Portuguese and Italian are Romance languages, direct descendants of Latin, originally the language of central Italy. The Senate, the upper house in countries like the United States and Ireland, is the Roman name for a Roman institution. The emblem of the United States and many now-vanished empires is an eagle, modelled on that of Jupiter, Rome's chief deity. The American motto, *E Pluribus Unum*, and the British motto, *Fidis Defensor*, are in Latin, the study of which was long considered essential for anybody with pretensions to education, and which is still useful for law and medicine.

Much of the world's law is derived from the legal codes of imperial Rome. The ideal of a world guided by common laws and international institutions, whether political, judicial or economic, owes much to Roman attempts, however imperfect, to create an empire based on law as much as force. The United States, the United Nations and the European Union – all implicitly reflect the influence of Roman universalism.

IMPERIALISM – HARD AND SOFT

Rome did not acquire or keep its empire by noble ideals or fine words. It was, first and last, a nation of soldiers. The triumphal arches the Romans erected around their empire celebrated bloody military victories. For a triumph, a general had to have killed at least 5,000 (sometimes 10,000) of the enemy. Our word emperor comes from *imperator*, victorious commander-in-chief, for emperors were above all the supreme generals of Rome.

As any of the peoples who revolted against Rome could attest, the Romans could be methodically brutal in their reprisals. Tacitus, greatest if gloomiest of Roman historians, has one Briton defeated by Rome's might say, "You made a desert and you called it peace." As Rome

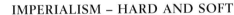

acquired its empire, it grew fantastically rich. By the 1st century AD, when Roman power was nearing its height, probably one person in three in the city of Rome was a slave. The whole Mediterranean world had to pay for the luxury and power of the conquerors, with money, goods and slaves. But if a few peoples rose in revolt, many others cooperated in what became a pan-imperial venture.

If Rome benefited from its empire – and empires are run, in the first instance, for the benefit of their rulers – then the advantages did not run all one way. As the empire matured, none of the privileges of being Roman was denied to former subject peoples. Rome was unique among ancient states in being ready to extend its citizenship to others. Under the empire, prosperity spread out in ripples, thanks to the benign aspects of Roman government. If people in the provinces paid taxes to Rome, these were often lighter than the taxes previously paid to their own rulers. In AD14, at the end of

his life, the first emperor Augustus was touched by a spontaneous demonstration. The passengers and crew of a ship just arrived from Alexandria put on garlands and burnt incense to him, saying they owed him their lives and liberty to sail the seas. These Alexandrians, from a great trading city but not Roman citizens, knew that their freedom and prosperity depended on the *Pax Romana*, the Roman peace that Augustus established and that his successors long maintained.

PAX ROMANA: THE ROMAN PEACE

It is easy to forget the benefits of external peace and internal security when they have become the accustomed way of life. Until well into the 19th century, however, most cities in continental Europe, like cities across Asia, were walled to protect them from attacks. What Rome gave the war-torn ancient world was unprecedented peace, security and stability for more than two centuries after Augustus reunited the empire in

Above: The empire in AD200, centred still on the Mediterranean, but now stretching from the Middle East to Scotland.

Below: The arch at Timgad, Algeria, commemorates Trajan, the city's founder. Cities were built across the empire with the full range of civic amenities: baths, theatres, amphitheatres, forums and triumphal arches.

Above: Rome's impact on Western culture has at times been almost overpowering. Pennsylvania Railroad Station in New York (built 1906–10, now demolished), simply recreated the interior of the huge baths of Caracalla in Rome, built 1700 years before.

Below: The Jefferson Memorial, Washington DC, repeats the form of the Pantheon in Rome of 1700 years earlier. This was a political and architectural homage, the young Republic saluting the ancient one.

30BC. Even the walls surrounding Rome were allowed to decay. Many cities across the empire also dispensed with walls, except for ceremonial perimeters. The Roman peace was upheld by a small army of some 300,000 men, perhaps half of one per cent of the population. The army itself was often occupied in building the network of *c.*50,000 miles (80,000km) of roads that stretched across the empire.

The Mediterranean Sea was cleared of pirates to become a marine highway dotted with seaside villas, a state of affairs not to recur until the 19th century. Land communications were better across Europe and western Asia under the Romans than at any other time until the coming of canals and railways. Lighthouses, from the great *pharos* of Alexandria in Egypt to many smaller examples, guided ships. With Rome's enduring peace, and its relatively light taxation, came novel prosperity. As city ruins show, some desert regions in north Africa and western Asia enjoyed under Roman rule a prosperity never to be repeated, while it took a millennium for most cities in western Europe to regain Roman levels of population and wealth.

MULTIRACIAL, MULTIFAITH

Much can be said against an empire that relied so heavily on slavery and a culture in which the chief entertainment of many citizens was watching men or animals fight one another, at times to death. But one accusation cannot be levelled against Rome: that of racism. When the Romans talked of "barbarians", the term simply denoted cultural and social backwardness and brutishness. The inhabitants of previously barbaric provinces, such as Gaul (France), North Africa and Spain, could and did become Romans, some eventually entering the Roman Senate – to the disgust of conservative senators. Several such "provincials" became emperors later in the empire. Racial background had no effect on a person's career. The emperor who presided over Rome's millennial jubilee in AD248 was called Philip the Arab because he came from Arabia Nabataea, now Jordan. Whole dynasties of emperors came from Libya, Spain and Syria. Rome extended the benefits of its empire ever wider, until finally in AD212 almost everyone except slaves acquired full Roman citizenship. Even slaves were being better treated by then, but slavery in a society with no colour bar was very different from that in 19th-century America. Many slaves were freed; a few prospered.

Romans, like most polytheists, were religiously tolerant. The myriad faiths of the empire were not suppressed but regulated, some being incorporated into the Roman pantheon. As long as subjects offered incense to the emperor – a political and not a religious gesture, as few educated Romans literally believed in the emperor's divinity – people had freedom of worship. The Roman suppression of Druidism in Britain, like the crushing of Jewish revolts in Judaea and later their intermittent persecutions of Christians, was political. The Druids potentially threatened Roman rule in Britain; the Jews had violently rejected Roman rule in Judaea and surrounding lands; and the Christians appeared to be disloyal.

Roman culture was so much influenced by the Greek that we often talk of "Graeco-Roman culture". This became effectively the cultural standard, even when influenced by local cultures – Roman civilization in Britain, for instance, was not identical to that in Syria. In the countryside especially, older beliefs and customs persisted beneath a Roman veneer. But it was possible to travel, unarmed, from Britain or Spain to Syria using one currency and speaking only two languages: Latin in the west and Balkans, Greek elsewhere. The traveller would have found that almost every city in the empire had its public baths, forum (market and meeting place), theatres, basilicas (halls), public games as well as students of Greek and Latin poetry and rhetoric. Rome conquered culturally as well as politically. Gauls, Spaniards, Africans and Britons adopted the Roman way of life as it seemed better than the alternatives. At the very least, this adoption helped the ambitious to rise.

ROME'S ENDURING LEGACY

The fall of the Roman empire in the west is irresistibly fascinating and rouses endless debate as to its causes. More significant is that the potent *idea* of the Roman empire did not expire in AD476. The Holy Roman Empire, created when Charlemagne was crowned by the Pope in Rome in AD800, attempted with some success to revive the empire, and it lasted for a millennium. Then Napoleon founded his short-lived empire, complete with eagles, triumphal arches and opportunities for other peoples to join the imperial regime. Perhaps, however, in the end the greatest heir of Rome was spiritual rather than military.

Within living memory, the Roman Catholic Church held all services in Latin, and the Pope still lives in Rome, in a line dating back almost 2000 years to St Peter, the first pope. As Eusebius, the "first Christian historian" (AD263–339), pointed out, it needed the peace and unity established by Augustus for Christianity to spread and establish itself. The Catholic

Church, with its hierarchy and its universalist ambitions, is the most obvious inheritor of ancient Rome.

Rome's greatest legacy is probably its universality, this longing to include all humanity within its realm. Rome's great poet Virgil voiced novel feelings for all human suffering. Rome's wars of conquest were often brutal, but the Roman peace atoned for this in the end. In the west especially, Roman culture went deep. Virgil's poetry was known to ordinary soldiers on Hadrian's Wall as evidence attests, not just to an elite.

> *"You created one homeland*
> *for the differing peoples*
> *Those without justice*
> *benefited from your rule;*
> *By allowing the vanquished*
> *to share in your own laws*
> *You made a city*
> *out of what was once the world."*

The words of the poet Namatianus, written around AD420, are poignant, as, only a few years earlier, the Goths had sacked Rome. His poem summarizes Rome's claim to be the universal city of humanity. To Rome as much as to Greece the world owes what has become Western civilization. The world without Rome would be unimaginably different. Arguably, it would be much the poorer.

Above: The Pantheon in Rome is among Rome's finest, best-preserved of temples, and its great dome has proved lastingly influential. It was built by the emperor Hadrian in AD118–28, but here it is shown as it was in the 18th century, with small towers.

Below: The Roman poet Virgil, flanked by two of the muses, was a protégé of the emperor Augustus. Virgil's greatest poem, the Aeneid, *became imperial Rome's epic, but it is an epic marked by concern for all humanity, not just the victors.*

TIMELINE

The history of Rome in its varying forms – as a tiny primitive kingdom, as an ever-growing republic, as a world-ruling empire and finally as the ghost or legend of that empire – stretches back to the early Iron Age. Its history really ends only in the 19th century, when the last Holy Roman Emperor abdicated and Napoleon Bonaparte crowned himself Emperor of the French in an obvious attempt to resurrect Rome's claims to universal empire.

The Romans themselves dated all events *ab urbe condita*, from the (mythical) foundation of the City by Romulus in 753BC – an event they saw, not without some reason, as being of world-transforming significance. Only in the 5th century AD did the present Christian calendar supersede the old Roman system.

Early dates down to at least 350BC remain very uncertain, but the broad sweep of Roman history remains unmistakeable and remarkable: the rise and ultimate fall of a mighty empire, whose memories lived on so potently that later rulers tried to resuscitate its titles and grandeurs.

Note: Very early dates, up to 350BC, are approximate.

753–451BC

753 Legendary founding of city by (mythical) brothers Romulus and Remus; Romulus reigns as sole king to 717, regarded by later Romans as actual founder of Rome.

***c*.650** The Etruscan kings (possibly Etruscan outcasts) arrive in Rome.

***c*.590** Solon reforms the Athenian constitution, making it semi-democratic.

578–535 Reign of Servius Tullius; forms the first Assembly, the *comitia centuriata*, on kinship lines.

534–509 Reign of Tarquinius Superbus, the last of the kings; building of first temple on Capitoline Hill.

509 Expulsion of Tarquin and end of Etruscan cultural predominance in Rome. Formation of Republic; kings replaced by elected officials, praetors and then consuls; first treaty with Carthage.

496 Rome defeats Latins at Battle of Lake Regillus; makes equal treaty of alliance with Latins.

494–440 Struggle of the Orders. Patricians (the 100 nobles supposedly chosen by Romulus) versus plebeians (everybody else).

493 First tribunes appointed to defend plebeian interests.

480 Greeks led by Athens defeat Persian invaders at Salamis; beginning of the classical age in Greece.

474 Battle of Cumae: Greeks defeat Etruscans and Carthaginians at sea; beginnings of Etruscan decline.

471 Creation of new Assembly of the Plebs, which elects tribunes annually.

450–300BC

450 Twelve Tables of the Law published; the first written laws help plebeians.

449 Tribunes increased to ten and their sacrosanctity legally guaranteed.

440 *Lex Cannuleia* establishes equality between plebs and patricians; institution of censors.

431–404 Peloponnesian War between Athens and Sparta; Athens defeated.

425 Fidenae (city) taken from Veii.

421 First plebeian quaestor.

405–396 Long siege and capture of Veii, the key to southern Etruria.

***c*.400** Celts (Gauls) invade northern Italy.

***c*.390** Sack of Rome by invading Gauls.

386 Rome grants citizens of Caere *hospitium publicum*, privileged status.

***c*.378** Building of Servian wall.

367 One consul must always be plebeian.

343–41 First war against Samnites, highland people.

338 Defeat of the Latins; Latin League dissolved; Roman power extends into Campania.

336–323 Alexander the Great of Macedon overwhelms Greek states and conquers Persian empire before dying in Babylon. His empire is divided between his generals, the Diadochi (successors).

329 Terracina becomes a Roman colony.

327–304 Second Samnite War.

321 Romans defeated by Samnites at Caudine Forks.

312 Censorship of Appius Claudius; building of first Roman road, the Via Appia to Capua, and Aqua Appia, Rome's first aqueduct.

299–200 BC

298–90 Third Samnite War.

295 Samnites defeated at Sentium.

287 *Lex Hortensia*: plebiscites (votes of the people) become law.

280–275 War with King Pyrrhus of Epirus.

275 Romans defeat Pyrrhus.

264–241 First Punic War.

260 Romans build their first fleet.

259 Roman victory at sea at Mylae.

256–55 Regulus invades Africa, but is defeated.

249 Romans defeated at Drapana.

241 Final Roman victory off the Aègates Islands; Sicily the first Roman province.

238 Sardinia and Corsica annexed.

223 Successful Roman campaigns in Cisalpine Gaul lead to first colonies there.

220 Censorship of Flaminius; builds Via Flaminia to Rimini and Circus Flaminius.

219 Hannibal besieges and takes Saguntum in Spain.

218–202 Second Punic War.

218–217 Hannibal crosses Alps; his army defeats Romans at Ticinus and later at Trebbia.

216 Roman defeat at Cannae; Hannibal forms alliance with Philip V of Macedonia; some allies abandon Rome.

214–205 First Macedonian War.

213–211 Siege of Syracuse.

211–206 Scipio campaigns in Spain.

209 Scipio captures Cartagena.

207 Hasdrubal leads army into Italy.

203 Scipio invades Africa, wins Battle of the Great Plains.

202 Scipio defeats Hannibal at Zama. End of Carthaginian overseas power.

199–100 BC

200–196 Second Macedonian War.

197–179 Gracchus ends wars in Spain; Spain organized into two provinces.

197 Philip V of Macedon defeated.

196 Flaminius declares "freedom of the Greeks" at Isthmia, near Corinth.

194 Romans evacuate Greece.

191 Cisalpine Gaul (northern Italy) conquered by Rome.

190 Seleucid king Antiochus III of Syria defeated at Magnesia; Seleucids expelled from Asia Minor.

184 Censorship of Cato the Elder.

179 Aemilian bridge, first stone bridge over Tiber, built.

168 Perseus of Macedonia defeated at Pydna; Macedonia becomes Roman dependency.

167 Direct taxation of Roman citizens abolished; sack of Epirus, 150,000 Greeks enslaved; Jewish revolt led by Maccabeus against Antiochus IV; Polybius arrives in Rome as hostage.

149–146 Third Punic War; Africa (northern Tunisia) becomes Roman province.

146 Corinth and Carthage sacked, Achaea and Macedonia Roman provinces.

141 Parthians capture Babylon: final decline of Seleucid empire.

136–32 First Sicilian Slave War.

133 Tiberius Gracchus killed; kingdom of Pergamum (western Asia Minor) left to Rome by last king.

107–100 Marius consul six times; reforms army, defeats Cimbri and Teutones and Jugurtha of Numidia (Algeria).

103–100 Second Sicilian Slave War.

99–1 BC

91 Beginning of Social War.

90 *Lex Julia*: full citizenship for Italians.

89–85 First war against Mithradates.

87 Marius seizes power in Rome.

86 Sulla sacks Athens.

82 Sulla becomes dictator; second Mithradatic War.

80 Sulla resigns dictatorship.

73–71 Slave revolt of Spartacus.

70 Consulship of Pompey and Crassus.

67 Pompey eliminates pirates.

66 Pompey given eastern command.

63 Consulship of Cicero.

60 First Triumvirate: Pompey, Crassus and Caesar.

59 Caesar consul for the first time.

58–51 Caesar's Gallic Wars.

55–54 Caesar "invades" Britain.

53 Crassus killed at Carrhae.

49 Caesar crosses the Rubicon.

48 Pompey defeated at Pharsalus; Caesar meets Cleopatra, and they become lovers.

44 Caesar assassinated.

43 Second Triumvirate: Antony, Octavian and Lepidus. Murder of Cicero.

42 Republicans defeated at Philippi: empire divided.

36 Octavian defeats Sextus Pompeius.

31 Battle of Actium.

30 Suicides of Antony and Cleopatra; Egypt annexed by Octavian; Roman empire reunited.

27 Octavian assumes title *Augustus*.

16–9 Annexations of Alpine and Balkan regions under Tiberius; Drusus reaches the Elbe.

12 Death of Agrippa.

AD1–49

4 Death of Gaius forces Augustus to recall Tiberius from exile in Rhodes.

6 Judaea becomes Roman province after death of Herod the Great (in 4BC); start of the Great Pannonian revolt (lasting until AD9), which distracts Tiberius from planned campaigns in Germany.

8 Poet Ovid exiled to Tomis on Black Sea.

9 Disastrous loss of three legions in Germany under Varus; frontier withdrawn to Rhine.

14 Death of Augustus; Tiberius succeeds as emperor; Germanicus quashes Rhine legions' mutiny and campaigns into Germany to avenge Varus' defeat.

19 Death of Germanicus, the designated heir, in Syria.

27 Tiberius retires to villa on Capri, fuelling rumours of his depravities there; Sejanus acts as his sole minister in Rome.

30 or 33 Crucifixion of Jesus.

31 Execution of Sejanus for conspiracy.

37 Death of Tiberius; accession of Gaius Caligula; birth of Nero.

41 Assassination of Caligula; Claudius succeeds him as emperor. Annexation of Mauretania (Algeria/Morocco) as two imperial provinces.

42 Abortive rebellion of Scribonus, governor of Dalmatia.

43 Invasion of Britain, which becomes province. Claudius increasingly relies on freedmen, who form the nucleus of imperial civil service.

46 Thrace becomes province.

49 Claudius marries his niece Agrippina; Seneca becomes Nero's tutor.

AD50–99

51 Caratacus, British prince, defeated and captured.

54 Death of Claudius; accession of Nero; Seneca and Burrus joint chief ministers.

59 Murder of Agrippina, Nero's over-powering mother.

60–1 Revolt of Boudicca and the Iceni in Britain; sack of London, Colchester and St Albans.

62 Death of Burrus and end of Seneca's influence; Nero increasingly extravagant

63–6 Settlement of Armenia and eastern frontier by Corbulo.

64 Great Fire of Rome; Nero persecutes Christians as scapegoats. Begins building the Golden House.

66–70 First Jewish War; Vespasian and Titus suppress Jewish revolt.

68 Suicide of Nero; accession of Galba.

68–9 Year of the Four Emperors: Galba, then Vitellius proclaimed emperor, then Otho, who commits suicide, leaving Vespasian sole emperor.

70 Capture and sack of Jerusalem.

79 Death of Vespasian; accession of Titus; destruction of Pompeii and Herculaneum by Vesuvius.

80 Inauguration of Colosseum at Rome.

81 Death of Titus; accession of Domitian.

85–92 Dacians check Domitian's campaigns and force subsidy payment.

88 Start of construction of *limes*, patrolled frontiers, along the line of the Neckar to cut off the Rhine-Danube re-entrant angle.

96 Assassination of Domitian; Nerva proclaimed emperor by Senate.

98 Death of Nerva; accession of Trajan.

AD100–199

101–6 Trajan's campaigns lead to new province of Dacia (Romania).

106 Annexation of Arabia Petraea (Jordan).

111–14 Construction of Trajan's column and forum at Rome; they are dedicated in 112–13.

113–17 War with Parthians. Conquest of Armenia, Assyria and Mesopotamia (Iraq).

115–17 Jewish revolt in Cyprus, Cyrene and Egypt.

117 Death of Trajan; accession of Hadrian.

118–28 Building of Pantheon, Rome.

121–2 Hadrian visits Britain; starts building of Hadrian's Wall.

131–5 Jewish revolt under Bar Kochba defeated; Jerusalem left a ruin.

138 Death of Hadrian; accession of Antoninus Pius.

142 Building of Antonine Wall across Scotland; Hadrian's Wall abandoned.

150–63 Revolt in northern Britain and abandonment of Antonine Wall.

161 Death of Antoninus; accession of Marcus Aurelius and Lucius Verus.

162–6 Parthian War. Ctesiphon and Seleucia sacked; plague brought back.

167 Marcomanni and Quadi, Germanic tribes, raid across Danube and reach Italy.

168–80 Wars of Marcus Aurelius.

180 Death of Marcus; accession of Commodus; peace with the Germans.

192 Commodus murdered; civil war.

193 Septimius Severus emperor in Rome.

195–9 Severus' Parthian campaigns.

AD200–299

211 Severus dies in York; leaves empire to sons Caracalla and Geta. Caracalla murders Geta.

212 *Constitutio Antoniniana*: Roman citizenship for all free men in empire.

217 Assassination of Caracalla, briefly succeeded by Macrinus.

218 Accession of Elagabalus.

222 Assassination of Elagabalus; accession of Alexander Severus; effective rule of Julia Mamaea, his mother.

235 Assassination of Alexander Severus; anarchy for almost 50 years – at least 30 emperors.

241 Shapur I (to 272), new Persian king, determined to revive old Persian empire.

251 Emperor Decius killed by Goths; plague ravages empire; persecution of Christians.

253–60 Valerian and Gallienus become co-emperors; Persian invasions.

260 "Gallic empire" formed. Valerian captured by Persians; sole reign of Gallienus; army reorganized, adminstrative capital moved to Milan.

268 Zenobia, Queen of Palmyra, breaks away with eastern provinces and Egypt.

270 Accession of Aurelian.

273 Zenobia defeated by Aurelian.

284 Accession of Diocletian; joint rule with Maximian as Augusti in 286.

286–96 Breakaway British "empire" under Carausius and Allectus.

293 Constantius I and Galerius appointed Caesars in new tetrarchy.

297–8 Persian War brings new Roman gains in east (now Kurdistan).

AD300–399

303–11 Last persecution of Christians.

305 Diocletian and Maximian retire.

306 Death of Constantius; his son Constantine I acclaimed emperor by troops but recognized only as Caesar of western provinces by other rulers.

312 Maxentius defeated at Milvian Bridge; Constantine sole ruler in west.

313 Edict of Milan: religious tolerance.

324 Constantine becomes sole emperor.

324–30 Foundation of Constantinople as New Rome.

325 Church Council of Nicaea presided over by Constantine.

337 Death of Constantine; empire split between his three sons: Constantine II (d. 340), Constantius II (d. 361) and Constans (d. 350).

355 Julian appointed Caesar in west.

361–3 Sole reign of Julian, pagan restoration; killed on Persian campaign.

364 Valens and Valentinian I joint emperors.

375 Valentinian dies of stroke.

378 Valens killed by invading Goths at battle of Adrianople; Goths occupy Roman territory south of Danube.

379 Theodosius I becomes emperor; accepts the Goths as federates.

382 Removal of Altar of Victory from Senate House; campaign against pagans.

394 Battle of the Cold River; Theodosius defeats rivals Argobast and Eugenius.

395 On his death, Theodosius divides empire between sons: Honorius emperor in west, Arcadius in east. Stilicho effective ruler in west.

AD400–535

404 Western imperial court moved from Milan to Ravenna, secure behind marshes.

406 German invaders cross frozen Rhine and sack Trier, the Gallic capital.

410 Last troops withdrawn from Britain; Visigoths under Alaric sack Rome; Alaric dies; Goths later settle in southwest Gaul.

421 Constantine III becomes effective ruler of western empire.

425 Valentinian III emperor in west; mother Galla Placidia at first is real ruler.

434 Attila becomes king of the Huns.

439 Vandals capture Carthage.

446 "Groans of the Britons": traditional last appeal by Romanized Britons for imperial help.

451 Battle of Châlons: Huns defeated by joint forces of Visigoths and Romans under Aetius.

452 Attila's invasion of Italy halted by Pope Leo I.

454 Murder of Aetius.

455 Death of Valentinian III; Vandals sack Rome.

476 Last emperor Romulus Augustulus deposed by mercenary chief Odoacer, who takes power himself. End of the western empire; imperial insignia sent to Constantinople.

493 Theodoric, king of Ostrogoths, becomes ruler of Italy.

527 Accession of Justinian I as emperor in Constantinople.

533 Belisarius, Byzantine general, reconquers North Africa from Vandals.

535 Belisarius begins reconquest of Italy.

PART ONE

ROME: THE WORLD'S FIRST SUPERPOWER

The rise of Rome, from the mythically simple beginnings of a few dwellings above the river Tiber to dominion over the whole Mediterranean world, was seen by Romans themselves as inevitable and divinely ordained. The qualities on which the Romans prided themselves – piety, fidelity and above all *virtus*, meaning courage, ability, strength and excellence – were what made their empire possible, indeed invincible. So long as its citizens retained them, Rome would remain mistress of the world. What is remarkable about Rome is that, almost without exception, it conquered all other powers, making it the sole superpower of the ancient Mediterranean world. This was a region where many of the great civilizations of antiquity – Egyptian, Babylonian, Carthaginian, Etruscan, Greek – converged, with only distant China ever rivalling Rome in stability, power and longevity. Rome was the heir of these ancient civilizations of the Middle East and Mediterranean, absorbing and propagating their cultures, while adding its own distinctive elements to make a civilization that was unique. When Rome finally fell, it not only left us its great architectural and engineering feats – aqueducts, arches, roads – but also the corpus of Roman law, the Catholic Church, and the idea of a universal empire that could extend its benefits to all under its sway, irrespective of racial background. Rome gave a huge area many centuries of peace, but it implanted also the ideal of a universal, basically benevolent state. This has made Rome an unrivalled cultural as well as political superpower, that continues to inspire and influence the world long after its fall.

Left: As Rome became the most wealthy and powerful city in the ancient world, it drew in foreigners as craftsmen, teachers, traders – and slaves.

CHAPTER I

AN EMPIRE OF FORCE AND LAW

Rome did not acquire its empire in a few dazzling victories, but piecemeal, sometimes unintentionally, if very rarely peacefully. Rome's growth from a small settlement on the Tiber into a great empire was largely due to its military prowess and ruthless aggressiveness. Military service was a central part of life for Roman citizens. Adaptable, superbly disciplined and incredibly tough, the Roman army made Rome an imperial power. This gradual and methodical process took many hundreds of years. While such an approach may have lacked glamour, it certainly created an empire that proved very long-lived.

If most Romans experienced army life, many were also lawyers. Roman respect for the law and legality, although there was no written constitution, long safeguarded the civilian basis of politics. For a surprisingly long time, the Roman army did not intervene in civilian affairs. Its generals, no matter how great their victories, had to relinquish their commands as they entered the city, becoming ordinary citizens again and liable to prosecution for any misconduct. Even the emperor did not claim to be above the law and wore a toga (civilian dress), not armour. Rome also freely extended its citizenship to ever more cities, one of the main secrets of its success as an imperial power.

Left: This detail from the Arch of Constantine in Rome shows Emperor Constantine addressing his army – the sometimes rebellious basis of Rome's imperial might.

LEGENDARY BEGINNINGS
753–509 BC

Above: Controlling the lowest crossing of the river Tiber, Rome was poised to dominate the valley of central Italy's largest river when it gained the power to do so. For long periods, however, the Tiber was as much a boundary as a route for expansion inland.

According to legend Rome was founded in 753 BC by Romulus and Remus, twin princes of Alba Longa, supposedly itself founded four centuries earlier by Aeneas, a Trojan prince. The twins, his distant descendants, were abandoned as babies on the orders of Amulius, who had usurped their kingdom and ordered their deaths. Miraculously, a she-wolf appeared from a wood to suckle them, and they were brought up by Faustinus, a kindly shepherd, on the Palatine Hill. When they grew up, they killed the usurper and together founded a new city: Rome. But they soon quarrelled, Romulus killing Remus for jumping over his ploughed boundary line. Romulus then populated Rome by inviting outlaws and homeless men to join him, and by abducting the young women of his neighbours in the famous "Rape of the Sabine Women". When the Sabine men marched back in force to reclaim their women, the latter, by now used to being Roman wives, intervened to prevent a battle and the two peoples intermarried. Romulus later ascended into heaven in a thunderstorm, becoming divine. From such violent, mythic beginnings sprang the Eternal City, Rome.

Right: According to legend, the twins Romulus and Remus, distant descendants of the Trojan prince Aeneas, were suckled by a she-wolf after they had been abandoned as babies. In 753 BC they founded the city of Rome, which bears Romulus' name.

THE EARLY SETTLEMENTS

Archaeology tells us that by the mid-8th century BC an unimpressive settlement existed on the Palatine Hill. The first Romans were actually Latin farmers or shepherds, the Latins being a subgroup of the Italian peoples, living in separate villages of small huts on the Palatine and the Esquiline Hills. Beneath and between these hills were marshy valleys. Despite later Roman propaganda to the contrary, this was not a particularly healthy or fertile spot, but an island had two advantages. In the midst of the fast-flowing river Tiber, it offered the first practical crossing upriver from the sea 16 miles (25km) distant, while the hills provided good defensive positions.

The settlements remained extremely primitive until the arrival – once again enshrined in myth – of the Etruscan Kings, who traditionally ruled Rome from 616 to 509 BC. Certainly, at about this time Rome came under the sway of the Etruscans. They were a civilized people who dominated Italy from Bologna to the Bay of Naples. Rome's strategic position on the Tiber meant the Etruscans, approaching the height of their power, inevitably wanted control over it. In close contact with the Greek cities to the south, whose art influenced but did not overwhelm their art, the Etruscans were a cheerful, even hedonistic, race, fond of the arts, women, banquets and athletics – or so their surviving bronzes and tomb paintings suggest. We still cannot fully read their language, even though, like the Roman alphabet, it uses a version of the Greek alphabet, but the Etruscans did not write very much.

A NEW CITY

It is probably true to say that the kings made Rome a city rather than a mere huddle of villages. The *Forum Romanum*, the market/meeting place, heart of the city and later of the empire, was established on drained marshland and paved, as was the *Forum Boarium* (cattle market) close to the river.

Tarquinius Priscus, the "good Tarquin", who ruled between *c.*616 and 579BC, held the first census. Citizens were organized into three tribes, each having ten *curiae*, or wards. From these 30 wards the kings chose 300 patricians, or heads of extended families, to sit in the advisory council known as the Senate. The first Assembly, the *comitia curiata*, is also thought to have emerged about this time, although its powers are unknown.

Priscus' successor, King Servius Tullius, reorganized the state, dividing Romans into five classes according to their wealth. Each class was subdivided into centuries, each century being roughly equal in wealth. All citizens were liable for army service, apart from those in the last and poorest class, who could not afford to arm themselves. A legion, or levy, had 6,000 infantry and 300 cavalry, the cavalry being provided by the richest century. In the newly appointed *comitia centuriata*, or Assembly by Hundreds, each century voted as a single block, with the richest (but smallest) century voting first. The vote was decided as soon as an absolute majority of centuries was reached, which inevitably gave the rich centuries the most influence and the poorest (and biggest) centuries the least. Rome never operated on the principle of "one man one vote".

At this time Rome acquired Ostia at the mouth of the Tiber as well as its first wooden bridge across the river. The period culminated in the construction of the first temple to Jupiter, king of the gods, on the Capitoline Hill. Originally simply constructed, the temple was later rebuilt ever more splendidly, and became *the* symbol of Roman power.

Above: The first Romans lived in simple huts, as shown in this mosaic of life on the Nile.

THE FOUNDING OF THE REPUBLIC

Around 509BC, the kings were suddenly and finally expelled, and the word Etruscan, like the word king, became an insult among Romans. According to legend, the last Etruscan king, Tarquinius Superbus, meaning "the proud", so angered the Roman nobles that they drove him out and declared a Republic, which they dominated through the Senate. From now on, the state was to be run by annually elected officials A new regime based on puritanical, patriotic *virtus*, or courage, was established that would serve Rome well through its coming struggles.

Below: This landscape is typical of the often wild mountains of central Italy east of Rome.

THE CONQUEST OF ITALY
501–266BC

After the expulsion of the Etruscan kings Rome became less wealthy and powerful. The other cities of Latium, which were similar in language (Latin) and culture to Rome, turned against her. Surrounded by enemies, especially the Samnites to the east and the Volscians to the south, Rome was forced to ally itself with them on equal terms – although it was never to accept equality with any city for long.

THE RISE OF THE PLEBEIANS
Inside Rome, the advent of the Republic caused an economic slump. This triggered a lengthy conflict, which was known as the Conflict of the Orders or classes, between the people (plebeians) and the patricians, the old heads of the family who traced their descent from the original Senate members and who still monopolized power. In 494BC the plebeians – who included some moderately rich citizens and many independent farmers or artisans – threatened to secede from the state and leave Rome. These people formed the core of the army, so it was a very serious

threat. After several attempts, the plebeians' threat worked and they acquired two tribunes of the people, special officials to defend their interests. Later, in 449BC, their number was increased to ten and they were given special status, regarded as sacrosanct or defended by the gods.

In 471BC the tribunes summoned a special Assembly of the Plebs to run alongside existing councils. At this time, only patricians could interpret the unwritten laws. Only in 450BC were laws written down on 12 tables of stone for everyone to see. These tables, often masterpieces of legal precision, became the foundation of Roman justice. In 421BC the first plebeian quaestors were elected, and from 367BC one of the two consuls (the top magistrates who led the armies) had to be a plebeian. The patricians tried to transfer some of the consul's powers to a new official, the quaestor, but from 337BC there was also a plebeian praetor. Finally, in 287BC a law, the Lex Hortensia (Roman laws were named after their proposer), declared that plebiscites, votes of the plebeian Assembly, could become law. This completed a social revolution without bloodshed – albeit with much dispute – and is an example of the Roman genius for pragmatism.

EXPANSION AND INVASION
Throughout this domestic turmoil, Rome steadily expanded its influence and territory. To the north, just across the Tiber, stood the wealthy Etruscan city of Veii, controlling a network of roads. Rome became involved in an intermittent 40-year war with this great rival. It ended only after Camillus, made emergency ruler, forced the army to campaign continuously – without even stopping for the harvest – and used a drainage tunnel to capture Veii in

Above: Rome alternately fought and treated with its often powerful Etruscan neighbours. This fresco from the 3rd century BC shows a treaty being agreed.

Below: The Via Appia, the first great Roman road, was built to connect Rome with Capua in 312BC and was later extended to Brindisi.

Left: Paestum was one of the first Greek cities in southern Italy to be conquered by Rome in the 4th century BC. Its magnificent temple of Ceres, with massive Doric columns, is one of the best-preserved of the early Greek temples and dates from c.500BC.

396BC. This was a very important conquest. Overnight, it almost doubled Rome's territory, and the way to Etruria (Tuscany/Umbria) was opened.

A few years later, however, Rome faced acute danger. A horde of Gauls, barbarous Celts, swept through Italy in 390BC. Rome sent the whole of its army – some 15,000 men – to face them, but the Gauls, twice that number and better fighters, destroyed it almost completely. The city lay defenceless and most Romans fled, apart from a garrison on Capitoline Hill and some elderly senators who, as Livy related, "went home to await the enemy, fearless". A general massacre ensued and Rome was burnt to the ground.

MASTERING PENINSULAR ITALY

After this disaster many were tempted to abandon Rome, but Camillus rallied them to rebuild the city. In 378BC the Servian wall was constructed. It was 12ft (3.6m) thick and 24ft (7.5m) high and enclosed 1,000 acres (427 ha) – then a huge area. Rome would not fall to barbarians again for 800 years. Troubles with Rome's Latin allies followed, however. After peaceful methods of dealing with them failed, a four-year period of dogged fighting ensued before the Romans gained final victory in 338BC. The Latin League was dissolved, with each city being linked to Rome while retaining internal autonomy. Many were given citizenship, without voting rights (*civitas sine suffragio*). This halfway status satisfied the Latin cities and was a stroke of political genius. Another series of wars against the Samnites lasted nearly 40 years, with Rome suffering a major defeat in 321BC. But again Rome rallied, the Latin cities remained loyal and the first great Roman road, the Via Appia, was constructed to supply the army in the south. The war ended in 290BC with Rome undisputed mistress of central Italy.

Rome now came into contact with the Greek cities of southern Italy. A dispute with the largest, Tarento, led to war in 280BC. The Tarentines hired King Pyrrhus of Epirus, a renowned Greek mercenary leader. Pyrrhus' army included war elephants, the first seen in Italy, and he defeated the Romans twice, marching right into Latium. But Rome adapted its infantry tactics to cope with the elephants and crack Greek spearmen. By 272BC Pyrrhus had left Italy, and Tarento and the other Greek cities accepted Roman alliance. Throughout peninsular Italy, Rome was supreme.

Above: After the Gauls sacked Rome in 390BC, the Romans built the great Servian Wall some 24ft (7.5m) high. When it was completed in 378BC, the wall made the city all but impregnable to later attacks.

THE GROWTH OF EMPIRE
264–133 BC

Above: The Carthaginians regularly used elephants, the "tanks of ancient warfare", in battle. The Roman legionaries soon learnt how to counter them, however, and they did not much affect the Punic wars.

Below: Lake Trasimene in Umbria was the scene of one of Rome's great defeats by Hannibal's armies in 217BC. The Carthaginians trapped the Romans by the lakeside and drove them into the water.

Facing each other across the Messina straits, Rome and Carthage had friendly treaties dating back to 509BC. But tensions soon developed between these two great powers of the western Mediterranean. Founded in *c.*800BC by Phoenician (Lebanese) traders, Carthage had extended its power along the African coast to Tangier and into Spain, founding Malaga and Cadiz. It also had control of most of Sicily. Larger and far richer than Rome, Carthage was ruled by a mercantile oligarchy whose faults showed up Rome's virtues. It relied on mercenary armies whom it often did not pay, led by Carthaginian generals whom it failed to support in success but always punished in defeat. However, as a city of merchants it had an excellent navy, while Rome, a land power, had no navy at all.

The clash came in 264BC when Messina appealed for Roman help against Carthage. Unusually, the Senate let the Assembly decide the issue. The Roman people voted for war and the first of three Punic Wars (the Roman name for Carthaginians) began. Lacking a fleet,

Rome decided to build one, copying a captured Carthaginian ship, but adding a new weapon: the *corvus*, or raven, a bridge fitted with spikes that crashed down and stuck on to enemy vessels. This allowed Roman soldiers to board the enemy ship and fight as if on land. With this weapon a sea battle was won off Mylae in 259BC, but the war turned against Rome when it sent an army to Africa under Regulus. After initial victories, he was crushingly defeated in 255BC and a relief fleet was lost in a storm. At immense cost the Romans built another fleet, and finally in 241BC routed the Carthaginians off the Agate Islands. In its defeat, Carthage was forced to abandon Sicily, which became the first Roman *provincia*, or imperial possession, apart from the great city of Syracuse. This became Rome's first client kingdom or protectorate. Rome had won by tenacity, adaptability and the loyalty of the Italian allies, who supplied Rome's armies with fresh recruits to replace those killed in battle.

A WAR OF ATTRITION

Carthage, plunged into chaos by a revolt of its unpaid mercenaries, stood by as Rome annexed Sardinia and Corsica, the former long a Punic possession. However, Hamilcar Barca, a Carthaginian general, carved out new territory in Spain, where he recruited a better army financed by Spain's silver mines. His son Hannibal took command in 221BC, determined to strike directly at Italy, the source of Rome's vast military manpower. In 218BC Hannibal marched his army, including 37 elephants, over the Alps in a snowstorm. Hannibal's skills, combined with Roman amateurishness, led to a series of Carthaginian victories, leaving Rome almost defenceless after the third annihilating defeat at Cannae in 216BC. Amazingly, only a few allied cities –

Capua, Tarento, Syracuse – changed sides, and Hannibal could not capture Rome itself, although he rode around its walls. With cool courage, the Senate then sent an army to Spain to strike at Hannibal's base. After some initial defeats, Cornelius Scipio landed in 210BC, and in 206 ousted the Carthaginians. Spain now became a Roman possession, divided into two provinces. Meanwhile, in Italy, the Romans had adopted the "scorched earth" policy of Fabius *Cunctator*, the Delayer. This denied Hannibal all resources, but also devastated Italian farms and caused massive homelessness. The war of attrition ended in 204BC when Scipio landed in Africa, and Carthage, which had seldom reinforced Hannibal, recalled its general. At the battle of Zama in 202BC Hannibal was defeated by Scipio, and Carthage accepted a humiliating peace.

ROME AND THE EAST
The Second Punic War was the most momentous in Rome's history. It determined that Rome would rule the western Mediterranean and be arbiter in the east. Rome had already been drawn east, for Philip V of Macedonia (northern Greece) had allied with Carthage in 214BC, when Rome seemed doomed. This First Macedonian War petered out in 205BC but five years later, fearing that Philip was growing too powerful, Rome intervened more decisively, defeating him in 197BC. The Roman general Flaminius then promised "the liberty of the Greeks", meaning self-rule, to the feuding southern Greek cities. Antiochus III, the Seleucid (Hellenistic) king (one of Alexander the Great's successors), was decisively defeated in 190BC when he tried to intervene in Greece, his pan-Asian empire reduced to a Syrian rump. Rome then established a free port at Delos, which soon became the commercial centre of the eastern Mediterranean, thronged with Italian merchants, and a centre of the booming slave trade. Rome defeated Macedonia again in 168BC when it tried to reassert itself, finally

making all Macedonia a province in 146BC along with Greece itself. When the last ruler of Pergamum, another wealthy Hellenistic kingdom in Asia Minor, died in 133BC, he bequeathed it to Rome.

A NEW IMPERIALISM
The sack of Corinth, Greece's richest port, in 146BC, revealed a new brutality and rapacity in Roman imperialism. Although the Senate enjoyed prestige and power both at home and abroad, it did not always act wisely. The final destruction of Carthage in the Third Punic War was partly due to Cato the Censor, a reactionary who ended every speech with "Carthage must be destroyed!" But it was also due to Rome's increasingly aggressive imperialism. Vast fortunes were being made by Roman nobles who returned from military triumphs, or even from provincial governorships, with huge amounts of booty, including slaves. The destruction of Epirus in 167BC brought in 150,000 Greek slaves alone. Very often these captives were better educated than their masters and helped introduce Greek culture to Roman society. However, the gains of war came at a cost. The stability of the Republic was threatened by the plight of tens of thousands of impoverished Romans, forced off the land during the Punic Wars and now unemployed in Rome.

Above: The meeting of the Roman general Scipio and his opponent Hannibal just before the Battle of Zama in 202BC is one of the most famous encounters in history. Scipio crushed Hannibal's army the following day.

Below: By the 2nd century BC Rome was developing its own distinctive architecture, shown here in the Temple of Portunus. Although influenced by Greek precursors, its layout was uniquely Roman.

VICTORY ABROAD, DISCORD AT HOME: 133–61BC

Above: Vital in transporting troops and goods, the Romans invested time, effort and money in developing a good road system. This is a view of the Via Appia to the south of Rome.

Below: A great soldier and military reformer, Marius was also very much a man of the people, often re-elected consul against the Senate's wishes. As a politician, however, he proved disastrously inept.

The problems of small farmers, the backbone of Rome's citizen army, became acute in the 130sBC. During the Second Punic War, many had been forced to abandon their farms. Unable to regain them when they came home, the farmers sold out to larger landowners and many migrated to Rome in search of work. But Rome had no industry and soon many farmers fell into the poorest class, thereby becoming ineligible for military service. This hardly worried the Roman oligarchy, itself growing ever richer.

AGRARIAN REFORM

In 133BC Tiberius Gracchus was elected tribune. A member of the aristocracy but schooled in Greek philosophy, Tiberius proposed that *ager publicus*, public land, often gained by conquest but which the rich had grabbed, should be redistributed to the poor in small lots. Such a proposal was half-expected, but what alarmed the Senate was that Tiberius proposed his reform directly to the Assembly, without taking it through the Senate, employing the *Lex Hortensia* to start a land commission. He then flouted custom by trying to have himself re-elected tribune. Tiberius also issued a challenge to the Senate's power over foreign policy. It was this, perhaps even more than his land reforms, that so enraged conservative senators, who mobilized their supporters and had Tiberius and 300 of his followers clubbed to death. Blood had been shed in Roman politics for the first time in nearly four centuries.

Ten years later Gaius, the more radical younger brother of Tiberius, re-enacted the agrarian reforms and proposed establishing colonies of landless citizens at recently conquered Carthage while subsidizing grain for the poor. To pay for this, he auctioned the rights to collect taxes in the new province of Asia to the knights (equestrians), to whom he also transferred control of the criminal law courts from the Senate. This boosted the knightly, or equestrian, order, the second richest class, which in turn increasingly challenged the Senate's powers. Gaius, too, paid for his reforms with his life. He failed to be elected for a third time as tribune and was killed as the Senate issued a *senatus consultum ultimum*, or Senate's final decree. From now on the Senate would be divided between the optimates, in reality reactionaries, and the *populares*, nobles and others who took the people's side or more often utilized popular support for their own ends. The struggle between these two factions in the end wrecked the Republic.

MARIUS AND SULLA

Rome's growing military weakness was starkly exposed by defeats in Mauretania (western North Africa), whose king Jugurtha proved invincible until the election of Gaius Marius as consul. Marius did not come from the nobility, and his frequent re-election as consul – seven times in all – revealed the new powers of the Assembly. Realizing that the legions badly needed recruits from proletarians, the landless citizens, Marius abolished all property qualifications for the army, while making it semi-professional with proper equipment. He encouraged legionaries to look to their generals, not the Senate, for rewards after service. This tie between general and army was fatally to undermine the Republic.

At first, Marius seemed the Republic's saviour. With his revitalized army he crushed the Cimbri and Teutones – barbarians who had overwhelmed two Roman armies – at Aix-en-Provence and in the Po valley in 102–1BC. The Senate then had to accept proposals that Marius'

Left: The Aegean island of Delos benefited from the Roman conquest, which made it a free port. Soon it was the most thriving port in the Mediterranean and a centre of the booming slave trade, until it was sacked by Mithradates' Greek allies in 88BC.

POMPEY AND CRASSUS

Spartacus, a gladiator, started a slave revolt at Capua in 73BC that spread throughout southern Italy. Crassus, notorious for his wealth, organized an army to suppress it, helped in the last stages by Pompey, once Sulla's youngest lieutenant. With their armies backing them, the two men became consuls in 70BC, and undid Sulla's measures, restoring the courts to the knights and reducing the Senate's powers. The problem of pirates threatening Rome's corn supply then became pressing, but Pompey, given overall command by the *Lex Gabinia* in 67BC, swept the Mediterranean clear of pirates in three months. His command was extended over the whole east, which he reorganized from the Caspian to the Red Sea. Returning home in 62BC, he disbanded his army but was annoyed at being denied his expected triumph by the Senate. He then formed the First Triumvirate, or Gang of Three, with Crassus and Julius Caesar, a rising *popularis* leader. From this moment, the days of the Republic were numbered.

veterans be given lands in Gaul, Greece and Africa as rewards when Marius marched south with some troops. In 90BC the Italian allies, who had been promised but had never received full citizenship, rose in revolt across Italy. The ensuing war was chiefly won by the *Lex Julia*, granting all free men south of the Po Roman citizenship. The war left more farmers uprooted and more ex-soldiers looking for rewards.

Lucius Cornelius Sulla, one of Marius' ablest generals but a die-hard optimate, went east in 86BC to defeat Mithradates, king of Pontus, who had invaded Greece. Meanwhile Marius, elected consul for the last time, massacred opponents with his troops before dying in January 87BC. The *populares'* triumph was brief. In 82BC Sulla returned from the east without disbanding his army and, after a battle outside Rome, revived the ancient office of dictator. He used it to proscribe (eliminate) thousands of opponents, rewriting the constitution to make it impossible for anyone to challenge the restored powers of the Senate. The guarantor of this regime was his own army, and when he retired in late 80BC, his reactionary settlement unravelled.

Above: Mithradates VI Eupator, King of Pontus (115–63BC), was one of Rome's most determined enemies in the east. His attempts to expand his Black Sea empire into Greece led to his defeat by Sulla and Lucullus, and he took his own life in 63BC.

THE END OF THE REPUBLIC
60–30 BC

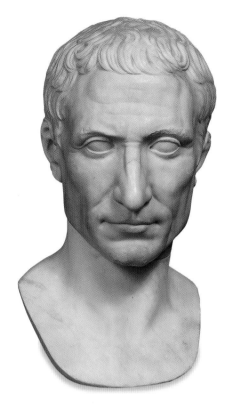

Above: Julius Caesar, dictator

Below: Rich but defenceless, Egypt fell to Rome in 30BC.

Julius Caesar was the third man in the secret but powerful triumvirate formed with Pompey and Crassus. Although a patrician, he supported the *popularis* faction, and was therefore hated by many in the Senate. However, he had made himself loved by the people through putting on lavish games, and had gained a reasonable military reputation in Spain. With the support of the other triumvirs he easily won election as consul in 59BC.

Once in office, Caesar quickly passed two land reform measures, giving Pompey's veterans their lands. He also revised taxes in the east, giving Crassus what he wanted for his own supporters, the tax-collecting knights. With Pompey and Crassus' support, his next step was to procure for himself proconsular command in the two important Gallic provinces (southern France and northern Italy) with their large armies, rather than the trivial command over "the woods and forests of Italy" that the Senate had decreed. Caesar pushed these measures through the Senate and Assembly ruthlessly and often illegally. It is reported that he once beat up his fellow consul Bibulus when the latter tried to oppose him. The support his fellow triumvirs had given him revealed the existence of their covert alliance, and Pompey married Julia, Caesar's daughter. Such political marriages were very common at the time.

THE END OF THE TRIUMVIRATE

In 58BC Caesar went north to take up his proconsular command and begin the lengthy conquest of Gaul, gaining for Rome one of its most important provinces. Meanwhile, the other two triumvirs were supposedly guarding his interests in Rome. The triumvirate was formally renewed in 56BC at Lucca. Crassus took up command in the east, keen for military glory to rival that of his fellow triumvirs. Disaster followed at Carrhae in 53BC. Crassus' legions were destroyed by the Parthians in the desert, and Crassus died with them. This left Pompey and Caesar in open and deepening rivalry, with the Senate backing Pompey as a lesser evil. In 49BC Caesar started civil war by crossing the Rubicon into Italy. Moving swiftly, he seized Rome, was appointed dictator by the people – in theory an emergency post – and followed Pompey and his other enemies to Greece, where he defeated them at Pharsalus in 48BC. Pompey, fleeing to Egypt, a nominally independent kingdom, was murdered upon arrival. Caesar, after encountering and being seduced by Cleopatra, then pursued and defeated the Republicans in Africa and Spain, celebrating a grand triumph in Rome while passing through.

CAESAR'S DICTATORSHIP

Once back in Rome, Julius Caesar embarked on a series of reforms including a general cancellation of debt and the founding of new colonies in Spain, Gaul, Greece and Africa – for his soldiers and the city's unemployed. He also reformed the calendar, began building the huge Basilica Julia, brought citizens from outside Italy into the Senate, started draining the Pontine marshes and reformed the currency – all this in a few months.

Early in 44BC Julius Caesar assumed perpetual dictatorship, revealing that his monopoly of power was not temporary, but permanent, like a king's. Like a king, too, was the way his image appeared on coins and statues. But this was anathema to all true Republicans. On the Ides (15th) of March 44BC, just before he left Rome for an eastern campaign, Julius Caesar was stabbed to death by a group led by Brutus, reputedly a descendant of the man who had driven out the last king in 509BC.

THE SECOND TRIUMVIRATE

Caesar's assassins, about 60 senators, had nothing realistic to put in his place, except more civil war. In the complex manoeuvrings that followed, Caesar's fellow consul, Mark Antony, formed the Second Triumvirate with young Octavian Caesar, the dictator's adopted son, and Lepidus, another Caesarean. Savagely proscribing many Republicans in Rome, they pursued the conspirators to Greece and defeated them at Philippi in 42BC. There followed a division of the empire, with Octavian ultimately taking control of all the west, and Antony controlling the east. Antony soon became enamoured of Cleopatra, the beautiful, intelligent queen of Egypt and the last Ptolemy ruler. Although officially married to Octavia, sister of his co-triumvir, Antony soon shunned her in favour of Cleopatra, and Octavia returned to Rome, humiliated.

Antony's military fame was tarnished by his failed campaign against the Parthians in 36BC. Meanwhile, Octavian was completing the basilica of the now deified Julius and establishing his own reputation as a patriotic Roman. The final showdown at the naval battle of Actium in north-west Greece in 31BC was an anti-climax, with many of Antony's supporters deserting. Pursued to Egypt, Antony and Cleopatra committed suicide, depriving Octavian of the joy of exhibiting them in his triumph, but not of the kingdom of Egypt, which he annexed personally. Two years later, Octavian returned to Rome to begin the immense task of the restoration of the Roman world after almost a century of civil war.

Above: The Battle of Actium in 31BC was the final stage in the long civil wars. Octavian's victory meant that the Roman world could at last be reunited and at peace after decades of civil wars. It also marked the completion of Rome's conquest of the Mediterranean world.

Below: The head of Julius Caesar on this silver denarius, a novel honour, shows the victor's laurel crown granted him by the Senate – which he wore all the time to disguise his growing baldness.

PEACE RESTORED: THE FIRST EMPERORS: 30BC–AD68

Above: Augustus, his family and friends are shown on the Ara Pacis, *or Altar of Peace, in Rome, in traditional Roman attitudes, symbolizing the restoration of "the Republic".*

Victorious after the long civil wars, Octavian finally returned to Rome in 29BC. His aim was to found a peaceful, effective but constitutional government, which the Republic in its last decades had failed to supply. The whole empire had suffered from the exactions of rival generals and was exhausted. As a cost-cutting exercise, he disbanded half his huge army, settling the soldiers in colonies around the empire. From now on, there would be a regular army of only 28–30 legions, or around 150,000 men, backed by equal numbers of auxiliary troops stationed in camps along the frontiers. To symbolize peace and to give the city room to grow, Octavian let most of the old Servian walls decay. Respecting Republican laws, he kept no troops in Italy – now extended to include the Po valley – but he retained nine cohorts of special Praetorian guards. Unlike Caesar, he seldom had a bodyguard in Rome. But he used his friends and colleagues, notably Agrippa, his general and son-in-law, and Maecenas, his cultural minister.

OCTAVIAN TO AUGUSTUS

In 27BC Octavian formally resigned his offices and announced "the transfer of the state to the Senate's and people's free disposal". He received them back with thanks, along with the title Augustus, meaning revered, auspicious, augmenting. He was elected consul and gave the Senate new powers as a high court and took part in its debates, becoming *princeps senatus*, leader of the Senate. Its functions became administrative, not political, in his disguised revolution. Augustus termed himself *princeps*, or first citizen, avoiding appearing royal or imperial. He gave up always being consul in 23BC after a serious illness. In its place, the Senate offered him tribunician power, making his person sacrosanct, and *maius imperium*, power over all the provinces. His *auctoritas*, personal prestige and authority, were key to his success, along with his old-fashioned probity, or *virtus*.

But the basis of Augustus' power was military, for he was also *imperator*, commander-in-chief. He used the army to expand the empire, annexing north-west Spain and the Danubian lands from the Alps to the Black Sea. Egypt also came under his control, while in the east he made a peaceful settlement with

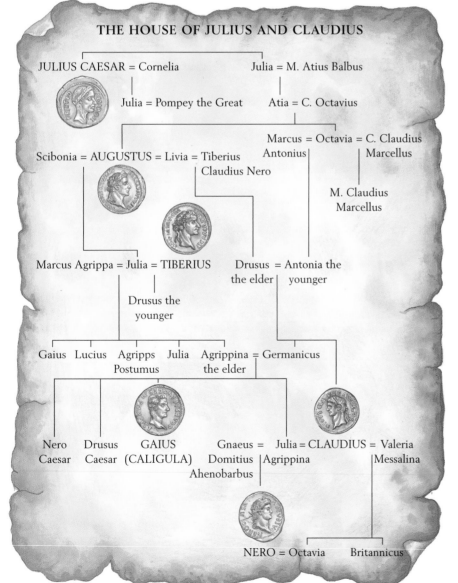

THE HOUSE OF JULIUS AND CLAUDIUS

JULIUS CAESAR = Cornelia   Julia = M. Atius Balbus

Julia = Pompey the Great   Atia = C. Octavius

Marcus = Octavia = C. Claudius
Antonius   Marcellus

Scibonia = AUGUSTUS = Livia = Tiberius
Claudius Nero

M. Claudius
Marcellus

Marcus Agrippa = Julia = TIBERIUS   Drusus = Antonia the
the elder   younger

Drusus the
younger

Gaius   Lucius   Agripps   Julia   Agrippina = Germanicus
Postumus   the elder

Nero   Drusus   GAIUS   Gnaeus = Julia = CLAUDIUS = Valeria
Caesar   Caesar   (CALIGULA)   Domitius   Agrippina   Messalina
Ahenobarbus

NERO = Octavia   Britannicus

the Parthians in 20BC. It was only in Germany that his expansionist policy was defeated when Varus was annihilated with three legions in AD9. This defeat plunged him into despair. His grandsons, his intended heirs, had both died and he had unwillingly adopted his stepson Tiberius of the proud Claudian family. None of the Julio-Claudian dynasty would ever repeat Augustus' golden age.

THE HEIRS OF AUGUSTUS

Tiberius, an excellent general, was an embittered man of 53 by the time he came to power in AD14. He continued Augustus' policies but lacked his *auctoritas* and charm. Instead, he relied on Sejanus, prefect of the Praetorian guard, as first minister, especially after Tiberius retired to Capri in AD26. There he was rumoured to indulge in fantastic sexual perversities. Probably untrue, such stories illustrate his unpopularity. Sejanus started treason trials that killed many in the imperial family before being executed for treason himself in AD31.

Tiberius' successor was his 24-year-old great-nephew Gaius, called Caligula after the little boots (a version of *caligae*, military boots) that he wore as a child. Very popular at first, Caligula abolished treason trials and proved as generous as Tiberius had been mean. But a serious illness six months into his reign seems to have driven him mad. He began a reign of terror, executing the Praetorian prefect Macro and many senators. His behaviour became increasingly eccentric – he joked he would make his horse consul. After he built a temple to himself as co-equal with Jupiter, he was assassinated in AD41.

While the Senate debated, a guard discovered a 50-year-old man hiding behind a curtain: this was Claudius, Caligula's uncle, passed over in the succession because of his bad stammer. But Claudius had a shrewd brain. Hailed by the Praetorians as emperor – he wisely offered them a bribe – his reign followed Augustan precedents, except for his conquest of Britain in AD43, which won

him military laurels. Claudius relied on freedmen as civil servants and began to centralize the government. But his personal life was less happy. His wife Messalina, notoriously promiscuous, was arraigned for treason in AD48. Claudius then married his niece, Agrippina, who probably poisoned him to make way for her son Nero.

Nero was only 17 when he succeeded his stepfather in AD54. At first guided by the philosopher Seneca and the Praetorian prefect Burrus, he ruled well, apart from murdering Britannicus, Claudius' son. He had artistic interests if not talents, and made a public performance as a singer in AD64. By then, with his mother murdered, Burrus dead and Seneca forced to commit suicide, Nero had become a tyrant to rival Caligula. The fire that destroyed half of Rome in AD64 was blamed on him by the people, although he scapegoated the Christians and had many of them burnt. He used the opportunity to build his Golden House, grandest of all the imperial palaces, but he also issued intelligent building regulations afterwards. Fatally, Nero neglected the army, and it was army rebellions that ended his rule in AD68. Abandoned even by his slaves, he committed suicide on 9 June AD68. The line of the Julio-Claudians died with him and civil war flared once again across the Roman world.

Above: The Pont du Gard, supplying Roman Nimes in southern France, is among the grandest surviving aqueducts and a monument to the blessings of the long Augustan peace. Beginning in 30BC, this period saw unprecedented prosperity spread around the empire, especially in the west.

Below: This fresco from the Golden House, the huge palace Nero built in the centre of Rome, illustrates the myth of the birth of Adonis – and also the high quality of Roman frescoes at the time.

THE FLAVIANS AND "THE FIVE GOOD EMPERORS": AD69–180

Above: Scenes from Trajan's Column in the Forum in Rome illustrate his victories in the Dacian wars and also provide us with detailed examples of Rome's army at its zenith.

Below: In AD124 the emperor Hadrian ordered the completion of the vast Temple of Olympian Zeus in Athens, started 650 years before. Hadrian favoured Athens in many ways, eventually becoming its archon *(mayor).*

Vespasian, emperor AD69–79, emerged victorious from the civil wars of AD68–9. A member of the Flavian family, his father was of equestrian not senatorial rank, but Vespasian proved a far better ruler than many Julio-Claudians. On reaching Rome in October AD70, he found that the state was almost bankrupt. To fill the coffers, he increased taxation and so earned a reputation for meanness – he even taxed the disposal of urine. Vespasian restored the frontiers and strengthened the eastern defences. He recruited from among non-Italians both for the Senate and the administration and made no pretence about the monarchical nature of his regime – only his sons could succeed him. He kept the consulate, still much coveted by senators, almost completely in the Flavian family.

Titus, who succeeded in AD79, had to deal with the Vesuvian eruption. Catastrophic and costly, it was fortunate for posterity, as it preserved Pompeii and Herculaneum almost intact. Charming and lavishly generous, Titus was generally popular and he completed the immense Flavian amphitheatre, or Colosseum, in AD80. But he died suddenly in AD81 and his younger brother Domitian, emperor AD81–96, succeeded him.

In some ways Domitian was an effective ruler, at least outside Rome. He extended the frontiers in south-west Germany and perhaps wisely curtailed Agricola's attempted conquest of Scotland. But at home he assumed a despotic manner, building a huge palace to rival Nero's. Becoming increasingly paranoid, he started a reign of terror that eventually led to his assassination in AD96.

THE ZENITH OF ROME

Domitian's successor, the elderly senator Nerva, realized that the army resented his accession and adopted Trajan, governor of upper Germany, as his son and heir. Trajan's reign (AD98–117) saw the empire at its peak geographically and perhaps economically. He was called *optimus princeps*, best of emperors, by the Senate. His building programme rivalled Augustus', while his care for the poor and sick showed a new imperial compassion. But Trajan was primarily a great soldier. Between AD101–6 he crushed the aggressive kingdom of the Dacians, finally annexing their land (Romania) and settling it with colonists. He then turned east, first annexing Arabia Petraea (Jordan), before dealing with Parthia, the old enemy in the east. Initial successes saw Roman armies reach the Gulf – their furthest advance. Mesopotamia (Iraq) and Armenia were added to the empire in AD115–17 but then abandoned.

Hadrian, Trajan's (probably) designated successor, spent much of his reign outside Rome, travelling round the empire. He visited Britain in AD122, building a

Left: Hadrian was the most peripatetic of emperors, traversing the empire from Egypt to Britain. Outside Rome at Tivoli, he also created the most spacious and luxurious of imperial palaces, with pools, colonnades and even temples – often replicas of what he had seen on his extensive travels.

Below: "Five Good Emperors" of the Adoptive and Antonine dynasties ruled Rome at its zenith in the 2nd century AD, adoption solving the problems of succession.

76-mile (122-km) long wall, to keep northern barbarian Britains out of the Romanized south. Hadrian admired Greek culture, and in Rome he built the Pantheon, one of the finest of all Roman temples. His successor, Antoninus Pius (emperor AD138–61), was an elderly senator who never left Italy. Under him the empire slept in a prosperous calm.

THE FIRST CRISIS

Ironically, under Marcus Aurelius, AD161–80, one of the last great pagan philosophers, Rome was engaged in a series of conflicts. The army was so weakened by the plague of AD166 that invading Germans were able to cross the Alps, while another band almost reached Athens. In a long series of wars, Marcus went on the counter-offensive, intending to annex what is now the Czech Republic and Slovakia. At the same time, he let some Germans settle inside the empire. He was still campaigning on the Danube when he died in AD180. He left the throne to his son Commodus: it was to prove a disastrous choice.

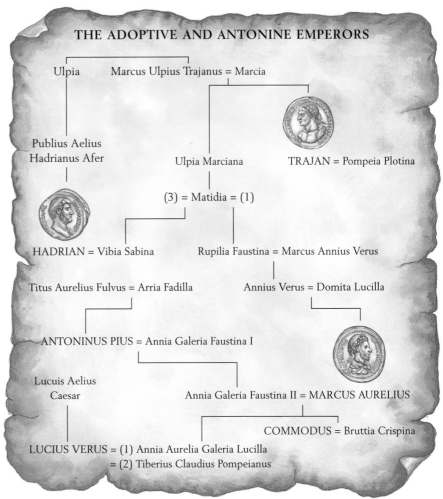

THE ADOPTIVE AND ANTONINE EMPERORS

Ulpia   Marcus Ulpius Trajanus = Marcia

Publius Aelius Hadrianus Afer

Ulpia Marciana   TRAJAN = Pompeia Plotina

(3) = Matidia = (1)

HADRIAN = Vibia Sabina   Rupilia Faustina = Marcus Annius Verus

Titus Aurelius Fulvus = Arria Fadilla   Annius Verus = Domita Lucilla

ANTONINUS PIUS = Annia Galeria Faustina I

Lucuis Aelius Caesar   Annia Galeria Faustina II = MARCUS AURELIUS

COMMODUS = Bruttia Crispina

LUCIUS VERUS = (1) Annia Aurelia Galeria Lucilla
= (2) Tiberius Claudius Pompeianus

CRISIS AND CATASTROPHE
AD180–284

Above: Under the debauched and incompetent Commodus, here shown dressed as the hero Hercules, the Golden Age ended in renewed civil wars.

Below: Septimius Severus, who came from Libya, founded a new dynasty that, through its Syrian connections, lasted for 40 years and produced a remarkable range of emperors.

Aged only 18, Commodus was the first emperor to inherit the throne from his father since Titus. Although Marcus Aurelius had groomed his son for his imperial role, Commodus soon shunned onerous public duties, ruling through all-powerful favourites. After an assassination attempt in AD182, he was reluctant to appear in public at all, preferring to spend his time in his palaces or country villas, where he indulged in sexual debauchery. When the last favourite, Cleander, had been sacrificed over a grain shortage in AD190, Commodus returned to Rome, where he ordered the deaths of many prominent citizens. His assassination in January AD193 caused fresh civil wars.

When Septimius Severus, commander of the Danubian legions, reached Rome in April AD193 two earlier claimants had been killed already. It took him four more years of wars before he defeated his rivals in the east and west and began reforging the monarchy. The first emperor of African origin (he came from Libya), Severus was essentially a soldier. He increased the army's size and improved its pay and conditions of service. He ruled as an autocrat, stationing a legion outside Rome and killing 29 senators. But as a general he was brilliant, leading an attack on Parthia in AD197, which captured the capital Ctesiphon (Baghdad). He died in AD211 in York after a northern campaign. On his deathbed, he reportedly told his two sons Caracalla and Geta to "pay the soldiers and ignore the rest".

Although Severus had told his sons to work together, Caracalla soon murdered Geta. Caracalla's reign, AD211–17, is notable for his law of AD212 which gave Roman citizenship to all free males in the empire. This law was probably passed for its taxation potential, as Roman citizens paid death duties, but nevertheless it was a significant move in the widening of Roman privileges. He also constructed the most grandiose baths in Rome.

Assassinated in AD217, Caracalla left no heirs, but the Syrian branch of the Severan family produced a 14-year-old boy, Elagabalus, whose reign (AD218–22) is notorious for his sexual promiscuity. This promiscuity was supposedly in honour of the Syrian sun god Baal, whose orgiastic worship Elagabalus introduced to Rome. His marriage to a Vestal Virgin impressed neither Senate nor people. Aware of the dangers, his grandmother Julia Maesa turned to another grandson, Alexander Severus, who became emperor at the age of 14 after Elagabalus' murder by the army.

Alexander reigned for 13 years – reigned rather than ruled, for real power lay with his mother, Julia Mammaea. She enlisted the Senate's support, but he failed to win the army's loyalty. An unconvincing general, he and his mother were murdered in AD235.

THE HOUSE OF SEVERUS

Publius Septimius Geta = Fulvia Pia

Julius Bassianus

(1) Paccia Marciana = SEPTIMIUS SEVERUS = (2) Julia Domna

Julia Maesa = Julis Avitus

Gaius Fulvius Plautianus

Julia Soaemias = Sextus Varius Marcellus

Julia Mammaea = Gessius Marcianus

CARACALLA = Plautilla

GETA

L. Seius Sallustius

ELAGABALUS = (1) Julia Cornelia Paula
= (2) Julia Aquila Severa
= (3) Annia Faustina

Sallustia Barbia Orbiana = ALEXANDER SEVERUS

TMRIS AND CATASTROPHE 33

THE 30 EMPERORS

In the 50 years of chaos that followed, at least 30 emperors, perhaps more, were proclaimed by armies around the empire. Assassination became the norm, as different armies – from the Danube, Syria and the Rhineland – fought each other, rather than the enemy. Barbarians responded with massive invasions, which worsened the economic and financial collapse. For a time, the whole concept of one empire looked doomed: the western provinces broke away to form the Gallic Empire from AD260 to 274, while the eastern provinces were overrun by a resurgent Persian empire under a new dynasty, the Sassanids. Rome's revival owed much to emperors from Illyria (the Balkans), who proved more energetically patriotic than the Romans themselves.

In AD248 the emperor Philip the Arab celebrated Rome's millennium, but there was little to celebrate. (Philip himself was murdered the following year.) The Goths, formidable horsemen from Sweden, crossed the Danube and ravaged the Balkans, Asia Minor and Greece. Plagues swept the empire, while the Persians, under Shapur I, invaded the eastern provinces and took Antioch, the great eastern trading metropolis.

Valerian, who became emperor in AD253, was captured in AD260 by the Persians, ending his life in humiliating captivity. However, his son and co-emperor, Gallienus, reorganized the army into a far more mobile and effective force. He annihilated a Gothic force in the Balkans in AD268, but was murdered shortly after. Gallienus' work was continued first by Claudius II, who again defeated the Goths before dying of the plague, and then by Aurelian, emperor AD270–5, who crushed two German invasions of Italy. Aware that Rome itself was threatened, Aurelian hastily erected the city walls that still bear his name. In AD272 he recaptured the eastern provinces seized by Zenobia, queen of the oasis trading city of Palmyra. Two years later he defeated the last of the separatist

Gallic emperors, Tetricus, reuniting Gaul with the empire. However, in AD270 he had to abandon Dacia as it was too exposed to invasion.

Aurelian promoted the worship of the Unconquered Sun, a semi-monotheistic deity to which he built a huge temple in Rome. He tried to restore the economy by issuing a new coinage. Inflation had reached terrifying levels – 1,000 per cent in the 17 years before AD275 – and the currency was almost worthless. This had led to payment in kind by the passing armies exacted from the peasants through whose lands they marched, or from the equally oppressed cities they were meant to be defending. Figures are lacking, but the economy and population of the empire shrank sharply during the chaos. However Egypt and North Africa did relatively well because they suffered few barbarian incursions. Emperor Aurelian was assassinated in AD275 but, although the empire half-relapsed into civil war, enough of his work remained for Diocletian, a soldier from Illyria, to use it as a base for reorganizing the government when he became emperor in AD284.

Above: The emperor Septimius Severus, here shown with his family, was the first Roman ruler to come from Africa, a part of the empire he favoured with lavish building projects and by advancing the frontier far into the Sahara.

Below: This bas-relief from Bishapur, Iran, shows the Persian king Shapur I humiliating the Roman emperor Valerian, who had been ignominiously captured in AD260.

RECONSTRUCTION AND REVIVAL: AD285–363

Above: The tetrarchs, the four rulers of the Roman empire, are here shown embracing each other in unshakeable amity. This system worked only while its founder, Diocletian, remained the senior emperor. Afterwards, the empire reverted to civil wars.

With Diocletian (reigned 284–305AD) the ravaged Roman world entered a period of relative stability and even revival. But in the long term this was at the cost of personal liberty, as the emperors strove to create a quasi-totalitarian state to counter the chaos of the preceding age. Diocletian, a soldier, became emperor in a bloody coup. He thought the problem of defending different frontiers would be helped by having more than one emperor. In AD286, he invited a comrade, Maximian, to become joint emperor and rule the western half of the empire. Both men took the title Augustus. In AD293 he added two junior emperors, with the title Caesar: Constantius I to rule under Maximian in the west and Galerius in the east. The Caesars became the official heirs to the Augusti and each emperor established his own court: Constantius at Trier; Maximian at Milan; Galerius at Thessalonica and Diocletian at Nicomedia in Asia Minor. Rome, still the capital in theory, was ignored.

Each new capital was richly adorned with palaces and basilicas, and anyone approaching the emperor had to prostrate himself. This deification of the emperor was designed to overawe subjects and keep them in their place The three sub-empires were not separate domains. They were all governed by the same laws and obeyed Diocletian, the senior Augustus. This system is called the Tetrarchy (from the Greek for four rulers) and at first it worked well.

LIFE UNDER THE TETRARCHY

In AD296, Galerius suffered a defeat on the troubled eastern frontier, but gained new lands the next year along the Upper Tigris. At the same time, Constantius invaded Britain, returning it to the empire after ten years of isolation. Such victories were helped by the tetrarchs' military reorganization. Each ruler had a mobile field force, the *comitatenses*, armoured cavalry who waged war. The other, larger, section of the army were the *limitanei*, permanent frontier troops who manned the much-strengthened border fortresses. German mercenaries became a regular part of the Roman army, and its manpower was increased to about 600,000 – twice its size under Augustus.

Such huge armies and courts cost money, and the tax burden became overwhelming. Diocletian tried to make reforms, issuing a new coinage in AD294,

Right: The dynasty of Constantine, who divided the empire between his three surviving sons from his marriage to Fausta, ruled the Roman world for nearly 30 years, although fratricidal strife rather than brotherly unity was the norm. Only Julian, Constantine's half brother, proved an able ruler.

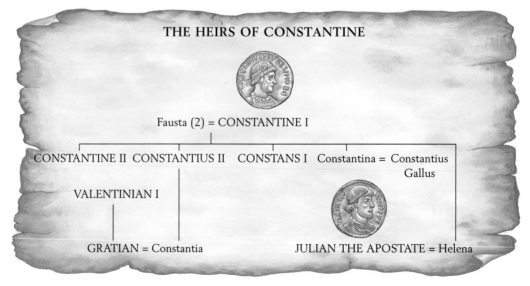

THE HEIRS OF CONSTANTINE

Fausta (2) = CONSTANTINE I

CONSTANTINE II   CONSTANTIUS II   CONSTANS I   Constantina = Constantius Gallus

VALENTINIAN I

GRATIAN = Constantia   JULIAN THE APOSTATE = Helena

to re-establish people's faith in the currency ruined by constant inflation, but there were not enough new coins to have much impact. Then in AD301 he issued his Edict of Maximum Prices, to try to fix a maximum price for goods and services. This did not work either, for goods simply vanished from the shops and inflation continued. But he had more success in making taxes regular, with annual revisions, and introduced new assessment methods.

In AD303 Diocletian launched the last and greatest persecution of the Christians. Their numbers had increased steadily in the 3rd century AD, until about 8 per cent of the population was Christian. Diocletian, like many in the empire, felt that the Christians' rejection of Roman gods was treasonous to an emperor who styled himself "companion of Jupiter". First the Christian clergy, then the laity had to sacrifice to the gods or face imprisonment and even death. Tired of his rule, Diocletian then made the unusual decision to retire, abdicating in AD305 to grow cabbages in his palace at Split. He made Maximian retire too. Constantius then became Augustus in the west and Galerius in the east. According to the terms of the Tetrarchy, the idea was that the two Augusti would abdicate in turn, to be succeeded by their Caesars.

THE CONVERSION OF EUROPE

When Constantius I died in AD306, his son Constantine I was declared Augustus by the troops in Britain. In AD312 Constantine defeated Maxentius, son of Maximian, and 12 years later overthrew Licinius, Augustus of the east, thereby reuniting the whole empire. Reputedly, before defeating Maxentius, Constantine had had a vision of the cross. In AD313 in the Edict of Milan, he and Licinius granted religious freedom to all faiths, including Christians. By AD325 he was actively presiding over the crucial Council of Nicaea (Iznik), and by the time of his death in AD337 he had come to see himself as the thirteenth apostle.

In AD324 Constantine had established the city of New Rome, or Constantinople (Istanbul), as his new capital. The former Greek city of Byzantium, superbly sited on the river Bosphorus, became almost impregnable behind its double walls. Constantine continued Diocletian's policies, dividing the empire between his three sons at his death, when he was finally baptized a Christian. Of the sons, Constantius II emerged the victor of 15 years of civil war, but he was no general. Faced by barbarian invasions and usurpers, in AD355 he appointed his half-cousin Julian, known only as a scholar, as his Caesar in the west.

Julian proved almost a military genius, repelling German invasions in a series of brilliant campaigns. He also tried to lighten the burden of taxation on the wretched peasantry. Growing jealous of his success, Constantius tried to recall him, but Julian was declared Augustus by his troops in AD360. Civil war was averted by Constantius' death, and Julian, revealing himself a pagan, ordered the old temples be reopened. However, his reign was too short for this to have any effect, for he was killed on a Persian campaign in AD363. Both the house of Constantine and the pagan reaction died with him.

Above: These fragments of a colossal statue of the emperor Constantine illustrate how the later emperors liked to depict themselves: semi-divine absolute monarchs – very different from the modest image Augustus had displayed.

Below: The massive fortress-palace on the Adriatic at Split (Spalato), to which Diocletian retired to die in his bed, survives almost intact.

THE FALL OF THE WEST
AD364–476

Above: From the mid-3rd century AD onwards, Roman fortifications became vastly more massive and imposing. Behind the huge walls of fortresses such as this at Portchester on the English coast, Romans now passively awaited barbarian attacks.

After his death in AD363, Julian was succeeded briefly by Jovian, and then by Valentinian I, who for military reasons divided the empire, with his brother Valens taking the east. Both men were fine soldiers and Christians, but while Valentinian was religiously tolerant, his brother fiercely persecuted pagans and non-conformists. Valentinian proved the last really effective emperor in the west, repelling and avenging German invasions until he died in AD375, leaving his young and incompetent son Gratian as his heir. Meanwhile, far-distant events were leading towards catastrophe.

In AD378, in a defeat by the Goths at Adrianople (Idirne), Valens and most of the finest Roman troops were killed. Gratian then appointed a Spanish officer, Theodosius, as Augustus in the east, who let the Goths settle *en masse* with their own rulers within the empire. In theory, they supplied men for the Roman army but in practice they proved uncontrollable. Theodosius defeated rebel emperor Magnus Maximus in Gaul, reuniting the empire, but he was called "the Great" chiefly for his ardent Christianity. In AD392 he banned all forms of pagan worship, as intolerance became official .

Theodosius, last emperor of a united empire, died in AD395, leaving the empire to his incompetent sons: Arcadius in the east, who died in AD408, and Honorius, who lived to AD423, in the west. But the real ruler of the west was Stilicho, of German descent. In December AD406 the Rhine froze solid; Vandals and other Germans poured across it and spread into Gaul and Spain. The Rhine garrisons that should have repelled them had been withdrawn to face a usurper from Britain. The Rhine frontier was never restored and Britain, too, was soon abandoned. But there were more pressing problems in Italy. Stilicho was murdered by Honorius in AD408, and in AD410 Alaric, the Visigoth king, sacked the city of Rome.

Although the Visigoths were relatively restrained in their conquest – they were Christians, respecting churches and nuns – the world was profoundly shaken. For

Right: The imperial dynasty founded by Valentinian I saw a further acceptance of the division of the empire into east and west. Disaster occurred when his brother Valens, the eastern emperor, was killed at the battle of Adrianople. Theodosius I founded another imperial dynasty but one dependent on Gothic support.

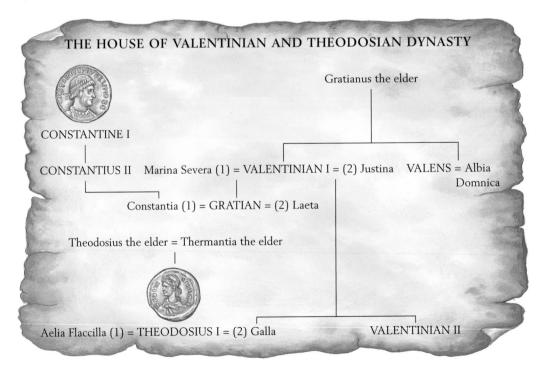

THE HOUSE OF VALENTINIAN AND THEODOSIAN DYNASTY

Gratianus the elder

CONSTANTINE I

CONSTANTIUS II   Marina Severa (1) = VALENTINIAN I = (2) Justina   VALENS = Albia Domnica

Constantia (1) = GRATIAN = (2) Laeta

Theodosius the elder = Thermantia the elder

Aelia Flaccilla (1) = THEODOSIUS I = (2) Galla   VALENTINIAN II

the first time in 800 years, Rome had fallen to the barbarians. Alaric stayed only three days, leaving with much booty and Galla Placidia, the emperor's half-sister. Alaric died soon after, and the Visigoths moved into southern Gaul. Constantius, a general, then took command and forced the Goths to return Placidia. After suppressing other rebels in Gaul, he married Placidia, against her will, and was proclaimed co-emperor in AD421. Constantius III died late that year and his son, Valentinian III, became emperor in AD425. Under his mother Placidia's control, Valentinian reigned for 30 years, and the empire continued to disintegrate.

HUNS AND VANDALS

The best efforts of Aetius, another Roman general, could not prevent the Vandals establishing themselves in North Africa. Gaiseric, the Vandal king, captured Carthage, the second city of the western empire, in AD439 and built a pirate fleet to terrorize the whole Mediterranean region. But Aetius' attention had been drawn north by an even worse threat.

The Huns, frighteningly effective horsemen, had built an empire from the Volga to the Baltic. Their greatest king, Attila, known in history as "the scourge of God" (*flagellum dei*), ravaged the eastern empire's European provinces in

BYZANTIUM SURVIVES

If the Roman empire collapsed in the west, it flourished in the east. Thanks partly to Constantinople's superb defensive position, the east Roman or Byzantine empire (the name comes from the original Greek city) lived on for another thousand years. Although invasions had stripped it of its outlying provinces by the 7th century AD, it remained wealthy and civilized, wholly Greek in language and deeply Christian in its religion. A Russian ruler married one of the last Byzantine princesses, assuming the title Czar, or Caesar.

the AD440s and then turned west. Attila retreated after a day's bloody fighting at Châlons-sur-Marne in AD451. This was the one defeat of his life. The next year he headed towards a defenceless Rome. Pope Leo I met him unarmed and the two talked in Attila's tent. What they said is not known, but the Huns turned back across the Alps. Two years later, Attila died and his empire collapsed.

After Aetius' death in AD454, Rome was once more leaderless, and the Vandals viciously sacked Rome. Increasingly, it was German chieftains who made and unmade emperors. Finally, in AD476, Romulus Augustulus, the last emperor of the west, was deposed by the German Odoacer, who declared himself king of Italy. The empire had ended in the west.

Above: The Hunnish king Attila, "the scourge of God", became known as the most terrifying of the barbarian invaders of the 5th century AD, renowned for his savagery. He was not the most effective invader, however, for he did not sack Rome and his empire died with him.

CHAPTER II

GREAT ROMANS

The Romans of the early Republic were shadowy figures of whom not much is known. A typical example was Cincinnatus. He was working on his farm when called on to become dictator and save the city in 458BC. Wiping the sweat from his brow and putting on his toga, he went off to be emergency ruler and defeat the most threatening enemies. That done, he returned to his plough.

Such self-effacing patriotism could not survive Rome's rise to world power from the 3rd century BC. The influx of wealth and contacts with the sophisticated Greeks gave Romans, too, the desire and opportunity to excel as individuals, to shine on the stage of politics or the arts, to become famous generals, politicians, philosophers or poets. The poet Horace, writing in the 1st century BC, was as much concerned with his posthumous literary fame as Julius Caesar was with his prestige and power when he was alive. Almost inevitably, the only Romans we know much about today came from the political or intellectual elite. We have almost no written records of other Romans to flesh out what archaeology tells us of their lives. What writings have survived, however, are enough to reveal much about the inhabitants of the world's first global city. Soldiers and statesmen, writers and thinkers, and powerful women, all come alive in the pages of historians such as Tacitus and Suetonius, which are at times as racy and bizarre as today's gossip columns.

Left: Julius Caesar, the most famous Roman of them all, receiving tribute from ambassadors of client states.

GREAT ROMAN GENERALS

Above: Scipio Africanus, who defeated the Carthaginians first in Spain then in Africa, was typical of many great generals of the Republic in the jealousy and attacks his feats roused back in Rome. These finally forced him into premature retirement.

While military service was a customary, indeed often inescapable, part of life for most Romans in the Republic, a few commanders stand out, either for saving the state or for transforming the armies. Some went on to intervene in civilian life, usually with disastrous consequences.

PUBLIUS CORNELIUS SCIPIO AFRICANUS (235–183BC)

Scipio was only 25 years old when given command of the Roman armies in Spain. Facing an invincible Hannibal in Italy, the Republic had decided to attack Hannibal's base, but the first Roman army sent to Spain was defeated and both commanders killed. They were soon avenged. Scipio captured Cartagena, the Carthaginian headquarters, in 209BC. The next year, he defeated Hasdrubal, Hannibal's brother, by using light troops as a screen for the heavier legionaries. Soon all of Spain went over to Rome, while Hasdrubal was later defeated in Italy. Consul in 205BC, Scipio then led an army to Africa and defeated Hannibal at the Battle of Zama in 202BC, overcoming Hannibal's war elephants by ordering his legionaries to open ranks and let the maddened animals pass between them.

Scipio made two significant military reforms. First, his armies in Spain adopted the short Spanish stabbing sword. Devastatingly effective, it became the standard weapon of Roman legionaries. Second, he reformed the maniple, of which there were 30 to each legion, at times allowing them to act in three separate lines. More than a mere soldier, Scipio was among the first Romans to appreciate Greek culture and to learn the language properly. Partly because of this, he was subject to persecution by Roman traditionalists such as Cato the Censor. In 190BC, accused of misappropriating booty from the Syrian campaign, he finally withdrew from public life altogether.

GAIUS MARIUS (158–87BC)

A great soldier but a disastrous politician, Marius came from an equestrian family. He made his fortune as a *publicanus* (tax-collector), and he was a tribune of the plebs in 119BC, and praetor in 116BC. He was appointed commander of the armies in Africa in the wars against King Jugurtha. Brilliantly successful, Marius became consul in 107BC, finished the war in 105BC and was made consul again the next year.

Marius was given sweeping powers, which he used to reorganize the army, introducing the cohort of six centuries (500–600 men), and giving each legion its silver eagle, which soon became an emblem of tremendous importance. He made the *pilum*, the throwing spear, break at its neck, to render an enemy's shield useless. Marius abolished the last property qualifications so making the army more attractive to the poor, who now, however, had to carry all their equipment – hence their nickname "Marius' mules". These soldiers looked to their general, not the Senate, for reward. Marius used his remodelled army to crush barbarian invaders.

Returning to Rome, Marius got entangled in the struggles between the *populares*, whom he supported, and the conservative optimates, and fled from Rome when Sulla marched on it. He finally returned to Rome – totally illegally – at the head of an army in late 88BC. Becoming consul for the seventh time, he slaughtered his opponents before dying in 87BC.

Right: Marius reorganized the army, giving each legion its silver, later gilded, eagle, which became the focus of intense loyalty.

Although Marius had shown that military competence did not lead to a successful political career, his political success was nevertheless unprecedented at this time. Despite the rules of the constitution, he had been consul seven times, five of them consecutively.

LUCIUS CORNELIUS SULLA (138–79BC)

An optimate, or senatorial reactionary, Sulla came from an old but impoverished patrician family. Appointed general by the Senate for the war against Mithradates of Pontus in 88BC, he used his army to march on Rome and expel the *populares* – the first military intervention in Roman history. He marched on Rome again in 82BC with a devoted army of 100,000 men. The proscriptions that followed became notorious. Sulla executed 40 senators, 1,600 equestrians (knights) and many other citizens, giving their lands to his veterans. To enact his revolutionary programme, Sulla became perpetual dictator.

He passed measures that robbed tribunes of their power, removed courts from the knights' control and issued new treason laws. All this was done to boost the powers of the Senate, which he expanded to 600 men. Behaving in many ways like a monarch – Sulla inaugurated a huge building programme, repaving the forum and rebuilding the Temple of Capitoline Jupiter – he suddenly resigned all power in 80BC and retired, dying a year later. His settlement at once began to collapse, his career serving as both a warning and an example to later Romans.

MARCUS AGRIPPA (63–12BC)

Augustus' greatest general and later his son-in law, Agrippa came from a modest background but from 44BC he was Octavian's closest companion and his indispensable military adviser. He was responsible for building and commanding the fleet that defeated Sextus Pompeius at Naulochus in 36BC, and for defeating Antony's much larger fleet at Actium in 31BC. He did this by using Liburnian galleys, which were smaller and much more manoeuvrable than the giant quinqueremes in Antony's fleet.

In 33BC Agrippa accepted an aedileship – although he had already held the consulship, the top post. In effect, he became Rome's first water commissioner: he erected the first public baths, supervised the extension and rebuilding of the *cloaca maxima*, the ancient drain of Rome, and built an artificial reservoir, or *stagnum*. Later he built a network of roads across Gaul. After Marcellus' death, Agrippa married Julia, Augustus' only daughter, and their two sons Gaius and Lucius became Augustus' official heirs. Agrippa died on 20 March 12BC, one of the finest generals and ministers who had helped transform the Republic into the Principate.

Above: Sulla, the dictator

Below: The capture of Reggio, a Greek city in Italy, as depicted by a medieval artist.

Above: A 3rd-century AD arch in Rome traditionally attributed to Drusus' victories.

Below: Germanicus

NERO DRUSUS (40–9BC)

The younger son of Livia and the stepson of Augustus, Drusus was the descendant of some of the proudest patricians in Rome and, like his older brother Tiberius, he was a formidable general. He first won military fame campaigning in Illyria. After the death of Agrippa in 12BC, although still in his early twenties, he was entrusted with the steadily advancing conquest of Germany. Drusus crossed the Rhine and invaded northern Germany, conquering territory up to the Elbe, which was designated as the new frontier. It is said he longed for the *spolia optima*, the highest military honours awarded to those who had killed an enemy commander in person, and so rode round the battlefields in search of a German chieftain to be his victim. This was probably slanderous, but he was certainly ambitious.

In 9BC Drusus' ambitions were curtailed by his early death in a riding accident. His death deprived the Julio-Claudian dynasty of a good general who was less morose and suspicious than his elder brother. It also deprived those senators still hoping for a republican restoration, for Drusus, according to Tacitus, was believed to be a secret republican. He had married Antonia, the daughter of Mark Antony and niece of Augustus, and they had two sons: Germanicus, who became a popular general, and the bookish Claudius, who later became emperor.

GERMANICUS (15BC–AD19)

The charming and popular son of Drusus and great-nephew of Augustus, Germanicus grew up partly among soldiers. Unlike his infirm brother Claudius, he was marked out early both as a general and as the successor to his father's reputed republican sympathies. By the time Tiberius became emperor in AD14, Germanicus had been appointed by Augustus as commander-in-chief of the Rhine forces, and Tiberius had had to adopt him as his son and heir.

At eight legions, the Rhine command was much the biggest in the army. Many of the legionaries had mutinied, and Germanicus restored order only with great difficulty and at peril to his own life. He led his armies into Germany, where Varus had lost his life and three legions in AD9. Germanicus buried some of the bones of the dead legionaries and defeated the German leader, Arminius, in a minor victory. However, Tiberius had no intention of resuming a forward policy, and in AD16 Germanicus was recalled. Tacitus has him say, "I achieved more by diplomacy than by war…as for the Cherusci and other savage tribes, Rome's vengeance has been asserted and we can leave them to quarrel among themselves." This proved true. In May AD17 Germanicus celebrated a triumph in Rome, then became consul with Tiberius before being sent to sort out problems in the east. On the way he visited Egypt, thereby arousing Tiberius' wrath, for senators were barred from Egypt without imperial permission. In Syria he soon quarrelled with the new governor, Gnaeus Piso.

When Germanicus died at Antioch in October AD19, it was rumoured that Piso had poisoned him. Whether scapegoat or villain, Piso was tried for murder and he committed suicide soon after. Germanicus left three children by his wife Agrippina, Augustus' grand-daughter, of whom one survived to become emperor: Caligula, the vile antithesis of his charming, urbane father.

GAIUS JULIUS AGRICOLA (AD40–93)

One of Rome's finest generals, Agricola was fortunate in having the historian Tacitus as a son-in-law to laud his life and career. Born in AD40 at Forum Iulii (Fréjus), Agricola's father was a senator and his mother a cultured woman who sent him to Greek schools in Marseilles. He first served as a military tribune in Britain under Suetonius Paulinus (AD58–61). As quaestor to Salvius Titianus, governor of Asia, he was shocked by the "mutual covering up of malpractice" among officials. After holding office in Rome, he returned to Britain as a commander. Governorship of Aquitania (south-west France) was followed by consulship under Vespasian.

When he became governor of Britain (AD77–83), Agricola, under orders from Rome, decided to complete the conquest of Britain. He first subdued North Wales before overawing the Brigantes in AD79 by sending two military columns on either side of the Pennines. He continued north into central Scotland, reaching the Tay. In AD82 he turned south-west, conquering that corner of Scotland and glimpsing Ireland, which he optimistically thought could be conquered by a single legion. In AD83 he continued north along the eastern edge of the Highlands, building forts as he went. Finally, in AD84 he met

the gathered Caledonian clans at Mons Graupius, perhaps near Inverness, defeating but not annihilating their forces. He then ordered the building of a major legionary fortress (for more than 5,000 men) at Inchtuthil above the Tay. But the emperor Domitian, suddenly needing troops for the Danube, recalled a legion and the conquest had to be abandoned. "Britain was completely conquered and immediately let go", was Tacitus' bitter comment, but the Highlands would have proved very difficult to conquer and hold.

Agricola was also a great peacetime administrator. He built over 1,300 miles (2,200km) of roads and 60 forts, repressed abuses, notably in the tax-collecting system, was lenient towards minor offences but hard on major ones, and encouraged the Romanization of Britain. According to Tacitus, he "encouraged individuals and communities to build temples, fora and houses… He had leading Britons' sons educated in the liberal arts… The result was that people who had rejected Latin now sought to be fluent and eloquent in it." Such eloquence was a vital Roman civic skill and spurred the development of a true Romano-British aristocracy. Agricola had no further important commands under the increasingly paranoid emperor Domitian, but at least he kept his life.

Above: The great popularity of the general Germanicus at the time of his sudden death in AD19 led to many arches being raised in his posthumous honour across the empire, such as this one at Pompeii in southern Italy.

Below: One of the greatest generals and governors of the Principate, Agricola conquered almost all Britain but suffered Domitian's jealousy. This Renaissance portrait, if more imaginative than accurate, testifies to his fame.

JULIUS CAESAR
101–44 BC

Above: This silver denarius with the head of Caesar – then a novelty in Republican Rome – dates from 44BC, the year of his assassination.

Below: The Forum and, bottom right, the Basilica Julia, which became Rome's chief law court and was perhaps Caesar's most imposing monument, although it was actually completed after his death by his heir Augustus.

Julius Caesar is probably the most famous Roman of all. Due to his early death, he achieved little as a ruler compared with his successor Augustus, yet he deserves his fame, for he was one of Rome's greatest generals and most far-sighted politicians. As a man, he was charming, urbane and often unscrupulous. As a politician, he was the first emperor in all but name. His career demonstrated that only monarchy – whether king, dictator or emperor – could save Rome from chaos. The charisma of his name, Caesar, was such that all his successors called themselves by it, even when totally unrelated to him. This practice continued long after the empire had ended and well beyond its reaches: in Germany up to 1918 (Kaiser is German for emperor) and in Russia (Czar also means emperor).

Gaius Julius Caesar was born on 13 July 101BC. Although a patrician, he was not from the highest Roman nobility. His marriage to Cornelia, daughter of Lucius Cornelius Cinna, linked him with the Marian *popularis* party, making him a wanted man under Sulla's dictatorship, so he withdrew to Asia. Returning to Rome after Sulla's death, he began his political career relatively slowly, supporting the repeal of Sulla's measures. He became quaestor in 68BC and aedile in 65BC, when he gave unusually lavish public games, both alarming the Senate and becoming heavily indebted to Crassus, Rome's richest man. He was now the leading *popularis*. In 63BC he became *pontifex maximus*, the chief priest of Rome, a prestigious post without many priestly duties. After becoming praetor in 62BC, and propraetor (governor) in Spain, he became a consul in 59BC, despite fierce senatorial opposition.

CONQUEROR OF GAUL
Caesar's election as consul was partly due to the support of Crassus and Pompey. Together the three men formed the First Triumvirate, initially a secret pact, always unofficial and essentially illegal. But Caesar's acts helpful to Pompey and Crassus revealed the existence of the triumvirate, so Caesar married his daughter Julia to Pompey to cement the alliance. Caesar often behaved unconstitutionally, forcing his conservative colleague Bibulus to resign. Caesar then got himself extended proconsular command in the "two Gauls".

The Roman provinces of Transalpine and Cisalpine Gaul (southern France and northern Italy) provided good recruiting grounds and opportunities for glory in Gaul itself, a huge area inhabited by warring Celtic tribes. After a victory over the Helvetii in 58BC, Caesar went on to defeat tribe after tribe. Although some

senators objected, the people loved his victories. No Roman had set foot in Germany before. Nor had they in Britain, Caesar's next target. His first invasion fleet in 55BC was damaged by tides, but he returned the next year with a larger force of five legions ferried by 800 ships. This force impressed the Britons, and Britain was claimed as a conquest. A huge final revolt in Gaul was suppressed in 52–1BC. The human cost was immense – over half of all Gauls of military age were killed – but Roman power had reached northern Europe. And Caesar had created an effective army, loyal only to him.

The triumvirate had been renewed in 56BC, but the deaths of Julia in 54BC and Crassus in 53BC undermined it. Pompey, jealous of Caesar, refused to let him stand for consul *in absentia* and gain immunity from prosecution. Caesar had either to accept political and even personal oblivion, or start civil war. On 10 January 49BC Caesar reluctantly marched his army across the Rubicon, the frontier of Italy. Civil war had restarted.

THE MAN AND THE DICTATOR
If slow to start war, Caesar was extremely fast to wage it. After an Asian blitzkrieg he uttered three infamous words "*Veni, vidi, vici*" (I came, I saw, I conquered). However, he spent the winter of 48–47BC besieged in Egypt, where he made Cleopatra his lover and installed her as queen.

As dictator in Rome he initiated a vast range of reforms. He overhauled the calendar, he cancelled interest on debts, and started construction of a basilica and forum. He ordered the draining of the Pontine Marshes and cutting of the Corinth Canal, but neither was accomplished. Around 80,000 landless Roman civilians and as many veterans were settled in 40 colonies around the empire. He issued a new coinage with his head on it and gave lavish games. The Senate was expanded to 900 with non-Italians from Gaul and Spain. A huge new library for Greek and Latin literature was planned. While he was preparing for a war with Parthia,

60 senators, led by Marcus Brutus and Cassius, stabbed him to death outside the Theatre of Pompey on 15 March 44BC.

Caesar had wrongly assumed everyone was won over by his generosity. One of the conspirators, Decimus Brutus, was named in his will and scheduled to be consul. But Caesar's growing personality cult was an outrage to republican sentiment; he had gone about with a large bodyguard, and when offered a regal diadem had not refused it convincingly. Caesar paid for his misjudgement with a life he may not have been too keen to prolong; he suffered from epilepsy and his health was worsening. Rome paid for it with another two rounds of civil war.

Caesar was tall, well built with dark eyes. Somewhat vain, he was delighted when the Senate voted that he could always wear a victor's laurel crown, as he was going bald. He was a noted womanizer but because of a youthful homosexual episode, he was throughout his life unable to escape being taunted with accusations of effeminacy. He was among Rome's best orators and a fine historian. A patron of the arts, he was perhaps the closest Rome produced to a "Renaissance man". His career has been an inspiration and a warning for many later rulers.

Above: Among Caesar's many projects for Rome was his new forum and a temple to Venus Genetrix, the goddess from whom the Julian dynasty claimed descent.

Below: This bronze statue at Aosta in northern Italy shows Caesar as the assured and triumphant general – a role he played to perfection.

POMPEY: CAESAR'S RIVAL
106–48 BC

Above: Pompey the Great. Undoubtedly a brilliant general and fine imperial administrator, in Roman politics Pompey often showed himself as being unable to decide between saving and overthrowing the Republic.

Below: Pompey was totally defeated by Caesar's numerically inferior armies at the Battle of Pharsalus. He fled to Egypt, only to be killed upon landing.

Caesar's greatest rival and one of Rome's finest generals, Pompey ended his career as the last defender of the Republic. Yet his own ambitions were fundamentally not so different from Caesar's. If he had won the civil war, he too could have ended up dictator, although he showed little of Caesar's statesmanlike vision.

Gnaius Pompeius Magnus, Pompey "the Great", was born in 106BC to a noble family on the Adriatic coast. He joined the reactionary general Sulla in 83BC and helped defeat the Marian faction in Rome, killing thousands of civilians. For this Sulla reluctantly granted Pompey a triumph, although he dubbed him *"adulescentulus carnifex"* (little teenage murderer). Given command against Spanish rebels in 77BC, Pompey defeated them, returning to Italy in time to deliver the final blow to Spartacus' slave uprising. Crassus then united with him to demand the consulship in 70BC. As consuls, the two men undid most of Sulla's reforms, restoring the tribunes' powers and reducing the Senate's control of the law courts, winning popular support if senatorial distrust.

When pirates began threatening Rome's corn supply in 67BC, Pompey was given command of 120,000 soldiers and 500 ships. He divided the Mediterranean into twelve zones and within three months had solved the problem. The *Lex Manilia* gave him similar powers over the east, where a war against Mithradates of Pontus had dragged on. Pompey, taking over Rome's armies in Asia, led them to a series of sensational victories: Mithradates committed suicide and Pompey united his kingdom of Pontus with the province of Bithynia. He then marched east as far as the Caucasus, deposing or installing kings, making them client states of Rome and founding 40 new cities. Turning south, he deposed the last Seleucid king and annexed Syria. Continuing into Judaea, he entered Jerusalem and even the Temple, to Jewish dismay. But he confirmed the Macabee dynasty on the Judaean throne, again as client kings. His settlement of the east was so well judged that it effectively lasted 120 years and boosted Roman imperial revenues by 40 per cent. In 62BC he returned to Italy, laden with glory and booty, with his victorious army behind him.

His return was feared, for he had been expected to emulate Sulla and march on Rome. Instead, he disbanded his armies and entered Rome as a civilian, expecting a triumph of suitable splendour and, even more important, land for his veterans. The Senate prevaricated for a year on the former and refused the latter. This proved fatal. Rebuffed, Pompey formed the First Triumvirate with his rivals, Crassus and Julius Caesar, marrying Caesar's daughter Julia to cement the alliance. As consul, Caesar gave Pompey's men their land, but his conquests of Gaul made Pompey jealous. During Caesar's absence, Pompey was effectively master of Rome, becoming sole consul in 52BC.

All he did with his power was to build Rome's first stone theatre, dedicated in 55BC, and side increasingly with the Senate, now dominated by Cato the Younger, a reactionary. When civil war broke out in January 49BC, Pompey reluctantly accepted command from the Senate. He retreated to Greece in the face of Caesar's superior forces, but at Dyracchium (Durazzo) he surrounded and nearly captured Caesar's army. However, in August 48BC he was decisively defeated at Pharsalus and, fleeing to Egypt, was killed as he stepped ashore. Pompey, a proud soldier if often uncertain of his course in Roman politics, might have preferred this end to being ignominiously pardoned by Caesar.

MARK ANTONY
83–30BC

Mark Antony (Marcus Antonius) was Julius Caesar's trusted follower, Octavian's rival, then his ally and finally his enemy. Lord of half the empire and greatest living Roman general, he was hailed as a god in Greek cities and achieved fame as the lover of Cleopatra, queen of Egypt.

Born in 83BC, Mark Antony started his career as an officer in Egypt in the 60s BC. From 54–50BC, he served under Caesar, becoming one of his most trusted officers. On the fateful Ides of March of 44BC, Antony was consul with Caesar and after Caesar's assassination, effectively became Rome's ruler. He used his position and rhetorical skills to drive the assassins from Rome but was outmanoeuvred by Octavian. Antony was too good a general to beat, however, and they came to terms. The Second Triumvirate was formed by Antony, Octavian and Lepidus, a necessary but powerless third. After the triumvirate had beaten the conspirators, Antony took the eastern half of the empire and Octavian most of the west.

From the start, relations were strained. Antony had greater prestige and larger forces but Octavian had Italy and Caesar's name. Antony married Octavian's sister, Octavia, and the triumvirate was renewed in 37BC. But it was obvious that Antony was entangled with a far more alluring woman, Cleopatra VII, queen of Egypt.

Cleopatra, Greek by culture and descent, was an intelligent woman and a shrewd ruler. Her wealth as much as her person initially attracted Antony, and he ostentatiously accepted her aid, ignoring Octavia whom he sent back to Rome. Deeply offended by this snub, Octavian began planning war and in 32BC read out what he said was Antony's will. In a ceremony in Alexandria, Antony gave many sub-kingdoms to Cleopatra's children by Caesar and himself, although confirming Pompey's eastern settlement.

Worse still, when Antony went north in 31BC for the showdown with Octavian, he took not only his Roman army and navy, but also Cleopatra, confirming his image of being under her thumb. In the stand-off between the two armies, Antony's men began deserting and the sea battle was an anticlimax. Both Antony and Cleopatra fled to Egypt, where they committed suicide when Octavian arrived in 30BC. If unsuccessful as rulers, Antony and Cleopatra became immortal as great lovers, not a fate that the great Roman general would have relished. Mark Antony's life ended in tragic failure. If he had triumphed, then an empire less narrowly Roman might have evolved.

Above: This statue in Vienna shows Antony as a debauched drunkard. In fact, he was a highly competent general.

Below: The banquets of Antony and Cleopatra, where pearls were dissolved in wine, were noted for decadence and luxury.

THE HISTORIANS' VIEW

The Romans recognized the power of history – that an imperial nation needs an inspiring, unifying myth, which history alone can provide. Among the fathers of Western history, Roman historians believed an individual's actions counted and that writing history had a moral purpose. As Tacitus, the greatest Roman historian, wrote, "Virtues should not be silently ignored, while the perpetrators of wrong actions… should be threatened with disgrace before posterity."

JULIUS CAESAR (101–44BC)

Caesar called his histories of the Gallic wars and civil wars *Commentaries* rather than full-scale histories. Although they had an obvious political purpose, the histories remain very readable. Written in the third person in a plain, concise style that only rarely becomes monotonous, they tell the gripping tale of Caesar's remarkable campaigns, with interesting geographical and cultural discussions about the Gauls, a people to whom he was not unsympathetic. He also related and praised his men's deeds as well as his own. The civil war commentary, which was not wholly written by Caesar, was more openly a defence of his actions in precipitating civil conflict.

SALLUST (86–34BC)

An active supporter of Caesar in his youth, Sallust took to writing history after being forced out of politics. He developed a terse, epigrammatic style inspired by Thucydides, the greatest Greek historian, but unfortunately most of his works, relating the history of the Republic down to 76BC, are lost.

Sallust was concerned with virtue and he repeatedly attacked the corruptions of his age, especially those of the luxury-loving aristocracy. Sallust himself had been a radical tribune of the plebs, although he later became a highly corrupt provincial governor.

LIVY (59BC–AD17)

At the age of 30, Livy began writing his life's work: a detailed history of Rome. Made up of 142 books, running from Aeneas' (legendary) arrival in Italy to the death of Drusus in 9BC, only 35 books survive intact, with fragments of others.

Essentially a conservative patriot, Livy retained a belief in Rome's grand destiny that won him both Augustus' approval and lasting popularity. He was the historian Rome had been waiting for. His style varied from the majestic to the vivid, while his imaginative sympathy for Rome's opponents makes him a humane writer. He, too, believed that history must instruct and elevate as much as inform.

Although not consciously dishonest, at times Livy attributed words and feelings to his characters that he had no way of knowing were true. Due to his own lack of military experience and partly, perhaps, to his imperfect Greek, he also made several military mistakes. For example, in describing the battle of Zama between Hannibal and Scipio in 202BC, he

Above: This bust of Caesar is unusually unflattering – unlike his two lively histories.

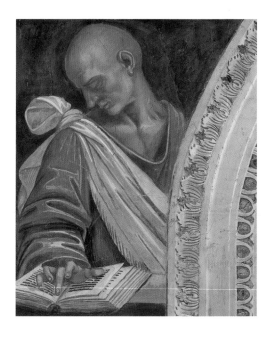

Above: The emperor Augustus approved of Livy's history of Rome's rise.

Below: Sallust turned historian only after leaving politics. His terse style recalls that of the ancient Greeks he so admired.

misinterpreted the Greek historian Polybius' description of Hannibal's third line as Italians, when they were in fact Hannibal's crack veterans from his Italian campaigns, held in reserve. But apart from this, and a tendency to accept legends of Rome's beginnings uncritically, he combined epic grandeur of language and lively description with the conscientious research of a true historian.

TACITUS (AD55– C.116)

Often considered the greatest Roman historian, Tacitus is admired and emulated by many subsequent writers for his style as much as his content. He came from northern Italy, where his father had been a tax-collector. He rose swiftly under the Flavians, entering the Senate under Vespasian and becoming consul in AD97 under Nerva. He wrote most of his histories under Trajan, his major works being the *Germania*, the *Agricola*, about his father-in-law, the *Histories* dealing with the Flavians and the *Annals* of the Julio-Claudians from AD14–64. Much of the last survives and forms a crushing, if unfair, indictment, especially of Tiberius, who slowly emerges as the brutal monster he always secretly was. Other characters – Sejanus, Claudius, Messalina, Nero – are also scathingly depicted. The action alternates between the imperial court at Rome and military camps on the frontiers and is filled with scenes of heroism or of villainy – with no mention of the provinces, which, for the most part, were growing peacefully richer. Tacitus was only interested in the grand themes of a period he saw as "rich in catastrophe, terrifying in its battles, rotten with mutinies". He carefully assessed all available sources before writing, but he was very biased, seeing Tiberius merely as Domitian's forerunner. His *Agricola*, by contrast, is a near eulogy focusing on Agricola's governorship of Britain, and ignoring almost everything else. His *Germania* paints the Germans as noble savages, in contrast to corrupt Romans. Master of the devastating postscript and

ironic put down, his style is intense and subtle, making him one of the great masters of Latin prose. His own gloomy fatalism stemmed from a nostalgic Republicanism coupled with an awareness that the empire had come to stay.

SUETONIUS (C.AD69–C.140)

The raciest and perhaps least serious of the major Roman historians, Suetonius is invaluable to posterity as he had access to imperial records that have since been lost. From an equestrian family, he rose in the imperial service, briefly becoming one of the emperor Hadrian's secretaries before his dismissal in AD119, reputedly for a scandal involving the emperor's wife. He spent the rest of his life writing. His two surviving works are *The Lives of Famous Men* and *The Lives of the Twelve Caesars*, the latter covering the Caesars from Julius to Domitian. He focused on highly entertaining, if not always reliable, accounts of each emperor's personal eccentricities, especially their habits in the bedroom or dining room, after dealing with the political events of the reign. He tended to highlight the former; for example detailing Caligula's remarkable antics in Rome while almost ignoring Claudius' conquest of Britain.

Above: One of the high points of Tacitus' Annals *describes the return of Germanicus's ashes, carried ashore at Brindisi by his widow Agrippina. Tacitus implied Tiberius had had his nephew murdered – almost certainly unjustly. But he hated Tiberius and blackened his reputation.*

Below: Suetonius took a racily biographical approach to history in his Lives of the Twelve Caesars. *He knew about court life, having been Hadrian's secretary.*

ROMAN PHILOSOPHERS
THE GREAT THINKERS

Above: Man of the world as much as philosopher, Seneca tried to apply Stoicism's noble tenets to real life – a doomed attempt that finally contributed to his death.

Below: Epictetus, shown in this medieval illustration talking to the emperor Hadrian, was one of the last and greatest Stoics.

In no area was Rome more indebted to Greece than in philosophy. This was perhaps inevitable, as philosophy was for long considered only a "footnote to Plato", the greatest Greek thinker. From the 2nd century BC on, many educated Romans studied philosophy in Athens, while the major schools of Greek philosophy, Epicureanism, Platonism and Stoicism, found imaginative adherents in Rome. They wrote in Greek as often as in Latin.

LUCRETIUS (C.96–55BC)
One of Rome's greatest poets as well as philosophers, Lucretius turned the dry, austere philosophy of Epicurus (341–271BC) into a lyrical, impassioned plea for a life free of political ambition and superstitious fears of death in *De Rerum Natura* (On the Nature of Things). Epicureans believed in avoiding political engagements, instead cultivating friendship in private communities. Radically, they admitted slaves and women as members, giving rise to ill-founded gossip. Far from indulging in orgies, they actually lived in sober modesty. The gods, according to Epicurus, exist but are unconcerned with human affairs, and human beings have free will. Lucretius writes with an intensity and richness of language, especially in his opening passage, "Delight of men and gods, life-giving Venus", which contradicts his supposed cool detachment. Epicureanism, although attracting the poet Horace, defied Roman belief in public service too deeply to spread far. Lucretius was Rome's great Epicurean poet but contributed little new in philosophy himself.

SENECA (4BC–AD65)
Although not an original thinker, Seneca, who also wrote plays, popularized Stoicism so successfully that his writings are still read today. Founded by Zeno (335–263BC), Stoicism taught universal brotherhood in harmony with a divine, rationally ordered universe. Seneca tried to live, and certainly died, according to his beliefs. Tutor, and also minister for five years, to the emperor Nero, Seneca was implicated in a conspiracy against Nero and forced to commit suicide, which he did with dignity and stoical courage. The essence of his teachings can be found in his letters to friends: "I was glad to hear that you live on friendly terms with your slaves, for so an intelligent, well-educated person like yourself should… Remember: the man you call your slave is of the same species and breathes, lives and dies under the same sky as you. You can imagine him as a free man, he can imagine you a slave… My advice in short: Treat your inferiors as you wish to be treated by your superiors." (*Epistulae Morales*, Moral Letters)

EPICTETUS (C.AD55–135)

As a slave, Epictetus was made lame by his master's abuse. He endured this without complaint, seeing the body as a mere "casing". Freed on Nero's death, in AD89 he was expelled from Rome and settled in Greece. He spent the rest of his life teaching an austere, yet compassionate philosophy. He attacked those who offered quick, easy cures for the human condition, believing that only those with the spiritual strength to cope with their own animal nature and with others' distressed souls and possessing the "counsel of God", could become true philosophers. He urged his followers to trust in divine providence through every misfortune, as he had. His ideas deeply influenced Marcus Aurelius.

MARCUS AURELIUS (AD121–80)

Plato's dream of an empire ruled by a philosopher-king seemed about to come true when Marcus Aurelius became emperor in AD161. Tragically, however, his reign was spent mostly in battles. His *Meditations*, written in Greek while on campaign, are the private records of a troubled man, who used philosophy to help him "as a man, as a Roman and as an emperor". They are also the last Stoic writings, but tinged with Platonism. "Say to yourself every morning: 'Today I shall encounter the officious, the graceless, the arrogant, the treacherous, the envious, the selfish. All this has affected them because they do not recognize the difference between good and evil.'" Marcus Aurelius had an absolute trust in divine providence and saw the universe as one great natural order whose laws men must accept and seek to understand.

PLOTINUS (C.AD204–70)

After studying philosophy in Alexandria, Plotinus settled in Rome, where he became a protégé of Gallienus, emperor from AD253. His writings, collected in the *Enneads*, were the most radically mystical since Plato's and today he is considered the founder of Neoplatonism.

Plotinus compared the universe to a huge fountain of light. An endlessly flowing source, the First Principle, the *monos*, or the One, descends radiantly like the light of the sun through ever lower levels of being until it reaches the very lowest, that of matter, at which point the cosmic dance moves back up towards the One. All human beings are capable of, indeed long for, reunion with the One, which Plotinus called "the flight of the One to the One" and claimed to have achieved three times. This can be experienced through inward contemplation rather than religious rites. Unlike the Stoics, Plotinus ignored completely the external world falling into ruin around him. Neoplatonism later influenced medieval, Renaissance and even Romantic thinkers.

Above: Philosophy continued to interest Rome's richer youths, here shown in debate with a philosopher on a 4th-century AD marble carving.

Above: Plotinus

ROME'S ENEMIES

As Rome's empire grew, it faced formidable opponents, both civilized and barbarian, who at times inflicted crushing defeats on its armies. But, until the empire finally collapsed in the west in the 5th century AD, Roman discipline, resilience and adaptability always won through and overcame earlier reversals.

HANNIBAL BARCA (247–183BC)

The Romans had no greater enemy than Hannibal, the Carthaginian general who came closer than anyone else to conquering them. While the First Punic War had been fought overseas in Sicily and North Africa, the Second was mostly fought in Italy, devastating the peninsula. The Romans called it "Hannibal's war".

Hannibal was the son of Hamilcar Barca, a Carthaginian general who established an empire in Spain to compensate for the loss of Sicily after the First Punic War. It is said that he made his young son swear enmity to Rome on the altar of Moloch, the chief Punic god, in Carthage. In 221BC, Hannibal took over the Punic army and attacked Rome's ally,

Saguntum. Wrong-footing the Romans, who were themselves planning a Spanish expedition, he then marched through southern Gaul and crossed the Alps in late 218BC, braving snowstorms that killed most of his elephants. Emerging into Cisalpine Gaul, he defeated the Romans at Trebbia in December and the next spring routed Flaminius' army at Lake Trasimene. His third, most devastating victory against much superior forces came at Cannae in 216BC. He won this by his tactical genius and professional army, which feigned a retreat in the centre before outflanking the Romans.

After Cannae, some large cities – Capua, Tarento, Syracuse – joined Hannibal, but the majority of Rome's Italian allies remained loyal and the Romans refused to despair. The Senate reappointed Fabius Maximus as dictator, and he waged a war of attrition. Hannibal had no siege engines to attack the walls of Rome, even though they were manned only by boys and old men, and Carthage would not send enough reinforcements. When his brother Hasdrubal finally reached Italy with an army in 207BC, he was defeated separately and his head thrown into Hannibal's camp.

Hannibal maintained his mercenary army's loyalty for another four years with great skill and in increasingly hostile country, before being recalled to Africa. At Zama in 202BC he encountered Scipio, conqueror of Spain, and was beaten in open battle. Hannibal guided Carthage through the dark days after defeat, but his proposed reforms aroused fierce opposition and he went into exile, first in Syria, then in Bithynia, where he finally committed suicide to avoid capture by Roman agents.

He was undoubtedly one of the very greatest generals of the ancient world, resourceful, tenacious and indomitable, with a smattering of Greek culture, like many nobles in Carthage.

Above: Monument at the site of the battle of Cannae, where Hannibal's troops defeated the Roman army in 216BC.

Below: Hannibal led a multi-racial army over the Alps, with Spanish, African and Celtic contingents, along with his elephants, only a few of which, however, survived the passage. Here he rides a small north African forest elephant, a breed now extinct.

Left: Antony met Cleopatra aboard her gilded barque on the river Cnidus, and, according to tradition, at once fell in love with her. But initially her wealth – Egypt was the richest kingdom in the east – probably attracted him even more than her person.

CLEOPATRA, QUEEN OF EGYPT (69–30BC)

Cleopatra VII, last of the Ptolemies, was portrayed to Romans as an oriental *femme fatale* who had lured the great Roman general Mark Antony to his downfall. In fact Cleopatra was Greek in language, culture and background, and she relied more on her intelligence and charm to captivate Caesar and then Antony than on her physical beauty. She wanted to acquire and then keep the throne of Egypt, and used Egypt's wealth to buy the support of Roman armies.

Cleopatra won Caesar's support against her brother Ptolemy XIII, supposedly her co-monarch, when he landed at Alexandria in 47BC. Legend says that Cleopatra was delivered wrapped in a carpet to Caesar's headquarters and they began an affair. Later, she had a son, Caesarion, by him. This liaison so enraged Ptolemy's supporters that they besieged the lovers in the palace. Part of the great library was burnt in the ensuing fighting, which led to Caesar installing her as sole monarch and a client of Rome. Cleopatra followed Caesar to Rome in 45BC, but returned to Egypt after his death.

When Antony met her, he was tempted as much by her wealth as her beauty, but he became her lover, the pair indulging in a life of sensual pleasure in Egypt, much to the delighted horror of opinion in Rome. After Antony had publicly snubbed his wife, the sister of his rival Octavian, he donated some provinces to his and Cleopatra's three children. Octavian's propagandists used this as evidence that Antony wanted to hand over the empire to Cleopatra – clearly not the act of a true Roman.

This famous love affair did not seem to affect Antony's plans for Rome's eastern frontier, but his political judgement was clouded. Instead of leaving Cleopatra behind when he assembled his troops for the final showdown, Antony let her come with him, leading many of his men to desert. The doomed pair escaped from Actium for a last winter of love, but Octavian followed. Cleopatra cheated him of his final victory by committing suicide, traditionally from an asp's bite, before she could be captured. Although Cleopatra may have affronted Octavian's puritanical patriotism, she presented little military threat to Rome.

Above: Antony and Cleopatra, the famous lovers, as played by Richard Burton and Elizabeth Taylor. The Roman soldier's and Egyptian queen's political views may have coincided also, for Cleopatra was determined to defend Egyptian independence while Antony perhaps envisaged a loose Roman hegemony over the east, not annexation.

Above: Boudicca, queen of the Iceni, in her chariot. Her revolt against Roman extortions – which included the rape of her own daughters – threatened Rome's hold of Britain, but the Britons were too chaotic to overcome Roman discipline.

Below: This coin struck by Zenobia of Palmyra as empress of the east in 270AD does not do justice to the famed beauty of this descendant of Cleopatra. Like her ancestor, Zenobia was beaten by Rome in the end.

BOUDICCA, QUEEN OF THE ICENI (DIED AD61)

The Iceni, a warlike tribe of Britons, occupied what is now Norfolk. Their king, Prasutagus, had accepted Roman rule, effectively becoming a client king. On his death, Prasutagus left his kingdom equally to his daughters and to the Romans. The imperial procurator, Catus Decianus, however, expropriated all Iceni lands and allowed Roman *publicani* – taxfarmers – into the kingdom. According to Tacitus, when Prasutagus's widow Boudicca objected, she was flogged and her daughters were raped. Her outraged subjects then revolted and marched on Camulodunum (Colchester), traditionally led by their redoubtable queen. "In appearance she was very tall and most terrifying, with a fierce glance and harsh voice; a great mass of tawny hair fell to her hips", wrote Cassius Dio more than a century later. Camulodunum had no walls and the governor, Suetonius Paulinus, was far away in Anglesey with the main Roman forces. After sacking Camulodunum, the Iceni, along with other Britons, almost annihilated the depleted Ninth Legion sent against them and marched on London, already the trading centre of Britain. They burnt it, together with Verulamium (St Albans), reportedly killing 70,000 Romanized citizens. Then, somewhere in the Midlands, the now huge British force met the Romans under Paulinus with 10,000 men. The Britons were so confident of victory that they brought their wives and children along to enjoy the spectacle. But Roman discipline won the day; the drunken, half-naked Britons fell before the steadily stabbing Roman short swords, and the fugitives became entangled in their own wagons. The legionaries killed every child, woman and even ox they found. According to Tacitus, Boudicca committed suicide soon after. Her revolt had accomplished nothing, except encouraging the Romans to reform their administration in the island and get rid of the *publicani*.

ZENOBIA, QUEEN OF PALMYRA (REIGNED AD267–71)

In the prolonged crises of the mid-3rd century AD, Rome's eastern provinces were invaded by the Persians, who overran Syria, Mesopotamia and Asia Minor, taking the emperor Valerian captive in AD260. The Persians were repulsed not by Valerian's son, the emperor Gallienus, but by Odenathus, king of the wealthy oasis trading city of Palmyra, officially part of Roman Syria. Odenathus, controlling heavy cavalry and mounted archers, now became the semi-independent "Governor of the East". When he died in AD267, perhaps murdered, his widow, Zenobia, a gifted and beautiful woman who loved hunting and drinking, succeeded him. But she was not content with junior status. She annexed Egypt and much of Asia Minor, and in AD270 declared herself Augusta and her son, Vaballathus, Augustus. For a moment it seemed that Rome's whole eastern empire was lost. But the emperor Aurelian marched east and routed the Palmyrene armies, first outside Antioch and then near Palmyra, capturing Zenobia as she was fleeing towards Persia.

Traditionally, she was taken back to Rome, where she walked in golden chains in Aurelian's triumph, before being allowed to retire to a villa at Tivoli. Palmrya itself never recovered its old glory.

ATTILA THE HUN (C. AD406–453)

The *flagellum dei*, or "scourge of God", Attila has gone down in history as a ferociously bloodthirsty savage. The Huns, exceptionally skilled horsemen, had exploded across the Eurasian steppes in the 4th century AD. Their empire then stretched from the Urals to the Danube. Attila started by extorting money from the Eastern empire. In AD448 he reacted to a cut in this subsidy by ravaging the Balkans, defeating armies sent against him. In AD450, aware that he could not capture Constantinople, secure behind its new walls, he turned west with 70,000 horsemen, herding the terrified Germans before him. He crossed the Rhine in AD451 and ransacked Gaul. The Roman general Aetius hastened north and, with the help of the Visigoths, fulfilling their duties as federates, met the Huns at Châlons-sur-Marne. The battle, which cost the Visigothic king Theodoric his life, lasted all day, but at the end the Huns withdrew. It was the only defeat in Attila's life. Attila returned to winter quarters on the Pannonian plains. Here, in a city of tents, he lived in an odd mixture of squalor and luxury. His captives brought a veneer of Graeco-Roman civilization along with plunder of the empire. Attila himself, reputedly even

Left: The great temple of Baal in Palmyra displays the sophistication and wealth of the city that challenged Rome in the east.

dirtier than most of his people but with diplomatic abilities, enjoyed receiving Roman dignitaries, although the pleasure was probably one-sided. Next year Attila turned south and crossed the Alps, sacking Milan and Aquileia, whose fleeing inhabitants founded Venice as a refuge. Aetius had no troops to repel him now. Instead, Pope Leo I rode north and met the Huns. What the Pope said to Attila is unknown but possibly he reminded him of the fate of the last man to sack Rome. Attila turned back and died a year later from a burst blood vessel after celebrating his marriage to his latest wife, a young Frankish princess. Within a few years the Hunnish empire vanished and the Huns passed into history and legend.

Below: Attila, advancing on Rome in AD452, reached and besieged Perugia in central Italy. No Roman forces could be found to oppose him, but Pope Leo I rode out to meet him and persuaded the Hunnish king to turn back, so saving Rome for that year.

CICERO
THE PEACEFUL ROMAN

Rome's greatest orator, lawyer and political thinker, Cicero was exceptional among the generals, consuls and warlords of the late Republic in never having been a soldier. He was, however, a fluent writer on subjects from astronomy to philosophy. Although his suppression of Catiline's conspiracy led to many citizens' arguably illegal deaths, he was a civilian and man of peace in an age of civil wars and naked military ambition. As his 800 surviving letters reveal, he was a man of genuine goodwill and optimism – over-optimism, as it turned out. Cicero attempted to apply Greek philosophy's ethical findings to Roman politics and human behaviour in general. Through Cicero's writings, much of Greek culture was transmitted to western Europe.

Right: Cicero, a novus homo, or self-made man, remains one of the greatest of all Roman writers and politicians, despite most unusually having no military career.

Marcus Tullius Cicero was born in 106BC in the small town of Arpinum, 60 miles (100km) south of Rome to a family of knights. None of his ancestors had held office in Rome, so his rise to the consulship made him a *novus homo*, a "new"or self-made man. He depended on his skills as a lawyer and orator but luckily won the friendship and support of Atticus, a rich banker. Cicero started his legal career by appearing in court against one of Sulla's freedmen in 81BC, risking the dictator's wrath. Wisely, he withdrew to Athens to continue his study of philosophy. He accepted the ethical precepts of Stoicism that all human beings had a spark of the divine in them.

Returning to Rome after Sulla's death, Cicero was elected a quaestor in 75BC. The Sicilians, finding him honest, asked him to prosecute Verres, an ex-governor of the island, for extortion in 70BC. Cicero's speeches were so devastatingly effective, driving Verres into exile, that the grateful Sicilians showered presents on him. He distributed these to needy citizens. Cicero became a praetor in 66BC, dealing with legal cases "fairly and honestly", as Plutarch put it. He also advised Pompey, then assuming his high command. Finally, in 63BC he was elected consul, the highest office.

Cicero owed his meteoric rise, unsupported by any great noble house, chiefly to his mastery of rhetoric – dramatic, impassioned public speaking, a key art of ancient civilization. Brilliant at ridiculing opponents, he used wit, irony and innuendo to overwhelm and seduce listeners. He also embodied the aspirations of the rising commercial equestrian class. Realizing that the senatorial class was too narrow, Cicero envisaged a *concordia ordinum*, a concord of the classes between senate and knights, which he later widened to a *consensus omnium bonorum*, a consensus of all good men. He regarded himself as a saviour of the Republic by his swift if brutal suppression of the conspiracy by the disgruntled patrician Catiline, who tried to overthrow the state in October 63BC.

Left: Cicero at the height of his rhetorical powers denounces the conspiracy of Catiline in the Senate. Cicero saw himself as the saviour of the Republic for this, but the subsequent executions were of questionable legality and harmed his later reputation.

Unfortunately, Cicero failed to win over the one man with the military power to support his *concordia*. Pompey returned in triumph from his eastern conquests to be snubbed by the Senate. On meeting him, Cicero talked only of his own achievements, annoying Pompey. In 58BC Cicero was forced into retirement, accused of acting illegally over the Catiline affair. Although recalled by Pompey, his political influence never fully recovered and he had to write the co-triumvir Caesar a grovelling letter promising he would not attack him again.

THE WRITER

Cicero's enforced leisure gave him time to write. His letters, mostly to Atticus his banker friend, reveal an urbane and cultured upper-class Roman, fond of dinner parties and literary discussions. His letter describing the visit of Caesar to his villa near Puteoli is a masterpiece. "What a guest! Two thousand troops in all… The villa was sealed off. But it went off all right. He was in a good mood and all the talk at table was of literature. Political subjects were avoided altogether. But once is definitely enough".

Cicero was also a family man. His son Marcus was clearly a problem, getting through a vast allowance in Athens. Cicero reserved his greatest love for his daughter Tullia, whose death in childbirth desolated him. He tried to console himself with a belief in the immortality of the soul, but was not totally convinced.

Cicero wrote copiously on philosophy and politics – not original stuff, "only the exact words are mine". *The Laws, The Offices* and *The Republic* deal with politics and the constitution, while *De Finibus* (The Highest Ends) summarizes much of Greek philosophy.

After Caesar's death in 44BC, in which he had no part, Cicero persuaded the Senate to appoint young Octavian to lead an army against Mark Antony. This was a mistake. Octavian, forming the Second Triumvirate, added Cicero's name to the list of those to be proscribed (killed), realizing that Cicero represented the Republic's last best hope. Cicero had set out on a journey to join the conspirators in Greece when Octavian's men overtook him and cut his throat. His severed head and hands were later exhibited in the Forum.

Below: Cicero's humane and liberal views had a profound influence on later western writers, as this illuminated medieval manuscript attests.

CHAPTER III

THE EMPERORS

Monarchs in all but name, the emperors of Rome are among history's most remarkable, often most colourful rulers, their unofficial position in control of a supposed republic giving them intoxicatingly unlimited powers. Originally reserved solely for the Julio-Claudians, one of the great families of the Roman nobility, the imperial throne gradually became the prize of other men. First there were the Flavians, from small Italian towns, then men born outside Italy, notably the Antonines, in the 2nd century AD. Finally, in the 3rd century AD, almost any halfway successful soldier might hope – or fear – to be chosen as emperor by his armies.

Sometimes Roman emperors were model rulers: among these imperial paragons Augustus, first and longest-lived, ranks high, as do Trajan, Hadrian and Marcus Aurelius. Balancing them are paranoids and near-maniacs, such as Caligula; playboy-buffoons, such as Nero; and the debauched – Commodus and the almost indescribable Elagabalus. Most emperors fall, like most human beings, into a category neither good nor bad. So Claudius, Vespasian and Domitian (initially but not later), Septimius, Diocletian and Valentinian I all proved humanly fallible. Undoubtedly, they worked hard if increasingly ineffectually at their task of governing the empire as they saw fit. In the end, the task grew almost unbearably onerous, becoming more a burden than a prize.

Left: A general of the 3rd century AD commanding his troops. The emperors remained above all army commanders, military prestige being vital.

EMPERORS OF ROME

Julio-Claudian emperors
Augustus 27BC–AD14
Tiberius AD14–37
Gaius (Caligula) AD37–41
Claudius AD41–54
Nero AD54–68

Year of the four emperors
Galba AD68–9
Otho AD69
Vitellius AD69

Flavian emperors
Vespasian AD69–79
Titus AD79–81
Domitian AD81–96

Adoptive and Antonine emperors
Nerva AD96–8
Trajan AD98–117
Hadrian AD117–38
Antoninus Pius AD138–61
Marcus Aurelius AD161–80
  and Lucius Verus AD161–9
Commodus AD180–92

Above: Vespasian

Above: Titus

Above: Domitian

Above: Trajan

Above: Hadrian

Above: Marcus Aurelius

Civil war
Pertinax AD193
Didius Julianus AD193

Severan emperors
Septimius Severus AD193–211
Caracalla AD211–17 and Geta AD211
Macrinus AD217–18
Elagabalus AD218–22
Alexander Severus AD222–35

Emperors of the age of chaos
Maximinus Thrax AD235–8
Gordian I AD238
Gordian II AD238
Pupienus and Balbinus AD238
Gordian III AD238–44
Philip the Arab AD244–9
Decius AD249–51

Above: Augustus

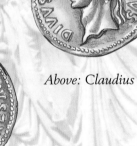
Above: Claudius

Above: Gaius Caligula

Above: Tiberius

Above: Nero

Trebonianus Gallus AD251–3
Aemilius Aemilianus AD253
Valerian AD253–60
Gallienus AD253–68
Claudius II "Gothicus" AD268–70
Quintillus AD270
Aurelian AD270–5
Tacitus AD275–6
Probus AD276–82
Carus AD282–3
Numerian AD283–4
Carinus AD283–5

"Gallic" emperors
Postumus AD260–9
Laelianus AD269
Marius AD269
Victorinus AD268–71
Tetricus AD271–4

The tetrarchs and their successors
Diocletian AD284–305
Maximian AD286–305 and AD307–8
Constantius I AD305–6
Galerius AD305–11
Severus II AD306–7
Maxentius AD306–12
Maximinus Daia AD310–13
Licinius AD308–24

Emperors of the house of Constantine
Constantine I AD306–37
Constantine II AD337–40
Constans AD337–50
Constantius II AD337–61
Julian AD361–3

Jovian AD363–4

Valentinian I (east) AD364–75
 and Valens (west) AD364–75
Gratian AD367–83
Valentinian II AD375–92
Magnus Maximus (usurper) AD383–8
Eugenius (usurper) AD392–4

Theodosian emperors
Theodosius I AD379–95
Arcadius (east) AD395–408
Honorius (west) AD395–423
Constantius III AD421
Theodosius II (east) AD408–50
Valentinian III (west) AD425–55

Last Western emperors
Marjorian AD457–61
Anthemius AD467–72
Romulus Augustulus AD475–6
Julius Nepos AD473–80

Eastern emperors
Marcian AD450–57
Leo I AD457–74
Zeno AD474–91
Anastasius AD491–518
Justin I AD518–27
Justinian AD527–65
Justin II AD565–78
Maurice AD582–602
Heraclius I AD610–41

With the advent of Heraclius, it becomes customary to talk of Byzantine rather than east Roman emperors, as the empire itself finally ceased to be Latin-speaking, even in the army.

Above: Diocletian

Above: Constantine I

Above: Julian

Above: Theodosius I

Above: Justinian I

Above: Septimius Severus

Above: Caracalla   *Above: Elagabalus*

AUGUSTUS: THE FIRST ROMAN EMPEROR

Above: Although he had won power by the sword, Augustus stressed the civilian aspects of his regime by wearing a toga.

Below: A temple to Augustus was built after his death in Istria – he was not worshipped in Italy while he lived.

The transition from ruthless battle leader to revered "father of his country" was one of the greatest achievements of Octavian, who became Augustus, first and greatest Roman emperor. In 44BC, the 18-year-old heir and adopted son of Julius Caesar, just assassinated, had only the lustre of Caesar's name as backing. Cicero, the leading senator, gave him an army command against Mark Antony. But Octavian soon changed sides to form the Second Triumvirate with Antony, gaining mastery of the western part of the empire and, after defeating Antony at Actium in 31BC, rulership of the whole Roman world, just as Julius Caesar had.

In January 27BC, Octavian resigned all his powers, to receive them back, as pre-arranged, from a grateful Senate along with the title *Augustus* (literally revered). We call him the first Roman emperor, but to his contemporaries he took pains to seem no more than *princeps*, first citizen of the Republic. He disguised his power so carefully that his claim to have "restored the Republic" seemed almost credible. Typical of his apparent modesty was his home: an average-sized house formerly belonging to the orator Hortensius. It was located on the Palatine Hill, the traditional aristocratic area. His 45-year reign laid the foundations of a regime that lasted almost 250 years. This – revolution, disguised as a conservative restoration – was typically Roman.

Octavian was very unlike his great-uncle Caesar. Aware that Republican feeling was strong and wanting senatorial support, Octavian cultivated an image of traditional Roman *virtus*, which roughly translates as courage, virtue and probity. He needed the senators' and equestrians' help to run the empire – he had no proper civil service, merely a few secretaries. The 27BC settlement gave him proconsular power in provinces with large armies, such as Gaul (France) and Syria, run by legates appointed by him. Senators governed peaceful, unarmed provinces like Greece. The administration was thus depoliticized, but Augustus retained control of the army, and the title *imperator*, effectively commander-in-chief, from which comes the word emperor. His own military reputation was mixed: he relied heavily on capable generals such as Agrippa, but he retained the crucial loyalty of the armies. They swore loyalty to him, not the Senate, and remained remarkably loyal to his successors.

At first Augustus was consul almost every year, until illness in 23BC made him rethink his position. From then on he had "perpetual tribunician power", which allowed him to convene the Assembly and Senate and propose or veto laws. In 19BC he gained *imperium maius* (supreme power) giving him overall control in the provinces. His settlement was so effective that he faced only one feeble conspiracy. In 2BC he was declared *pater patriae*, father of his country, by the Senate.

THE AGE OF AUGUSTUS

Contemporary writers saw the Augustan era as a golden age in almost every sense – politically, economically and also culturally. Augustus fostered the empire's economic recovery by restoring and ensuring peace. Guided by his cultural minister, Maecenas, he took a direct interest in cultural affairs, and Virgil's epic account of Rome's origins, the *Aeneid*, was a fruit of the age. A great building programme was inaugurated in Rome, completing Caesar's projects such as the vast Basilica Julia. In *Res Gestae*, his list of accomplishments, Augustus claimed to have restored or built 82 temples in one year, including one to Mars, the war god, and one to Apollo, the Greek god of poetry and science. Agrippa, his general, started Rome's first large public baths. Augustus boasted that he had found Rome a city of brick but left it a city of marble.

At heart, Augustus was a social conservative. He wanted to restore the traditional Roman virtues of piety and fidelity, or so propagandists proclaimed. He also wanted to raise the falling Roman birth rate. In the *Lex Julia* of 18BC, he made adultery a crime, penalized celibacy and childless marriages and gave tax breaks to families with three or more children. He banished even his own daughter, Julia, for adultery and the poet Ovid for general licentiousness. He also revived the sacred "secular" games and other old religious festivals.

THE MAN BEHIND THE IMAGE

Augustus was slim, rather short, but well proportioned, "unusually handsome and exceedingly graceful", according to Suetonius, with curly golden hair. Although his health was poor, he nevertheless lived to the age of 77. Ruthless in his youth, he later mellowed. He was a modest gambler and a sociable family man, enjoying dinner with friends. Surviving letters to Gaius, his grandson, calling him "my dearest little donkey", reveal paternal affection. His last years were unhappy, however. Not only did family problems distress him, but the Varus disaster in Germany in AD9, in which three legions were destroyed, shook him badly. He advised Tiberius, whom he had adopted reluctantly in AD4, to expand the empire no further. After his death in AD14 – almost certainly from natural causes – he was given a splendid funeral and declared a god by the Senate. He became the paradigm against which all later emperors would be measured.

FAMILY PROBLEMS

As emperor, Augustus inevitably involved his family in dynastic politics. In 36BC he married Livia Drusilla, who ignored his frequent infidelities and acted as a moderating influence on him. He had only one child, Julia, by his first marriage. Keen to pass on power to a direct descendant, he married Julia to his nephew Marcellus. When Marcellus died in 23BC, Julia, still only 16, was made to marry Agrippa, 24 years her senior. Their five children included two sons, Gaius and Lucius, whom Augustus adopted as his sons. But when Agrippa died in 12BC, Augustus turned to Tiberius, his gloomy stepson who was forced to divorce his wife, Vipsania, whom he loved, and marry Julia, whom he loathed, to be a guardian to the young princes. Disgusted, Tiberius withdrew from public life and Julia began a series of affairs which led to her exile. The premature deaths of the two young princes – Lucius in AD2, Gaius in AD4 – forced Augustus to recall Tiberius to favour. The resulting Julio-Claudian dynasty lasted until AD68.

Left: This cameo gemstone shows Augustus and the goddess Roma. Augustus was often worshipped in association with the goddess of Rome in the provinces but never in the city of Rome itself. After his death he was officially deified by the Senate.

Below: Augustus as the triumphant Roman imperator, *or commander-in-chief. In fact, he was not a brilliant general and in later years never led his armies in person, relying on his very capable generals.*

ORGANIZERS OF EMPIRE

Although the lives and reigns of some emperors were relatively undramatic, they played such vital roles in organizing or restoring the empire, expanding or stabilizing its frontiers and widening its citizenship, that they stand out as truly exceptional emperors. Two of the most notable were Claudius and Hadrian.

Left: On the assassination of Caligula, gangly, stammering Claudius was declared emperor by the Praetorian guard.

CLAUDIUS (REIGNED AD41–54)

Already 50 when the Praetorian guard declared him emperor on 24 January AD41, Claudius's appointment was an event that probably surprised him as much as everyone else. Tall, gangly, with a stammer and a tendency to dribble, Claudius had been kept in the background until his nephew, the new emperor Caligula, half-jokingly made him consul in AD37. After the assassination of Caligula, however, Claudius was the only Julio-Claudian available as next emperor.

Claudius was intelligent if bookish – he had written histories of the Carthaginians and Etruscans, which are now lost – and initially at least he had good intentions. He abolished treason trials and set about restoring public order, which had been shaken by Caligula's excesses, trying to work with rather than against the Senate. However, he had no military experience – a big disadvantage for a ruler whose power ultimately depended on the army, although his brother, the general Germanicus, was fondly remembered by soldiers. One of his first acts was to order the invasion of Britain, which Julius Caesar had

Below: The emperor Claudius is shown here in the guise of the god Jupiter – an implausible role for such a physically unimpressive and ungainly man, but one that became increasingly expected of all the emperors.

attempted and of which both Augustus and Caligula had talked. This proved remarkably successful. Part of southern Britain was overrun in AD43, and Claudius hastened north to celebrate its conquest. Conquests of Mauretania (north Algeria/Morocco) and Thrace in the Balkans made him the most expansionist emperor since Augustus and popular with the army and the people.

To please the volatile populace further, Claudius built an entirely new harbour near Ostia, with breakwaters and a lighthouse, greatly facilitating Rome's troubled grain supply. He also completed two aqueducts that had been started by Caligula. What displeased many in the Senate was his liberal policy of making "Gauls" – Roman citizens from Gaul, sometimes of Gallic ancestry but always Romanized – senators, and extending Roman citizenship widely. (Claudius himself was born in Lyons.) The Senate also criticized his reliance on Greek-speaking freedmen: Pallas looked after finance, Narcissus foreign affairs and Callistus the law. At first, Claudius kept his secretaries under control as they built up departments that foreshadowed the bureaucracy of the 2nd century AD. His love life was unhappy, however. His third wife, Messalina, on whom he doted, was 30 years younger than him and notoriously adulterous. She finally plotted to make one of her lovers emperor and was executed for treason in AD48. In his later years, in declining health, Claudius was ruled by his last wife, Agrippina, who probably poisoned him. Hostile historians have depicted him as hopelessly in thrall to his wives and freedmen, but provincials and later emperors like Vespasian remembered him as an unusually effective ruler.

HADRIAN (REIGNED AD117–38)

Perhaps Rome's greatest emperor devoted to peace rather than war, Hadrian is best known for his wall across northern England, but this is only one aspect of a many-faceted man. A distant relative of the emperor Trajan, whose niece Sabina he married, Hadrian was born in Spain in AD76. He distinguished himself in Trajan's Dacian campaigns and was governor of the key province of Syria during Trajan's eastern wars (AD114–17). When Trajan died, he was proclaimed, on rather debatable grounds, as his chosen heir.

Widespread Jewish revolts and Parthian counter-attacks led Hadrian to abandon all conquests east of the Euphrates, although he retained Dacia (Romania) and Arabia Nabatea (Jordan). He adopted a general defensive policy, personally overseeing the strengthening of the frontier defences in his journeys around the empire – he spent over half his reign outside Italy. On his British visit in AD122, he ordered the building of a stone wall 76 miles (122km) long and 20ft (6m) high, manned by 15,000 troops to keep the barbarians out of Romanized Britain. He also constructed less durable fortifications in Germany and Syria.

He built lavishly, reconstructing the Pantheon, Rome's finest temple, building his huge mausoleum (now the Castel Sant'Angelo) and a luxurious villa complex at Tivoli that included 160 acres (64ha) of gardens and pavilions. In Athens he added a new quarter to the old city, being such a passionate philhellene (lover of Greece) that he was nicknamed Greekling. Initiated into the Eleusinian mysteries, the most important in Greece, Hadrian became archon (mayor) of Athens, which he made head of a new Panhellenic League. He also ordered the completion of the immense temple of the Olympian Zeus, started by Pisistratus more than six centuries earlier.

Sexually Hadrian "ran to excess in the gratification of his desires", according to the 4th-century AD *Augustan Histories*, most notoriously in his passion for the beautiful young boy Antinous, who drowned mysteriously in the Nile. Hadrian thereupon founded a city in his lover's memory, Antinouopolis.

Hadrian got on badly with the Senate from the start, executing four senior senators early in his reign for alleged treason, and he was too obviously cultured to please the Roman populace. But he was a superb administrator and legal reformer. His jurist, Salvius Julianus, drew up a "Perpetual Edict", which codified previously unwritten laws. Hadrian also extended Nerva's and Trajan's policy of poor relief. Despite these achievements, he remained unpopular with the Senate, although there were no conspiracies against him while he was away on his long travels. The empire probably reached its economic peak during his reign, in which the eastern provinces finally recovered their political self-confidence and economic strength.

Above: Hadrian was one of the wisest and most conscientious, as well as cultured, emperors.

Below: Hadrian's most lasting achievement in northern Europe was the wall he built across northern England.

BEST OF EMPERORS

Above: Trajan was the most popular of all emperors.

Below: Trajan's Column in Rome celebrates and records his Dacian victories.

Traditionally, the reigns of the "Five Good Emperors" from Nerva to Marcus Aurelius (AD96–180) encompassed Rome's golden age. The differing fortunes of Trajan and Marcus Aurelius, the two great emperors at each end of the epoch, however, indicate that the empire was indeed passing through its zenith.

TRAJAN (AD98–117)

Born in Spain in AD53, Marcus Ulpianus Traianus was the first non-Italian emperor, although his family were Romans of senatorial rank. He was adopted as the son and heir of the emperor Nerva in AD97 as the elderly senator was so unpopular with the army. Trajan already had a distinguished military and civil record and proved an inspired choice. Affable and handsome, he was equally at ease with the Senate, people and army, but it was military matters that occupied him first.

In AD101 Trajan attacked Dacia (Romania), forcing Decebalus, the king of Dacia, to accept a humiliating peace. But Trajan renewed the war, and by AD106 he had captured the Dacian capital. Decebalus committed suicide. Huge quantities of Dacian gold were taken to Rome, along with Decebalus' head on a pole. Dacia became a Roman province, its lands settled by Romans, its gold mines protected by forts. In AD106 Trajan annexed Arabia Nabatea (Jordan).

With an improved and bigger army, Trajan turned to Parthia. Twin armies swept down the Tigris and Euphrates in AD115 to take the capital Ctesiphon (Baghdad). Trajan marched on to the Gulf, the only emperor to do so. Back home, the Senate voted him perpetual triumphs – a unique but empty honour. But he failed to take Hatra, a key city, revolts flared behind him and the Parthians counter-attacked. In AD117, his conquests across the Euphrates already abandoned, Trajan died of a stroke in Asia Minor.

THE GREAT BUILDER

Trajan was also a great peacetime ruler. He created special funds for helping poor children and built on a massive scale. Some projects were utilitarian, such as the new harbour at Ostia, and some were ornamental, such as his column, whose frieze relates his Dacian wars. Others, including his huge forum, his two libraries and his baths, were both. His correspondence with Pliny the Younger, governor of Bithynia, reveals Trajan's humane good sense. Although reputedly fond of boys and wine (as well as hunting and war), Trajan was never seen as drunk or promiscuous and there were few who disputed his right to the title *optimus princeps*, best of emperors, granted him by the Senate.

MARCUS AURELIUS (AD161–80)

Brought up by Stoic philosophers, high-minded, ascetic and self-sacrificing, Marcus Aurelius seemed destined to become Rome's true philosopher–king. But tragically his reign was filled with almost continuous warfare, and he spent much of it fighting. Born in Spain in AD121 to an aristocratic Roman family, Marcus was chosen as Hadrian's sole heir when he was only six. Antoninus Pius, the next (elderly) emperor, adopted him in AD138. Marcus became consul at the age of 18 and then Caesar (junior emperor). Lucius Verus, nine years younger, was his adoptive brother. When he became emperor in AD161, Marcus persuaded the Senate to make Verus co-Augustus alongside him.

Almost immediately, Parthia invaded Armenia. Lucius Verus went east and the Parthians were repelled – mostly by the governor of Syria, Avidius Cassius, Verus preferring the fleshpots of Antioch – and Ctesiphon and Seleucia-on-the-Tigris were sacked in AD165. The total destruction of the latter, a Hellenistic city, was thought to have aroused divine wrath, manifest in a terrible plague that the

Above: Marcus Aurelius, a philosopher by inclination, spent his reign in endless warfare.

Meanwhile, the Germans had rallied and Marcus had to continue his gruelling Danubian campaigns, spending each winter in camp, finding time between campaigns to administer the empire and write his famous *Meditations*. He decided to annex the whole area up to the Carpathians, forming a continuous new frontier that might prove more defensible. But his health, never strong, was now failing – he probably had cancer – and he died in camp near Vienna in March AD180. Commodus, his worthless heir, quickly abandoned his father's campaign and high ideals.

Below: The world-weariness of the philosopher–emperor Marcus Aurelius can be glimpsed even in these panels celebrating his (incomplete) triumph against the Marcomanni. The contrast with the unalloyed martial vigour of Trajan's celebratory column is very obvious.

victorious troops brought back with them. This ravaged the empire, weakened the army and overshadowed Verus' triumph.

An unexpected German invasion across the Danube, which reached Aquileia in north-east Italy in AD168, triggered a financial and military crisis. Marcus armed gladiators and slaves and went north with Verus. Lucius Verus' sudden death in AD169 did not affect operations, in which Marcus showed himself a very competent general despite having no earlier military experience.

THE DANUBIAN WARS

For five years, Marcus struggled with the Marcomanni and Quadi, Germanic tribes in the modern Czech Republic and Slovakia. He had almost defeated them, campaigning through bitter winters – one battle was fought on the frozen Danube itself – when a revolt by Avidius Cassius in Syria distracted him. Avidius had been misled by a rumour of Marcus' death into making a bid for the empire, in which the empress Faustina was perhaps involved. Avidius was murdered by troops loyal to Marcus before civil war could develop, so Marcus merely toured the east with his 14-year-old son Commodus before returning to Rome for a belated triumph in AD176. The column later erected by Commodus to mark this victory echoes Trajan's, but its overall atmosphere is sombre, rather than jubilant. Marcus rides his chariot with a weary, resigned air.

EVIL EMPERORS

The fact that the emperor's powers could appear unlimited encouraged some emperors – usually those who had inherited the throne young – to become power-mad or paranoid, or both, and to behave in ways that were capricious or despotic, if not arguably insane. Others, later in the empire, were simply brutal thugs, despite having undoubted military talent. All met violent ends.

CALIGULA (AD37–41)

When Augustus' great-grandson Gaius Caligula (literally "little military boots", a nickname he got from the boots he wore as a child) succeeded Tiberius in March AD37, Rome was jubilant. Aged 24 and son of the much-loved general Germanicus, Caligula promised to end the terror of Tiberius' later years. His reign started auspiciously: he recalled all exiles, burnt the police files and even made his uncle Claudius, embarrassingly clumsy, fellow consul.

That autumn, however, he became seriously ill, and when he recovered, his behaviour had changed completely. The illness could have unbalanced his mind, as Suetonius believed; alternatively, it could have brought out a latent paranoia and brutality. What appeared first was a reckless extravagance. He gave extremely spectacular games, at times appearing as a gladiator himself, and lavished attention on his favourite racehorse, Incitatus, who lived luxuriously in a marble stall. Caligula declared that he would make Incitatus a senator, even consul – only half a joke, for his relations with the Senate were deteriorating and in AD39 he dismissed both consuls for treachery. That summer he built a useless bridge of boats 2 miles (3km) long across the Bay of Naples and drove a chariot across it – a gesture typical of his extravagance, and perhaps indicative of growing insanity.

Spindly and prematurely bald, Caligula was insanely jealous of men with a good head of hair. Dressing in effeminate, gaudy silks, he generally did not impress people physically. Although he had had a military childhood, he felt his lack of military glory. In September AD39 he visited the Rhine legions before turning back abruptly, seemingly panic-stricken at being on the German side. He also talked of invading Britain, but when his army reached the Channel, he ordered the legionaries to collect seashells. After celebrating this "victory" over Neptune the sea god, he returned to Rome determined to be worshipped as a god himself. He built a temple to himself and forced senators to become its priests. Some historians suggest that in this he was emulating eastern monarchs, who were worshipped in their own lifetimes. Some emperors indeed were, but not in Rome. Finally, disgusted by such caprices, Caligula's courtiers and officers conspired to kill him on 24 January AD41 as he was leaving the games.

Above: Nero, the would-be artist and actual playboy, became one of Rome's most notoriously debauched and despotic emperors.

Below: The antics of Caligula introduced a capricious madness to the Principate that very nearly destroyed it.

NERO (AD54–68)

Just 17 years old when he succeeded the elderly Claudius in AD54, Nero promised to revive the spirit of Augustus' Principate. At first, guided by the philosopher Seneca, his former tutor, and the Praetorian prefect, Burrus, he seemed to rule well. Trajan later referred approvingly to Nero's first fine *quinquennium* (five years), although he may have been thinking only of Nero's building projects. Despite two family murders – the first in AD54 of his step-brother, Britannicus, the second of his mother, Agrippina, in AD59 – the new regime appeared to run smoothly enough.

In fact, Nero spent much of his time engaged with dramatic pursuits. For these he had a real passion if not talent, vastly admiring Greek culture, at least in its more histrionic aspects. At first Nero performed only before select private audiences, as a noble Roman forfeited all dignity by performing in public. He later alienated the upper classes by appearing on stage, first in half-Greek Naples in AD64, where he made his debut as a singer, and later in Rome itself.

After the death of Burrus in AD62, Seneca retired from court, aware that his influence over Nero was fading. Nero was free to give full vent to his passions, including satisfying his bisexual appetites and penchant for the rough trade. He had a boy, Sporus, castrated and then married him in a mock wedding ceremony. He abused married women and freeborn boys equally (slaves being thought "fair game"). Falling for Poppaea, wife of his crony (and later briefly emperor) Otho, he divorced and executed Octavia, Claudius' daughter, but then viciously kicked Poppaea to death in a rage. This last action lost him much popular support.

Nero's discovery of the senatorial Piso conspiracy against him in AD65 led to savage reprisals. When fire ravaged Rome in AD64, Nero was reputed – wrongly – to have started it and then "fiddled" or sung over the flames. In fact, his fireproof rebuilding regulations were very sensible but his new palace, the Domus Aureus (Golden House) appeared intolerably lavish and vast, sprawling over central Rome. To divert his unpopularity, Nero ordered the first recorded persecution of Christians. Most Romans had no fondness for this new sect but they grew disgusted when they saw Christians being coated with pitch and ignited as human torches in the circus to please the emperor.

Nero loved the glamorous absolutism of Hellenistic monarchies, but Rome was not ready for this. To pursue his artistic vocation, he went to Greece in AD66 and participated in the Olympic Games. He fell out of his chariot, but was declared the winner of every prize, the logic being that if he had not fallen out, he would certainly have won! By the time he returned, reluctantly, to Rome in late AD67, he faced revolts. Some collapsed of their own accord, but Nero dithered fatally, finally being declared a public enemy by the Senate. He committed suicide on 8 June AD68, crying, "What an artist dies in me!" Despite a few good ideas, such as cutting the Corinth Canal and restoring "liberty" (self-government) to the Greek cities, he had no concern or understanding of the army and left a half-bankrupt empire in the grip of civil war.

Above: Nero was popularly – but wrongly – supposed to have fiddled while Rome burned during the fire of Rome in AD64.

Below: After the great fire of Rome in AD64, Nero tried to make the newly recognized sect of the Christians into scapegoats. His plan backfired when their sufferings in the arena roused Roman pity.

Above: Domitian, the grim, sometimes paranoid, emperor

Below: Commodus posed as his favourite hero Hercules in the last years of his reign.

DOMITIAN (REIGNED AD81–96)

Depending on the observer, Domitian was an emperor whose reputation varied greatly. To the Senate and its supporters, including Tacitus, and also to many equestrians, he was an increasingly paranoid autocrat and priggish despot. To the army and to many people in the provinces, he was a conscientious and efficient emperor, albeit lacking the charm of his brother Titus, who had died after a reign of only two years. Although 30 years old when he succeeded Titus, Domitian had had little experience of office. He soon showed that he was a conscientious judge, if one of a marked puritanism. He forbade the castration of boys (for sexual purposes), and he punished homosexuality among senators. He also condemned to death four of the six supposedly chaste Vestal Virgins for having lovers, some incestuously. (One was buried alive in the traditional manner.) This was perfectly legal – as *pontifex maximus*, such cases were his responsibility – but the emperor's conservative rigour shook many in easy-going imperial Rome. What hurt the Senate far more was the way he openly treated them as mere subjects and demanded to be addressed as *dominus*, or lord.

He assumed the title of Perpetual Censor in AD85 and summoned all his officials to the palace, rather than meeting them in the *Curia* (Senate House) or Forum. He rebuilt the imperial palace on the Palatine Hill in a style reminiscent of a Hellenistic monarchy – and Nero – where he entertained lavishly. Although he enforced a public puritanism, he kept many concubines himself, whom he personally depilated.

Aware of the need to keep his soldiers' loyalty, Domitian increased their pay by a third, and, lacking a military record, embarked on a perhaps unnecessary war in AD83 against the Chatti, taking the honorary title Germanicus for a modest victory. According to Tacitus (a biased source), only Domitian's jealousy prevented Agricola from completing his conquest of northern Britain in AD84. In fact, Domitian needed Agricola's troops to quell an uprising in the Danube region. Coupled with a senatorial conspiracy in AD87, this revolt made Domitian increasingly paranoid.

In AD93, fuelled by informers' reports that reached him in his palace – whose mirror-like walls allowed him to watch everybody – he began a reign of terror that spared none. Finally, his closest attendants turned against him, encouraged even by the empress, Domitia. He was murdered in the imperial palace on 18 September AD96. However, the army and Praetorians mourned him.

COMMODUS (REIGNED AD180–92)

Whatever the truth of the rumours that Marcus Aurelius was not the real father of Commodus and that the empress Faustina had slept with a gladiator, Commodus was certainly very unlike his industrious, disciplined and ascetic predecessor. Yet Marcus raised Commodus, his sole surviving son, as a future emperor, making him joint ruler in AD177.

Upon his accession in March AD180, Commodus abandoned Marcus' forward policy in central Europe. Back in Rome he soon showed his distaste for the tedium of government by handing over power to a series of favourites, usually his lovers. He later often had them executed to defuse outbursts of popular unrest. He meanwhile amused himself with his immense seraglio – allegedly containing 300 girls and 300 boys – mostly in luxurious villas outside Rome.

A botched assassination attempt in AD182, probably instigated by his elder sister Lucilla, fuelled his paranoia about the Senate, and he became more openly tyrannical. His chief favourite after AD185 was Cleander, a former slave from Phrygia (Asia Minor) who openly sold offices; in one year he sold the consulate 25 times, enriching himself with the proceeds. A severe shortage of grain in AD190 led to his downfall, when Commodus sacrificed him to the angry mob. In his last years, Commodus emerged from his seclusion to participate in gladiatorial contests – something that deeply shocked many Romans – and was frequently portrayed as the divine hero Hercules, complete with lion skin and club. He also demanded worship as a living god.

Physically, Commodus was "of a striking appearance, with a shapely, manly body and a handsome face", according to Herodian, but the *Augustan Histories* describe him as having a drunkard's dullness of expression. After a serious fire damaged the city in AD191, Commodus decided to refound Rome as Colonia Commodiana (Colony of Commodus) on 1 January AD193. Such rampant megalomania led to a conspiracy among his closest courtiers. Eclectus, the imperial chamberlain, Quintus Laetus, the Praetorian prefect, and his favourite concubine, Marcia, together planned his assassination on 31 December AD192. Marcia gave him poison but he vomited it up, so a gladiator had to strangle him to death. The Senate then damned Commodus as "more cruel than Domitian, more foul than Nero", but four years later Septimius Severus deified him as part of his campaign to adopt himself retrospectively into the Antonine dynasty.

ELAGABALUS
(REIGNED AD218–22)
Born in Syria in AD204, Elagabalus was perhaps the most bizarre of all Rome's emperors. As a child he assumed the hereditary high priesthood of the Semitic sun god, taking its name, Elagabal. He was proclaimed emperor as Marcus Aurelius Antoninus Pius in May AD218 by a lover of his grandmother, Julia Maesa, sister-in-law of the former emperor Caracalla, who was still revered by the army. Elagabalus did not reach

Rome until AD219, which he entered in company of a divine black stone that the Syrians claimed had fallen from heaven, walking backwards before its chariot, which was drawn by white horses. He installed this meteorite in a new temple on the Capitol and made it the supreme god of Rome, even above Jupiter. This was not a popular move, and the new god's often orgiastic worship, rumoured to include secret human sacrifice, principally of small children, alienated the city further, as did Elagabalus' marriage to one of the sacred Vestal Virgins. Elagabalus' almost pathological sex life perhaps indicates transexuality, for he used to prostitute himself to men in cheap bordellos and asked his doctors to cut an artificial vagina into his body. Such bizarreness completed his unpopularity. Only the semi-competent government of his mother and grandmother, and the prospect of his very different cousin Alexander Severus as successor, delayed his assassination until 11 March AD222.

Above: The temple of Jupiter Heliopolitanus in Baalbek in the province of Syria, from where the later Severans came.

Below: Elagabalus was only 14 when he came to the throne, but already depraved.

SAVIOURS OF THE EMPIRE

With the murder of Alexander in AD235, the empire began to glide into chaos. Rival emperors formed separatist realms while, amid endless civil war, barbarian invaders penetrated deep into the empire. Most emperors were army men, acclaimed by greedy legionaries, then casually murdered. But a few, whose efforts helped save the empire in its darkest hours, stand out and deserve to be remembered as restorers of Rome.

GALLIENUS (AD253–68)

Although his reign saw chunks of the empire break away, Gallienus is now seen to have laid the foundations for its subsequent recovery and to have been a patron of the arts. On becoming co-emperor with his father, Valerian, in AD253, he took over the west while his father took the east. Valerian had initial successes against the Persian invaders in Syria, but he ended his life as a Persian captive. Gallienus was unable to revenge this because of barbarian invasions over the Danube. He repelled these but had to accept Postumus' separatist empire in Gaul and Spain. However, Gallienus rescinded his father's anti-Christian edicts and was a patron of the Neoplatonist philosopher Plotinus. He also encouraged a new style in sculpture that revived Augustan classicism, besides being a poet himself. His significant reforms, however, were military. He banned senators from army command and made Milan, closer to the threatened frontiers, capital in all but name, leaving Rome increasingly a ceremonial city. Finally, he created the empire's first armed reserve, a mobile force of crack troops called the *comitatus* (retinue). He also minted new coins to pay them in place of the debased currency. With this new model army, he crushed the Goths in AD268 at Nis in Serbia, killing 50,000, although he was assassinated soon after by his own troops.

AURELIAN (AD270–75)

Commander of Gallienus' new cavalry wing, and possibly involved in the plot against him, Aurelian was one of the Illyrian emperors, tough capable soldiers from the Romanized Balkans who helped save the empire. After turning back another German invasion in AD271, he decided to refortify Rome, three centuries after Augustus had removed most of the Servian walls. The new Aurelianic walls, still standing, ran for 12 miles (19km) and were rushed up, often incorporating older structures. After a victorious campaign against Zenobia of Palmyra in the east, he defeated the Gallic separatists at Châlons in AD274, reuniting the empire in just four years. Aurelian celebrated by building a huge temple in Rome to *Sol Invictus* (the Unconquered Sun), decorating it with booty from Palmyra's temples. Solar monotheism was popular with the army and he presumably hoped the new cult would help unify the empire. The next year, preparing to fight Persia, he was murdered by his secretary for unknown reasons and was mourned by both the army and the Senate.

Above: Under Gallienus, the empire seemed to touch rock bottom. Then, largely due to his new ideas, it began its long, slow recovery, although he himself was soon murdered.

Below: The walls with which Aurelian hastily encircled Rome in the 270s incorporated existing older buildings such as the Claudian aqueduct.

DIOCLETIAN (AD284–305)

Diocletian was one of the greatest of Rome's later emperors, recasting the empire in a bureaucratic, half-oriental mode that essentially lasted three centuries, an achievement for a man who remained, beneath his imperial splendour, a simple Illyrian soldier. Diocletian realized that the empire's crucial weakness lay in the fickle way the armies made and deposed emperors, and the lack of any principles for the succession. In AD286 he made his fellow soldier, Maximian, co-Augustus. They divided the empire, Diocletian taking the east, and both began campaigning energetically, if not always successfully. In AD293 Diocletian adopted Galerius as Caesar, his junior emperor and heir. Maximian did the same with Constantius I in the west. A Caesar was to succeed his Augustus in this Tetrarchy, or quadruple rulership. Each tetrarch adorned his administrative capital – Trier and Milan in the west, Thessalonica and Nicomedia (north Turkey) in the east – with palaces, basilicas and monuments. Each court's elaborate rituals were based on Persian models, elevating the emperor to semi-divine status to help guard against assassination. A two-tier administrative system was adopted. Provincial governors lost their military powers and their provinces were split and then grouped into 12 dioceses, or super-provinces. The army was expanded and reorganized along Gallienus' lines, with fixed frontier troops and *Palatini*, mobile forces directly under the emperor. The new system was successful; the Persians were defeated and the frontier extended further east in AD297, while Britain was restored to the empire by Constantius.

FINANCIAL REFORMS

This extra government came at a huge cost. Diocletian tried to make the tax burden more predictable and equitable, but was unable to check inflation. His notorious Edict of Maximum Prices in AD301, which fixed prices and wages, merely meant that goods disappeared from the markets, although workers were increasingly tied to their jobs like serfs. Nor was Diocletian's religious policy successful. Persecution of Christians, who were seen as unpatriotic blasphemers, even traitors, for their refusal to worship the gods of Rome, began in AD298 and became more savage in AD303. In the west, Maximian and Constantius hardly persecuted them, but in the more Christianized east, several thousands were martyred from AD303 to AD311 and many more abjured their faith. But in one area Diocletian was outstandingly successful: he died peacefully. In AD305, worn out, he abdicated – the first Roman emperor to do so – and retired to his vast fortified palace at Split in Dalmatia. He emerged only once, in AD308, to try to restore peace among his quarrelling successors, for the principles governing succession in the Tetrarchy did not work at all as intended. He died perhaps disappointed at the way his scheme was unravelling, but at least he died in his bed. His basic reforms underpinned the whole later empire.

Above: Under Diocletian, the empire entered a new, less chaotic phase marked by increasing bureaucratization and official attempts to control all aspects of life.

Below: Not least of Diocletian's achievements was being able to retire peacefully to his specially built palace at Split on the Adriatic, although his plans for the succession soon fell apart.

Above: Father of Constantine the Great, Constantius Chlorus was an effective ruler in his own right, regaining Britain for the empire and ruling it and Gaul wisely for many years as a Caesar, or junior emperor. He showed religious tolerance.

Right: Constantius received an enthusiastic welcome from Londoners after his troops reached the city in time to prevent its sack by the usurper Allectus' Frankish mercenaries.

CONSTANTIUS I, CAESAR (AD293–305), AUGUSTUS (AD305–06)

Constantius I, nicknamed "Chlorus", or pale – possibly from the leukemia that finally killed him – is often seen merely as the father of Constantine the Great. In fact, he was a successful ruler in his own right, most notably in his restoration of Britain to the empire. The Augustus Maximian's Praetorian prefect, he was made his heir and Caesar (junior emperor) in AD293, and made Trier his capital. He married Maximian's daughter Theodora, putting aside Helena, the mother of Constantine, who may not have been his legal wife. His first major task was to remove the separatist British empire of Carausius. He drove Carausius from Boulogne in AD293 and then invaded Britain in AD296. His troops reached London in time to stop Frankish mercenaries sacking it, which so pleased Londoners that they struck a medal hailing Constantius as the "restorer of light". A restoration of the whole province followed, ushering in a prosperous half century. Nine years later, Constantius, now a full Augustus, returned to Britain and led a campaign to crush the Picts, before returning to York to die of illness in July AD306. Constantius was notably tolerant in religious matters, ignoring the great persecution of Christians started by Galerius and Diocletian. He was a worshipper of *Sol Invictus* (the Unconquered Sun), a form of solar monotheism popular in the army at the time.

JULIAN "THE APOSTATE" (AD 361–3)

As a 24-year-old philosophy student in Athens, Julian had no political or military experience, being noted only for his inky fingers and his unfashionable beard, when his distant cousin Constantius II summoned him to rule the west as a Caesar in AD355. Julian had grown up partly in a remote castle in Cappadocia, where he studied the Greek classics and recoiled from the machinations of the court. Because the court was also avowedly Christian, Julian began to see all Christians as corrupt and murderous. Constantius, surviving son of Constantine – his two brothers had been murdered – could not deal both with a Gaul overrun by Germans and with the eastern frontier. To great surprise, Julian proved very successful as a general, repelling the Alamanni at Strasbourg in AD357 and marching across the Rhine, emulating Julius Caesar. Julian also reformed the administration, reducing some of the crushing taxes on civilians. Jealous, Constantius tried to recall him in AD360, but Julian's troops proclaimed him Augustus. Civil war was averted by Constantius II's death in AD361, when Julian became sole emperor. He now declared himself a pagan; he had long secretly worshipped the old gods. Although he never persecuted Christians, he forbade them to teach, hoping to reverse the rising Christian tide by excluding them from Greek culture, still overwhelmingly important for anyone with pretensions to learning. Julian himself wrote some philosophy and even a satire. Early in AD363 he invaded Persia with a huge army. He reached, but could not capture, its walled capital Ctesiphon (Baghdad). He then turned back for some reason and was killed, probably by a Christian in his army, on the retreat. His pagan restoration, like his several attempts at administrative reform, died with him, but religiously and militarily he had gained a few years more for Rome and her gods.

Above: The emperor Julian, bearded like ancient Greek philosophers, whose attempted pagan restoration died with him.

VALENTINIAN I
(AD364–75)

A man of the people, Valentinian was another Danubian soldier. He had risen through the ranks to become one of Julian's senior commanders, although the two had not got on well. Tall, fair-haired and blue-eyed, he had a commanding presence and a vigorous personality. Decently educated, he became perhaps the last great emperor in the west.

After the brief reign of the emperor Jovian, who died of natural causes, Valentinian was unanimously acclaimed emperor by the army and civil service in Constantinople. At once dividing the empire, he generously gave his younger brother Valens the east, which was by then much the richer half. He himself moved to Milan, and began to campaign vigorously against Germans who had crossed the Rhine. Driving them back, he marched up the Neckar valley and won a victory in the Black Forest. Then he moved north to Trier, which became once again the capital of the whole western empire. This proved fortunate for Britain, suffering barbarian attacks. Valentinian sent Count Theodosius north in AD368 to restore order. Following an illness in AD367, Valentinian had raised his 8-year-old son Gratian to the throne with him. This was not an inspired choice. Gratian proved an ineffectual emperor, chiefly interested in religion. Valentinian was generally noted for being a poor judge of men, and for having a violent temper. The latter proved fatal. In AD375 he was in Pannonia to repel German invaders. Angered by the insolence of some German envoys, he died of a stroke. Valentinian was also noted for two things seldom associated with late-Roman emperors: a genuine compassion for the poor, whom he tried to help by extending the system of public health in Rome; and, despite his Christian faith, a religious tolerance that was becoming increasingly rare. Meanwhile, his brother Valens in the east was persecuting pagans, and also the Christian majority who did not agree with his version of Christianity, which denied the divinity of Christ. Valens led Rome's forces to a catastrophic defeat at the hands of the Goths at Adrianople in AD378, a defeat from which the empire never fully recovered.

Below: The base of the Egyptian obelisk in the hippodrome in Constantinople, the new eastern capital, shows the emperor Theodosius I receiving the submission of barbarian tribes. Theodosius spent most of his reign (AD379–95) fighting his numerous Roman rivals, but he was the last emperor to rule the whole empire.

CONSTANTINE THE GREAT

Above: Founder of the city of Constantinople and the first Christian Roman emperor, Constantine regarded himself as the "thirteenth apostle".

Below: Constantine was almost the last emperor to adorn Rome with edifices such as baths, a basilica and this triple arch.

Now famed for being the first Christian Roman emperor and for founding Constantinople as the "New Rome", later the capital of the eastern or Byzantine half of the empire, Constantine was, above all, a supremely competent general and a ruthlessly ambitious politician.

Like many other Roman emperors, Constantine's background was that of a soldier. Born c.AD276, his father was Constantius I, "Chlorus" (pale), one of Diocletian's junior emperors. Rumours that his mother was a prostitute can probably be dismissed, although Helena was not the saintly Romano-British noblewoman of legend. Constantine was serving with Diocletian's army when his father became Augustus in May AD305. Hastening across the empire, he joined Constantius in Britain.

On Constantius' death at York in AD306, his troops hailed his son as Augustus – prematurely, for at first he was only accepted as Caesar of the west and Constantine initially established his

Above: Emperor Constantine converted to Christianity late in life, yet his role as the founder of the Byzantine civilization is indisputable. Along with his mother Helena, he is still revered by Greek Orthodox Christians as a saint.

capital at Trier in Gaul. In the ensuing struggles, Constantine was victorious over Maxentius, ruler of Italy, at the Battle of the Milvian Bridge in AD312. He attributed his victory to a dream in which Christ had appeared telling him to mark his soldiers' shields with a cross (or so the story goes). Henceforth, Constantine's soldiers always fought under the cross – at least according to Eusebius, an almost contemporary Christian writer anxious to portray Constantine as a true Christian.

In AD313 Constantine, now Augustus of the west, declared religious tolerance for Christians and pagans alike, although he was already moving towards Christianity. In AD324, when he became sole ruler of the empire, he forbade public sacrifices and ritual prostitution and looted pagan temples to finance his church-building programme, which included the first basilica of St Peter's in Rome. He also presided over the Council of Nicaea (Iznik) in AD325, in vain trying to promote religious unity before finally agreeing to persecute those declared heretics by the Council.

Although Constantine's conversion was almost certainly genuine – he saw himself as the "thirteenth apostle" – religious conviction was also much reinforced by political convenience: the Church's highly effective social organization impressed him, as did the prospect of despoiling pagan temple treasures.

DIOCLETIAN'S HEIR

A revolutionary in religion, Constantine continued with Diocletian's army reforms and further elaborated court ritual, wearing a bejewelled diadem and, allegedly, in later years a wig. If personal vanity was a failing, so was paranoia, for he had his son Crispus by his first wife executed for adultery in AD326. Rumours that the current empress Faustina had intrigued against her stepson – either to advance her own sons or because Crispus had rejected her advances – seemed born out by her suicide soon after, when the emperor's mother, Helena, convinced Constantine of Faustina's guilt. (In the new, ever more elaborate "Byzantine" court, eunuchs played an increasingly vital role as major officials. They appealed to absolutist rulers because they could never found rival dynasties themselves.)

Constantine minted the first *solidus* coin, which, at 72 to the pound (454g) of gold, provided a stable gold currency for many centuries, although inflation continued. Otherwise, his financial policies burdened civilians even more heavily. A new tax, the *chrysagryon*, payable in gold or silver, was levied every four years on citizens. It was so onerous that fathers allegedly sold their daughters to pay it, but money was needed for the huge court, army and building programme. Constantine completed Maxentius' gigantic Basilica Nova in Rome and constructed his own arch – plundering other arches for its decoration. He also built the Baths of Constantine, the ancient city's last grand building, and a palace for the pope. But Constantine did not find Rome, with its proudly pagan memories, sympathetic.

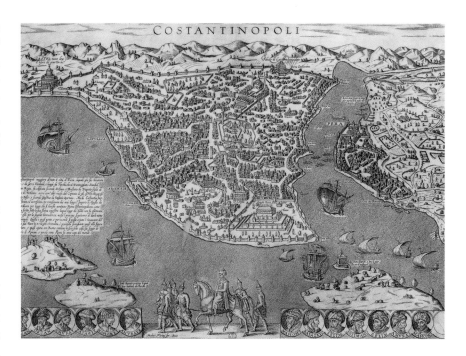

CONSTANTINOPLE

Byzantium had been a small Greek city for almost 1,100 years when it was chosen as Constantine's new capital in AD324. Easy to defend and superbly sited between Europe and Asia, this New Rome, or Constantinople (Istanbul), became a great city. It was later given a Roman-style Senate and its citizens received handouts of free grain and circuses. Constantine liberally adorned his new capital with artworks taken from Greek cities and built new palaces, fora and churches, as well as temples dedicated to Jupiter, Juno and Minerva, echoing those of Rome.

The Byzantine civilization was a fusion of Greek, Roman and the emerging Christian tradition. For this achievement alone, Constantine deserves the title "Great". When he died in May AD337, he was buried in the Church of the Holy Apostles in Constantinople. However, the Senate in Rome deified a ruler who had not resigned the old pagan title of *pontifex maximus*, higher priest, held by every emperor since Augustus. Such a contradiction demonstrates Constantine stood halfway between the old pagan empire of Rome and the deeply Christian Byzantine empire that replaced it and which lasted another eleven centuries.

Above: One of Constantine's greatest feats was the founding of Constantinople. For over a millennium it was one of the greatest cities on earth.

Below: Constantine was a fine general. This ivory shows him triumphing over his enemies.

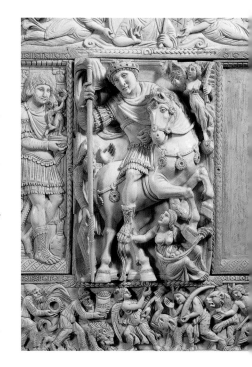

WOMEN BEHIND THE THRONE

Above: Mother of the emperor Nero and last wife of the ageing Claudius, Agrippina aspired to rule through both. But although she (probably) murdered Claudius, her son soon tired of her and had her killed in turn.

Below: Livia, wife of Augustus and mother of Tiberius, had great influence if not power while her husband lived. But after Augustus' death during the grape harvest, Tiberius increasingly ignored her.

Although women in Rome could never hold office or vote, by the late Republic they could own, manage and inherit property. They also joined men at dinner parties and shared Rome's political and cultural life. If their men were of high status, women could also aspire to become powers behind the throne, even occasionally becoming effective rulers.

LIVIA DRUSILLA (59BC–AD29)
In 38BC Livia Drusilla became Augustus' third wife, having divorced her first husband, Tiberius Claudius, by whom she had had two sons: Tiberius and Drusus. As she and Augustus had no children, Augustus adopted first his nephew Marcellus, then his grandsons Gaius and Lucius as his heirs, and only last, when the others had died, Livia's son Tiberius. Because of this, she was suspected of procuring their deaths, although this may be unjust – mortality rates were high at the time – and is certainly unprovable. We do know that Livia gave Augustus invaluable support and stability. The clemency he showed to his (few) enemies in later life was said to stem from her advice. She also tolerated his frequent infidelities, even when he left for Gaul in 16BC accompanied by Terentia, his then mistress. When Tiberius succeeded Augustus in AD14, Livia was rumoured to have poisoned him and his last surviving grandson, Agrippa Postumus. But it is probable that Agrippa, excluded from the succession for psychopathic tendencies, was killed by Tiberius. Livia died at the age of 88, a Julio-Claudian matriarch.

JULIA AGRIPPINA
A sister of Caligula and great-granddaughter of Augustus, Julia Agrippina had married Domitius Ahenobarbus, a great-nephew of Augustus, which made their son Nero doubly descended from the first emperor. Once divorced from Domitius, Agrippina married her uncle, Claudius, in AD49, who had had his third wife, Messalina, executed for plotting against him.

Agrippina plotted to have Nero succeed in place of Britannicus, Claudius' son by Messalina. In AD51 Nero became *princeps iuventutis* (leader of youth), with Seneca, his tutor, and Burrus, one of Agrippina's protégés, head of the Praetorian guard. All was ready for Nero's succession when Agrippina (probably) had Claudius poisoned in October AD54. Britannicus was executed and she hoped to rule through the 17-year-old Nero. At first he showed her respect, but in AD55 she was expelled from the palace and exiled. In AD59 Nero tried to murder her by having a specially built ship sink under her. However, she swam to shore and it took a freed man of Nero's called Anicetus to finish her off. So perished "the best of mothers", as Nero had once called her.

JULIA MAMMAEA
When Alexander Severus succeeded his assassinated cousin, the depraved Elagabalus, to become emperor in AD222, he was only 14 years old and under the sway of his mother, the Syrian princess Julia Mammaea. He never managed to

escape her maternal domination, but at first Julia ruled very effectively. She reversed all Elegabalus' scandalous policies, chose 16 distinguished senators as advisers and relied heavily on the famous lawyer Ulpian, also from Syria, whom she made commander of the Praetorians. However, Ulpian proved unable to control the Praetorians, and was finally murdered by them in AD228.

Meanwhile, Julia had become madly jealous of her son's wife, Barbia Orbiana, whom Alexander had married in AD225, and whose father he had made Caesar or co-ruler. Julia had her daughter-in-law thrown out of the palace and her father executed. Being still dominated by his mother, Alexander accepted this, but Julia could not control foreign attacks. After an inconclusive expedition to repel a Persian invasion in AD232, mother and son went north to deal with a German attack. Alexander so alienated the Rhine legions by his military feebleness and his meanness about their pay that they chose the giant Maximinus as emperor in AD235. Troops sent to kill Alexander found him clinging to his mother in a tent. Mother and son were butchered together, so ending the Severan dynasty.

GALLA PLACIDIA (AD392–50)

Daughter of Theodosius I the Great, grand-daughter of Valentinian I and half-sister of the emperor Honorius (one of the feeblest emperors), Placidia herself was a far stronger character than her half-brother. However, her efforts to preserve the empire foundered partly on her own likes and dislikes. Abducted by the invading Visigoths in AD410, she was carried off to Gaul and forcibly married to the Visigoth king, Ataulf. She owed her return to Italy to Constantius III, a general who took control of the western empire in AD413 and forced the Visigoths to settle around Toulouse. In AD417 he married Placidia against her wishes. However, his death in late AD421 left their infant son the official emperor: Valentinian III (AD425–55).

After a brief interregnum, troops from Constantinople helped Placidia to gain control of Ravenna, the new imperial capital, and she began ruling through her son, Valentinian, trying to maintain imperial power amid the gathering chaos. She had to rely, however, on the armies of the general Aetius, a highly effective soldier whom she for some reason came to loathe. She embroiled him in a dispute with Boniface, governor of North Africa, that had terrible consequences. Boniface enlisted the support of the Vandals, a German tribe who had settled in southern Spain. This was disastrous, for after their entry into Africa in AD429 they were never dislodged. In AD439 they captured Carthage, cutting off Rome's grain supply. Aetius proved more successful in Europe, defeating the Huns in AD451 at Châlons. By then Placidia was dead. She did not live to see the end of her dynasty, for Valentinian proved fatally incompetent. Jealous of Aetius, he had him murdered before being killed himself by two of Aetius' officers in AD455, leaving no heirs. Shortly afterwards, the Vandals landed near Rome and sacked it, carrying off Valentinian's widow and thousands of Romans. The empire soon ceased to exist.

Above: The ruins of Baalbek (Heliopolis) in Syria, the home province of Julia Mammaea, who in reality governed the empire for 13 years during the reign of her ineffectual young son, Alexander Severus.

Above: Daughter of emperor Theodosius, Galla Placidia was far more determined than her half-brother, the emperor Honorius, but she was too often swayed by her personal feelings to pursue effective imperial policies and actually hastened the empire's fall.

CHAPTER IV

GOVERNING THE EMPIRE

Seeing Rome for the first time in 166BC, the Greek historian Polybius was struck by the apparent excellence of its government, thinking it combined the best aspects of democracy in its Assembly of the people, of aristocracy, embodied in the Senate, and monarchy, in its elected officials or consuls. This seemingly perfect system of checks and balances made Rome's status as ruler of the Mediterranean world look well deserved.

But during the Republic and Principate, Rome never had a written constitution. Real power lay in the informal network of alliances and *clientalia*, the web of dependants that each Roman noble needed for a political career. The Senate, dominated by the interests of its noble elite, failed to cope with the problems of governing an expanding empire. This led to the Republic's downfall and its replacement by the emperors. Under imperial rule, the Senate became increasingly ceremonial and the Assembly disappeared, while the provinces rivalled Rome in power and privilege, if never in prestige. By the 4th century AD, the Roman empire had become an absolute monarchy, albeit one where the emperor (at least in theory) obeyed the laws. The full codification of laws by Justinian in the 6th century AD meant that the Roman legacy transmitted to the Middle Ages was more autocratic than democratic, an inspiration more to rulers than the ruled.

Left: At the very heart of Roman life and of the whole empire lay the Forum Romanum, adorned with monuments such as the triple triumphal arch erected by Septimius Severus.

A SELF-GOVERNING CONFEDERACY

Above: The Maison Carrée at Nîmes, France, one of the finest temples of the Augustan era, testifies to the prosperous sophistication of such colonies founded by Rome but growing into confidently self-governing cities that contributed to the empire's strength.

Below: Ostia, at the mouth of the Tiber, was Rome's first colony, the forerunner of many hundreds planted around the Mediterranean and Europe. Later its nearby port became Rome's greatest harbour, supplying the voracious capital.

Rome ruled its growing empire with the minimum of government by co-opting the aristocracies of other cities, first in Italy then around the Mediterranean, into ruling on Rome's behalf. In essence, the empire became a confederation of internally self-governing cities. Defence and foreign affairs were transferred to Rome's control, however. Unlike other ancient cities with empires, notably Athens, Rome was generous in granting citizenship to other towns in Italy. As its empire spread to the less urbanized parts of Europe, it planted colonies of Roman citizens or made existing cities into Roman colonies, so that the empire ended up as an agglomerate of more than 1,000 cities. (New cities without this status, were founded as well.) Urbanization helped spread Roman culture around the empire.

In 381BC the Romans seized Tusculum, a Latin city, and part of the Latin League of cities around Rome. All its citizens were granted Roman citizenship, which they happily accepted, later supplying many consuls. But there were limits to granting full citizenship, if existing Roman citizens were not to be outnumbered. Another type of citizenship, *civitas sine suffragio*, came with all rights except the franchise, and was imposed on cities of the Latin League after their defeat in 338BC. These cities retained internal autonomy, electing their own magistrates, who often got full citizenship. They had to supply troops to Rome when required, serving under their own officers. If they settled in Rome, they became Roman citizens. This halfway house to full citizenship long satisfied the Latin cities.

Rome now began founding colonies of self-governing settlements, both Latin colonies of mixed Latins and Romans, such as Calvi near Capua, and wholly Roman ones, such as Ostia in *c.*350BC. Between 343 and 264BC, about 60,000 colonists received allotments of land in some 40 colonies throughout Italy, from Cremona to Brindisi. Peoples of Italy not thought worthy of Latin citizenship, such as the rough Samnites, were made *socii*, allies, bound to Rome by bilateral treaties. They lost control of their foreign policy and had to supply troops but retained autonomy. The effectiveness of this system was revealed in the cities' loyalty during the Punic wars, when Rome looked doomed. A century later, Italians pressed for full citizenship. The war of the Allies, the Social War, gained full citizenship for all Latins and Italians in 89BC.

COLONIES OVERSEAS

Among the more radical proposals of Gaius Gracchus was the founding of a colony overseas for some of Rome's landless citizens on the site of Carthage, destroyed 23 years earlier. This proposal came to nothing, as did a similar idea for overseas colonies by Saturninus, a Marian tribune, in 102BC. Only under Caesar was the planting of colonies of Romans resumed, mostly for retired legionaries, but his plans included settling 80,000 unemployed Romans abroad. Arles, Tarragona, Fréjus, plus Carthage and

Corinth rising from their ruins, were among his foundations. Under Augustus, who had even more veterans to settle, colonies of ex-legionaries were founded at Turin, Avignon, Nîmes, Cologne and Zaragossa, among others. All have flourished ever since, showing that Augustus and his legates, like Caesar before him, had a good eye for cities. These colonies were self-governing cities with Roman rights, and include Timgad in Algeria, founded by Trajan for his veterans, and Camulodunum (Colchester), founded by Claudius as capital of Britain.

In the east, an old Hellenistic city such as Tarsus might win Roman rights for some (including St Paul), but it was in the west that Roman colonization really bore fruit. Places like Vienne and Lyons acquired Roman rights and grew into fine cities, with theatres, baths and forums. A grade lower were *municipia* with Latin rights, whose magistrates became full Roman citizens. Below them were *civitates*, urban settlements. The tendency was to upgrade any city that proved worthy. London started as a mere *civitas*, but became a *colonia* and the provincial capital.

Above: The Temple of the Spirit of the Colony at Timgad in Algeria, a colony for veteran legionaries founded by the emperor Trajan.

THE OLIGARCHICAL REPUBLIC

Above: This bronze dating from the 5th century BC supposedly portrays Brutus, one of the nobles who helped – according to legend – to expel the last Etruscan king, Tarquin.

Right: The Romans were intensely conscious of their ancestors. They kept their busts in their houses and at times they would parade solemnly with them in public. This statue dates from the 1st century BC.

The three-fold constitution that Polybius so admired – the people, gathered in the *comitia*, or Assembly; the Senate, or Council of Elders, composed of older nobles; and the magistrates themselves, annual officials elected by the *comitia* – had existed in that form since only 287BC, although parts of it may have predated the expulsion of the kings in 509BC. Certainly the Senate itself went back at least to the 6th century BC.

In theory, the people, as constituted in the *comitia*, or Assembly, were sovereign and had unlimited powers. In practice, they met only when summoned by magistrates and could vote, without discussion, only on measures put before them. These restrictions meant that Rome was never a democracy in the sense that many Greek cities were in the classical age (480–322BC). This did not seem to concern the people, for they usually had little desire to guide the state. Their main interest was to be protected from any unjust or arbitrary actions by magistrates and nobles and to gain redress for their economic and legal grievances. Later in the Republic, when Rome had an empire to exploit, they also expected entertainment in the form of free, or very cheap, public games and grain – the so-called *panem et circenses* (bread and circuses). This aspect of Roman life survived the end of the Republic and was transplanted to Constantinople in AD330.

The *comitia centuriata*, or Assembly, was traditionally created by the kings, and continued into the Principate. Its origins were military (the kings wanted to establish an army based on heavy infantry), and it was structured corresponding to army divisions. The citizenry was divided into five classes and each class was subdivided into varying numbers of centuries, except the lowest or poorest class, which was exempt from military service. From the start, the Assembly was heavily weighted in favour of the richer citizens, for the more affluent centuries outnumbered the poorer ones in voting power, if not in numbers. As voting on every proposal started with the richer centuries and ended when an overall majority of centuries had voted, the poorest often did not vote at all. This was a long way from a one-man, one-vote democracy.

The Conflict of the Orders, or Class War, which lasted intermittently from 494 to 287BC, was about this democratic deficit and also economic problems. In the 5th century BC Rome suffered economically, partly due to the reduction in trade at the end of the monarchy, partly because of land shortages and partly because endless wars made it difficult for the citizen-soldier, often fighting during the summer, to tend his farm properly. Many poorer citizens grew so heavily indebted that they became serfs, or *nexi*, of their creditors. Because of problems of this sort they threatened to secede – traditionally five times; the first in 494BC, when they gained new tribunes of the people, magistrates outside the senate-dominated run of offices who could veto measures on their behalf. The writing down of the Twelve Tables of the Law in 450BC was meant to help, but it took a range of measures, culminating in the *Lex Hortensia* of 287BC, by which the decrees of the *concilium plebis*, Council of the People, were to be binding on the whole state, for the conflict finally to be settled.

This did not mean that Rome had become in any way democratic, however, for richer citizens generally dominated the *concilium plebis* too, while the eminent plebeians who had, by law, been elected as one of the two consuls since 367BC, formed the so-called plebeian nobility. Further, the tribunes, once the people's defenders and leaders, were now increasingly co-opted into the Senate, first just to listen to debates but finally to initiate them. The tribunes, who were normally among the richer and therefore often the more ambitious of plebeians, thus joined the plebeian nobility, allied to the Senate rather than opposed to it, and the tribunate increasingly became just one office among others. If former tribunes began entering the Senate themselves, this reduced their effectiveness as champions of the poor, but it made for a welcome amity and unity in a state facing horrendous external threats. Under the emperors, the people finally lost their right to choose magistrates in AD14, and the *comitia* became a mere rubber stamp on the Senate's and emperor's decisions. But the informal powers of the people of Rome long remained a major force in Roman politics. Their approval, most vocally expressed in the amphitheatre or circus, was courted for as long as Rome remained the real capital.

THE MAGISTRATES

With Sulla's reforms in 82BC the *cursus honorum*, or ladder of office, was finalized, but before that the Roman system was oddly informal. The highest magistrates were always the two consuls, elected annually by the Assembly. They each had equal powers and could veto the other's, but this rarely happened. No one could (legally) be consul in successive years. In theory, no one under the age of 42 could become consul, but this check on youthful ambition was unsuccessful. Beneath the consuls were the praetors, whose numbers were steadily increased to eight under Sulla and under Caesar to 16. One praetor supervised the administration of justice, while another praetor dealt with foreigners. Propraetors, like the proconsuls, governed provinces after their year's office. To assist consuls there were quaestors, the most junior rank on the *cursus honorum*, and there were also two censors, elected every five years, who took a census of every citizen's wealth, including senators', demoting or promoting citizens. There were also four aediles who looked after the city's policing.

As the astute, if notably reactionary, senator Cato the Censor (234–149BC) justly observed, the Roman Republic was "not made by any one man, but by many; not in a single lifetime but over many centuries". Considering the overlapping of duties and powers, the Roman Republic worked remarkably well until its last century. But what made it work and lay behind the often fleeting powers of the magistrates and the often inchoate desires of the Assembly was the immense and enduring prestige of the Senate.

Below: Aulus Metellus, an orator of the late Republic (c.90BC), here declaims with a gesture typical of Roman public speaking. Rhetoric was always vital to Roman public life, essential not only for aspiring politicians but also lawyers and ordinary citizens.

ROME'S RULING CLASSES

Under the emperors, Rome was administered by its two upper classes, the Senate and the equestrians (knights). Although the Senate was older and more distinguished, equestrians came to play an increasingly crucial role in the state. The Roman people lost all political power.

THE SENATE

Unlike the senior house of modern republics, the Senate in Rome was not the upper house, for there was no lower house, only the Assembly. Nor was the Senate directly elected. However, as it consisted of men who had once been magistrates – elected by the Assembly – there was a democratic element in it under the Republic. Traditionally, the city's founder, Romulus, chose 100 senior heads of important families as a royal council or Senate. Roman conservatism ensured that this ancient body survived not only the end of the Republic but even the passing of the emperors themselves. The Senate was still debating in the 6th century AD under the Ostrogoths.

The Senate of the early Republic was composed of 300 *patres familias*, or heads of households. They were joined by other prominent men, known as *patricii*, to form a proud nobility of about 1,000 families. From the 4th century BC, plebeian (new) nobles entered the Senate, intermarrying with the older nobility.

Magistrates in the Republic entered the Senate after a year in office as quaestor, the lowest rank. Unless the censors decided to the contrary, they held their seats for life. The Senate's formal powers – to preselect who could stand as magistrates, to approve measures before they went to the Assembly, to advise and consult – made it powerful enough, but this was eclipsed by its informal *auctoritas* (prestige, authority). The Senate expounded its views in a *senatus consultum*, the report of a debate. This had no legal authority, but magistrates normally accepted it. A late development was the *senatus consultum ultimum*, a decree to end all debate.

The Senate guided the Republic effectively through the Punic and later wars. When Hannibal camped outside Rome in 213BC, the Senate's *sang froid* helped save Rome. At that time its members were still recruited from an almost closed circle of *c*.2,000 men. Although they disagreed at times, they did not form destructively divisive factions. But by the time of the reformist Gracchi brothers (133–121BC), the consensus was breaking down and disputes led to violence and murder. From then on, the Senate's control of the state began to

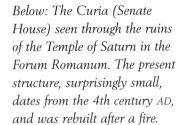

Below: The Curia (Senate House) seen through the ruins of the Temple of Saturn in the Forum Romanum. The present structure, surprisingly small, dates from the 4th century AD, and was rebuilt after a fire.

weaken. The coups and counter-coups of the 80s BC revealed that the Senate no longer controlled the generals. Despite Sulla's attempts to limit the latter's powers, the Senate lost control of Rome.

THE SENATE AND THE EMPERORS

Augustus tried to restore the Senate's dignity in running the empire. He held real power, but the Senate retained, and sometimes gained, important duties, including presiding over law courts and choosing governors for about a third of the provinces. Senators also continued to be appointed legates – meaning they held power delegated from the emperor – as governors of "imperial" provinces such as Gaul and as generals of legions. By AD100 almost half the Senate was composed of provincials – citizens born outside Italy – and most consuls were not Italian born.

Senate-respecting rulers such as Trajan were balanced by despots such as Caligula or Domitian. Hadrian, a humane emperor, soured his relations with the Senate because he executed several members. The Senate sustained a nostalgia for Republican government long after this was remotely practicable. Augustus was punctilious in attending senatorial debates, but few of the later emperors paid it such attention. They were often too busy to do so.

SENATORIAL ORDER

To become a senator was to attain the highest honours in the state, except that of emperor. To win entry into the Senate, its members had to have a fortune in property (not cash) of one million sesterces. Many had far more. In practice, Senate membership in the Principate was mainly hereditary. The son of a senator started his career at the age of 20 as a military tribune and could enter the Senate as a quaestor at the age of 25 if chosen by the *princeps*. He then worked his way up the *cursus honorum* until, if he was lucky, becoming consul at the age of 43. Under the empire, a consul did not hold his office for a whole year but retired to let another fill the post. None of the offices carried a salary, but the governorship of a major province such as Africa did (one million sesterces a year), making it a coveted post.

Senators formed a class above normal Romans. They wore a special toga, which had a broad purple stripe, had the best seats at the theatre reserved for them and were often promised by a new emperor that their members would not be summarily arrested and executed. Until Diocletian, senatorial estates in Italy were free of tax, and even later senators retained many privileges, remaining immensely wealthy.

Above: The ancient Rostra (literally, ships' prows), from which magistrates made speeches in the Forum, Rome.

Below: Roman senators taking part in a procession for a consul's assumption of office c.270AD. Although by that date the Senate had lost almost all its political powers, it nevertheless retained immense prestige and wealth.

Above: While the equestrians as an order failed to maintain their distinctive status in the later empire, senators such as this 5th-century noble retained their importance and their regular meetings in the Senate House well into the 6th century.

Below: Head of a priest of Aphrodite, dating to the 1st century BC. Many of these local cults flourished under the Roman Empire, sometimes attracting the attention of senators from Rome.

THE EQUESTRIANS

Immediately beneath senators in prestige and dignity, and sometimes individually richer, were the equestrians, or knights. Originally, they had supplied the cavalry for the armies of the early Republic, being those relatively few citizens rich enough to equip themselves as horsemen. By 200BC they had lost this role to auxiliary cavalry. Excluded entirely from the *cursus honorum* of the senatorial nobility, they turned instead to making money. The big advantage they had over senators was that they were not barred from all forms of business. As the empire expanded south and east in the 3rd and 2nd centuries BC, literally golden opportunities arose for equestrians in banking, commerce, tax-collecting and bidding for the many government contracts – building bridges and harbours, supplying armies – that were farmed out. Most profitable of all was tax-farming. When the radical tribune Gaius Gracchus, presumably heedless of longer-term consequences, granted the equestrians the tax-collecting contracts for the Asian provinces in 122BC, he was rewarding his immediate political allies. But he also vastly boosted a powerful new class of businessmen who soon began to challenge the Senate's monopoly of office and power, and generally supported the *popularis* reformist party. Sulla, a keen *optimate*, or senatorial reactionary, proscribed (killed) 1,600 equestrians – compared to only 40 senators – when he tried to re-establish senatorial supremacy, but even he was forced to recruit from equestrian ranks for his much-enlarged Senate. Equestrians and their tax-collecting agents, the *publicani*, were among those massacred by angry Greeks in Delos and the cities of the Aegean in 88BC at the instigation of Mithradates.

Caesar made frequent use of equestrians, using them both to fill the Senate and as administrators, some of them being non-Italian multi-millionaires such as Lucius Balbus of Cadiz. By then, equestrians were numerous – there were 500 men of equestrian status in both Padua and Cadiz in Augustus' time. They provided a perfect source of enterprising, often enthusiastic men to run the empire under the Principate, for they had no senatorial-type nostalgia for the days of the Republic. Augustus employed equestrians widely, either as procurators or financial secretaries in charge of the finances of imperial provinces who could control the senatorial legate, or else as governors of those provinces such as Egypt where he wanted to exclude the Senate. In Rome he revived the annual mounted processions of equestrians that took place on 15 July, when up to 5,000 of them would ride past on their ceremonial horses. Tiberius' chief minister Sejanus was an equestrian – but he overstepped the mark, for

CURSUS HONORUM

Originally very flexible, this official career ladder or succession of magistracies was codified by the *Lex Villia Annalis* of 180BC and confirmed a century later by Sulla. After an initial ten years' military service and his 30th birthday, a well-connected Roman could hope to be elected one of the 20 quaestors, whose duties were chiefly financial. A quaestor automatically became a member of the Senate and might then hope to become an aedile. By the age of 38 he might be elected praetor and only at the age of 43 (39 before Sulla's reforms in 81BC) could he stand for the consulship. After being consul, he could become a governor of a province as a proconsul or perhaps a censor, one of two magistrates elected every five years to conduct a census of the Roman people, classifying them according to wealth and conduct. No office could in theory be held until at least two years had elapsed since his previous term of office. The aim, which failed disastrously in the end, was to stop men such as Marius, Pompey or Caesar becoming too powerful.

Tiberius, proudly conscious of his descent from the great Claudian family, struck Sejanus down.

To rank as an equestrian required a fortune of 300,000 sesterces, less than a third of a senator's. Equestrians could be recognized by the narrow purple stripes on their togas; they wore a special gold ring and had the second best seats in the theatres. To belong to the equestrian order did not require residence in Rome, unlike the Senate, and many in fact lived outside the city, either in Italy or in the provinces, often respected members and patrons of the local city magistracy. The sons of equestrians, though not automatically admitted to the order, in practice usually were, first serving as army officers, often in unglamorous posts such as remote frontier forts, then in civilian posts such as customs, finance and general administration. The leading treasury officials under the Principate were most often equestrians, as were the very highest posts in the empire: the prefectures of the corn supply, the *annona*; of the fleet; of the *vigiles*, the night watchmen/firemen; and last and most powerful, the Praetorian prefect, head of the Praetorian guard. Salaries for these posts were considerable, coming in grades of 60,000, 100,000 and 200,000 sesterces. Freedmen and centurions were sometimes given equestrian status and could hope to rise meritocratically. Hadrian (AD117–38) made extensive use of such new equestrians. Unlike senators, however, they had no *curia* (Senate house) as a focus for their class, and their name and status did not survive the end of the empire.

Below: Typical of the new business opportunities for the equestrians, who were allowed to take part in commerce, was the free port at Delos in Greece, which became the busiest entrepôt in the late Republic. Reputedly, Delos could handle the sale of up to 40,000 slaves a day.

THE SECRET WORKINGS OF ROMAN POLITICS

The oligarchic reality of the Republic, which negated its seemingly democratic constitution, depended on the huge web of patronage called *clientalia*. This was an informal, but openly acknowledged, system by which each noble commanded the loyalties of hundreds, or even thousands, of retainers bound to him in reciprocal relationship. This enabled the nobility to manipulate the Assembly, which otherwise could have shown signs of democratic independence. The tenacious network survived the end of the Republic, although it was the emperors who became its ultimate beneficiaries.

As early as the 5th century BC, possibly even under the kings, *clientalia* was an important part of Roman life. At its simplest, it was a personal relationship of mutual obligation between the *patronus*, the patron, who was generally a great aristocrat or patrician, and his *clientes*, or dependants, humble and usually impoverished plebeians. In the Republic's later years, such clients came to include freedmen, usually former slaves of the *patronus*, who formed an increasingly numerous group. But unless these freedmen became Roman citizens – and so able to vote – they were second-class *clientes*. Only a full Roman citizen could expect to receive the *sportula*, regular little presents in cash or kind that a client expected from his patron.

The patron would look after his clients in many aspects of life – if they went to law, needed to borrow money, needed advice in general or a guardian for their children. In return, a client gave his patron political support, both by voting for him and his allies in the Assembly and also by augmenting his personal following. The patron saw himself as a *paterfamilias* in relation to his clients, as head of an extended family, and their relationship had the same sort of highly charged feelings of *pietas* (piety) and *fides* (faithfulness) expected in a family.

For the ordinary Roman in a city grown impersonally vast, being a client offered certain advantages besides the obvious financial and legal help a great man could give. It gave a client a feeling of belonging and participating in the affairs of one of the great families who ran the growing empire. By 200BC the major noble families were organizing their bands of *clientes* on a professional basis, mobilizing them in great blocks to vote as required, and to cajole and threaten other voters when required. Tiberius and

Below: Most of public life, not just political, but also social and legal, took place in the Forum Romanum. Here too the networks of clients and patrons could be renewed, cemented or extended.

Gaius Gracchus were murdered by clients of the optimate senators, not by the senators themselves. The system continued in an apolitical way even after Tiberius had removed the Assembly's last political powers of electing magistrates.

The concept of *clientalia* spilt over into Rome's dealings with its allies and subjects. When Quintus Flaminius declared "freedom" for the Greek cities in 196BC, the sort of relationship he saw between the Greeks and Rome was not total independence but the symbiotic client–patron relationship that worked so well in Rome. The Greeks did not see it this way, having known real freedom, and it took brutal repression by Rome before they accepted the new status quo. But later, when Rome extended its power east to less liberty-addicted kingdoms in western Asia, this informal, essentially personal, system worked well.

MILITARY *CLIENTALIA*

The army was for a long time outside the client system, as of all political life – armies were not allowed into Italy and weapons could not be carried openly in Rome. But from the time of Marius' reforms in 106–102BC, soldiers, now recruited even from the poorest classes, began looking to their generals for rewards for their loyalty in exactly the same way that civilian clients did. The results proved disastrous for the Republic. Caesar's army also formed part of his *clientalia*, as, in a different way, did all his supporters, most of them definitely new men – equestrians or men from the Italian municipal aristocracies or people from even further afield.

Octavian went even further. Preparing for the war with Antony, the climax of his struggle for supremacy, in 32BC, Octavian pressed all the leading men throughout Italy – not just the senators and equestrians in Rome but the local aristocracy of the *municipia* – to swear an oath to him. *"Tota Italia in mea verba iuravit"* (All Italy swore an oath of loyalty to me) he later recorded in the *Res Augustae*, which list his accomplishments. Having sworn such an oath, these men, the ruling classes in the widest sense, became in effect his clients, bound to him by ties of reciprocal fealty. When soldiers swore loyalty to the *princeps* as their supreme commander – although Octavian was never much of a general – the armies, too, effectively became his clients. This personal tie underpinned the Principate throughout its existence; many civilian client–patron relationships had long been hereditary. For the Principate as much as the Republic, therefore, *clientalia* acted as a sort of invisible glue.

Above: As princeps, *or the leading citizen of the state, Augustus was the greatest patron of them all – a role he extended into military life, also binding the army to him.*

Below: Life in the insulae, *the often cramped apartment blocks where most Romans lived, could be grim. Being the client of a rich patron offered a small chance of improvement or at least some support.*

THE PRINCIPATE
A MONARCHY IN DISGUISE

Above: The arrival of Vespasian in Rome in AD69 marked the advent of the second dynasty of emperors: the Flavians. Shorter-lived than the Julio-Claudians, this era ended when Domitian, the last of the Flavians, was assassinated in AD96.

Below: The dramatic public murder of Julius Caesar in 44BC was a stark warning to later emperors to exercise their (unofficial) power with greater discretion and tact. Many failed to do so – and paid the inevitable price.

In February 44BC Caesar, victor of the civil war, had himself created perpetual dictator. Partly because of this latest, most blatant, addition to his powers, he was assassinated soon after. Octavian, later Augustus, was wiser, disguising the absolutist foundations of his new regime so carefully that the Senate could go along with his restoration of the Republic – meaning a stable constitutional government, not rule by the "Senate and People of Rome". Gradually the emperor appeared more and more as an autocrat, whose power depended on force. In the turmoil of the 3rd century AD, the trappings of absolutism finally emerged until, under Diocletian and Constantine, the emperor became a superhuman being, surrounded by genuflecting courtiers.

"If Caesar with all his genius could not find a way out [of the crisis], who can possibly do so?" Gaius Matius, one of Caesar's followers, asked Cicero in a letter soon after Caesar's assassination. It took two more rounds of civil wars before Augustus found an answer. His Second Settlement of 23BC meant that he no longer monopolized the consulate, but let other members of the Senate hold this much-desired office. In fact, it became customary for the first consul of the year to make way for a second. Augustus did his utmost to restore the forms of the Republic – he was ostentatiously first among equals, the *princeps* – and to breathe new if restricted life into its institutions. He offered the senatorial nobility careers running the empire, army and Rome itself. Although Augustus' own household, along with his public behaviour, was notably modest – in reality his wealth, like his power, was vast.

Augustus' successors lacked the tact, patience and *auctoritas* to dissemble so successfully. Tiberius, the next emperor and in many ways deeply traditional, unwittingly revealed the real nature of the Principate by making Sejanus his effective prime minister, although Sejanus was a knight, not a senator, disqualified for high office. Tiberius withdrew to Capri for the last decade of his life and ruled through secretaries, demonstrating again the monarchical reality of power. Tiberius was, however, a morose recluse. The real problems lay elsewhere.

HELLENISTIC GOD–KING OR ROMAN MAGISTRATE?

What often tempted Augustus' heirs was the glamour of the newly conquered Hellenistic monarchies (Alexander the Great's successors) in the eastern Mediterranean. In these empires, it was usual for kings to be hailed as gods while still alive – more agreeable to impatient young princes than waiting until after death. Also, there was no tedious rigma-role of recruiting officials mainly from the ranks of worthy senators and knights. If charming freedmen (ex-slaves), such as Pallas or Narcissus under Claudius, seemed to be the right choice, they could run government departments.

Above: Marcus Aurelius, sacrificing before the Capitoline Temple in Rome. The emperor was also pontifex maximus, *highest priest.*

AD69–79), solidly Roman in his virtues if honest about his dynastic intentions, the constitutional forms were partly revived. But Vespasian passed on power to his sons, first the charming but short-lived Titus, then his second son, Domitian (reigned AD81–96). Domitian soon revealed himself as a paranoid autocrat, who demanded to be addressed as Lord and God. A vast Flavian palace arose on the Palatine, from which he issued orders. Domitian, inevitably, was assassinated.

Under the "Five Good Emperors" (AD96–180) the Principate seemed to have reached some sort of stability with the Senate. Yet the trend towards absolutism continued. Amid the chaos of the 3rd century, the need for effective rule drowned all forms of opposition until the emperor appeared as he really was: a supreme autocrat.

Below: Trajan was an immensely popular emperor – with the army, the Senate, people in Rome and in the provinces. This detail from a triumphal arch in Benevento, southern Italy, commemorates his services to commerce.

Germanicus, Tiberius' heir, discovered in AD19 that people in the east were still enthusiastic about worshipping a Roman general as a god if he let them. Germanicus did not, but his son Caligula, his head turned by seemingly unlimited prospects of power if not by illness, did, forcing senators to become priests of his own cult. This was unacceptable and Caligula paid for it in AD41. So, too, did Nero, whose paranoia after the senatorial conspiracy of Piso led to a vicious spiral of reprisals and further conspiracies. Nero succumbed in other ways to the lure of Hellenistic god-kingship. His Domus Aureus, or Golden House, built after the great fire of AD64, was a palace of truly imperial size, eating up acres of prime land in central Rome, with a colossal statue of Nero as sun god just outside it.

The palace was half-demolished after his death. In its place symbolically rose the Flavian Amphitheatre, or Colosseum, an amphitheatre for the people, started by Vespasian. Under Vespasian (reigned

REPUBLICAN EXTORTION, IMPERIAL PROBITY

The Roman talent for pragmatism was revealed in governing its huge empire. Through a system of trial and error – at the provinces' expense – the Roman Republic found efficient ways of governing its provinces without a large bureaucracy. But by AD300 the empire was being governed on an almost uniform basis by the central government. By then, the skeletal secretariat of the Republic had been replaced by the top-heavy bureaucracy of the Tetrarchy.

Below: The theatre of Pergamum, the kingdom bequeathed to Rome by its last king in 133BC, which became Rome's first province in Asia.

Above: The fortifications of Syracuse, the greatest Greek city in Sicily, date back to 380BC. When Rome finally captured Syracuse in 211BC, it completed its conquest of the island, making it its first true province.

Rome, gaining control of Sicily after the First Punic War in 241BC, faced a new problem. Sicily was large, wealthy and urbanized – mostly by Greek cities but with Punic strongholds in the west, plus rustic Sicel peoples inland. Instead of founding colonies with Roman or Latin rights, as in Italy, Rome created its first *provincia* – literally, sphere of command – appointing former consuls or praetors as governors, with the minimum of staff. Syracuse, the island's largest city, an independent client state until 211BC, offered in its *decuma*, or 10 per cent tax on grain production, a model for revenue-raising. But although many governors corruptly enriched themselves, they also found themselves managing local finances and handing out justice. Sicilian cities, like most cities later in the east, kept much autonomy, being administered by local elected officials later called decurions. These local oligarchs allied with Rome, while Sicily proved an invaluable granary for Rome's hungry citizens. In Spain, too, acquired in 197BC, cities like Cadiz remained client states. A 5 per cent tax on grain output and the development of its silver mines later made Spain into a valuable province, while its tough peoples supplied auxiliary forces. In Italy the Po valley was dominated by warlike Gauls, threateningly close to Rome itself, but offered potentially fine farmland. Another approach led to the founding of such Roman or Latin colonies as Parma and Bologna. By 150BC the Gauls and Ligurians were being driven back into the Alps. By 78BC the area was almost part of Italy in fact if not law; the poet Catullus was born there.

Rome's conquest in the 2nd century BC of the eastern Mediterranean, richer and more civilized than Italy, led to no radical changes in provincial policy. Corrupt governors faced only a small chance of prosecution after their term in office, even if they had flagrantly abused provincials. Cicero's famous lawsuit against Verres, infamous governor of Sicily, was a rare exception. In another speech to the Senate, Cicero pointed out, "Words cannot say how deeply we are hated by foreigners because of the foul behaviour of the men sent out in recent years to govern them." Cicero himself tried to govern Cilicia justly and warned his brother Quintus, on becoming governor of Asia, of the problems caused by well-connected *publicani*, tax-farmers. The burden of Roman taxes, if levied justly, was often no greater than when independent – in the case of Macedonia it was less. But the rapacity of the *publicani* could so enrage provincials – in Greece and Asia Minor in the 80s BC or a century later in Judaea – that they led to anti-Roman uprisings.

PROVINCES UNDER THE EMPIRE

Augustus, who had won the war against Antony as a champion of Italy, could not appear over-generous to provincials. But he still managed to transform provincial administration, usually abolishing the *publicani*. Instead, he levied the *tributum soli*, or land tax. Cisalpine Gaul became part of Italy, and the rest of the provinces

were divided into two groups. Provinces such as Sicily, Africa or Asia were directly under the Senate's jurisdiction, governed by proconsuls, while other regions, such as Gaul and Spain, were part of the *princeps'* giant province, governed by his legates – normally senators, sometimes knights. The founding of cities – whether as colonies of veterans or *civitates*, county towns – made administration easier.

Even in senatorial provinces, good emperors kept a careful eye on governors, as letters between Pliny the Younger, governor of Bithynia, and Trajan show. "Can you send out a land surveyor? A lot of money could be regained…if accurate surveys were made" asked Pliny. Trajan replied, "I regret not. I need all available surveyors here in Rome. Find a reliable one in your own province", and "What is to be done about the unfinished theatre at Nicaea can best be considered and decided by yourself on the spot." But if disaster struck, as when 12 cities in Asia were destroyed in AD17 by an earthquake, even the parsimonious Tiberius promised ten million sesterces in aid and a five-year remission of all taxes, along with a senatorial commission to help in reconstruction.

Above: The temple of Apollo at Corinth, the Greek city sacked by Roman legionaries in 146BC but later reborn as the capital of the province of Achaea. Such a fate was typical of many Greek cities.

Below: These Roman soldiers of the 1st century AD came from Gaul, by then a half-Romanized province.

TAXATION

Above: A cloth merchant displays a piece of fabric, seen on a sarcophagus from Trier in the 4th century AD. The steady growth of textile industries in Gaul and other provinces shows that economic activity was not yet crippled by taxes.

Below: This early 6th-century mosaic from Ravenna was made under Gothic rule. By then, maritime trade had shrunk dramatically, although for centuries maritime taxes had been a major source of revenue for Rome.

"It is a statesman's duty not to impose the *tributum soli* on the people", Cicero declared, voicing the sentiments of the Roman people. The *tributum soli* (property tax) had been the main tax on Roman citizens supposedly levied only in emergencies, and the 3rd century BC had seen one emergency after another. But by the time generals were returning with their booty from a ransacked Greece after the Battle of Pydna, the need for it had passed, and in 167BC it was abolished. Taxes remained controversial throughout the Republic, became less so under the Principate and then, under the later emperors, grew into a crushing burden.

Originally, both Romans and their Latin associates contributed to the Roman state through fighting for it, providing their own arms and armour. Indirect taxes such as customs duties paid for minimal peacetime government, with the *tributum soli* raised in wartime. When the acquisition of Sicily in 241BC allowed the Romans the luxury of taxing subject foreigners, they copied the efficient Syracusan 10 per cent tithe on farm produce. In the wealthier provinces of the east Mediterranean, major problems arose.

PUBLICANI – HATED PROFESSION

In 146BC Achaea (South Greece) and Macedonia were formed into provinces, and 13 years later the last king of Pergamum left his wealthy realm in Asia Minor to Rome. The Republic proved incapable of administering, especially of taxing, these new provinces fairly or honestly. Gaius Gracchus' short-sighted assigning of the tax concessions to the equestrians allowed a ruthless type of tax-collector to emerge: the *publicani*, or tax-farmers (the "publicans" of the New Testament), who could, in effect, levy whatever taxes they liked. The Greek cities supported Mithradates of Pontus in 88BC because of these extortions. Some Romans such as Cicero realized this. Writing to his brother Quintus as the new governor of Asia, Cicero admitted that, "however sympathetic and conscientious you may be in everything, there is one immense obstacle – the *publicani*". After Sulla had driven Mithradates out of Greece in 85BC, he fined the Greek cities five years' back taxes – a sum they could pay only by resorting to Italian money-lenders charging interest at exorbitant rates of 50 per cent or more.

IMPERIAL HONESTY

Julius Caesar and Augustus recognized and tried to remedy this abysmal situation. Augustus could not at first completely abolish the *publicani*, but he regulated them closely. Italy and Rome were exempt from the chief direct tax of the empire, the *tributum soli*, a flat-rate percentage tax on supposed land values, but all parts paid the 1 per cent sales tax, the *centesima rerum venalium*, and customs duties, the *portorium*, levied at 2–2½ per cent and tolls at varying levels in ports. Figures from AD90 from the Red Sea port of Coptos, a terminus for the trade with India, show that a sailor paid tolls of 5 drachmae and a captain 8 – but a prostitute paid 108 drachmae.

A 5 per cent death duty was paid by every Roman citizen, which was one reason why the emperor Caracalla in AD212 granted citizenship to most free people in the empire. Another significant tax was the 5 per cent tax on sales of slaves, again levied throughout the empire. In Egypt, Syria and other parts of the east, Rome also continued to levy the *tributum capitis*, or poll tax, based on censuses that Augustus organized. The emperor Vespasian, restoring the general finances, notoriously put a novel tax on urine collection.

Augustus and his successors had other important sources of income, which supplied the *aerarium militare*, the imperial military treasury. One was from Egypt, long considered separate from the empire, a major source of wheat and other products such as linen and papyrus. Many mines also became imperial possessions, some of the very few large-scale industrial operations in the Roman world. The silver mines near Cartagena in Spain employed 40,000 miners, many of them slaves. The *princeps* had a huge *patrimonium*, or private estate, acquired from legacies or confiscations.

All these together supplied enough, in good times, to pay for the army, the slim civil service and entertaining the Roman populace, without, at first, oppressing the provincials. But it left no surplus for bad times.

THE BURDENSOME LATER EMPIRE

Septimius Severus (AD193–211) raised army numbers to *c.*400,000 men and increased its pay, and under the tetrarchs numbers topped 500,000. There were now four courts to support, and the tax burden increased on a shrinking economy. Ignorant of economics, emperors debased the coinage, hitting the administration worst of all with raging inflation that made soldiers' pay worthless. Gallienus (AD253–68) had to issue a new coinage for his crack troops. Other emperors resorted to the *annona militaris*, military supplies, seizing goods directly.

Diocletian undertook a reform of the whole tax system, not completed until after his death. Realizing that the *annona* (the successor to the *tributum*, the tax on land holdings) and the *capitatio*, the poll tax payable in cash, were grotesquely regressive, hitting the poorest hardest, he established a new system: the *capitatio-iugatio*. This was based on the ancient *iugerum*, a plot measuring 60 x 40 yd (55 x 37m). Land and labour were combined to provide a tax unit that varied according to soil quality and use as vineyard, pasture or cornfield. Five *iugera* of vineyards were worth 20 *iugera* of grain land or 60 of rough pasture. Every five, then every 15, years, a general census, the *indictio*, fixed the tax units, and every year a revised budget and tax demand were issued. Italy lost its tax exemption almost completely. Diocletian aimed to make the burden of taxation not lighter but fairer and more predictable, with some success. Taxes from customs dues and sales continued. He also attempted to stamp out corruption among tax officials and fix maximum prices with an edict in AD301. Under his successors, taxes grew ever heavier until tax collectors were feared and hated more than the barbarians.

Above: A tax-collector from the Rhineland, then under Roman rule, counts his money.

Below: Entrance to the Horrea Epagathiana, a 2nd-century AD warehouse in Ostia. Customs duties at 2½ per cent contributed greatly to imperial revenues.

CHAPTER V

ROME AND THE LAW

The Romans prided themselves on the excellence of their laws, with some reason, seeing law as a field in which they were superior to the Greeks. In its imposing entirety, Roman law is one of Rome's great glories and legacies. However, it did not emerge fully formed, but evolved slowly, from custom and experience, and reached its final form only with the codification of laws by the east Roman emperor Justinian (reigned AD527–65) after the collapse of the empire in the west.

Originally, Roman laws were not at all democratic or concerned with concepts of liberty and justice, but were as pragmatic as the Romans themselves. As early as the 5th century BC, the Romans showed a hard-headed grasp of the day-to-day relations of one citizen to another. For long there was no distinct profession of lawyer and judge, separate from that of law-maker, as today. Cicero was a brilliant barrister, magistrate *and* politician. Under the Principate and later empire, the emperor himself frequently judged cases. Paradoxically, as life in the later empire became increasingly brutal and the imperial administration more despotic, the law became more humane. It was revised and amended by a series of outstanding jurists, influenced by Greek philosophical ideas. Roman law increasingly fused the practical and the idealistic. Its universality, clarity and relative humanity have inspired later jurists and legislators from the Middle Ages to today.

Left: The immense Basilica Nova in Rome became one of the great law courts of the later empire.

LAW IN THE EARLY REPUBLIC
THE TWELVE TABLES OF THE LAW

Above: The altar on this coin, struck at Lyons, the Gallic capital, was for the combined worship of Augustus and Rome itself. The emperor found himself forced to judge more and more law cases, despite the many other demands on his time.

Below: Traditionally, the ten men charged with drawing up the Twelve Tables of the Law in 451BC visited Athens for inspiration, although such a long journey seems improbable for the time.

In the Republic's early decades, there were no written laws. This greatly favoured the patricians, who monopolized the offices of both the *magistrati* and *pontifices*, the priesthood that presided over many law cases, meaning that they alone could interpret laws. *Magistratus* meant both an official and a judge, for the Romans for a very long time made no distinction between judicial law – both criminal and civil – and constitutional laws. *Lex*, a constitutional law, expressed the will of the people (stated by the Assembly, but guided by the Senate), and could be applied to widely differing purposes, such as redistributing land, declaring war or appointing a commander. But a magistrate could also, on his own initiative, issue edicts that had legislative effect. Sitting on a *tribunal* that was literally a platform, the consuls and lesser magistrates were the heirs to the kings, as the emperors were later heirs to the consuls, and heard criminal or civil cases brought before them by plaintiffs. Law,

therefore, in some ways predated actual legislation, being an emanation of Roman *imperium* – authority or power that was thought of as semi-divine in origin.

However, there was nothing mystical about the Twelve Tables. These were drawn up by the decemvirs, a commission of ten patricians who wrote down all Rome's laws on twelve stone tablets in 451BC to placate the plebeians. The laws of the Tables, couched in plain, exact language, remained the basis of Roman law for many centuries, and were learnt by generations of schoolboys. For Livy they were still "the source of entire public and private law". Although possibly influenced by the Greek example of writing down laws, the Twelve Tables' subject matter, as well as their language, is very Roman, a mixture of general principles and minutely detailed private and public law. Among the laws was the *ius provocationis*, the citizen's right to appeal to the Assembly against any magistrate's judgement involving a capital penalty or exile. Later this mutated into "appealing unto Caesar". But this protection was of limited use, as magistrates could still in certain circumstances have a criminal summarily executed without any trial.

Many other laws dealt with the facts of rural life, referring to trees cut down or animals that wandered off – most Romans were still small farmers – but all laws were administered by urban officials. The Twelve Tables generally confirmed the far-reaching paternal power of the father, the *paterfamilias*, over all his children. No matter how mature or important they might be in civil life – even if they had become consuls – sons could not make wills or take part in any legal transaction as long as their fathers were alive. In theory, a father's powers extended to killing his children, although this was

Above: Statues line the great Via Appia to Capua, built by Claudius Appius, who wrote a handbook of legal procedure in 326BC.

rarely exercised. Infanticide (the exposure of children who were unwanted because they were deformed or simply superfluous), on the other hand, was common, especially with baby girls. But women, or at least a *materfamilias*, or wife, did have some rights: for example, on reaching the age of 25 a woman regained the right to manage her own property.

LAW REFORMS

Such stark spelling out of the laws did not help to defuse social tensions, as the decemvirs had hoped, for the plebeians could now see for themselves the iniquities of many existing laws. To redress this, about 30 laws were passed as *leges*, statutes named after their proposer, over the next four centuries, on matters ranging from inheritance to citizenship, sometimes revoking or amending earlier laws considered unjust. A good example of such old laws was that of the *nexus*, in which a debtor who did not repay his

debts risked becoming a *nexus*, or serf – effectively a slave – of his creditors. This law was abolished by the *Lex Poetelia* of 326BC. In 304BC Claudius Appius, a former consul and one of the great radical patricians of Roman history, published a handbook of the correct forms of legal procedure. As the law had until then remained a patrician monopoly, this was another democratizing step.

An even more important decision was made by Titus Corunianus, the *pontifex maximus* in 253BC. The supreme priest (the law was long seen as a manifestation of sacred power) now admitted students to his legal consultations. The priestly monopoly of legal knowledge had already been broken 50 years before by the publishing of judicial procedures, and there was now a need to train others to deal with the expanding number of law cases. These *iurisprudentes*, or lay jurists, were not professional lawyers, but were other citizens, sometimes ex-consuls such as Manius Manilius. Manilius published a book, *Venalium Vendendorum Leges* (Terms of Business for the Sale of Marketable Goods), which attempted to codify and clarify the laws. Attending court cases, the *iurisprudentes* acquired a broad knowledge of the law, which they could use to advise praetors and other magistrates. Their revisions, enlargements and interpretations of the original Twelve Tables, plus their legal formulation of many customary laws that had not been committed to stone, greatly enhanced Roman law. Later they would sit on the *quaestiones*, the special law courts.

Around the same time, in 242BC, a new office of praetor was created, the *praetor peregrinus*, or praetor to deal with legal cases in which at least one of the parties was not a Roman citizen but either a foreigner or subject of Rome. This praetor helped formulate the *ius gentium*, or law of foreign nations, dealing with other nationalities. This was very timely, for Rome had already begun to deal with foreigners who lived not just outside Rome but outside Italy.

Below: One of the strengths of Roman law, from the Twelve Tables of 451BC onwards, was its attention to minute practical detail, which allowed even poorer citizens, such as this woman grocer from Ostia, to practise their trade freely and relatively peacefully.

HOW THE LAWS WORKED IN TIMES OF CRISIS

Above: The law De Baccanalis *was passed in 186BC to control deteriorating public morality, banning the orgiastic worship of the wine god Bacchus. Later on, the worship of Bacchus, as of many other new foreign gods, was safely regulated.*

The events of the century after the start of the Second Punic War in 218BC, when Rome attained Mediterranean predominance and ever-growing wealth for the aristocratic few, saw huge changes in Roman society. The concentration of masses of usually impoverished citizens in Rome – mostly former farmers who had returned from years of fighting abroad to find their land had been occupied by richer neighbours or had gone to waste – led to a dramatic increase in crime, often violent crime. At first, the authorities simply reacted savagely. Hoping to make an example of those they caught, they appointed *tresviri capitales*, triumvirs to deal with capital offences. Such offences included, however, not only the obvious crimes of murder, arson and theft but even the mere carrying of arms with alleged criminal intent or the possession of poisons. If the accused was caught red-handed or confessed his guilt, he would normally be summarily executed. If he pleaded innocence, he would be tried before a praetor or his deputy, or by a triumvir. In both cases, a *consilium*, or advisory commission of jurors, discussed the case and gave advice. In any case, there were no long-term prisons in the Republic and there was a deep repugnance to having armed officers inside the city itself.

As the political situation became more troubled, extraordinary judicial courts (*quaestiones extraordinariae*) were set up to deal with especially egregious cases of corruption, mass crimes, misgovernment and conspiracies against the state. A consul or praetor would preside over these special courts. Finally, from the middle of the 2nd century BC, *quaestiones perpetuae*, or permanent criminal courts, were established to deal with specific offences such as abuse of office by magistrates or conspiracies against the state. The *Lex Sempronia Iudicaria* of 122BC allowed the *equites*, the richer middle class or knights, to sit on the juries, a move made essential because of their rapid growth in number. Although the knights lost control of the courts under Sulla, who restored the Senate's monopoly of them, they were soon reinstated by Pompey and Crassus in 70BC. However, the composition of the juries of the courts remained contentious down to the end of the Republic. Crimes examined by the *quaestiones* included *peculatus*, embezzlement of public funds; *maiestas*, high treason; *de falsis*, forgery of wills and counterfeit coining; *iniuriis*, or violent crimes against the person, and *repetundae*, extortion in the provinces.

THE COURTS

In the courts of the late Republic, which continued under the early Principate, the presiding magistrate would first decide whether a case was worth proceeding with; all prosecutions were still brought by private individuals. He came to his decision after consulting with the members of his *consilium*, the jurors. Jurors for each case were chosen by lot (to avoid corruption or undue influence) to form a panel of up to 75 jurymen, but both prosecution and accused had the right to object to individual jurors, who might be

Right: Marcus Tullius Cicero (106–43BC), orator, writer, statesman and the greatest lawyer of Republican Rome, rose to fame for his attacks on the corrupt governor Verres. His eloquence and rhetoric have given his legal speeches the status of literature.

their personal enemies. During the trials the jurors did nothing but listen, leaving the often vituperative courtroom drama to the accused and to the individual prosecutor. Private citizens had either to prosecute and prove their case, or hire somebody else as their advocate, as the Sicilians famously did with Cicero in 70BC. Cicero, who was both a brilliant barrister and a magistrate, a politician and a senator, made Verres lastingly notorious by his speeches against him, accusing him of every kind of crime, from conniving with pirates to stripping the island of so many statues that it damaged the tourist trade. (Verres went into exile rather than face conviction.) Few cases were as colourful as his, however.

In fact, the procedures actually gave some advantages to the accused. Not only was he entitled to several advocates, but he was allowed 50 per cent more time to speak than the prosecution. The jury finally voted in secret on the accused's alleged guilt or innocence. If found guilty, the penalty fixed by the law was ordered by the magistrate. If it were only a matter of a fine, the jurors might meet again to decide the exact amount. Death was the supposed penalty for many offences, but in practice only slaves and people of the lower orders were normally executed. Generally, other citizens were permitted to escape into exile. As life in Rome was widely believed to be the only life worth living, exile seemed punishment enough.

The jury system of the *quaestiones* normally ensured a reasonably fair and balanced dealing with most criminal cases. But these criminal cases were often time-consuming and laborious and could drag on for years and years. Under the Principate, therefore, the *cognitio extra ordinem* of the imperial law court grew in importance. This was an extraordinary criminal procedure without a jury. By the 2nd century AD, jury courts had begun to fade away. Augustus, at first unwilling to involve himself in judicial affairs, increasingly found himself called

on to give judgement in courts, something that a legalistic-minded emperor like Claudius later positively welcomed. In reality, of course, the *princeps* could judge any case, for even in imperial times there were no professional judges; the supreme civil official was also the supreme judge (*iudex*). Through his tribunician power, the *princeps* could also have laws passed, and his decrees were anyway treated as law. The emperor's concern with law continued, indeed intensified, under the later emperors, culminating at last in the emperor Justinian's great code.

Above: A lictor, or ceremonial official, who preceded consuls, is shown carrying the fasces. *This was a bundle of rods with an axe head at one end, symbolizing the powers of capital and corporal punishment that such magistrates wielded.*

THE GREAT IMPERIAL CODIFICATIONS

Above: Roman law was not automatically enforced on the provinces. But its superior appeal as the law of Rome meant, as these inscriptions of AD209 from Africa show, that most provinces soon adopted it.

Below: Roman public buildings included great basilicas, where judgements were heard. Their form and plan was adopted by early Christian builders, as at this basilica on the Via Nomentana, Rome.

As the empire grew and more and more subjects became full citizens and fully subject to Roman law, legislation inevitably became more complicated. The need to harmonize accumulated laws variously derived from the Twelve Tables, from magistrates' and emperors' edicts and from the numerous *leges* (statutory laws) became pressing.

THE FIRST CODIFICATIONS

As early as the 1st century BC, Mucius Scaevola, consul in 95BC, produced a handbook on civil law that was long regarded as the standard work. But it was not until the 2nd century AD, under the great organizing emperor Hadrian, that determined attempts were made to codify the law. Hadrian initiated a series of codifications that continued into the 6th century AD.

Iuventius Celsus, who had been consul for the second time in AD129 under Hadrian, wrote 39 books of *digesta* (classified legal decisions). In them, he pronounced numerous celebrated legal definitions and pithy maxims, such as the famous formula *impossibilium nulla obligatio* (*Digesta*, 50), "there can be no legal requirement to do the impossible". Salvius Julianus, who became consul in AD149, collected and revised the edicts that successive praetors had declared during their year in office in his *Edictum Perpetuum*, or everlasting edict, which was the first real codification of Roman law. From that time on, imperial edicts could be recognized as permanently valid legally. His publication helped spread a wider understanding of the legal safeguards protecting the inhabitants of the empire and also revealed a growing humanitarian concern for the empire's subjects – at least on paper.

Slaves now had more legal protection, which circumscribed their owners' rights to treat them completely as chattels. This was partly because they were becoming scarcer and therefore more valuable, but it also marked a change in attitudes. Although both pagan and Christian thinkers abhorred slavery, their views did not reflect a general revulsion, and on economic grounds slavery appeared indispensable. One of Salvius' pupils, Gaius, continued Salvius' work in his *Institutes*, while under Marcus Aurelius (reigned AD161–80), Cervidius Scaevola continued the task of interpreting and codifying the corpus of Roman law. The new basilicas, such as that of Maxentius in Rome, now served as courts where the emperor gave judgement.

Despite the growing political and military troubles of the 3rd century AD, the work of codifying and moderating the laws was carried further. Aemilianus Papinianus, the prefect of the Praetorian guard for ten years (AD203–213) under the militaristic Severans, became famed

for his great compendia of the legal decisions that comprised the laws, the *quaestiones* and *responsa* (investigations and findings). Under the emperor Alexander Severus, Domitius Ulpian was a noted lawyer and writer, and adviser to Julia Mammaea. As the emperor's mother was effectively the regent, Ulpian also became Praetorian prefect. His huge works, which endeavoured to cover the full gamut of the laws, are extremely clear and reveal his easy and lucid mastery of very complicated material.

Other distinguished lawyers of the age were Herennius Modestinus, who was prefect of the Vigiles (watchmen) from AD226 to AD244, and Paulus, whose copious writings include the *Sententia* (opinions). Many of these writers either came from the eastern, Greek part of the empire or were deeply influenced by Greek philosophical concepts. Their philanthropic and, in some ways, democratic beliefs modified ancient Roman concerns which had centred on private property and the sanctity of contracts. Paradoxically, just as these high-minded men were writing, the empire was collapsing into a bloody chaos that made all such idealism seem useless.

THE IMPERIAL DIGESTS

Although the empire in the west finally collapsed in the 5th century AD, urban life continued unchecked in the richer and more civilized east. Here, the school of Beirut (in the Lebanon) had emerged as the leading centre of Roman law studies – mostly in Latin – and provided the lawyers who helped draw up the two final grand digests of Roman law. Building on the achievements of Ulpian and other jurists, this led to the Theodosian Code of AD438, issued under the eastern emperor Theodosius II. Accepted in both parts of the empire, this combined humane and enlightened ideals with savagely repressive measures, repeating ineffective laws passed many times before. The majesty of the law was no longer so respected by people in real life.

In the 6th century AD, the eastern empire enjoyed what seemed a golden age under Justinian I (reigned AD527–65). He reconquered half the western empire and enriched Byzantium with numerous palaces and churches, most notably the cathedral of Hagia Sophia. But perhaps his greatest achievement was his enduring *Digest of Roman Law*. Justinian appointed a committee of 16 lawyers to summarize and amalgamate the whole of Roman law. Over 11 years, from AD528, the lawyers compressed three million lines of older laws into a mere 150,000 lines. This gave the Byzantine world its laws for the next millennium, and profoundly influenced law in the then barbarous west. When medieval western Europe rebuilt itself as a civilization, its rulers looked to this great compilation. The jurists who emerged from Europe's oldest university – the University of Bologna – from 1100 onwards, revived and expanded this *Codex* of Roman law. Although it tended to elevate governmental efficiency above individual rights, its comprehensive clarity proved very attractive to successive states, some of them democratic. Under the Napoleonic empire (1803–14), it became the law of almost all continental Europe and, later, of many parts of Latin America.

Above: The Emperor Napoleon's famous legal Code was consciously modelled on Roman law. It forms the basis of much continental European law to this day.

Below: The eastern emperor Justinian I reconquered half the west and built many fine churches, but his greatest achievement was his final codification of Roman law.

POLICE AND SECRET POLICE

Above: The increasingly suspicious emperor Tiberius centralized the crack Praetorian guard in a special camp in Rome, where they were controlled by Sejanus, who was for a long time the emperor's most trusted confidant and minister.

For a long time, the Romans lacked two aspects of civil life that seem essential to modern eyes: a professional local or national police force, with some form of central criminal detective agency, and, perhaps even more notably, a prison service to incarcerate criminals for long-term punishment.

KEEPING ORDER

Under the Republic, from 367BC, policing the (still quite small) city was a task for the four aediles – two plebeian, two patrician – who were elected each year and who maintained public order. Later, the *praetor urbanus* helped deal with the growth in crime. This patchy attempt to deal with crime was common, not just in the ancient world, but right up to the 19th century. (Britain had no proper police force until well into the 19th century and used to

Right: Although theoretically part of the regular army, the Praetorians were in reality treated quite differently. Paid more and retiring earlier, they lived in Rome and often, like this guard, were not obliged to wear full armour.

deport those criminals it did not execute, as did the Russians.) In Rome, under the generally light government of the early Principate, minimalist policing worked reasonably well at first, with troops from the Praetorian guard always available as a back-up force. From the time of the Severans (AD193–233), however, secret police, who had already appeared under tyrannical rulers such as Domitian and Commodus, multiplied. The later empire effectively became a police state, whose horrors were limited only by its corruption and incompetence.

In the city of Rome itself, whose population must have passed the million mark in the 1st century AD, some sort of police force was clearly necessary, as Augustus realized. Due to the almost total lack of street lighting – Antioch was the one large city in the empire that had some sort of crude street lights – Rome became a dangerous place at dusk, although the rich went out with their own bodyguards, not over-concerned about what happened to lesser citizens. Augustus created two new forms of police; the *cohortes urbanae* and the *vigiles*. The *cohortes urbanae*, or city cohorts, who comprised first three, then four, cohorts of 500 men, were commanded by a senator, the prefect of the city. The only armed force left directly under the Senate's control, it kept order of a sort in public places. More effective at night were the *vigiles*, or night watchmen/firemen, seven brigades of 1,000 men (one for each two of the city's 14 wards), initially recruited from freedmen, who patrolled the streets at night. They seem, however, to have been more concerned with fighting fire than crime, for they carried buckets and pumps with them, but on their regular patrols through the city they must have also acted as some sort of deterrent to crime. But, despite this, we can assume that Rome remained dangerous at night.

Backing up these unimpressive forces were the formidable cohorts of the Praetorians, the special guard recruited only from Roman citizens of Italy until the reign of Septimius Severus (AD193–211), paid twice the usual rate and under the command of the Praetorian prefect, the highest post an equestrian could hope to reach. Augustus stationed its nine cohorts around Italy, but under Tiberius they were centralized by Sejanus into a large camp in the north-east of Rome. These were the imperial guard, however, not used for day-to-day policing but to suppress popular riots or conspiracies. Although the *Pax Romana* established by Augustus meant an end to large-scale brigandage, there were still plenty of robbers around, even in the mountains of Italy, and at times small-scale military operations were needed to suppress them. Elsewhere in the empire, the army was occasionally called in to deal with major uprisings: from the Sicilian slave revolts of 135BC, when 70,000 slaves united under their "king" Antiochus to defy the Romans for three years, to the revolt of the Bagaudae (literally, brigands) who, from the 3rd century AD on, terrorized central Gaul, setting up their own courts. In between such uprisings, decurions, the local magistrates of the cities around the empire, dealt adequately with local crime on a smaller scale, acting as judges.

THE POLICE STATE

Like all military dictatorships, the emperors made use of *delatores*, spies or informers, who discovered or invented conspiracies, and *speculatores*, special mounted intelligence officers of the Praetorian guard – regular officials, unlike the *delatores* – who sometimes travelled around the empire. But the wiser emperors did not rely too much on such doubtful sources. Despite this, Trajan – *optimus princeps*, or the best of emperors, in the Senate's view – started a new form of intelligence service, the *frumentarii*. This grew rapidly under Septimius

Severus, augmented by similar officials, who set up the sinister office of the *agentes in rebus*, literally those active in public affairs; the *stationarii*, or place-holders, and *collectiones*, or tax-collectors. These special police were usually soldiers, indicating the militarization of society under the Severans. According to the early 20th-century historian M.I. Rostovtzeff, they did not "care a straw for the people", but hunted down those who had defaulted on their taxes or gone into hiding to escape government extortions.

Diocletian's bureaucratic reforms encouraged a huge growth in the number of these officials. Later, in the 360s, the emperor Julian introduced measures to try to reduce their numbers. Such agents were solely concerned with protecting the government and lining their own pockets, not with dealing with normal crime or helping the people, whose well-being and safety held no interest for them. Bribery was the normal means by which most subjects of the later empire dealt with such imperial officials.

Above: Trajan created a new form of intelligence officer, the frumentarii, *who thrived under later, less benign emperors.*

Below: The arch of Septimius Severus, the militaristic emperor in whose reign the secret police multiplied.

PUNISHMENT

Above: This mosaic of the 3rd century AD shows gladiators battling. Due to the inevitably high mortality rate of this, perhaps the most brutal spectator sport ever devised, many criminals were condemned to be gladiators.

Below: The Romans' formidable organizing powers are exposed in the underground network of passages that kept the Colosseum in Rome working smoothly in the long games that filled so many days.

Two things characterize Roman attitudes to punishment. First, there was no real equality before the law, which we tend to take for granted. Second, keeping criminals imprisoned for long periods was impractical, on grounds of expense, and other penalties were the norm.

BREAKING THE LAW

There was a marked division between the way Roman citizens and non-citizens were treated, both under the Republic and under the early Principate. Later, after almost everybody had become a citizen in AD212, an even starker division grew up between the treatment of the upper classes, *honestiores*, and the lower, *inferiores*. Even in the Republic, richer citizens such as senators and knights were better treated than poorer ones.

Roman jails were normally manned by soldiers, and used only in the short term as a place for suspects awaiting trial. Punishments were often gruesome, especially for non-Roman citizens or *inferiores*. In civilian life, Roman citizens, and later the *honestiores*, could not be flogged or crucified, for example, and

could "appeal to Caesar", as St Paul did when kept on remand. And while it was widely believed that slaves would tell the truth only if they were severely tortured, citizens were exempt from torture.

Early Rome was essentially a primitive rustic society, and most penalties in the early and middle Republic were draconian, with crude punishments that seem violent to our modern sensibilities. In Rome's deeply conservative culture, such punishments long remained on the books. For example, Vestal Virgins were chosen from high-born Roman maidens around the age of 7 to tend the fire of Vesta, the goddess of the hearth. The girls had to remain virgins for their 30 years of service, by which time they were regarded as being well past marriage. Inevitably, some lapsed and had sexual liaisons. If they were discovered, they faced the potential sentence of being buried alive. Much later, Domitian's revival of this archaic punishment shocked the then more tolerant Romans. Parricide also incurred punishments that reveal the deep religious revulsion that it aroused. The offender was tied up and bundled into a sack with a snake and a cock and then hurled off a rock.

Many penalties, of course, related to civil laws. An article from the Eighth Table of the Law, concerned with penalties, states, "If any man mutilates another's limbs, he must suffer the same, unless he agrees to pay compensation to the injured man." This *Lex Talionis*, the law of an eye for an eye, extended to other crimes, such as arson: arsonists themselves should be burnt alive. The Tables even stipulated the death penalty for any patron – who was almost always a nobleman – who cheated his client, though this was not often enforced. In all these types of cases, it was not the Roman state but individual citizens who brought the actions, the state merely supervising their private pursuit of justice.

EXILE

Although death was a penalty for many offences, it was not always enforced, especially for more important Roman citizens. Instead, exile remained a common and potent penalty. Not only did it end a Roman's political life – for the time being, anyway – but it meant banishment from the one city on earth that really mattered to all true Romans. The incorrigibly metropolitan poet Ovid was exiled to the barbarous remoteness of Tomis on the Black Sea by Augustus in AD8, possibly for involvement in the affairs that led also to the banishment of Augustus' own daughter Julia.

LIONS AND GLADIATORS

Although the image of Christian martyrs being thrown to the lions – tied to a stake in the arena and there chewed to death – remains powerful, Christians in fact made up only a few of the people who were sentenced to this *damnatio ad bestias,* or condemnation to the wild beasts. This form of punishment was anyway not thought particularly entertaining by Romans, the most exacting of audiences.

Many criminals condemned to death ended up in the arena as gladiators, people utterly without rights. From the 2nd century BC on, Rome was developing an insatiable appetite for gladiators, who had a high mortality rate. The games Titus gave for the inauguration of the Colosseum in AD80 required several thousand pairs, some of whom were killed during the day's entertainment. But gladiators were very expensive to train, and combat did not inevitably end in death. Those who survived three years in the games were normally given their wooden sword of freedom.

Special schools of gladiators, with ferocious discipline, were established. One of the most famous of these was at Capua, and it was here that the last great slave revolt broke out in 73BC, organized by the Thracian gladiator Spartacus. Displaying genuine leadership, he united his fellow outcasts and for two years

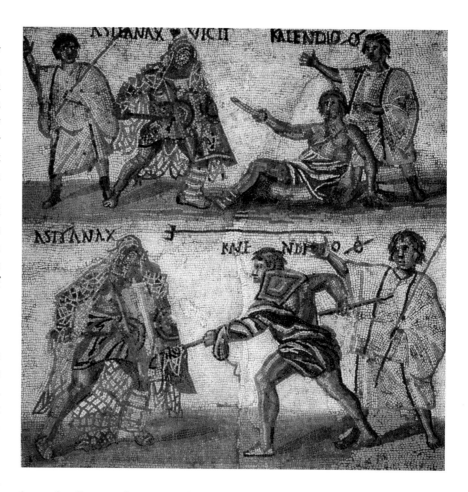

kept the forces of Rome at bay, moving around the mountains of southern Italy until Crassus cornered and killed him in 71BC in Apulia. Along the great Via Appia from Capua to Rome, 7,000 ex-gladiators were then crucified as a ghastly warning to other potential rebels.

CRUCIFIXION

The last, worst and most degrading punishment of Rome's sadistic society was crucifixion. An excruciatingly slow torture (for few had their deaths hastened by a spear like Jesus Christ), crucifixion was adopted by the Romans in the 2nd century BC, probably from the Asian monarchies. Julius Caesar had the pirates who captured him crucified, the normal punishment for such heinous crimes as well as for conspiracy. After the conversion of Constantine and his successors to Christianity in the 4th century AD, crucifixion was discontinued, but this was on religious rather than humanitarian grounds.

Above: Special training schools for gladiators were established in the late Republic to satisfy the insatiable demand of the Roman populace for such brutal thrills.

Below: Crucifixion was a common, if horrifically painful, form of death penalty. It was used for many crimes, from piracy to conspiracy.

CHAPTER VI

FOREIGN POLICY

Although Rome had no foreign office or state department, it certainly had policies towards the non-Roman world. While well-meaning Romans such as Cicero liked to believe that Rome acquired its empire chiefly in wars of self-defence, others must have seen it differently, as they watched the smoke rising from Carthage, Syracuse, Corinth – all cities sacked by Rome.

Yet for a long time Rome, unlike the Persians or the Macedonians under Alexander, initiated few wars of deliberate conquest. From *c.*300BC to Pompey's eastern command in 66BC, Rome's foreign policy was more reactive than pre-emptive. Only when control of foreign policy slipped from the Senate's grasp did clear signs of expansionist imperialism appear, first under Pompey and then under Caesar and his successors. After that, Rome followed an aggressively expansionist policy until it could do so no longer and was forced to go on the defensive in the 2nd century AD.

All other cities had to be subordinated to Rome and were regarded as foreign, even when they were Latin-speaking neighbours. However, the privileges of Roman citizenship were gradually extended to inhabitants of other city-states, first in Italy, then across the Mediterranean world. Ultimately, after the conquest of Egypt in 30BC, there were no foreign powers worthy of the name, except for the Parthians in the east. Instead, there was the Roman world – and the barbarians.

Left: A sculpted head from the ruins of Carthage, the North African city that was for long Rome's deadliest enemy.

EARLY BEGINNINGS
THE CONQUEST OF ITALY

Above: The Via Appia, the first and archetypal Roman road, was designed for the conquest of southern Italy as much as for communication.

Below: This fresco from a 4th-century BC tomb near Paestum, southern Italy, shows warriors armed like the Samnites. The Samnites were Rome's most threatening enemies in the region, taking three wars to subdue.

Although it may sound grandiloquent to talk of the foreign policy of a state whose territory in 500BC was roughly only 10 miles (16km) across, Rome regarded all those beyond its sacred *pomerium*, or city boundary, as foreign. By binding such cities to her in treaties, at times granting them citizenship or alliance, Rome's approach became less "divide and rule" than "conquer and assimilate". Even large, relatively distant cities such as Capua could be incorporated by this incremental method, Rome's most original idea in conquering Italy.

Rome signed a treaty with the cities of the Latin League in 493BC, but she did so only because mountain enemies were threatening farms in the lowlands. These tribes were only ejected from the key Algidus Pass in about 430BC, after a 50-year war. They were overcome by establishing chains of *coloniae* – defensive settlements of farmer–soldiers who received land. At first these were federal Latin colonies, with Romans merely among other settlers, but later Rome began founding her own colonies, which then became civilian settlements too.

Another way of dealing with enemies was assimilation. The Sabines were other menacing neighbours in the hills north-east of Rome, but around 505BC the Sabine nobleman Attus Clausus settled by invitation in Rome, reputedly taking 4,000 followers with him and increasing the city's population. He became a Roman patrician and changed his name to Claudius, founder of the Claudians. Afterwards, the Romans imported the Sabine god Sancus, which symbolized the fusion of the two peoples.

A less malleable threat was Veii. Just 11 miles (18km) north of Rome, this wealthy Etruscan city controlled a network of paved roads and blocked Rome's way north. Wars started in 479BC, until finally the Romans began such a long siege – traditionally, ten years from 406–396BC – that the army had to be paid for the first time. Veii was destroyed, its people killed or enslaved and its patron goddess Juno taken to Rome, thereby symbolizing triumph in a total war. This extermination of a city – along with taking its land for the *ager publicus*, public land – was often repeated.

All such successes seemed to be overthrown by the invasion of the Gauls in *c.*390BC, who sacked the still unwalled city. In despair, some citizens even talked of abandoning their burnt city for Veii until Camillus rallied them. The small city of Caere helped Rome recover and in return received *hospitium publicum*, reciprocal rights with Roman citizens in judicial and financial matters. Rome later extended this formula to other cities. In 378BC Rome fortified itself with the

Samnite League 298 BC
Roman territory 298 BC
Carthaginian possessions *c*. 260 BC
Roman colonies by 272 BC
Under Roman control 270 BC
Annexed by Rome 263 BC

Left: By 265BC Rome controlled the whole of peninsular Italy south of a line from Pisa to Rimini. Besides territories directly part of the Republic and full Roman colonies – strategically planted from Rimini in the north to Brindisi in the south and often linked by roads – there were allied territories, enjoying either Latin or the less prestigious Italian status. All these cities proved a source of vital strength in Rome's forthcoming contest with Carthage, but important long-established Greek cities such as Tarento were sometimes disloyal.

Below: The Etruscans were Rome's most impressive and powerful neighbours. They were wealthy, civilized and had a high level of culture as shown in this life-size terracotta sculpture of a married couple from a 6th-century BC Etruscan tomb.

Servian walls, but it was already expanding again. In 381BC Tusculum, a Latin League city, received full Roman citizenship to keep it loyal to Rome. This novel generosity was later extended to other cities, also usefully boosting the numbers of citizens for military service.

In 343BC Capua, the wealthiest city of fertile Campania, appealed to Rome for help against Samnite raiders. Initially, the war went badly. Roman troops mutinied at having to fight so far from home, and the Latin League, alarmed at Rome's power, joined the Volscians against her. Four years of bitter fighting were required to defeat the Latins by 338BC. Then Rome dissolved the League, treating each city differently. The citizens of Lanuvium, for example, received full Roman rights, as did three other deserving Latin cities. The Volscian city of Antium on the coast, a pirate stronghold, had its ships destroyed – their beaks went to adorn the *Rostra* in Rome – and a Roman colony was planted, which the Volscians were allowed to join. Capua and four other Campanian cities then received Roman citizenship *sine suffragio*, without the vote. The Romans showed themselves fair and pragmatic in these treaties, winning the abiding loyalty of most cities.

OVERLORD BY DEFAULT

Above: Two Greek hoplites (heavy infantrymen) from an Attic vase. Adaptable Roman legionaries repeatedly defeated Greek hoplites massed in the inflexible phalanx, *a major reason for Rome's final total success in the eastern Mediterranean region.*

Below: The Colossus of Rhodes, a giant statue reputedly straddling the harbour entrance, symbolized Rhodes' maritime wealth and power. When its power was wrecked by Rome's expansion, piracy flourished, no longer checked by the Rhodian navy.

There seemed little reason for a major conflict between the Roman Republic, a land power controlling peninsular Italy, and Carthage, a mercantile power based in modern Tunisia, with trade routes extending to southern Spain. Treaties going back to the first days of the Roman Republic were renewed as late as 279BC. But when Rome faced Sicily across the Straits of Messina, it faced new dilemmas. An appeal to Rome by a party in Messina for help against Carthage left the Senate undecided until the Assembly, exercising its right to declare war, decided for action. The bloody wars made Rome hegemon (ruler) of the Mediterranean.

One reason for supporting Messina was that the Greeks of southern Italy wanted Roman help for Greeks in Sicily, but this counted for little compared with a new aggressive mood in Rome itself. Carthage, too, had been trying to extend its control over all Sicily from its base at Palermo in the west and was determined to control the Straits of Messina. About three times larger than Rome, an immensely wealthy city, with a huge professional fleet and mercenary armies, Carthage was Rome's one significant rival power in the western Mediterranean. As such, Rome was unlikely to ignore it indefinitely.

Victorious after the First Punic War in 242BC, Rome's policy towards Carthage was mixed. Rome helped Carthage suppress a massive revolt by unpaid mercenaries in 239BC, for social order had to be maintained. But it then took advantage of Carthaginian preoccupation to annex Sardinia and Corsica, both in the Carthaginian sphere, in an act of aggression. Marseilles, a Greek city allied to Rome, was worried about growing Carthaginian power in Spain that threatened Ampurias, its colony in Catalonia. (Possibly Hamilcar Barca signed a treaty in 227BC accepting the river Ebro as his northern frontier in Spain.) When Hannibal attacked Saguntum in 219BC, independent if south of the Ebro, Rome decided on war – superfluously, as it turned out, as it was Hannibal who launched the catastrophic Second Punic War.

The final act, the Third Punic War of 146BC, showed Rome at it most odious. Carthage had regained its wealth through agriculture and trade but, lacking a large fleet, posed no threat. However, the Romans, even without reminders from Cato the Censor that *Carthago delenda est* (Carthage must be deleted), had grown greedy. They destroyed Carthage after a long siege, enslaving its citizens. By then, Rome was mistress of the middle sea.

ARBITER OF THE EAST

The eastern Mediterranean around 200BC was dominated by three great Hellenistic kingdoms ruled by descendants of Alexander's generals: the Ptolemies in Egypt, the Antigonids in Macedonia and the Seleucids, whose huge Asian empire centred on Syria. Smaller Hellenistic states included Rhodes, a cultured trading republic, the Aeotolian

Above: Hoplites formation from a Greek amphora from Chigi, Italy. By adopting new tactics, Rome defeated such Greek armies.

Confederacy in Greece and the Attalid kingdom of Pergamum in Asia Minor. For a century these states had been involved in complex alliances and wars that seldom caused serious damage. Upon entering this civilized sphere, Rome proceeded to wreck it through myopic fear, suspicion and greed that together made it look more imperialist than it really was.

Philip V of Macedonia had rashly allied himself with Hannibal in 215BC, angering Rome, although the First Macedonian War involved little fighting. When Philip made a secret treaty with Antiochus III of Syria in 202BC to divide Ptolemaic lands, Rome intervened. Flaminius defeated Philip at Cynoscephalae in 197BC, where Roman legions out-manoeuvred the Macedonian *phalanx*, but he merely reduced Macedonia's size. To the cities of Greece proper, Flaminius promised liberty. This promise was genuine, except that he envisaged a sort of patronage, not the total independence the delighted Greeks assumed. From this misunderstanding came much grief. Meanwhile Antiochus, until then a successful ruler, made a series of clumsy mistakes: he seized the Gallipoli peninsula, although Rome had told him to keep out of Europe; he welcomed Rome's arch-enemy Hannibal to his court in 195BC; and sent a force into Greece in 192BC to support the rebellious Aetolians. Rome, alarmed that he wanted to recreate Alexander's empire, sent armies to defeat Antiochus at Thermopylae and again, massively, at Magnesia in 190BC. Antiochus lost all land west of the Taurus Mountains and paid a huge indemnity. Rome was now arbiter of the east, a point ruthlessly brought home to the next Seleucid, Antiochus IV, when he invaded Egypt in 168BC. The Roman envoy Popilius Laenas drew a circle around the king and told him not to move until he agreed to Rome's terms. Antiochus humbly accepted.

Rome did not fill its hegemonic role well. Many Romans enriched themselves in Greece, while Rome still declined to govern Greece. When the Achaean League rebelled in 146BC, Rome sacked Corinth, Greece's richest city, enslaving its citizens and creating a province. Rome treated its allies scarcely better. Fearing the growing power of Rhodes, it created a free port at Delos that wrecked Rhodes' maritime wealth. With Rhodes in decline, piracy flourished unchecked, also hurting Rome. Attalus III, last king of Pergamum, accepting the inevitable, bequeathed his kingdom to *imperium populi Romani*, the empire of the Roman people, in 133BC.

Below: The Acropolis of Pergamum, the capital of the wealthy Eumenid kingdom in west Asia Minor. Pergamum was long Rome's chief ally in the east, its cavalry helping to defeat the Seleucids at the Battle of Magnesia in 190BC.

DEFENSIBLE FRONTIERS
THE RHINE AND THE DANUBE

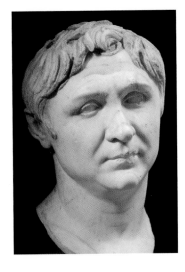

Above: Pompey, one the Republic's finest generals, added a whole string of provinces and client states to Rome's eastern empire.

Below: A bend of the River Rhine in Germany. Fast-flowing, the Rhine offered a natural but not inevitable frontier for the empire in northern Europe. It effectively marked Rome's north-western boundary for almost 450 years.

The intermittent expansion of the empire in the middle Republic gave way to rapid, even reckless expansion in the 1st century BC. Between 66 and 63BC, Pompey extended the Roman sphere of influence from the Caucasus to the Red Sea. Caesar conquered the huge area of *Gallia Comata* ("long-haired Gaul") a decade later, and claimed Britain as a client state. Augustus annexed Egypt, the richest kingdom of the Mediterranean, in 30BC. His later wars of conquest added north-west Spain to the empire by 23BC, the Alpine lands by 15BC and most of the Balkans and Danubian territories by 6BC. Later, Tiberius and Drusus conquered as far as the Elbe by AD5, while Roman fleets even nosed into the Baltic. Roman power seemed set on an endless advance. The question was, where would the *termini imperii*, the frontiers of the empire, finally be set, if the empire were not to continue to advance north-east indefinitely? Fixed frontiers, a new concept for Rome, required choosing defensible lines, tactically and strategically.

There was no compelling reason to regard the Rhine or the Danube as definitive frontiers. Despite Caesar's claims in his *De Bello Gallico* about the importance of the Rhine, neither of these two great rivers marked a real cultural or political divide. Augustus, while happy to ignore Britain beyond the seas, decided to conquer Germany between the Rhine and the Elbe, presumably to create a line running roughly from Hamburg through Dresden and Prague to Vienna (none of these cities existed then, of course). This would usefully shorten the frontier, as later emperors realized. Accordingly, a pincer campaign was launched in AD6. Tiberius was to advance north through Bohemia, while other troops moved up the Elbe and others up the Main valley past what is now Frankfurt. But a massive revolt in recently conquered Pannonia recalled Tiberius for three years' bitter campaigning, the worst, according to Tacitus, since the Punic Wars. Then Varus (an army commander) and his three legions were betrayed and massacred by Arminius of the Cherusci in the Teutoburg Forest in AD9. Augustus, now an old man, was shattered by the news and called a halt to all further expansion.

Tiberius followed Augustus' advice to stay within the bounds of the empire to the letter, keeping the Rhine–Danube lines, but this was not very practical. Although both rivers were large, the L-shaped re-entrant angle between their upper reaches was vulnerable to invasion. Claudius, eager for military glory, invaded Britain in AD43, embroiling Rome in a province with a frontier problem in its north that was not settled until Hadrian's visit in AD122. Apart from the suppression of a large-scale revolt by Civilis on the lower Rhine in AD70, Germany was ignored until Vespasian and his sons, especially Domitian, began a

new campaign. Systematic and inglorious, this was mocked by Tacitus, but proved of lasting value. In the Chattan War of AD83–5, Domitian pushed the Rhine frontier east, along the line of the Taunus Mountains, creating a fortified frontier that sheltered the Rhineland behind and projected Roman power deeper into Germany. The frontier then ran south along the Neckar to join the upper Danube. Further additions to extend this new area of Agri Decumates to the Danube at Regensburg came in the 2nd century AD, reducing the Rhine–Danube lines by 150 miles (240km) in total; legions could now move far more swiftly from one frontier to another.

DANUBIAN PROBLEMS

Domitian had been distracted from his German campaign by a Dacian attack in AD85. Well organized, rich (thanks to gold mines) and well protected by their mountainous terrain, the Dacians were a growing threat. After Domitian's campaigns produced a stalemate, it was left to Trajan to deal with Dacia. An initial campaign in AD101 with 13 legions (totalling over 150,000 troops) seemed to have made Dacia an obedient client state, but the settlement, weighted in Rome's favour, failed to last. Trajan prepared for another full-scale invasion by building an immense bridge and road. The final storming of the Dacian capital in AD106 meant Dacia became a province, protected along its northern flank by the Limes Porolissensis, a new fortified frontier along the Carpathians. By creating this great bulwark of a province protruding north-east almost on to the Russian steppes, Trajan divided the tribes on either side of it, so safeguarding the Danubian lands for generations. Beyond them, of course, lay Italy itself, almost unprotected.

The Danube frontier collapsed when the Quadi and Marcomanni (from the modern Czech Republic) poured into Italy in AD166. In a series of campaigns, Marcus Aurelius painstakingly drove

them back. Despite being distracted by a rebellion in Syria in AD175, Marcus won a great final victory over the Marcomanni and Quadi in AD179 and was seemingly about to create two new trans-Danubian provinces, Marcomania and Sarmatia, when he died – and with him died his expansionist plans.

Renewed barbarian pressures in the 3rd century AD saw a general retreat on the northern frontier: Aurelian evacuated Dacia by AD275 and the Agri Decumates were abandoned by c.AD265. In their place came new, heavily fortified capitals near the frontiers, such as Trier and Sirmium, with other massive fortresses that barbarians could bypass but never capture. The whole empire had in some ways become the front line.

Above: Roman troops on the Danube embarking supplies. The Danube became Rome's longest, and ultimately most vulnerable, frontier.

DEFENSIBLE FRONTIERS
ASIA

The best advice for western generals is, "Never invade Russia." For Romans, the advice should have been, "Don't invade Parthia", for it proved fatal to many military reputations. Parthia's huge empire, which stretched from the Syrian frontier to central Asia, was unimpressive militarily. Its kings faced revolts from over-mighty subjects in its Iranian lands, while the Hellenistic cities of Mesopotamia (Iraq) felt little loyalty to it. Its large armies were not professional like the Romans', although their cavalry was well suited to the terrain. Such weakness allowed Rome to invade Parthia at times, but geography – the huge distances, the deserts, the way

the Iranian highlands outflanked the Tigris–Euphrates valley – in the end prevented it ever from holding more than north Mesopotamia. Unfortunately, the precedent of Alexander the Great, who had conquered half of Asia, lured Roman generals east. When the formidable Sassanian dynasty replaced the Parthians in the AD220s, Rome faced worse problems. What had been a quiet frontier became a perilous burden. Yet the frontier between the upper Euphrates and the Tigris fluctuated remarkably little for six centuries.

Rome and Parthia first clashed after Pompey annexed the Syrian rump of the Seleucid empire in 64BC. Crassus, who was

Above: Petra was a wealthy trading city (now in Jordan), and it was annexed under the emperor Trajan.

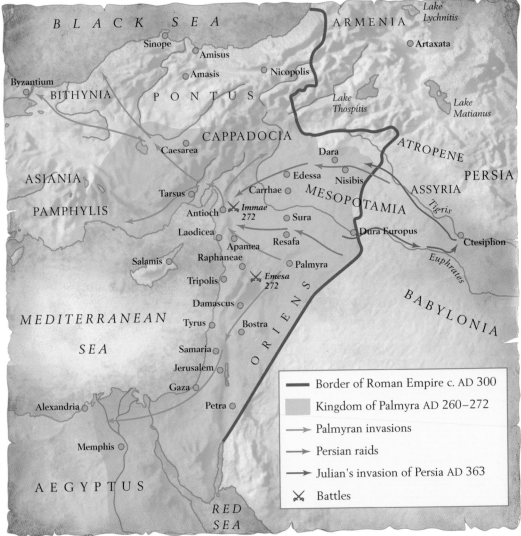

Right: The Eastern frontier c.AD300. Palmyra's short-lived empire (shaded), did not alter the eastern frontier, but Julian's defeat led to the ceding of Nisibis and half of Roman Mesopotamia to Persia.

Map legend:
- Border of Roman Empire c. AD 300
- Kingdom of Palmyra AD 260–272
- Palmyran invasions
- Persian raids
- Julian's invasion of Persia AD 363
- Battles

governor of Syria and eager for glory, marched east, to be destroyed with his army by Parthian horse archers in the desert near Carrhae in 53BC. Caesar was preparing an immense invasion of Parthia in 44BC when he was assassinated. Antony, in control of the east after 42BC, decided to attack by the mountain route but failed to capture the key city of Phraapsa in 36BC, when his siege engines were cut off. He had to beat a humiliating retreat harassed by Parthian horsemen. Augustus, after settling other frontiers, was expected to resume the eastward drive but wisely contented himself with a diplomatic triumph in 20BC. This saw the lost legions' eagles (along with a few prisoners) ceremoniously returned and a Roman protégé installed on the Armenian throne. Such client states served as useful buffers between the two powers. For a century, Augustus' successors remained west of the Euphrates, although Vespasian annexed some client states.

BETWEEN TWO RIVERS

There was therefore no need for Trajan's grand eastern venture that began in AD114 with the conquest of Armenia. Mesopotamia may have looked similar to Syria – a fertile land, Aramaic-speaking peasants, Greeks in the cities – and there was talk of securing the trade routes east, but it was Alexander's example that really counted. Failure to take Hatra, right in the middle of the new conquests, signalled that the Parthians were not totally defeated and they began to attack the now long-exposed eastern flanks. Even without the many Jewish revolts behind, these new frontiers were indefensible. Hadrian pulled back completely, apart from Nabatea. The status quo was restored, except that Arabia Nabatea was fortified.

In AD165 the Romans retaliated to the Parthian attack by sacking both Ctesiphon (Baghdad), the Parthian capital, and Hellenistic Seleucia-on-the-Tigris, bringing home a crippling plague and almost wrecking Hellenism in Iraq. But the only significant change was to advance the

frontier to Dura-Europus, a fortified city on the Euphrates. This left the rest of the frontier as before, between the upper Tigris and Euphrates, stretching from the Black Sea to the Red, with Palmyra as a client state. But there was one possible line that offered Rome a defensive frontier that Septimius Severus saw and seized. In AD197 he captured Ctesiphon but sagely withdrew, annexing only upper Mesopotamia, following the line of the Khabur river as it flowed south into the Euphrates, then east along the escarpment of the Jebel Sinjar to the Tigris north-east of Nisibis. This territory gave Syria, with its wealthy cities, far more protection and also helped Rome to control Armenia, blocking the Parthians' lowland route to it.

This proved a lastingly defensible frontier. Despite the newly aggressive Sassanid Persian dynasty – it claimed all the old Persian empire's lands up to Macedonia – the Romans retained this new province of (upper) Mesopotamia throughout the 3rd-century crises.

Above: The ruins of Dura-Europus, Syria, a vital fortress on the Euphrates, captured and destroyed after a siege by the Persians in c.AD256 and never reoccupied. The defence of the eastern frontier depended heavily on such fortified trading cities.

CLIENT AND BUFFER STATES

Above: Giant heads c.50BC proclaim the power of the client kings of Commagene.

Below: Pompey entered the Temple in Jerusalem, thereby desecrating it in Jewish eyes.

When Pompey marched through western Asia from the Caucasus to the Red Sea in 66–63BC, annexing and rearranging kingdoms, he recognized many existing smaller kingdoms as client states or allies. The careful use of client or buffer states allied to and to varying degrees under the control of Rome became a characteristic policy of Roman imperialism in the late Republic and early Principate.

Such statelets – most were very small – could supply reinforcements when called for, rather than perpetually requiring costly garrisons themselves. In AD67, Vespasian's legions were reinforced by 15,000 lighter troops from nearby client states for the Jewish war. For Augustus and his heirs, this was an attractive way of defending the empire on the cheap. It resembled the client system in Rome itself and meant, furthermore, that the states concerned often became half-Romanized, or further Hellenized, before being incorporated into the empire. Armenia was the one significant exception to this trend.

Most client kingdoms lined the indeterminate eastern frontier, beyond which loomed the Parthian empire, Rome's only civilized rival. In northern Europe the various German tribes were, for the most part, too fragmentary or impermanent to be able to create stable kingdoms. Here subsidies and treaties kept these barbarians in check or at each others' throats, but they were not proper client kings.

The major eastern client states, established by Pompey and confirmed by Mark Antony and Augustus, included three vital border crossings: Pontus, on the south coast of the Black Sea, Cappadocia in central Asia Minor, annexed in AD17, and Commagene, controlling the vital passage across the upper Euphrates. This latter was ruled by a dynasty of Hellenized monarchs called Antiochus, whose gigantic heads adorn their hilltop mausoleum at Nemrud Dag. Further south, Arab client kings included Palmyra, rising to wealth, and flourishing Arabia Nabatea (Jordan), with its capital at Petra.

Most important and troublesome was Judaea, later Palestina. Herod I the Great ruled from 37 to 4BC, rebuilding the Temple in Jerusalem and building a second coastal capital at Caesarea Maritima, which became a typical Hellenistic city. He was a tyrannical but effective ruler. After his death, his kingdom was divided between his less competent heirs, until its central portion became a Roman province in AD6. (Its most notorious governor was Pontius Pilate.) It returned briefly to Jewish rule under Cornelius Julius Agrippa, Herod's nephew, and his son Cornelius Agrippa II. As their names suggest, these rulers were half-Romanized.

Another client state was Mauretania (northern Algeria/Morocco), formed partly from the old kingdom of Numidia. Its monarch, Juba, became an exemplary Hellenizing king in his new capital at Caesarea and married one of Cleopatra's daughters. It was annexed by Claudius, who also annexed the client state of Thrace in the eastern Balkans. On the north Black Sea, the Bosphoran kingdom was part-Scythian but had Greek cities on the coast. It remained an important client state to Rome because of the grain trade from the Ukraine.

Vespasian annexed Commagene and other smaller client states in a fit of centralizing enthusiasm in AD69–79 until only the tiny kingdoms of the Caucasus – Iberia in the Caucasus, and Colchis – plus Palmyra and Arabia Nabatea remained. This required the deployment of more troops and the building of more forts to face Parthia directly. Trajan annexed Arabia Nabatea in AD106.

ARMENIA: THE EXCEPTION

On the high plateau between Iran and Asia Minor, Armenia formed a natural buffer state between Rome and Parthia (later Persia). Almost independent, it leaned worryingly towards Parthia, being more Iranian than Hellenic with a feudal aristocracy and few towns. Its key position above Syria and Mesopotamia meant that it could not be ignored. Lucullus was the first Roman to enter Armenia, pursuing Mithradates in 69BC. In 65BC Pompey added Armenia to his clients, but Antony's attempt to win it failed. Yet when Augustus staged a triumph in the east in 20BC that returned the legionary standards lost by Crassus at Carrhae, Parthia (temporarily) recognized Armenia as a Roman protectorate. Nero's fine general Corbulo imposed a compromise in AD63 in which Parthian princes would be the kings of Armenia but invested (crowned) by Rome. In AD66 Nero invested Tiridates as king of Armenia in an extravagant ceremony in Rome. Trajan used the Parthian replacement of a Roman-approved king in Armenia in AD114 as a pretext for his grand eastern campaign, annexing the kingdom. Hadrian then evacuated it with other eastern conquests. This seesaw continued with minor variations over the next two centuries. When Armenia became the first Christian kingdom – a few years before Constantine's conversion – it became more pro-Roman. It was finally divided between Persia and Rome in AD383, with Persia getting most of it.

Above: Arches of the aqueduct at Caesarea Maritima on the coast of Judaea (Israel) that were restored under Trajan.

Below: One of Herod the Great's proudest feats was the building of a Hellenized city at Caesarea Maritima with a huge Roman-style aqueduct.

RELIANCE ON THE GERMANS
THE *FOEDERATI* AND THEIR DANGERS

Above: Barbarians, such as this captive from Trajan's campaigns, could often be turned by the Romans into useful subordinate foederati.

Below: Stilicho tried to use Visigoths as foederati, *with catastrophic results.*

When Rome was sacked by the Visigoths in AD410, it was by troops formerly in the pay of the Roman emperor: *foederati*, federate or allied troops. Events in the 5th century showed that such allies were often as dangerous to the empire as its open enemies, but they seemed better than no troops at all when it seemed the only way of protecting the empire.

Foederati means those who have made a *foedus* (literally treaty), so it was a term encompassing many types of barbarian. The employment of barbarians as auxiliary troops in small groups had a long history. Julius Caesar used German cavalry in his conquest of Gaul, and Trajan recruited cavalry from the Arabs for his eastern campaigns. Crucially, however, such troops remained firmly under Roman control and were normally as loyal – or disloyal – as any legionaries or other auxiliaries.

Marcus Aurelius faced acute problems after the plague and invasions of AD166–7. His plans included settling numbers of barbarian tribes in Pannonia and Moesia, who would in exchange return devastated land to cultivation and serve as auxiliaries. Later emperors also let barbarians settle in lands they themselves had devastated, hoping that they would supply recruits for the army. Constantine recruited so many barbarians into his elite force, (the *Scholae Palatinae*, who replaced the Praetorians), that he was accused of "barbarizing" the army. However, the barbarians remained under imperial control and sometimes became Romanized officials of high rank, such as Stilicho. Son of a Vandal general who had fought on the Roman side at Adrianople, Stilicho became totally Romanized, marrying Theodosius' niece Serena. He was, however, an exception, for the balance between Roman master and German hireling changed drastically in the late 4th century AD.

ADRIANOPLE AND AFTER

The Huns came from the heart of eastern Asia. They drove the Ostrogoths out of the Ukraine and into the Roman empire in AD376. Some 200,000 Goths, including Visigothic cousins living in Dacia, crossed the Danube, being allowed to settle in depopulated lands in Thrace. Their annihilation of the main Roman army under Valens at Adrianople two years later meant that the Goths now faced no real check on their activities.

The new emperor Theodosius' appeasement of the Goths seemed inevitable. Not everyone was convinced, but Theodosius' Gothic federates proved their worth by fighting at the Battle of the Frigid River in Slovenia in AD394. By the time Theodosius died in AD395, the Goths were settled as *foederati* en masse, under their own leaders *inside* the empire,

supposedly loyal to an empire no longer their military superior. The first decade of the 5th century AD revealed the full dangers of such a policy.

While Stilicho intrigued to be guardian of the young emperor Arcadius in the east as well as of Honorius in the west, Alaric, king of the Visigoths, played off one court against the other, escalating his demands for land, money and titles. Escaping Stilicho's pursuit in AD395, he had himself made *magister militum per Illyricum*, general of the army for Illyricum, by Constantinople, gaining access to Roman supply depots in the Balkans. So strengthened, he marched into Italy in AD401, attacking Milan. Defeated by Stilicho the next year, Alaric again escaped. Concentration on the Gothic threat weakened the Rhine frontier, where Suebians, Vandals and Burgundians crossed into Gaul in AD406. Some reached as far as Spain. Meanwhile, the pretender Constantine had landed in Gaul, denuding Britain of its garrison to pursue his imperial claims. Stilicho turned to Alaric, still supposedly a *foederatus*, for help against the barbarian invaders of Gaul and the usurper from Britain.

Alaric demanded 4,000lb (1,814kg) of gold in return for the mere promise of his help. This deal with a barbarian so scandalized many Romans that it led to Stilicho's assassination in August AD408 and an end to the appeasement policy. In response, in October AD408, Alaric crossed the Alps again, marching on Rome. He probably intended not to attack the city directly but to starve it out – it was well defended and the Goths were bad at sieges. On his third attempt, in August AD410, some Romans opened the gates to the Goths. For the first time in 800 years an enemy army possessed Rome.

Alaric stayed in Rome for only three days – the city had no food for his army – and died soon after. Yet the Visigoths, after further disputes, finally did help the imperial government, driving the Suebians and Vandals into westernmost

Iberia. In return, they were granted lands around Toulouse. Finally, at the Battle of Châlons-sur-Marne in AD451, Visigothic *foederati* proved themselves worthy allies by helping to repel the Huns.

Other German *foederati* proved less amenable. The Vandals crossed into Africa in AD429. There, through conquest and extortion, they gained control of the richest provinces in the west – a loss the imperial government tried to disguise by titling them *foederati*. The Vandals went on to seize the great port of Carthage, cutting off Rome's grain supplies.

Above: Marcus Aurelius receiving homage from barbarians AD176, some of whom he enlisted as foederati. *Useful mercenaries, so long as the Romans retained the upper hand, the* foederati *became a threat when the Romans lost control after AD378, and the empire was seriously imperilled.*

AT THE EMPIRE'S EXTREMITIES
EGYPT

Above: The temple of Horus at Edfu is the only Egyptian temple to survive almost intact. The Romans continued to support the ancient priesthood to maintain the social status quo.

Below: The annual flooding of the Nile enriched its banks with silt brought down from central Africa, making it the chief granary of the ancient world. Egypt's grain went to feed the Roman populace after its conquest in 30BC.

When Octavian occupied Egypt after defeating Antony and Cleopatra in 30BC, he decided that this immensely rich, ancient and, to Roman eyes, strange land should become his personal property or private kingdom. This meant that the *princeps* became the heir of the Ptolemies, themselves heirs of nearly three millennia of pharaonic rule. Augustus was depicted and worshipped as a pharaoh. Later emperors at times restored or extended temples, as Trajan did at Philae, although the powers of priests were generally circumscribed. The Romans wanted Egypt as a granary for Rome.

Egypt, with a population of about eight million under the early Principate, was second only to Italy in size. A Praetorian prefect governed the province from Alexandria, and senators were forbidden to visit it without the emperor's express permission. The first prefect, Aelius Gallus, led a campaign deep into the Sudan, making grandiose claims for his conquests. This so angered Augustus that

Gallus was forced to commit suicide. Later prefects were more cautious, and the frontier remained fixed for centuries near Aswan. The bulk of the population, the *fellahin*, or peasants, were tied to their land and governed by a combination of priests and local bureaucrats, as they had been for millennia. Their forced labour continued to supply the wheat and other products – linen, cotton and papyrus, the precursor of paper found only along the Nile's banks – that now went to Rome rather than their own government; but for a long time they posed little problem. Most Egyptians paid the *laographia*, or special poll tax; only the three Greek cities – Alexandria, Ptolemais and Naucratis – were exempt. At first 27,000 troops – three legions plus auxiliaries – were kept to control the country, with a flotilla on the Nile, later reduced to just one legion (needed in turbulent Alexandria), for there was almost no external threat. The native Egyptians still spoke their ancient language, now known as Coptic, and were separate from the two newer populations, the Jews and the Greeks, whose disputes caused the Romans many problems.

Both Jews and Greeks had been in Egypt for some time. The first Jews had been settled by the Persians in the 6th century BC as military colonists around Old Babylon (Cairo), as the Persians were unpopular rulers in Egypt. When Alexander the Great founded Alexandria in 331BC, he invited Jews to settle there. Later, under the Ptolemies, whose empire stretched to the Lebanon, many Jews moved to the metropolis. By the 1st century BC, around 8–10 per cent of the population of Egypt was Jewish. Alexandria must have had a larger Jewish population than any city in Judaea itself. Many Jews prospered in Alexandria and, although they had their own quarters

and kept their religion, some of them were influenced by Hellenism. Most famous of these was the philosopher Philo (*c*.25BC–AD45), whose attempts to reconcile the teachings of the Torah and Plato in works such as *The Contemplative Life* influenced later Christian thinking. Philo also took an active role in politics, leading the embassy of Jewish Alexandrians in AD40 to persuade Caligula not to enforce the worship of his own divinity on Jews. (Jews had been exempted from emperor-worship.) Caligula pronounced that those who could not see he was a god were more to be pitied than hated.

Philo's deputation to Rome was needed because of unceasing disputes and rivalries between Alexandria's Jews and its Greek-speakers, jealous of Jewish privileges. There were further riots between the two groups under Claudius. Under Nero, 50,000 people were killed when the Jews tried to burn down the amphitheatre and the governor had to send in two legions. In AD115 the whole Jewish population rose in revolt, causing immense destruction.

ALEXANDRIA: COSMOPOLIS AND CHRISTIAN CRADLE

With nearly one million inhabitants, Alexandria was almost as large as Rome under Augustus, and was still very much the centre of Greek scientific life. Heron invented the world's first steam engine there in the 1st century AD and Ptolemy drew up a map of the heavens a century later. Its famous library contained 500,000 papyrus rolls, the largest in the world, and its *pharos* (lighthouse), reputedly 400ft (120m) high, was the tallest structure in the world. Alexandria was the centre of trade routes stretching across the Mediterranean and east to India, its markets filled with exotic goods and peoples. Its grand boulevards, such as the Canopic Way lined with porticos, long eclipsed anything to be found in Rome. But it lacked what even the smallest *municipium* had: an elected council and magistrates.

This derived from the extremely autocratic government of the Ptolemies. Augustus continued without a council, which had to wait for Septimius Severus visiting Egypt in AD200–01. When the Alexandrians were not involved in commerce or sectarian strife, their thoughts turned to philosophy or religion. Plotinus, founder of antiquity's last great school of philosophy, was born there in AD204. But Egypt was also one of the most fertile grounds for early Christianity, which appealed both to native Egyptians and to erudite citizens of Alexandria.

The Greek theologian St Clement of Alexandria (*c*.AD150–214) was a bishop of Alexandria (later called Patriarchs). His pupil Origen (AD185–253), one of the first original Christian thinkers, castrated himself to avoid sexual temptation. Many early Christians went to the desert as a solution to this problem, with certain areas becoming almost crowded with hermits. Another Alexandrian bishop St Athanasius (AD295–373) attended the Council of Nicaea in AD325. Constantine accepted his views on the single nature of Christ, which became orthodox Christianity. Religious disputes continued to rack the city nearly as badly as the Greek–Jewish conflicts of earlier times.

Above: The Pharos of Alexandria was one of the Seven Wonders of the Ancient World. Reputedly 400ft (120m) high, it was the prototype of many such structures built by the Romans throughout their empire. This fanciful later picture understates its height.

Below: The bulk of the Egyptian population under the Romans remained fellahin, *or peasants, working the land and paying taxes mostly in kind. Only the advent of Christianity really affected them.*

AT THE EMPIRE'S EXTREMITIES
BRITAIN

Above: The ruins of Vindolanda, one of the many fine stone forts in Hadrian's wall country, built to mark the province's northern limits.

Below: Part of the Mildenhall Treasure, one of the most spectacular examples of Roman art in Britain, dating from the 4th century AD.

Although the English Channel formed one of the best natural frontiers the empire ever had, Britain had tantalized the Romans since Caesar's two brief expeditions of 55 and 54BC. The second, with five legions, had temporarily crushed some Britons, but did not lastingly affect its warring, if artistically gifted, Celtic tribes. Claudius, lacking a military background because of his disabilities, was eager to gain glory in this mysterious and reputedly rich island. Strabo had summed up Britain's exports as "hunting dogs, slaves, gold", but the Romans overestimated Britain's wealth. The cost of its large garrison – up to 30,000 troops – probably exceeded its revenues at first, but recent research suggests Britain contributed much more than was once thought to the empire.

The death in AD41 of Cunobelin (Shakespeare's Cymbeline), who had ruled much of south-east England from Camulodunum (Colchester), led to disputes between his sons, which helped the Romans. The invasion force of AD43 under Aulus Plautius, made up of four legions plus auxiliaries – about 40,000 men – landed at Richborough, moved north to the Thames, crushing all British resistance, then waited until Claudius hurriedly joined them before advancing. Claudius then established Camulodunum as the capital for his new province, and, hailed as *imperator* by his troops, proudly returned home.

Several client kingdoms acknowledged Roman suzerainty: the Iceni in Norfolk, the powerful Brigantes in northern England and the Regni in Sussex. The young general Vespasian led the Second Legion south-west, storming 20 *oppida* or hill forts. Meanwhile, the Ninth Legion moved north to Lincoln, which became a colony in the reign of Nerva (AD96–8). London, St Albans and other towns sprang up in the wake of the army in the AD70s, and the Fosse Way from Lincoln to Exeter marked in effect the first provisional boundary of Roman Britain.

This boundary proved temporary. Caratacus, one of Cunobelin's sons, escaped to rally opposition in Wales and drew the Romans west. Captured in AD51, he was taken in chains to Rome where he marvelled aloud that such a magnificent city should covet his poor land. Traditionally, Claudius, impressed by his courage, spared his life. A new governor, Suetonius Paulinus, decided to eliminate the Druid stronghold at Anglesey in AD58. The Romans rightly saw these priests, who practised human sacrifice, as inspiring British resistance. The revolt of the Iceni under Boudicca in AD60 made Suetonius Paulinus return in a hurry to crush them, but Roman policies were changed: the *publicani* were removed and a conciliatory attitude was adopted. Soon the burnt towns were rebuilt and British grandees began adopting Roman ways (as the near-palace at Fishbourne suggests), despite a total lack of imperial interest under Nero.

THE NORTHERN FRONTIER

The Brigantes, suddenly turning hostile under Venutius, their new king, were defeated at Stanwick in AD71, and Rome's northward advance resumed. Agricola, governor from AD77 to 83, encouraged the civilizing of lowland Britons, settling them in *civitates*, or towns, rather than hill forts, complete with theatres, forums and baths, and teaching them Latin. The Silures in Wales moved from their hill fortress to a new Roman town at Caerwent. Agricola then turned north to complete the conquest of the still mysterious island. He pushed deep into the Highlands, routing the assembled Caledonians at Mons Graupius (near Inverness), nearly completing the conquest of Britain. He then sent a fleet to circumnavigate the north and started to build a large legionary fortress at Inchtuthill, Tayside. It was never finished, for Agricola was soon recalled by Domitian and his northern forts were then abandoned.

When Hadrian visited Britain in AD122 he found the frontier in flux. True to his retractive instincts, he established a new 76-mile (122km) Tyne–Solway line. Intended to be permanent, it was built in stone in its eastern part, the western part being built initially in turf. In AD139, south Scotland was reoccupied and the turf Antonine Wall (named after emperor Antoninus) was built across the waist of Scotland along the Forth–Clyde line. It was abandoned by AD163, and Hadrian's Wall once again became the northern frontier. The emperor Septimius Severus marched north in AD209 and reached Aberdeen, but on his death in AD211 Scotland was again evacuated.

By AD130, a pattern of military garrisons had been established, with legionary forts at Chester, York and Caerleon and auxiliary troops along the walls and round Wales containing the still barbarous tribes. In lowland Britain urban life developed rapidly, if normally quite modestly. However, the great basilica and forum in London, built under Hadrian, were gigantic in size. The baths at Aquae Sulis (Bath) have an elegant opulence that suggests a sophisticated society, as does the large theatre at Verulamium (St Albans). Mining was developed – far more iron, lead and coal were produced than gold – along with farming and trade. Britain escaped the catastrophes of the 3rd century AD relatively lightly, although most towns now built themselves stone walls. But a new threat was emerging: Saxon raiders along the east coasts who would one day conquer the province.

Above: Housesteads was a typical fort on Hadrian's wall, with a garrison of one cohort of auxiliaries (c.500 men).

Below: A sea-god dominates the centre of a floor mosaic from a Romano--British villa. Such villas flourished up to the mid-4th century AD.

PART TWO

THE POWER OF ROME

The Romans called their empire *imperium Romanorum*. This translates rather appositely as the power of the Romans. From the Latin word *imperator*, or commander-in-chief, comes our word emperor. For contemporaries, there was no escaping the military fact of Roman power. Certainly, subject peoples who incurred Rome's anger knew that the heavy weight of Rome's military machine could descend on them with exemplary force.

The Roman army was indisputably the best armed force in the ancient world – at least in those areas it knew – although its navy was of very minor importance. For a period of more than half a millennium, from the defeat of Hannibal in 202BC to Rome's own stunning defeat by the Goths at Adrianople in AD378, Rome was generally undefeated. Individual Roman generals could be outmanoeuvred or outwitted, and at the empire's extremities – in northern Britain, the deep forests of central Germany or the deserts of Asia – Rome's power seemed to reach its limits. But elsewhere, no other army could in the long term resist Roman military might; it was relentless, unflinching and genuinely invincible. Rome's army was not just the first fully professional army on a global scale; for a very long time it was probably the only such force deserving the name. Certainly Europe and the Middle East would not see such a force again until the 17th century at the earliest. In many ways, Rome's example was not to be surpassed until the career of Napoleon Bonaparte, who openly and repeatedly borrowed aspects of Roman power when creating his own militaristic empire with its eagles, arches and client states. Above all, the Romans were remarkably disciplined soldiers. This helped make them and keep them highly effective imperial rulers.

Left: Capturing a city that had not surrendered when summoned, Romans often killed every living thing, even dogs – a brutality calculated to terrify.

CHAPTER VII

THE ROMAN ARMY

The growth of the Roman army, from an unpaid citizens' militia to a world-conquering professional force, made possible the growth of the Roman empire. The Roman army was Rome's greatest institution. The city, surrounded by enemies from the start, survived by taking the offensive. Two factors distinguished the Roman army in its long prime from the mid-4th century BC until after AD200: flexibility and tenacity. As the long, often catastrophic war against Hannibal (218–202BC) showed, panic was a Greek word seldom found in a Roman's vocabulary. In the later Republic, almost constant wars turned a part-time self-defence force into a full-time army. Deficiencies, revealed in wars in Africa, called for radical reforms provided by Marius, who opened the army to the poorest citizens as a career. From 100BC the army became fully professional and under the Principate was paid by the *princeps*. In return, soldiers swore allegiance to the *princeps*. Military and civilian careers long remained intertwined. Young Roman nobles served in the army before starting political careers, retaining vital links between civilian and military life. But from the mid-3rd century AD on, soldiers and civilians were segregated by emperors to prevent revolts. Disarmed, the citizens grew ever more timid, while soldiers became more detached from, and openly contemptuous of, the civilians whose taxes supported them and whose lives they supposedly were protecting.

Left: Officers and soldiers of the Praetorian guard, the elite imperial bodyguard stationed in Rome.

THE PEOPLE'S ARMY

Above: Mars, the god of war, was appositely the god of the early Roman state, forever at war with its neighbours.

Rome, surrounded by land-hungry tribes, was frequently at war. Appropriately, Mars, god of war, was originally its chief god. If its early wars were little more than glorified raids, when the Roman army grew larger it soon distinguished itself from other armies by its tenacity and readiness to innovate, taking what it needed from other people's customs.

Under its first kings, the army of Rome consisted of individual warriors fighting mostly on foot, led by aristocrats. King Servius is credited with having effected a "hoplite revolution" in the mid-6th century BC. He regrouped the citizens into six classes, calculated according to wealth rather than lineage, divided into centuries (of 100 men originally). The last class was exempt from military service, as it could not afford to arm itself, although later its members served as rowers in the usually insignificant navy.

In civil life these centuries formed the *comitia centuriata*, the main form of the Assembly. The bulk of the fighting was now done by men of the classes who could equip themselves as armoured infantry. They probably used hoplite armour and arms – round shield, cuirass (body armour), sword and long spear – derived from Greek models. The equestrians, those able to pay for a horse, formed the small cavalry. This Roman version of a hoplite revolution increased the size of the Roman army and survived the fall of the monarchy. Romans were less attached to the hoplite army than Greek or Etruscan cities, whose hoplite armies met for set battles in a *phalanx*, a rigid formation of spearmen. Instead, they seem to have fought more flexibly from early on in a *legio*, or legion.

The word *legio* means levy, the call-up of heavy infantry in 30 centuries, plus 300 cavalry recruited from the richest citizens and *velites*, light troops recruited from the poorest eligible class or the very youngest. By about 300BC, a legion had a total of *c*.4,200 spearmen, commanded by one of the two consuls. Troops paraded and drilled on the Campus Martius just outside the city, for no arms could be carried inside Rome, although the levy took place on the Capitoline Hill. In the mid-5th century BC there was a change in army command. The two consuls, until

Below: The four types of soldier of the early and mid-Republic, of whom the first three fought in the acer triplex *(triple line). The last were poorly armed skirmishers.*

then only the generals, were partly supplanted by six military tribunes, presumably more professional. Such professionalism was needed, for in about 435BC Rome began its first serious long war with its powerful Etruscan neighbour, Veii, which had formidable defences, both natural and man-made. It was not until Camillus took command that Veii was captured. He made the Romans fight continuously – previously they had returned to their farms for the harvest – and introduced pay. By 342BC the Roman army was involved in fighting in Campania, a place that seemed so distant that the troops at first mutinied. By now, however, Rome had established a novel form of fighting that enabled it to survive defeats by technically superior enemies.

THE TRIPLE LINE (*ACER TRIPLEX*)

According to Polybius, the Greek historian brought to Rome as a hostage in 167BC, the Roman army of the middle Republic fought in three lines determined by age and experience. The first line consisted of the youngest soldiers, the *hastati*, literally spearmen. Behind came men in their late 20s or 30s, in the prime of life, called *principes*. In the rear were the veterans, the *triarii*, the third line. All lines wore bronze helmets; the richer ones wore a mail cuirass, others simply had a bronze breastplate. All carried a long semi-cylindrical shield. Roman infantrymen were primarily swordsmen. Their sword was the *gladius hispaniensis*, with a blade less than 2ft (60cm) long, well suited for both cutting and thrusting. The first two ranks carried the *pilum*, a weighty javelin with a wooden shaft about 4ft (120cm) long, surmounted by a 2–3ft (60–90cm) narrow iron shaft with a pyramid-shaped point. This tiny point gave the javelin enough impetus to smash through a shield. Each legionary had two *pila*, with a maximum range of about 100ft (30m).

Each of the three infantry lines was divided into ten *maniples*. Those of the *hastati* and *principes* had about 120–60 men each, while the reserve of *triarii*

made up maniples of 60 men. During battle, the maniples were arranged like a chess-board in a *quincunx*, a five-fold formation, in which the *principes'* maniples guarded the gaps between the units of the *hastati*. In the rear, the *triarii* covered the gaps in the *principes'* lines. In front of the *hastati*, skirmishers engaged the enemy, retreating between the *hastati maniples*, who then threw their javelins and charged the enemy. When exhausted, they retreated between the gaps between the *principes*, who also charged, throwing their javelins. The *triarii* had to fight only in extremis. A saying that things "had come to the *triarii*" meant things were in a terrible state.

The triple line of maniples made for a more flexible, mobile formation than the *phalanx*, which could be easily upset. Triple lines proved their worth, first defeating Samnite cavalry in gruelling wars (343–290BC), then the crack *phalanx* of Pyrrhus of Epirus. Typically, the Romans, then facing war-elephants for the first time, learnt how to open their ranks to let the enraged beasts pass through.

Above: This detail from the Column of Marcus Aurelius in Rome shows well-trained Roman soldiers fighting barbarians on the Danube in the 2nd century AD.

BATTLE HARDENING

King Pyrrhus was astonished less by his defeat at the hands of a non-Greek city, than by the Romans' refusal to accept the rules of war as then understood by Greeks. By the 3rd century BC, these had become relatively civilized. Wars were fought between mercenaries, who were not expected to fight to the last drop of blood. By contrast, the disciplined Romans (whom Pyrrhus acknowledged were "not barbarians"), fought with grim determination both on the battlefield and in the political arena. Rome would tolerate high casualties in its citizen armies, but would accept no compromise treaties with enemies strong enough to recover and possibly challenge her again. Unconditional surrender or total destruction was the choice offered to rival powers. This might be brutal, but it proved devastatingly effective.

When Rome and Carthage went to war in 264BC, Rome had no fleet to combat the Mediterranean's greatest maritime power. Carthage's wealth enabled her to hire huge armies of mercenaries. The Romans, however, set about building a

fleet for what proved to be a naval war. Wars at sea were fought by galleys, rowed by oarsmen. The Romans copied a Carthaginian galley that had run aground, training rowing crews – poorer citizens – on land while they built 140 cloned ships. The first naval clash proved a disaster, and the Romans realized that they could not out-manoeuvre the experienced Carthaginians. Instead, they devised the *corvus*, or raven, a boarding ramp with an iron spike that fell and stuck into the enemy's deck, locking the two galleys together. Naval skills became redundant as Roman legionaries charged across and got down to hand-to-hand combat.

At the Battle of Mylae in 260BC, a larger Carthaginian fleet was totally defeated, losing 50 ships including its flagship thanks to this unnautical novelty. The Romans defeated the Carthaginians again in 256BC at Ecnomus. The Romans went on the offensive, landing an army under Regulus in North Africa. However, Regulus was defeated in 255BC and taken prisoner. A relief fleet was sunk by a storm, as were other fleets because the

Below: Only in the First Punic War did the Roman fleet play a crucial role. Thanks to the corvus, *which bound ships together, Rome defeated Carthage repeatedly at sea.*

corvus made galleys top-heavy. Finally, the Romans raised another fleet and won the decisive battle of the Aegates Islands in 242BC. Carthage gave up Sicily and her fleet. Her ruling families, like the Barcas, however, were determined on revenge.

ENDURANCE AND INNOVATION

In Hannibal Barca, Rome encountered a military genius. Hannibal recruited his army from the best fighting nations – Numidian cavalry, Spanish and Celtic infantry. Against such a force, Rome fielded its superior militia. Rome still carried out a fresh mobilization each year, and still appointed amateur generals from that year's consuls. Rome's only obvious strength was the huge supply of recruits from her allied cities – 700,000 men.

Hannibal's three swift victories – at Trebbia, Trasimene and, most devastatingly, at Cannae in 216BC – should have won the war. But they were not cheap victories: Cannae cost Hannibal 5,700 men. The Roman maniples' triple lines helped soldiers to keep fighting even in defeat. So did their discipline. Rome, with its belief in its gods, fought on. Although it might have seemed wiser to keep troops at home, legions were sent to Spain. Fabius Maximus wore Hannibal

down by avoiding open battle and reconquering the south. The long sieges of Capua, Tarento and Syracuse showed Roman inventiveness at its best. Scipio took the offensive in Spain, adopting Hannibal's own tactics (placing heavy legions on the wings with light troops in the centre) to crush the Carthaginians at Ilipa in 206BC. He then defeated Hannibal at Zama in 202BC, where the Romans outfought the Carthaginians, after turning back their elephants.

Above: The scene from the Temple of Neptune in Rome c.100BC shows soldiers of the late Republic equipped with long shields, plumed helmets and, for the officer by the altar, a cuirass. Soon after this time, Roman soldiers stopped providing their own armour.

Below: Roman troops cross water using a bridge of boats.

THE FALL OF THE REPUBLIC

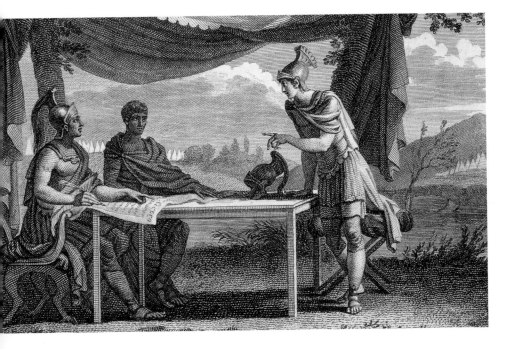

Above: A standard of a cohort, the subdivision of the legion.

Below: Lepidus, Mark Antony and Octavian formed the Second Triumvirate in 43BC.

Success can breed complacency, as Rome discovered in the later 2nd century BC, when it struggled against adversaries who were often less formidable than those it had already overcome. The army's lack of full professional status was one of the main problems. Essentially, most Roman soldiers still expected to return to their farms at the end of a campaign – although these were usually ruined by often long periods of absence. This left many men without property, making them and their sons ineligible for further military service, and so weakening the army. These shortcomings were corrected by Marius' army reforms. In the long term, these proved fatal to the Republic's existence.

Military problems first became apparent in the Third Punic War (149–146BC). Disturbed by Carthage's economic – not military – resurgence, Rome engineered war after Carthage became entangled with its aggressive neighbour Numidia, officially breaking its treaty with Rome. The Roman armies suffered repeated reverses until Scipio Aemilianus (the adopted grandson of Scipio Africanus) took command and stormed Carthage, destroying the city.

Worse followed in Spain, where Iberian tribes fought each other and Rome endlessly. Another revolt against Rome, based in the northern city of Numantia, proved intractable. Untrained Roman armies were defeated until Scipio assembled and trained an army of 60,000 men. Even then, he did not dare face the Numantians in open battle but used siege tactics to capture and destroy their city in 133BC. Such brutality had become a hallmark of Roman imperialism but was now coupled with military semi-competence.

Back in Africa, another challenge to Roman power arose with Jugurtha, a fine general and king of Numidia (northern Algeria). He defeated a Roman army in 110BC, forcing it to "pass under the yoke". He proved so successful at eluding superior Roman armies that treachery was suspected. Roman troops deserted in droves, as their commanders appeared incompetent or corrupt. The arrival of the martinet Quintus Metellus restored discipline and morale, but he failed to catch Jugurtha. Impatient for a successful conclusion, the Roman Assembly chose Marius, a *novus homo*, or "new man", from an equestrian family.

MARIUS AND HIS REFORMS
After serving under Metellus as consul in 107BC, Marius was given the African command the next year. Before leaving Rome, he appealed for volunteers from the propertyless class, the *capite censi*, helping to turn a citizens' militia into a career army that appealed to landless poorer citizens. With a much increased supply of recruits, Marius won victories in Africa that revealed his own military talents. But he failed to corner Jugurtha until treachery led to his capture and final execution in Rome in 104BC.

Meanwhile in the north, two large Germanic peoples, the Cimbri and the Teutones, annihilated twin Roman armies at Arausio (Orange) in 105BC. In the

Left: The Colosseum, Trajan's Column, the Forum, a severed head and streams of blood feature in this depiction of The Massacre of the Triumvirate, *by Antoine Caron, a 16th-century painter.*

worst disaster since Cannae, 80,000 men were reported lost. Marius was again given command by the Assembly and in three years radically restructured the army.

The three lines based on experience and age were abolished. All legionaries now had a *pilum* (javelin) plus the short *gladius* (sword) and had to carry supplies on their backs, hence the new nickname "Marius' mules". The basic sub-unit became the cohort of 480 men, which was divided into six centuries of 80 men each commanded by a centurion, officers who became the backbone of the army. Each legion had its own standard, a gilt eagle, that embodied the legion's *esprit de corps*. The legions themselves became more permanent, and, most importantly, these full-time legionaries started looking to their generals for reward, the Senate having failed to look after its demobilized soldiers.

This new-style army proved far more flexible than its predecessor. Marius used his uniformly equipped cohorts to crush the Teutones in a bloody battle at Aix-en-Provence in 102BC and the next year to rout the Cimbri in northern Italy, reportedly killing 100,000 of them. The most alarming barbarian invasions until the 3rd century AD had been repelled and Marius was (unconstitutionally) re-elected consul yet again.

THE RESULTS OF THE REFORMS

After Marius, no one won supreme power in Rome (as opposed to just becoming consul) without an army to back him. Powerful Roman generals – first Marius, then Sulla, Pompey, Caesar, and finally Antony and Octavian – built up armies that were loyal to them rather than to the state, and could use them for personal reasons. Sulla, once Marius' lieutenant in Africa, led the army he had been assigned for war against Mithradates against Rome itself in 88BC, the first of many such "marches on Rome". From Marius' reforms until the end of the Republic, Rome's armies were used against each other almost as much as against foreign enemies. This wrecked the Republic.

The *military* consequences of Marius' reforms were almost wholly positive, however. The Social War with the Latin allies of 91–87BC had given the allies Roman citizenship and greatly increased the numbers eligible for legionary service. These professional legions made a superb permanent army. Reorganized and supplemented by increasing numbers of specialized auxiliaries – from Balearic slingers to African cavalry – they continued Rome's conquest of the ancient world, successfully defending it until the mid-3rd century AD with only minor changes in their structure.

Below: The eagle-standard introduced by Marius became the focus of loyalty among legionaries. To lose one in battle was a disgrace, and the aquilifer, *eagle-bearer, was an important soldier. But loyalty to the legion did not always mean loyalty to the Republic.*

LEGIONS AND PRINCIPATE

When Octavian, victorious after the lengthy civil wars, returned to Rome in 29BC, a pressing problem was how to deal with a huge army of nearly 70 legions, plus a large fleet. Such swollen forces were unsustainable by an empire exhausted economically, and unnecessary when Rome faced no major external threats. They also posed a potential future threat to the stability of his regime should they become loyal to a successful and ambitious general. Although Octavian had risen to power by the sword, he did not wish to advertise the fact. Above all, he wanted to ensure the loyalty of the army to himself and later to his family, to avert any recurrence of civil war.

Octavian decided on demobilization, reducing the army's size to only 28 legions (around 150,000 regular soldiers). This meant that he needed to find a way of paying off some 300,000 veterans with

Above: A legionary of the 1st century BC *with his* pilum *(javelin) and* gladius *(sword).*

grants of land in ways that did not anger too many existing landholders. Augustus, as he was titled from 27BC, did this by founding colonies of veterans, often outside Italy – in Spain, Sicily, Gaul, Greece, Syria and Pisidia (central Turkey). He also established 28 colonies in Italy, some of which became famous in his lifetime. Turin is a good example. His vast wealth allowed him to pay fair prices for land in Italy. The revenues of Egypt flowed directly into the imperial purse and he owned vast tracts of land taken from enemies. In AD6 Augustus set up the *Aerarium militare*, a special military treasury, to meet legionaries' retirement pensions from indirect taxes.

The 28 legions – reduced to 25 after the Teutoburg disaster – were stationed in troubled provinces such as Tarraconensis (northern Spain) and along the frontiers, especially the Rhine and Danube, where permanent fortresses were established, later to develop into towns such as Cologne or Vienna. The Rhine was the early crucial frontier, with eight legions stationed along it, some in double camps such as Xanten. Later, the Danube became the most important. Under the Principate, legions were commanded by legates, who held delegated power (*imperium*) from Augustus. He kept only nine cohorts of the elite Praetorian guard in Italy and stationed only three of them in Rome – a tiny military force for a city of nearly a million inhabitants. Along the frontiers, the lower-paid, more lightly armed auxiliaries, recruited from non-Roman citizens, supplemented the legions.

This frontier deployment meant that there was no central reserve, at least until Septimius Severus (AD193–211) based a legion near Rome. Although criticisms

Left: Legionaries of the Principate, with curved shields, lorica segmantata *armour, short swords and* pilum, *the javelin with the thin neck.*

Right: A Roman centurion as imagined in the Italian Renaissance, with his sword on his left and wearing ornate armour.

have been levelled against Augustus for this lack, in practice it probably made little difference given the length of the frontiers and the slow progress of marching legionaries. The army remained *potentially* on the offensive, ready to move along or across the frontiers. A central reserve under an ambitious commander might also prove a threat to the emperor. Augustus did establish three fleets to keep the Mediterranean free of pirates as well as flotillas on the Rhine, Danube and Nile, but naval power was always secondary to land power.

LOYALTY TO THE *PRINCEPS*

All new recruits swore a *sacramentum*, or oath to the *princeps*, rather than to the Senate. But, unlike Caesar or Pompey, Augustus was not a great general. He owed his earlier victories (over Sextus Pompeius and Antony) principally to Marcus Agrippa, his chief minister and closest ally. After Actium, Augustus campaigned only in northern Spain in 23BC. He fell seriously ill there and seldom again took the field, but troops did not swear allegiance to the general Agrippa. The image of the emperor or of one of his family was carried by an *imaginifer*, a standard-bearer ranking behind only the *aquilifer*, the eagle-bearer. The emperor's name was coupled with that of *Roma Dea* (Rome the goddess) in sacrifices and his image appeared on busts and coins. Such reiterated expressions of loyalty to the *imperator* or Caesar, helped to cement Augustus' settlement, enabling it to survive the antics of Caligula and even, for a surprisingly long time, those of Nero. Nero's almost total neglect of the military was a major cause of his downfall.

Augustus was fortunate that in his stepsons Drusus and especially Tiberius (from AD6 his adopted son) he had extremely competent generals who campaigned steadily on the Rhine and Danube. Their military successes reflected on the *princeps*. Later emperors were less lucky but faced few serious challenges from army commanders until AD68 and the Year of the Four Emperors. Thereafter, dynastic continuity, coupled with generous donations at each emperor's accession, helped to keep the legions loyal. When a general did revolt, like Saturninus in AD89, he was quickly quashed. This contributed to the success both of the Flavians and of the Five Good Emperors – all of the latter being adopted sons. Ironically, when Marcus Aurelius made Commodus (whom he believed to be his actual son) his heir, the dynasty came to an end and the ensuing civil wars, longer and more damaging than in AD68–9, weakened the empire.

Below: The imperial guard as they appear on the base of the Obelisk of Theodosius I, a 4th-century AD emperor, in Constantinople (Istanbul).

ARMY OF THE LATER EMPIRE

Above: Light-armed auxiliary troops, with clubs but no armour, supplement the legionaries on this detail from Trajan's Column in Rome.

Below: The massive walls of Richborough, Rome's chief port of entry to Britain and part of the Saxon Shore defences of the 3rd century AD, show the empire was on the defensive.

During the mid-3rd-century AD crisis, it became obvious that the traditional deployment of the army had become inadequate. Withdrawing legions from one frontier to fight on another left the exposed frontier intolerably vulnerable. The persistent and well-organized Sassanid Persians were more deadly than the earlier Parthians. The Germanic Goths, who first appeared on the Danube delta in AD242, were also formidable. Over the next 30 years they penetrated into the empire's Mediterranean heart, sometimes seizing ships. Athens, far from any frontier, was sacked in AD268 by the Heruli, another tribe that was wandering the empire almost at will.

At least 30 emperors held power between the murder of Alexander Severus in AD235, and AD284, the accession of Diocletian. Only one died a natural death (Claudius Gothicus in AD270). Many more usurpers were acclaimed by mutinous legions throughout the empire. A few, like Postumus in Gaul and Carausius in Britain, formed breakaway empires that lasted years. The lack of a central reserve and the intertwining of civilian and military careers now appeared terrible weaknesses.

Around AD200, Septimius Severus had begun building a reserve in Italy, doubling the Praetorian guard and stationing a legion near Rome. This created a mobile force of around 18,000 men. Later, Gallienus (AD253–68) banned senators from holding senior commands and began building up a mobile cavalry force in northern Italy, drawing on *vexillationes* (detachments). Like his removal of the government to Milan, close to the Alpine passes and the Rhine–Danube frontiers, this concentration of forces around the emperor set a precedent. Gallienus was murdered before he could employ this force to lasting effect, but his successors, Claudius II and Aurelian (AD270–75), used it to defeat the Goths, Palmyrene rebels and the separatist Gallic empire. Aurelian also accelerated the programme of refortifying cities, notably the capital itself. These steps marked the start of a radical change in tactics and strategy that was completed by Constantine.

CRACK TROOPS – AND THE REST

Constantine (AD324–37) continued to make the army more mobile, dividing it into two groups that were distinct in armour, pay, prestige and role. The low-paid *limitanei* were the frontier guards and the elite *comitatenses* were mobile forces grouped around the emperors. The latter were often cavalry: scale-armoured *cataphracts* or *clibanarii* with plate armour. Such horsemen looked imposing but were often ineffectual. Julian had to discipline cavalry units for cowardice during his Persian campaign in AD363 and the indiscipline of Valens' cavalry was partly responsible for his defeat at Adrianople in AD378. Before the widespread adoption of the stirrup – now known not to have occurred much before AD600 – heavy cavalry was of limited use, for lances could not be used in charges. The impact of hitting an opponent would have unseated a stirrupless rider.

FORTIFICATIONS PROGRAMME
To protect the vulnerable cities of the interior, new fortresses or fortified towns – known as *burgi*, a German word – became nodal strong points, usually invulnerable to direct attack by barbarians. At York, old walls were replaced by thick defensive walls capable of carrying pieces of artillery. This huge fortification programme was replicated across the empire. Behind these huge walls, frontier troops could await the arrival of the mobile relief forces. Large landowners began fortifying their villas or farms, so that invaders, even if undefeated in the field, would face starvation outside the walls.

Constantine created *palatini*, imperial Palatine guards, to replace the Praetorians. Many of these were German horsemen. This increasing dependence on Germanic mercenaries is symbolized by the adoption of "dragon standards" – long, wind-sock-style banners – and German war cries. By AD379, when Theodosius became emperor after Adrianople, the Goths had become *foederati*, or allies, with whole tribes enrolled *en masse*. When imperial government divided after Theodosius' death in AD395, the Goths turned against their Roman allies and started the chain of events that led to the sack of Rome in AD410.

The empire in the 4th century AD still had about 60 legions, each now made up of only about 1,000 lightly armed men. The infantry no longer wore much body armour and used darts rather than the *pilum* (javelin). Nonetheless, properly led and trained Roman armies could still defeat their enemies, as victorious campaigns from Galerius' victory over the Persians in AD297 to Valentinian's campaigns against the Germans in the AD360s showed. Often, however, Rome's armies were deployed against each other.

The *limitanei*, stationary frontier troops garrisoning the new forts, were unimpressive. Many were expected to grow their own food, as they were not paid all year round. Nonetheless, some of these frontier troops continued to fight for the western empire right up to the end in the AD470s. In AD534, after the eastern empire had reconquered North Africa, the emperor Justinian ordered the re-establishment of the *limitanei* to defend the long frontiers. But the actual reconquest of the west – Africa, Italy, southern Spain – was carried out by smallish numbers of cavalry. An army of 20,000 men was by then thought large.

How effective the army of the later empire was is debatable, but it was certainly more expensive, and the taxes to pay for it contributed to the alienation of subjects from the imperial government. But as Roman civilians were increasingly loath to fight – there are reports of men of military age mutilating themselves to avoid conscription under Constantine – there seemed little alternative. The continued survival of the eastern empire, and its 6th-century revival, suggests that the late-Roman army could fight effectively at least at times.

Above: York was for long a legionary headquarters and the capital of northern Britain. Two emperors – Septimius Severus and Constantius Chlorus – died in the city, and Constantine I was proclaimed emperor there by his troops.

Below: This scene from the Arch of Galerius in Thessalonica, Greece, commemorates Galerius' victory over the Persians in AD297. Elephants, often used by the Persians, can just be glimpsed in the background.

CHAPTER VIII

INSIDE THE ARMY

As the Roman army became a world-conquering force, it evolved an original system of organization. Based on the legion, this model had the flexibility to overcome much larger, and often technically superior, enemy forces. Above all, it was indomitably aggressive. From the earliest wars of the Republic in the 5th century BC up to the 3rd century AD, its core troops were the legionaries: highly disciplined, well-armoured, heavy infantry-men who could fight in many different ways, from storming fortresses to outfacing charging elephants or even, as marines, fighting onboard ships.

The Roman army was notorious for its tough discipline and rigorous demands. However, for its age it was also oddly meritocratic, and in some ways continued to represent the voice of the Roman people after the Republic had ended. In effect, it spoke, as well as fought, for the people of the whole empire, not just Rome. The legions were often remarkably long-lived – some units lasted more than 300 years. In so doing, they became the unwitting agents of a process of Romanization that transformed western Europe through the towns that sprang up around their camps, or in the peaceful hinterland guarded by them. Many of the bridges, aqueducts and walls around the former provinces were built by legionaries in the long periods of peace that their fighting had established. The Roman army was more than just an army: in some ways it became the heart of Rome itself.

Left: Legionaries, besides being professional soldiers, often also became skilled builders, constructing many forts and roads.

ORGANIZING THE LEGION

Above: A Roman optio, *the second-in-command to a centurion, with his distinctive plumed helmet, worn by a member of the re-enactment group the Ermine St Guard. Officers such as the* optio *and the centurion were the army's backbone, and they received higher pay.*

Below: The symbol of the 20th Roman legion, Valeria Victrix.

Legio means levy, and originally a legion was the levy of all eligible Roman citizens between the ages of 17 and 46, arranged in centuries (literally 100 men). The Roman army of around 500BC numbered around 4,000–6,000 men, hoplite heavy spearmen, like the Greeks. Over the next centuries, however, the legion proper emerged as a new, more adaptable unit that enabled Rome to conquer and hold the Mediterranean world.

By *c.*320BC, the legion of the Republic had been established. According to Polybius and Livy – who do not always agree – a legion had five elements: cavalry, light infantry and three sorts of heavy infantry. The richest citizens made up the cavalry of about 300 men, socially prestigious but too few to affect battles. The all-important heavy infantry, about 4,200 men who could afford their own armour, was divided into three lines. The first line had the youngest soldiers, the *hastati* (literally "armed with a spear", although they carried javelins and swords). Next came the *principes*, men in their prime, and last came the *triarii*, the veterans. Behind the *triarii* were deployed less dependable troops, *rorarii* and *accensi*. All soldiers wore bronze helmets and had a long shield of wood covered with leather. The *hastati* and *principes* were armed with the *pilum*, or javelin, and the *gladius*, or short sword, about 20in (50cm) long. The *triarii* appear to have had longer spears. The *velites* were light infantry too poor to equip themselves with full armour.

All three lines were organized into ten maniples. This, the smallest fighting unit, had two centuries, commanded by the senior centurion. Maniples of the *hastati* and *principes* numbered about 120–60 men each, while the *triarii* made up ten maniples of about 60 men. Each maniple also had about 40 *velites*, or lightly armed troops. In battle, the maniples were arranged in the *triplex acies* (triple battle-order) of a chequerboard formation. The maniples of the *principes* covered the gaps between those of the *hastati*, and their own gaps were covered by those of the *triarii*. The *velites* seem to have been used as skirmishers. Each legion of Roman citizens was augmented by an equal number of allies (about 4,000–5,000 infantry and 900 cavalry), commanded by Roman officers. These were called *alae* (wings) because in battle they were put on the wings of the main legions.

The *triplex acies* proved its virtues by defeating the numerically and technically superior armies of Pyrrhus, the Macedonians and the Seleucids. The flexibility and discipline of the maniples – opening up to let hostile elephants or cavalry through, for example – was very nearly invincible. When the Romans were defeated, notably by Hannibal, it was due to Roman amateurism, for the armies were disbanded after each campaign and had to be recruited afresh. When armies remained in existence for a long time under a great general such as Scipio Africanus, they were superb, as the run of Roman victories from Zama in 202BC to Pydna in 168BC showed.

THE CLASSIC LEGION

Rome's military reputation was dented by defeats in the later 2nd century BC, which culminated in disaster at Arausio (Orange). Twin armies were annihilated by the Cimbri and Teutones in 105BC with the loss of 80,000 men. Such a defeat led Marius, recently emerged as the people's general in the war against Jugurtha, to reorganize the legion radically. He had already abolished the property qualifications. Now he got rid of all distinctions based on class or age: both the *velites* and the cavalry disappeared. All legionaries were identically armed with the *pilum* and *gladius*, and had mail armour and a long shield. The maniples ceased to be the

basic unit, although they remained in existence for a while. Instead, the chief tactical sub-unit became the cohort, ten of which made up a legion.

Each cohort had about 480 men divided into six centuries of 80 men led by a centurion. Later the first cohort was usually double strength, raising a legion's total strength to 5,280 men. *Alae*, no longer allies but cavalry wings recruited from auxiliaries, were specialist, increasingly well-regarded units either 512- or 768-men strong. Ten cohorts were easier to command than 30 maniples and could be deployed as wanted. The cohort did not command the same loyalty as the century and the legion. Marius introduced the silver (later gilt) *aquila*, or eagle, as each legion's main standard, symbolizing its pride and identity. Legions now became permanent, offering a career to landless citizens who volunteered. These became highly professional soldiers, who looked to their generals for substantial reward after their service. This had huge political as well as military consequences.

Above: The principia, headquarters, at the legionary fort of Lambaesis (Tazoult) in modern-day Algeria.

CENTURIONS AND OFFICERS

Centurions may be seen as the equivalent of sergeant-majors in the modern British army. Yet they were even more important, effectively ranking between a contemporary captain and a major. Beside them, a legion's senatorial officers and commander could appear semi-skilled amateurs.

Centurions needed to be not only excellent soldiers but literate, for they had to read and write orders and could have political or diplomatic roles. A letter of introduction from someone influential helped one become a centurion; in the Roman army, as in the Roman state, personal connections counted for a lot. Former members of the Praetorian guard in Rome and, more rarely, equestrians applied for centurions' posts. But some centurions rose from the ranks of the legion, staying 40 years in the army.

There were 59 centurions in a legion, one for each ordinary century of 80 men in the normal nine cohorts and (from *c.*50AD on), five for the first cohort of five double centuries. This cohort's centurions, the most senior in the legion, were known as *primi ordines*, of the first rank. In ascending order these were the *hastatus posterior* (a name recalling the extinct *maniples*), the *princeps posterior*, *hastatus*, *princeps* and *primus pilus*. The *primus pilus* was the most important officer in the whole legion. He had to be at least 50 years old and held his post for only a year, after which he might retire, his gratuity of 400–600,000 sesterces elevating him to equestrian rank. (A normal legionary received about 3,000 sesterces on retirement under Augustus.) Some went on to become

Above: The most vital of officers in the Roman army, a centurion was colourfully, even resplendently, armoured, with crested helmet and medallioned cuirass. Note the vine branch in his right hand – used for beating his men.

Right: This tombstone commemorates the centurion Marcus Caelius of the Eighteenth Legion, who was killed fighting at the age of 53 in the Teutoburg Forest ambush in Germany in AD9.

prefect of the camp, another very important post, others became *primus pilus* again, adding *bis* or *ter* (second or third) to their title; a few became provincial governors or fleet commanders; one or two even became prefects of the Praetorian guard.

A centurion was distinguishable by his silvered armour, his greaves (shin armour, also worn by legionaries) and his transverse-crested helmet. He wore his sword on his left and his dagger on the right, but still carried a shield. Centurions were responsible for maintaining Roman discipline, using their *vitis* (vine cane) often to ferocious effect on their men. This could make them very unpopular. One centurion was killed by angry legionaries during the mutiny on the Danube in AD14. He was known as *cedo alterum* (Get me another!) due to his habit of beating soldiers until his cane broke. Centurions often took bribes from their men, for granting leave or exempting them from fatigues. But they paid for their privileges in blood, suffering disproportionately high casualties in battle, as they were expected to stand their ground to the end.

Beneath the centurions were the standard-bearers: the *aquilifer* (the eagle-bearer), the *signifer* (the emperor's image-bearer) – who also looked after soldiers' pay and savings – and the *vexillarius*, (legionary standard-bearer). All were important posts, especially the *aquilifer*. When Caesar's troops hesitated before disembarking on the shores of Britain, the *aquilifer* leapt into the water shouting, "Follow me, comrades!" And they did. Like these officers, the *optio*, the second-in-command of each century, was on double pay. Each century also had a *tesserarius*, responsible for the important sentry rota, and a *librarius* (clerk). At legionary headquarters there was a staff of clerks and orderlies, including the *exactores* (exactors of payments) and clerks with special duties such as the *librarii horreorum* (clerk of the granary records).

OTHER OFFICERS

The other officers in a legion, although theoretically senior, were less professional. Each legion had six tribunes, the senior being a *laticlavus*; the broad stripe on his toga indicated he was accepted for the Senate. He would be under 25, having his first military experience for a year or so before returning to civilian life. The other five tribunes, *angusticlavii*, or narrow stripes, came from the equestrian order and were generally older and far more experienced. They had often commanded an auxiliary cohort already. They had general administrative duties and, if competent, might go on to command large *alae* (500 or 1,000 men) of auxiliary cavalry. The commanding officer, the *legatus legionis*, was a senator in his 30s or 40s, appointed by the emperor and serving for three years. He might have had no military experience since serving as tribune long before. He was sometimes also the provincial governor. A legate relied heavily on his *primus pilus* and camp prefect for advice, but, as Varus in the Teutoburg ambush in AD9 showed, amateurish legates could not always be relied on to make sound military judgement in crises.

Above: Disciplined Roman swordmanship – stabbing more often than cutting – was a vital part of repeated Roman successes often against vastly superior numbers of barbarians. Better armour also played a part in Roman victories, although single combat like this was uncommon.

TRAINING AND DISCIPLINE

Above: Re-enactment of combat by Roman legionaries. In full armour, they are using their swords, the short but (in the right hands) lethal gladius.

What most impressed foreign commentators about the Roman army was its exceptional discipline and training. Their battle drills were like war. "It would be fair enough to call their drills bloodless battles and their battles bloody drills" wrote Josephus, the captured Jewish leader who became a Roman citizen in AD67. Training and discipline were what made Roman armies so often victorious, not superiority in arms or numbers. When this combination began to break down in the 4th century AD, the army too began to disintegrate.

Every new recruit swore a *sacramentum* (oath) to his general, by which he abrogated all his civilian rights for his 26 years of service. The oath was renewed every year. From then on, his life was in the army's hands. According to Vegetius, writing on military affairs around AD400, a recruit was taught how to march in step and keep his place in formation. Regular route marches of 20 Roman miles (*c*.30km) in five hours, and of 24 miles (*c*.36 km) in the same time at quick step, helped to get a recruit fit.

Drilled twice a day, he learnt how to vault on to a horse and how to mount and dismount fully armed from either side. He was taught to use his weapons by practising cuts and thrusts against a man-sized wooden stake. Initially, he used a heavy wooden sword and shield to strengthen his muscles. He would then fence with other recruits, the tip of his sword covered, before entire units waged mock battles against each other. The climax of such contests came with the mock-cavalry battles, the *hippaka gymnasia*, which were among the army's grandest spectacles. But above all, he was taught how to fight in formation without panicking, becoming so drilled in such discipline that it became second nature.

Training was not restricted to new recruits or to wartime. Repeated drilling kept the army at the peak of efficiency. The legionary was also taught other skills, including swimming, slinging and pitching camp. From *c*.100BC specialist sub-officers in each legion learnt more technical skills, such as building roads. All these were designed to produce an adaptable, tough, reliable soldier, skilled in swordsmanship and adept at keeping formation under exacting circumstances, and always obedient to military discipline.

Left: A Roman garrison on the River Nile from a 1st-century BC *mosaic. Egypt was one of the empire's softest postings.*

PUNISHMENTS AND REWARD

Death was the punishment for a wide range of offences: dereliction of guard duty (by falling asleep or going absent without leave), desertion, theft (from a comrade), perjury, homosexual acts with another soldier and cowardice. After a brief trial, the guilty soldier was hit with a staff by the tribune, a cue for the other soldiers to club or stone him to death. If he did not die at once, he was thrown outside the camp and abandoned. If an entire unit was found guilty of cowardice or mutiny, it might be decimated. Every tenth man, chosen by lot, would be bludgeoned to death and the remainder of the unit disgraced, pitching their tents outside the main camp and being fed barley rather than wheat. But there were other, less severe and probably more common types of punishment: reduction in rank, loss of privileges gained over years of service, corporal punishment and discharge with ignominy and no gratuity.

The Roman army did not rule solely by punishment; it offered rewards too. Booty from a successful campaign would be shared among the soldiers – although this obviously dwindled during peacetime – and there were occasional individual donations to worthy soldiers. The army also handed out military decorations such as silver or gold chains and *phalerae*

(medallions) of bronze or gold worn on the breastplate. Various *coronae* (crowns) were also awarded: the *corona civica* for personally saving the life of a Roman in battle, the *corona muralis* for the soldier who first scaled an enemy city's wall and the *corona vallaris* for the first to cross the entrenchment of an enemy fort. Under inspired generals, competition for such prizes could be intense and were sometimes shared, as at Cartagena in 210BC. From the time of Vespasian on, legionaries could also expect a donation from a new emperor on his accession.

Above: A modern-day re-enactment of Roman legionaries forming a testudo, *or tortoise shield roof, used when approaching walls. The discipline required to maintain such formations – it was said to be possible to walk on the locked shields – was learnt painfully during long army training.*

Left: A Roman legionary's training centred above all on learning how to use his gladius *(stabbing sword) to devastating effect. He would start with a wooden sword, which he jabbed at a pole, before progressing to a real iron weapon.*

PAY AND CONDITIONS

Above: Emperor Caracalla, who twice raised the soldiers' pay in the 3rd century AD.

Below: The Palestrina mosaic from the late 1st century BC shows soldiers, perhaps in a scene from a romantic myth.

Nobody could call the ordinary legionary of the Principate overpaid or pampered. After 26 years' service, he received a gratuity in land (not always where he wanted it) or in cash. This came to 3,000 denarii under Augustus and had only increased to 5,000 under Caracalla 200 years later. For most soldiers, yearly pay was also modest. According to Suetonius, Caesar doubled the pay of rank-and-file legionaries to 225 denarii a year in 49BC at the start of the Civil War, to keep them loyal. Basic pay remained at this rate until Domitian (AD81–96) raised it to 300 denarii. It then stayed unchanged throughout the 2nd century AD, despite steady inflation, until Septimius Severus and then Caracalla raised it twice early in the 3rd century AD. During that century,

rocketing inflation devalued the currency. The government responded by paying soldiers in kind – often letting them seize goods from civilians – or in gold currency, which alone retained its value.

Pay rose less with seniority than with promotion. According to Vegetius, a *tesserarius* received one-and-a-half times a normal legionary's pay, an *optio* twice and so on up the scale to centurions, the most junior of whom received at least five times the basic pay. The elite Praetorians were paid twice the basic rate, auxiliaries only half, although some cavalry *alae* (detachments) probably received at least as much as ordinary legionaries.

Supplementing the legionaries' annual pay were the *donativi*, or largesse, that most emperors gave out after their accession, or after a great – or purported – victory. Caligula, for example, gave all legionaries an extra four gold pieces (100 denarii) after his abortive "invasion" of Britain. Although weaker emperors undoubtedly resorted to bribery – according to Suetonius, Claudius gave the Praetorians who had spared his life 150 gold pieces (3,750 denarii) each – even Augustus left 75 denarii to each soldier in his will.

Out of their meagre pay, legionaries had to buy clothes, food, weapons and tents as well as bribes for the centurion. One of the centurion's chief perks was indeed taking bribes in return for granting leave or exemption from fatigues (chores), a practice that disciplinarians like the emperor Hadrian tried to stamp out. Discontent seems to have been widespread in AD14: Germanicus was almost killed stopping a mutiny among the Rhineland legionaries who had been engaged in campaigns for many years.

For food, Vegetius lists as staples corn, wine, vinegar and salt in plenty at all times. The men mostly ate porridge, bread and beans, supplemented by other vegetables and eggs, with meat on the numerous feast days, plus any obtained by hunting. When campaigning they ate hardtack, long-lasting wholewheat biscuits. Such hardships were made more acceptable by the way many generals, even those from the imperial family such as Tiberius or Julian, shared their troops' hardships while on campaign, sleeping on the ground and eating basic rations.

At first under Augustus, legionaries slept in simple timber huts or even in their leather tents. Soon, however, proper stone fortresses were built, often with amphitheatres just outside and with baths within or nearby. Bathhouses were regarded as absolutely essential, and the remains of a typically impressive one on a basilican plan have been found at Chester. Even more impressive are the baths at Caerleon, the largest military baths in Britain. The amphitheatres, in contrast,normally made of turf and timber in northern Europe, seldom saw full-scale gladiatorial games (since these were too expensive) but were used for festivals and animal displays.

Townships soon sprang up outside the larger camps, where men off duty could go to eat and drink in *tabernae* (taverns), and, of course, to meet women. These settlements (*canabae*) often grew into sizeable towns and a few became *coloniae*. But legionaries, although they often started and supported their own families, were not allowed to marry legally while on service until the reign of Septimius Severus. However, their partners were often recognized by people around them and could inherit a soldier's belongings. Their sons, too, were normally accepted as Roman citizens if they enrolled in the legion. The marriage ban probably stemmed from official reluctance to pay for army widows' maintenance.

MEDICAL TREATMENT

Although the legionary's life was tough, his medical treatment was remarkably good – in fact, the Roman army's medical care was probably superior to that of any army until the 20th century. As all armies used to lose more men to disease than to

enemy action, this was a major advantage. The care the Romans took with their water supply and drains, seeking out good supplies of fresh water and piping it down to the camps, then carrying the sewage to a spot on a river below any watering place, averted many diseases. They also isolated sick, possibly infectious, soldiers and treated them in special hospitals. At Inchtuthil, the northernmost legionary fortress in Scotland, a special *valetudinarium*, or medical wing, has been revealed with spacious wards and double internal walls, presumably for both thermal and acoustic insulation. Doctors (*medici*) were specially trained and became specialists at operations to remove arrowheads and sling-stones from their legionary patients and at cleaning and binding their wounds. Here the Romans continued the medical traditions of the Greeks, which went back to Hippocrates in the 5th century BC. Roman courage must have been needed on the operating table, as there were no anaesthetics.

Above: These soldiers from the 4th century BC are carrying a dead comrade. From the earliest times, the Romans were willing to accept very high casualties in their wars.

Below: The worship of Mithras, the saviour-god of Persian origin, became very popular in the Roman army.

AUXILIARY TROOPS

Above: The auxiliaries, often drawn from such conquered peoples as shown here in this Hellenistic sculpture, provided much of the cavalry used by the Romans. They did not have stirrups and, although they had spears, fought more with long swords.

Below: Specialized auxiliary troops such as these archers played an increasingly important role in the Roman army from the 1st century AD onwards. In the east, the Romans often used horse archers from Palmyra.

Legionaries, the army's backbone, were solely heavy infantry. Intended to fight major battles, they were originally recruited exclusively from Roman citizens. During the Republic, legionaries were supplemented by equal numbers of soldiers from the Latin and Italian allies: the auxiliaries. These supplied lighter troops, including much-needed cavalry. With the extension of the full franchise to the allies in 90BC, they no longer provided such troops, seeking the more prestigious and lucrative posts in the legions. However, auxiliaries became increasingly important as Rome began to defend, as opposed to simply expand, its empire. From Augustus' reign onwards, auxiliaries were systematically recruited from non-Roman citizens. One of their big advantages to the government was that their pay was considerably less (an auxiliary infantryman was paid about half a legionary's rate).

Numidian (North African) cavalry, used to rout Hannibal at the Battle of Zama in 202BC, and other non-Italian auxiliary cavalry, were commonly employed by the mid-2nd century BC. Caesar had made use of the Gallic and German horsemen he encountered in Gaul to help defeat Pompey. But these remained exceptions. In the war between Antony and Augustus in 31BC, their huge forces were still overwhelmingly made up of legionaries. Reducing the army to only 28 legions, or about 150,000 men, and establishing permanent frontiers, Augustus began to employ auxiliaries, chiefly as frontier and policing troops.

The Romans employed auxiliaries as specialists to supplement their heavy infantry: Cretan or Syrian archers, slingers from the Balearics and Numidian, Gallic and later Sarmatian cavalry, 3,800 of whom were sent to Britain to repel an invasion. Auxiliaries can clearly be seen on Trajan's Column, which displays the army of the Principate at its peak in the early 2nd century AD. But most auxiliaries were not specialized forces. By Trajan's time they consisted predominantly of infantry equipped, like the legionaries, with mail shirt, cross-braced helmet, sword and javelins. The major difference was that their arms and armour were cheaper and of lesser quality. Reviewing the Sixth Mounted Cohort of Commagenes in Africa, Hadrian commented dismissively that their appearance and the condition of their weapons matched their (low) level of pay, but he added that they compensated for their scruffiness by their enthusiasm in military exercises. There was a major exception to the inferiority of auxiliaries in Rome's increasing use of cavalry, especially mounted archers, from eastern cities like Palmyra. Many of these auxiliaries started off as levies supplied by client kings on Rome's eastern frontier. They became more important as

the eastern frontier itself became a problem in the 3rd century AD, and by then were paid more than, in some cases much more than, legionaries.

MANNING THE FRONTIERS

Auxiliaries were organized into smaller units than legions. The infantry was grouped into cohorts of 500 or 1,000 men and cavalry into similarly sized *alae* (literally, wings). These smaller sizes made it easier to move them around, although many resented being transferred, and at first auxiliary cohorts were stationed near their land of origin. A cohort of raw recruits from the Lower Rhine, whom Agricola had stationed in south-west Scotland, revolted at being displaced, murdering their officers and then sailing back to Germany. Shipwrecked and captured by pirates, they ended up as slaves back on the Rhineland. Some auxiliaries recruited from Britain served outside the island, presumably to ensure their loyalty. Auxiliary cohorts became ethnically mixed, with recruits from different areas, although they kept their original names.

The organization, discipline and training of auxiliaries mirrored that of the legions, although the command structure was simpler. Centurions were recruited from the ranks and spent their lives with the same unit. These cohorts were commanded by equestrian tribunes starting off their military careers, or else by decurions from the local aristocracy. The commander of an *ala* of cavalry was a *praefectus alae*, quite a senior post. Mixed cohorts, *cohortes equitatae*, containing about 80 per cent infantry and 20 per cent cavalry, were well suited to the low-intensity policing duties that mostly occupied them. Hadrian's Wall, typical of a fortified frontier, was manned entirely by auxiliaries. There were about 12–15,000 of them housed in forts ranging from tiny towers to big 1,000-men cohort camps such as Housesteads.

Military orders were always given in Latin and sacrifices to the emperor were compulsory (hence overtly practising Christians were at first uncommon in the army). After completing 26 years of military service, auxiliaries were rewarded with full Roman citizenship, recorded on a bronze tablet called a *diploma*, and this was a status that their sons inherited. Occasionally an entire cohort received Roman citizenship for outstanding services. Auxiliaries helped spread the Roman way of life. After Caracalla's grant of nearly universal citizenship in AD212, the distinction between auxiliaries and legionaries soon grew blurred.

Above: Memorial to Longinus, a Roman cavalryman of the 1st cohort of Thracians, who died in AD49, aged 40 after 15 years service, and is buried at Colchester. Longinus came from Sardica (modern Sofia) and served a long way from home. The tombstone was found in 1928, but the face was only discovered in 1996.

PITCHING CAMP

Roman discipline and methodical planning were epitomized by the way that every evening, after marching all day, Roman soldiers constructed elaborate marching camps, always on a rectilinear plan, often for only one night. (These camps left few traces.) Such effort in all conditions required exceptional organization and discipline. Pyrrhus of Epirus realized how formidable his foes were after watching the Romans pitch these camps in 280BC. A century later, Polybius was equally impressed. Such was Roman conservatism that the practice continued throughout the Principate.

One of the best descriptions of the marching camp appears in Pseudo-Hyginus, written in the late 2nd century AD. Every afternoon, towards the end of the day's march, a tribune with centurions would scout ahead to choose the location for that night's camp, ideally a rectangle about 800 yd (731m) long of raised land, clear of trees and with running water nearby. They marked the *praetorium* (the commander's tent) and *principia* (headquarters) with a white flag and then planned the rest of the camp from this centre, using a *groma*, a surveying instrument. The two main streets, the *via principalis* and the *via praetoria*, running through the middle of the camp, were 60ft (18m) wide, lesser ones 50ft (15m) wide. With these streets defined, the lines of the ditch and rampart would be established by spears stuck into the earth at intervals.

Every legionary carried two to three *pila muralia*, palisade stakes about 7ft (2m) long with sharpened points. After they had dug their *fossa* – a trench normally about 3ft (1m) deep and 5ft (1.5m) wide (but deeper and wider if under immediate threat), they planted their stakes in the *agger*, the low rampart formed by the excavated earth, intertwining them so any intruders could

Above: Stout stakes with sharpened points lined the palisades of the more heavily fortified camps.

Right: A ditch, rampart and palisade separated the camp from the world outside. A similar arrangement was also used for some frontier installations, here, in a reconstruction of a section of the German frontier, with a watchtower.

not easily remove them. The camp's ramparts, although hard to penetrate and impossible for a unit in formation, did not form defensible barriers but marked it out from its surroundings. Just inside lay the *intervallum*, the space at least 100ft (30m) wide always left empty, to enable the legionaries to deploy within the camp and to bar enemy missiles reaching the tents. All camps were laid out in exactly the same pattern wherever they were. Legionaries camped on either side of the *via praetoria*, the cavalry facing the *via praetoria*, the other auxiliaries and non-Romans being put with the baggage train and cooking tents beyond the *via principalis*. Only the four entrances were more heavily fortified. The legionaries marched out of their allotted gates already armed and in formation.

The *contubernium*, the basic legionary tent, slept eight men. Made of leather, with front and back access, these tents could be rolled up into a sausage shape and carried by mules or ponies. Larger, more elaborate tents were provided for centurions and other officers. That of the general was large enough for administrative and military offices.

Keeping watch was vital. Every evening a guard from the *maniple* or century chosen for the first watch was taken to the tribune's tent and given a *tessera*, a small marked tablet. He surrendered this to a cavalry trooper who made his rounds at fixed hours, collecting the *tesserae* from each guard. If the sentry was absent or asleep, the trooper got witnesses to this. At dawn they reported to the tribune, who checked the *tesserae*. If one sentry had not returned his *tessera*, then he would be tried and cudgelled to death by his comrades, whose lives he had endangered by his inattention. As Polybius dryly commented, "the Roman army's night watches are most punctiliously kept".

Such repeated entrenchments might seem laborious, even wasteful, but they gave the Romans many advantages. By shutting out the possibly alien world and creating a model of Roman order, it helped give soldiers a good night's sleep, protected from surprise night attacks, and left them fresh to face the enemy next day. It also reduced the risk of disease through the properly dug latrines and, not least, impressed possibly hostile observers.

Above: Excavations at Caerleon, the legionary fortress in South Wales, have revealed the network of latrines and waterways at the barracks, a testimony to Roman concerns to keep their army healthy and fighting fit.

ROADS, CANALS AND BRIDGES

The Roman network of roads was both practical and impressive. The empire was united by 53,000 miles (85,000km) of roads from Scotland to Syria. Often built by legionaries, the roads were designed for troop movements, but civilians soon followed. Under many roads across Europe today lie Roman roads. It was not until the 19th century that Europe saw such a comprehensive road system.

The Greeks had built short stretches of paved roads and in the first Persian empire (c.539–331BC) the Royal Road linked the Aegean provinces to the capital Susa, 1,500 miles (2,400km) distant. But none approached the audacious scale of Rome's roads. The first road was the Via Appia, dubbed "Queen of Roads", built in 312BC by Claudius Appius the Censor. Running at first 164 miles (264km) from Rome to Capua to supply armies fighting the Samnites, it was later extended to Brindisi, another 234 miles (377km). It had the hallmarks of a classic Roman road: running as straight as practically possible, it crossed marshes on stone bridges and had a gravel top-dressing (replaced in 295BC by paved stones), good foundations and a proper camber to let water drain away, making it usable in all weathers. It was followed by many others, such as the Via Flaminia in 220BC, running across the Apennines to Rimini. Some roads had overt military intentions. The Via Aemilia, built in 189BC and running unblinkingly straight for 150 miles (240km) from Rimini to Piacenza through northern Italy, was intended to overawe Gallic natives and reassure Roman settlers. It did both. Rome's imperialist road-building did not stop with Italy. In 130BC the Via Egnatia was constructed across the top of Greece from Durazzo to Thessalonica and on to Byzantium (Istanbul). It remained a great imperial highway for 1,200 years.

All roads in the Republic, which helped unite and Romanize a very disparate Italy, were built by *publicani*, contractors working to orders from the state, who would inspect the roads on completion. (The same term applied to tax-farmers.) Under Augustus, the road-building programme became more systematic and ever more impressive. He restored many of Italy's roads and built new ones, some high across Alpine passes such as the St Bernard and Mt Genèvre passes, whose bridge and viaducts still impress travellers. In Gaul, important cities such as Lyons became hubs for a network of roads across the province – north to the Channel, north-east to the Rhine, south to Provence. London became the hub of a similar, if smaller, network, as did Antioch in Syria.

Above: The Romans built to last, as this still-surviving, if battered, road across the moors in northern Britain reveals.

Below: The 2nd-century AD road in Petra, the trading city in Jordan. Many roads survive intact in desert areas.

Left: The Roman bridge of Alcantara over the river Tagus in western Spain was built in the early 2nd century AD by Caius Julius Lacer for eleven local towns. It still stands and carries traffic today, which must make it one of the world's oldest functioning bridges.

Along the indeterminate desert frontiers of Arabia Petraea (Jordan), a road built under Trajan acted as a *limes*, a guarded frontier patrolled by cavalry. A similar pattern of patrol roads as *limes* can be seen both in North Africa and in Germany. Along the pan-imperial highways galloped the emperor's emissaries. They changed horses at the imperial posting stations, where they were also fed at the local population's expense. All roads were similarly maintained by corvées of forced labour until the end of the empire. Ironically, Rome's invaders benefited from its excellent paved roads.

CANALS AND BRIDGES

Even for Romans, it was always cheaper to move goods by water than by land. The Mediterranean, with its obligingly many inlets, combined with large rivers – the Rhône, Rhine, Danube, Nile, Tagus – provided a network of waterways. The Rhine and Danube were great military routes with fleets patrolling. The Danube fleet was divided in two, one flotilla operating downriver from the Iron Gates. Rivers were sometimes supplemented by short canals, although there was no canal-building programme. Caesar, like Nero, talked of digging a canal through the rocky mass of the Corinth isthmus, but this vision taxed Roman technology. Traces of Nero's attempt were found when the Corinth Canal was dug in the late 19th century. His builders had stopped when they hit bedrock.

Bridges were not beyond Roman technology and carried Rome's roads across gorges and rivers so successfully that some still stand. The great bridge over the Tagus at Alcantara in Spain was built by the combined efforts of eleven Lusitanian towns in Trajan's reign. Its builder, Caius Julius Lacer, proclaimed in an inscription that his bridge would last forever. In contrast, Caesar threw a timber bridge across the Rhine, then destroyed it, a feat meant to impress Roman audiences as much as Germans. But the most impressive Roman bridge was that built across the Danube at Drobeta by the architect Apollodorus for Trajan's Dacian campaign. With 20 massive stone piers, each 160ft (49m) high, driven into the fast-flowing river over 1000 yds (1000m) wide, and a timber superstructure, it was seen as one of the wonders of the world. Hadrian pulled it down on becoming emperor for reasons of prudence – he said barbarians might cross by it – or through jealousy of Trajan.

Above: Roman soldiers under Trajan (AD98–117) built a remarkable bridge across the Danube, pulled down soon after by Hadrian, and a supporting road along the Iron Gorge's steep cliffs.

FLEETS AND SHIPS

The Mediterranean, which the Romans called both *Mare Internum*, the inner sea, and *Mare Nostrum*, our sea, might appear to be at the centre of the Roman empire. In fact, however, the Romans were never great sailors. Unlike the Greeks, they only turned to controlling the seas when they were forced to. Rome's navy was always markedly inferior in status to its army and the might of the empire was built on land. But in order to conquer and then control their expanding empire, the Romans needed to gain sufficient mastery at sea, having, at the very least, modest permanent fleets – a fact Augustus finally accepted.

Like the other Mediterranean naval powers, the Roman navy consisted of galleys, which were rowed by poorer citizens or allies and very seldom by slaves. By the 3rd century BC these galleys were quinqueremes, with five rows of oars, or triremes, with three rows, arranged in a pattern that is still not entirely clear. Before the development of proper cannon in the 16th century, naval warfare – chiefly ramming and boarding – made galleys the only effective warships in the landlocked waters. However, their large crews of about 300 oarsmen, together with the lack of living space on board, meant that they normally had to be beached at night. Fleets therefore hugged the coasts whenever they could.

The Romans had no navy until their wars against Carthage began in 264BC. As Carthage ruled the western Mediterranean with an efficient navy of galleys mass-produced in its superb double harbours, Rome realized it must build a fleet of its own to fight it. According to Polybius, the Romans modelled their galleys on a stranded Carthaginian ship, quickly building 100 quinqueremes and meanwhile training their oarsmen on tiered benches on land. But their inexperience led initially to defeat, even in harbour. Accepting that they could not match Punic seamanship,

Below: This Roman pharos (lighthouse) lies within the ruins of medieval Dover Castle in England. It was one of numerous lighthouses built along the coasts of the empire.

the Romans ingeniously devised the *corvus*, the raven, a boarding ramp fitted with a heavy spike which swivelled on a pole set on the ship's prow. This ramp, about 40ft (12m) long and 4ft (1.2m) wide, was swung over the deck of the enemy ship and dropped on to it, locking the two galleys together. Roman marines – 120 of them to a galley – then swarmed across to overwhelm the Carthaginians.

This tactic won several victories over the startled Carthaginians, beginning with Mylae in 260BC and continuing at Ecnomus in 256BC, where each side mustered over 300 ships according to Polybius. The Romans then grew over-confident, sending huge invasion fleets to Africa to support Regulus' invasion, most of which were sunk in storms. The *corvus* may have made the galleys – always fragile vessels – top-heavy, and the Romans never used it again after finally defeating the Carthaginians in 241BC.

Under the terms of the subsequent treaty Carthage gave up most of her navy, and during the Second Punic War (218–201BC) her ships tried to avoid the now indisputably superior Romans, as did the Macedonian ships. Philip V's 100-strong fleet sailed into the Adriatic in 216BC but fled at the sight of only ten Roman quinqueremes. From the mid-2nd century BC the Romans let their fleet decay, as there seemed to be no naval rivals left. They relied instead on Greek ships to transport their troops, failing to realize the importance of the Rhodian fleet in maintaining freedom of the sea. Rhodes' navy declined after the opening of Delos as a free port in 168BC, and pirates took advantage of this, raiding right up to Ostia and capturing two praetors in 68BC. Pompey was appointed emergency commander under the *Lex Gabinia* to quash them, with a fleet of 200 galleys, which were mostly supplied by Greek cities. With this fleet he swept the seas clean, but in the subsequent civil wars

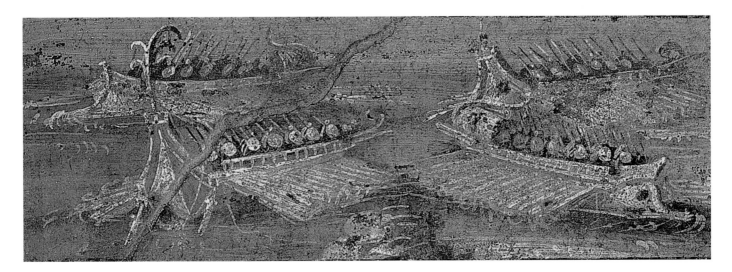

(49–30BC) fleets multiplied. Sextus Pompeius had a large fleet with which he cut Rome's grain supply until defeated with the aid of Antony's ships at Naulochus in 36BC. The final battle in the civil wars was the naval contest at Actium, in which Antony and Cleopatra's Roman-Egyptian fleet was cornered and defeated by Agrippa, Octavian's general, who traditionally used smaller Liburnian galleys against Antony's quinqueremes.

THE IMPERIAL NAVY

Augustus disbanded most of the huge fleets that victory brought him – some 700 ships – but, needing to safeguard Rome's grain imports, he did not close down the navy. Instead, he set up three small fleets at Misenum in the Bay of Naples, at Ravenna and at Fréjus, using the mainly Greek ships and crews he already had as their core. The fleet at Fréjus shrank to a mere flotilla. There were also river fleets on the Rhine, Danube and Nile and a small fleet on the Black Sea. Later a fleet, the *classis britannica*, was created to patrol the English Channel and southern North Sea. From the mid-3rd century AD this British fleet was used chiefly against the Saxon pirates who were becoming increasingly common. Commanded by prefects under imperial orders, the navy offered a similar career to the army's auxiliaries. After 26 years, sailors received Roman citizenship at the end of their service.

Ships were commanded by *trierarchs*, squadrons by *navarchs*, both names indicating the Greek origins of the fleet.

For a long period, the whole of the Mediterranean was kept peaceful by these measures, essential for the empire's well-being. If it was sometimes swifter to move troops by sea than by land, it was almost always cheaper to transport goods by ship. The 3rd-century AD crisis revealed that these fleets had become inadequate, however, as Goths and other barbarians seized shipping and turned pirate, and they were expanded. Later, the Byzantine empire relied heavily on its navy, but the Byzantine empire was predominantly Greek, and the Greeks always retained a strong maritime tradition.

Above: Navies in the ancient world consisted of galleys such as these biremes. They had huge crews of up to 300 oarsmen (not usually slaves in either Greece or Rome), essential to propel the ships to ram and board opponents.

Below: The main port of Rome at Portus, north of Ostia, with the artificial harbours built by Claudius (right) and Trajan (left) to help the import of grain. The canal linked the port with the Tiber, while the pharos guided shipping into port.

CHAPTER IX

ARMS AND THE MEN

The Roman army was one of the most effective fighting forces in history, but its weapons were not normally superior to those of its enemies. Most Roman weaponry was simple: a short sword, a javelin, a coat of mail or armour plates, greaves (leg armour), and a rectangular or oval shield. Against often more numerous northern barbarians, the Romans did have some technical advantages: their armour was better, their catapults alarmingly formidable. All these, however, were secondary to Roman discipline and courage. How the Romans used their weapons was what counted; and it was their *virtus*, their courage and ability, that Romans celebrated, not their technological prowess. When necessary, they made other people's weapons, be they catapults, slings or armour, part of their own standard equipment. This Roman adaptability, coupled with ruthless determination and refusal to surrender, were Rome's real secret weapons.

In only two spheres were the Romans true innovators: the maniple and the cohort, tactical formations within the legion that helped them beat Hannibal and the Greeks, and the massive fortifications of the later empire. These constituted the most formidable walls yet seen anywhere in the world. The proof of their effectiveness is shown by the thousand-year survival of Constantinople, whose walls enabled the new Rome to live on when the old Rome fell.

Left: The Romans made good use of catapults and other artillery in siege warfare. Encircling siege walls was also frequently used to prevent movement from the besieged town or camp.

ARMOUR

*Above: The higher grades of cavalry (*alae*) wore elaborate helmets to mark their rank. This is a 3rd-century AD cavalry helmet.*

Below: The long, curved shield was standard issue for legionaries in the Principate from the 1st century AD.

Roman armour in the early Republic (5th century BC) was influenced by Rome's neighbours, the Etruscans, who in turn emulated the Greeks. Etruscans adopted the Greek hoplite method of fighting – heavily armoured spearmen grouped in *phalanxes* – and their armour reflected this. It consisted of greaves (shin armour), a bronze cuirass (breastplate) and a helmet with long cheek guards and high crests. However, as the Romans evolved their own uniquely flexible system of *maniples* and legions after 400BC, they began to develop their own lighter armour, which varied according to the wealth of the Roman concerned, for at that time and for long after, each soldier armed and armoured himself.

The first two lines of heavy infantry in each *maniple* – the *hastati* and *principes* – wore a modest-sized square breastplate called a *pectorale* (breast guard) and one greave for the left leg, the one that was thrust out when fighting. Wealthier legionaries, especially those of the *triarii*, sometimes wore mail shirts, but these could be very heavy, weighing over 30lb (14kg). After the Roman defeat at Lake Trasimene in 218BC, some soldiers who tried to escape by swimming were drowned by the weight of their armour. The legionaries all wore bronze Montefortino-type helmets (named after the place where some were found). These had two tall, feathered plumes 2ft (60cm) high sticking out of them to make the soldiers look taller, long cheek guards and a double chin strap. For defence, the legionaries depended on their long, semi-cylindrical body shields. These were about 4ft (1.2m) long and about 2ft (60cm) wide. Reconstructions show that these shields weighed at least 22lb (10kg). They were made of two sheets of wood glued together, covered with canvas and calf skin. The shields could also be used as weapons to knock the enemy over. The *veles*, light infantry

recruited from the poorer citizens, had no armour and so they wore animal skins over their helmets to help their officers recognize them.

From the time of the late Republic (100BC), after Marius' reforms, legionaries were far more uniformly equipped and armoured. The ordinary legionaries wore long mail coats and Montefortino-style helmets, but with horsehair plumes that hung down, and carried long oval shields very similar to the earlier shields. Officers (centurions and tribunes) often wore "muscled" – modelled to the body – cuirasses with greaves over leather tunics, ribbons of rank around their waists – a Greek idea – and elaborate Italo-Corinthian helmets. Some of the armour of this period was of poor quality, probably reflecting the massive demands made on armourers by the fast-growing armies of the civil wars.

By the early 1st century AD, with the Principate firmly established, workshops were set up to mass-produce the body armour the legionaries needed. The standard helmet evolved from the jockey type, which recalled a reversed jockey's cap in the late Republic, to the "Imperial Gallic helmet". Partly inspired by Gallic examples, the latter had an enlarged neck guard and long cheek guards, with a reinforcing strip across the front of the cap to protect the face from a downward cut. With added ear guards, this became the standard Roman infantry helmet over the next two centuries. It was usually made of iron, which was always cheaper than bronze, if less durable. Such a helmet gave a high degree of protection while allowing soldiers to hear and see clearly.

Equally flexible and protective was the *lorica segmentata*, the name given to a type of banded armour developed in the 1st century AD, the first full example of which was excavated at Corbridge. This had bands of soft untempered iron plates forming a corselet, or cuirass, which was buckled on. Such armour was brilliant at

absorbing blows and not too heavy – it weighed about 20lb (9kg). This made it lighter than the cheaper, more easily maintained, main alternative, the *lorica hamata*, a mail coat worn by some legionaries and by the auxiliary infantry. The *lorica hamata* was heavy, weighing over 30lb (14kg). In the 1st century AD, the oval shield was replaced by a rectangular curved shield, made of three layers of thin strips of wood, encased in leather and covered with a linen layer, its rim reinforced with bronze. The handgrip in its centre was reinforced by an iron or bronze boss. Auxiliaries normally had a simpler version of the Imperial Gallic helmet and a flat oval shield.

ARMOUR IN THE LATER EMPIRE

The types of armour in the later empire reflect the increasing divergence between the mobile *comitatenses* and elite *Palatini* – and the lowly *limitanei* (frontier guard). The Romans encountered real heavy cavalry, the *cataphracti*, around AD100 when Sarmatian riders appeared on the Danube. They were soon employed as auxiliaries, and in the 3rd century AD the Romans began to imitate them. The typical *cataphract* wore mail weighing at least 60lb (27kg), covering him from hooded head to knee; his horse also wore mail armour. An even more heavily armoured cavalryman wore the *lorica squamata*, scale armour, according to graffiti from Dura-Europus. Such armour looked magnificent when well polished, but must have been uncomfortably hot – *clibanarius* means "oven man". The infantry, meanwhile, demoted from their primary battle-fighting role, wore crude iron *intercisa* helmets and relatively little armour. Apparently this was partly a matter of choice – for they now found it too heavy to march or drill in armour – but it made them less effective.

Above: By the 1st century AD, most legionaries wore a type of armour called the lorica segimentata. *This, with banded soft iron plates, was laced at the back and gave excellent protection, but it was expensive.*

Above: Sword and dagger.

ARMS: SWORDS, DAGGERS, BOWS, *PILA* AND SLINGS

The Roman soldiers of the early Republic (509–*c*.350BC) were armed in the prevailing Greco-Etruscan style as hoplites – heavy spearmen with long pikes and swords and small round shields. However, by the 4th century BC the new legions of maniples, the army's smallest fighting units, who were starting to fight in the *quincunx*, or chequerboard pattern, required quite different types of arms.

The basic weapon the Roman legionary now acquired, and which he was to use to create the Roman empire, was the *gladius hispaniensis*, the "Spanish sword". This may have been inspired by Spanish examples, but it was probably being used before Rome had any direct experience of Spain. This sword, which had a blade less than 3ft (1m) long, was wickedly sharp and well suited to both cutting and thrusting. Its long, tapering point of highly tempered steel meant that it could pierce most opponents' armour. Roman swordsmanship was generally much better than that of their adversaries, but the legionaries were also helped by having swords of a quality that only chieftains could afford among most of their enemies.

The *gladius* evolved from the Mainz-type *gladius* to the slightly longer Pompeii type, which could cut as well as thrust. (These swords are named after the places where examples were found.) Roman cavalry, for a long time very secondary in importance, used a longer sword, the *spatha*, which was about 3ft (1m) in length. In the later empire, this longer sword was adopted by most Roman infantrymen, but by then infantry had become very inferior to cavalry. Legionaries wore their swords on their right, probably because their heavy shields on their left would have made it awkward to draw after hurling their other principal weapon. In contrast, centurions, wore their swords on the left, possibly because they carried their shields only some of the time.

Almost equally important to the legionary of Rome's golden age of military might was the *pilum*, the javelin or throwing spear. Each legionary in the first two rows of the earlier legions, the *hastati* and the *principes*, carried two *pila*, which came in two thicknesses according to Polybius. The *pilum* had a thin wooden shaft about 4ft (1.2m) long, with a pyramid-shaped barbed iron head on top of a thin iron neck. When thrown,

Left: A slinger in the Dacian wars, one of the many auxiliary soldiers.

this could often go right through an enemy's shield, but if it did not, the point would stick in the shield and the neck bend, so making the shield useless. An enemy would then have to throw it away, leaving himself exposed to the merciless cutting thrusts of the legionary. (Marius later revised the *pilum* by making it bend even more effectively. It is possible that he was also responsible for adding the weights halfway down the *pilum*'s shaft.)

A *pilum*'s absolute maximum range was about 100ft (30m), although its effective range was only half that. Roman troops painfully acquired the discipline required to wait until the enemy was that close before discharging a devastating volley. The *triarii* were armed with long spears that could be used as pikes until Marius' reforms, when all legionaries received the same equipment. Although primarily intended for throwing, the *pilum* could also be used as a stationary weapon to repel cavalry, when the first row would kneel, bracing the butts of their *pila* on the ground so that they formed a spiked barrier. Behind them, other rows would launch their *pila* at the cavalry, whose horses would not cross such a seemingly solid barrier. Legionaries also had the *pugio*, a dagger about 8in (20cm) long, which was worn on the left hip, but this seems to have been given up in the Principate. Such simple but devastating weapons, when used in the right hands, made the Roman legionary appear almost invincible.

THE AUXILIARIES' WEAPONS

Auxiliary infantrymen of the Principate used much the same weapons as the legionaries, but the other, more specialized, types of auxiliary obviously had different kinds of weapons. Slingers, traditionally recruited from the Balearic islands, used simple slings, as did the club men, both being skirmishing light troops, but they were not significant parts of the army. However, the archers whom Rome employed, at first from Crete but later from many sources including Syria, were at times vital. They normally had composite bows, made of bone and sinew as well as wood, which fired arrows further than simple wooden bows.

The *alae* (literally, wings) of auxiliary cavalry also gained increasing importance. Although they often charged with spears or lances, their impact was small compared to later cavalry charges owing to their lack of stirrups, for which the "horns" of their saddles only partly compensated. This must have hampered the effectiveness of the heavily armoured *cataphracts*. The stirrup is first mentioned only in the *Strategikon*, a military manual written by the East Roman (Byzantine) emperor Maurice (AD582–602). In the later empire, the *limitanei* carried several *mattiobarbului*, lead-weighted darts, which they kept inside their shields, instead of the *pilum*. These smaller missiles would have been particularly useful when defending forts, which was now the chief duty of *limitanei*.

Above: This detail from the Roman triumphal arch in Orange, southern France, shows hand-to-hand fighting with the gladius.

Below: Roman legionaries used many varieties of sword, all based on the gladius hispaniensis, or Spanish stabbing sword. These two examples date from the 1st century AD, near the zenith of Roman power.

ARTILLERY

In the earlier Republic, Rome's armies had little in the way of artillery or catapults. In the epic siege of Veii (406–396BC), the formidably well-fortified Etruscan city, for example, they relied chiefly on surprise to capture the city, eventually digging a tunnel under the walls and crawling up an irrigation channel by night. But in their expansion across the Mediterranean after 264BC, the Romans came across the varied catapults developed by the Greeks (especially by Philip II of Macedon) and learnt how to employ such "artillery", the only kind there was before gunpowder.

The Romans' lack of development in such armaments mirrored the general lack of technological progress in civilian life. Compared to medieval Europe, or even to the Greeks, Roman civilization made few technological innovations. Nonetheless, the Romans adopted earlier discoveries, often to good effect. After the disaster at the Battle of Adrianople in AD378, for example, the Goths were dissuaded from further attacks on the walls of Adrianople by a single bolt fired from a Roman scorpion-type catapult.

WEAPONS OF BOMBARDMENT

There were two basic types of artillery, according to Vitruvius, who was writing in the 1st century BC. The first was the catapult type, among which was the typical *catapulta*, a two-armed torsion catapult firing either bolts or stones. Similar was the *scorpio*, a light, bolt-shooting *ballista*. Both operated on the crossbow principle, with a pair of vertical coil chambers at the front; the bow was drawn back by a windlass and held by a rack and pinion. When the bow was released, the bolt shot along a groove and out through an opening in the front in a flat trajectory. These stationary catapults could fire iron bolts up to 300yd (275m) with some accuracy. In AD363 during the Persian campaign, an officer standing next to Julian was killed by a bolt aimed at the emperor. The Persians used much the same weapons as the Romans.

The *carroballista* was a *scorpio* mounted on a mule-drawn cart; it could be used in the field to fire bolts with large heads up to 1ft (30cm) long, which made a formidable arrow. According to Vegetius – who, writing around AD400, may not be completely accurate – each century of the traditional Roman army had a *carroballista*. Used on the flanks of the legion, they fired barrages over the heads of the legionaries.

The other, much heavier, type of catapult was nicknamed the *onager* (wild ass) because of its kick. This was a slower-firing, lower-tension catapult, based on the principles of a sling rather than a crossbow, but one capable of lobbing huge stones at walls or troops. Josephus records that at the Siege of Jerusalem in AD70, the Tenth Legion had machines that could hurl stones weighing a *talent* (55lb/25kg) about 400yd (360m).

Battle stones found at British forts, such as High Rochester, north of Hadrian's Wall, weigh over 100lb (45kg).

Above: The onager *(wild ass) was a primitive but highly effective catapult, capable of lobbing large weights surprising distances. It was used mostly in sieges and for defending fortresses, being too immobile for battlefield use.*

Below: This complex late Roman catapult, a ballista fulminalis, *could shoot its bolt or spear up to 300yd (275m). While slow, such catapults could be devastating, terrifying barbarians.*

THE SECRET WEAPONS THAT ROME IGNORED

As Romans in the 4th century AD knew too well, the empire faced unremitting threats from without and ever-growing manpower shortages within. Although most Roman armies remained better equipped than their barbarian opponents, this did not make up for their lack of numbers. Attempts to cope with the shortage of Roman recruits by recruiting barbarian *foederati* were not only inherently risky but were also leading to the de-Romanization of the army itself. Vegetius, the best-known military writer of the period, advocated a return to the stringent discipline of earlier years, which had underlain Roman triumphs down the centuries, without success.

However, the anonymous writer of *De Rebus Bellicis* (About Wars), who probably lived in the middle of the 4th century AD, had different and more ingenious ideas. He proposed what were in effect a variety of super-weapons with which the Romans might make up for their lack of numbers and their decline in fighting spirit. One such weapon that he proposed was a horse-drawn, arrow-firing catapult that could be swivelled around completely on a four-wheeled cart, and which could be mechanically elevated or lowered to control the trajectory of fire. Another super-weapon he proposed was a mobile armoured shield beneath which attackers could approach a wall – a development of the *testudo*, tortoise formation, of locked shields. He also envisaged a variety of armoured chariots, one with scythed wheels – almost looking back to the scythed chariots once used by Celts and Persians – pulled by armoured horses. At sea, where there was a shortage of oarsmen for the galleys, he cleverly thought of using ox-power to turn a capstan on deck. Through a series of cogs and gears this would have powered two paddle-wheels, one on each side of his novel warship, which he called a *liburna*. Whether or not his schemes, at times anticipating more recent war machines, were at all practical given the technology and resources of the time, nothing came of them.

Only one much later invention really worked: that of *Greek fire*, which was a flame-thrower, using the siphon principles to project a form of liquid fire, highly effective against ships and siege engines. This invention traditionally helped to save Constantinople from Arab attacks at the end of the 7th century AD.

Above: Roman legionaries loading an onager-*type catapult at the siege of Alesia in Gaul in 52*BC, *one of the epic Roman sieges. These cumbersome stone-throwing catapults were normally only used in sieges, or later for defending fortresses.*

Below: Roman legionaries, played by re-enactors, loading a carroballista-*type catapult. A bolt-firing machine on the same principles as the crossbow, this was mobile enough to be used in battle, but its chief role was for attacking or defending forts.*

Special reinforced platforms were built for firing such machines from within forts in the later empire. Technically, the *onager* was a relatively crude machine: its arm was pulled back, tightening the coiled ropes that propelled it, and a sling at the end of its arm was filled with a stone and then released, with a tremendous kick, to be stopped by a padded beam. According to Vegetius, perhaps overstating ancient strengths, each legion had ten *onagri*, one for each cohort, drawn on carriages by oxen. Used *en masse* they were highly effective in siege warfare, either for offence or defence, but they were too immobile to be of much use on the battlefield, unlike the *carroballista*.

SIEGE WARFARE

Above: This detail from Trajan's Column in Rome shows legionaries assaulting walls during the wars in Dacia, a formidably well-defended kingdom.

Below: Legionaries building double wooden walls to bi-circumvallate Alesia, to prevent Gaulish armies from relieving the besieged inside.

The Romans brought to siege-craft their customary determination and aggression. Our word siege comes from the French *siège*, sitting out. In contrast, the Roman word *oppugnatio* means assault, attacking a city relentlessly. In contrast to elaborate Greek siege machinery, the Romans preferred simpler methods. These included bi-circumvallation, building double walls to stop relief getting in. They were also masters of battering rams.

When the Romans attacked the large Greek city of Agrigento (Acragas) in Sicily in 262BC, they built a line of forts around the city, connected these by walls with watchtowers and starved the city into surrender. If an enemy army was in the field, they built a second wall facing outward. They first used bi-circumvallation besieging Lilybaeum in the First Punic War. The greatest bi-circumvallation was at Alesia in 52BC, where Caesar bottled up Vercingetorix and defied a relief Gaulish army.

At ports such as Lilybaeum in Sicily, where complete enclosure was impossible, the Romans tried to close in the harbour with earth, although at Lilybaeum this was washed away by the sea and they captured the city by assault. Syracuse, changing sides after Hannibal's victory at Cannae, presented Rome with its biggest challenge in scientific siege warfare in 213BC. Marcellus, the Roman commander, controlled the sea, but Syracuse harbour was heavily fortified. The Romans made a simultaneous attack by land and sea, using 50 galleys filled with archers, slingers and javelineers. Eight galleys were tied together in pairs and on each a wide ladder was raised. This was the same height as the walls. But the scientist Archimedes, masterminding Syracusan defences, arranged catapults to fire at fixed ranges so that the Romans faced devastating fire. Marcellus tried a night attack to avoid this, but Archimedes designed huge cranes that swung out

from behind the walls and dropped stones on the Roman galleys. Others lowered giant grappling hooks, which pulled the ships up and released them to capsize. Finally the Romans captured Syracuse by stealth. Archimedes was killed in the sack of the city.

Roman tenacity caused many cities to capitulate before the siege started. A story relates how a Roman commander, about to besiege a city, was told by its envoys that they had enough food for ten years. The Roman replied that in that case he would capture the city in the eleventh year. The city surrendered. If it did not surrender, a city faced obliteration. According to the current rules of warfare, once the head of a battering ram touched the enemy's walls or gate, no mercy could be expected and Romans never gave it. From Cartagena in 209BC to Jerusalem in AD70, the Romans systematically killed every living thing in the cities they captured – even dogs – apart from attractive women and children, whom they raped and sold into slavery. Such exemplary terror generally worked. However, Roman commanders preferred to starve a city into submission, because its booty became theirs, whereas in an assault the troops were permitted to sack a city and take what they could.

BATTERING RAMS

The Romans excelled at battering rams, the most basic siege tool. The name comes from its head, a massive iron hammer in the shape of a ram's head. It was fixed to a huge beam in a very strong shed, often on wheels, with a steep-pitched roof covered in hides from animals recently butchered so that their wet skins would repel any fire arrows. Vitruvius and Vegetius describe similar sheds of varying sizes, sometimes called *testudo arietaria*, after the tortoise. This name was also given to formations of men carrying linked shields above their heads. High towers of timber could be rolled forward to protect them by shooting arrows and javelins. If effective against

Mesopotamian mud and Mediterranean stone walls, metal rams were of little use against the timber and turf ramparts of north Europe. Caesar describes a *murus Gallicus* (Gallic wall), stone-faced but its centre filled with soil. Laced with timbers, it was impervious to normal rams. Usually other forms of assault had to be found.

The other great siege tactic was mining a wall. A mine would be dug under a city wall, supported by wooden props that, when ignited, caused the tunnel and the wall above it to collapse. As defenders could hear the tunnellers, they often made counter-mines, causing the attackers' tunnel to collapse. The besieged also mined under the bulky towers of the attackers, causing them to keel over. On the eastern front, especially when the Sassanids replaced the Parthians, there were long and elaborate sieges, as at Dura-Europus in *c.*AD256 and at Amida in AD359. In both cases, these fortified Roman cities fell to the Persians only after long, expensive sieges.

Above: A Renaissance view of a triumph of Julius Caesar shows the spoils and varied war engines used in his conquest of Gaul, including the siege of Alesia in 52BC.

Below: A medieval drawing of a Roman four-wheeled horse-drawn carroballista, *the mobile type of catapult used in battle as well as siege warfare.*

TRIUMPHS AND OVATIONS

On returning to Rome after defeating a (foreign) enemy, a general of the Republic could expect to be awarded the highest accolade, a triumph. According to legend, this celebration dated back to the birth of Rome and Romulus' defeat of Acron, king of the Ceninenses. Wearing a laurel wreath, Romulus led his men singing in triumphant procession to thank Jupiter. The ceremony was influenced by the Etruscans, who added a chariot and other details, including the ceremonial clothes and red-painted face of the *triumphator*, the triumphant general. As the empire grew, the ceremony also grew in splendour. It continued far into the Principate, but by then only members of the imperial family received a full triumph.

The *triumphator* was clad in the *toga picta*, a purple toga edged with gold, over a purple tunic and gilded shoes. He carried an ivory sceptre topped by an eagle, the bird of Jupiter, and an olive branch while wearing a laurel wreath, on his solemn procession to Jupiter's temple to give thanks for his victory. The procession started in the Campus Martius (field of Mars) just outside the *pomerium*, the sacred boundary. At its head were magistrates and senators; next came the horn-blowers, heading a long train of bearers laden with booty. They were followed by models or paintings of captured cities or battles won. Next came priests leading the white sacrificial oxen with gilded horns, with children carrying the *paterae*, golden saucers to catch the oxen's blood. Then came the captives in chains. The *triumphator* brought up the rear in a horse-drawn chariot, with his children beside him and surrounded by crowds of *ludiones*, Etruscan-style dancers. To balance all this, a slave standing behind the *triumphator* whispered in his ear, "Remember, you are mortal." Behind the general came any citizens whom he had

Below: Caesar's final triumph, as depicted in this Renaissance painting. His many victories were celebrated with unparalleled magnificence and splendour.

TRIUMPHAL ARCHES

Among the most distinctive features of the Roman empire were the triumphal arches built to proclaim its victories. The most famous arches are in Rome itself. The Arch of Titus, dedicated in AD81, is among the best preserved; it graphically commemorates Titus' capture of Jerusalem in AD70, and shows the seven-branched candlestick taken from the Temple. Arches, of which many survive, were erected right across the empire, from Jordan to Britain. A vast arch almost 100ft (30m) high and square was erected at Richborough, the chief port of entry to Britain, probably during the AD90s to celebrate Emperor Domitian's supposed conquest of the north of the island. Cased in Cararra marble with gilded bronze statues, it did not long survive Domitian's assassination in AD96.

Above: This Arch of Trajan dominates the ruins of the colony for veterans the emperor founded at Timgad in Africa.

freed from captivity, and last of all his victorious soldiers, wearing olive wreaths and singing verses that alternately honoured and mocked their general.

The procession entered by the Forum Boarium (cattle market) and wound through the Circus Maximus, round the Palatine Hill and up the Sacred Way to the Forum, before ascending the Capitoline Hill. Here the leading captives were taken away and sacrificed with the oxen. However, after Aemilius Paullus' triumph in 167BC, they were normally spared if they had fought bravely. Only those who had broken their word to Rome, like Jugurtha the Numidian king and Vercingetorix the Gallic leader, were executed. Caratacus, the British prince, and Zenobia, Queen of Palmyra, were both spared to live in comfortable obscurity. Cleopatra, however, chose suicide over such ignominy.

Under the Republic, triumphs became more splendid, each successful general proclaiming his – and his family's – glory ever more grandly, despite the efforts of senators to curtail it. Their monuments, statues and, from the mid-3rd century BC, temples all along the triumphal route formed a permanent memorial to their achievements, beautifying the city.

In the Principate, triumphs were reserved for the emperor, and generals had to be content with an *ovatio*, an ovation, in which they sacrificed on the Alban hill and entered Rome on a horse the next day. With this came the grant of *insignia triumphalia*, triumphal ornaments, the right to wear triumphal uniform and a laurel wreath at official ceremonies and have a statue among former triumphators. From Trajan's reign on, all consuls seem to have had the right to such triumphal dress, which must soon have devalued it.

Below: Wearing a special painted toga and clutching a golden sceptre, the triumphant general Scipio Africanus, who had beaten Hannibal, is escorted through the streets of Rome to the Capitoline Hill, where captives were traditionally sacrificed.

Above: Reconstruction of a tower and the walls of the legionary camp at Xanten on the Rhine in Germany. This was originally a two-legion camp. The tower, like most built in the Principate, has a wide gate and was not designed for prolonged defence.

Right: Another view of the partially reconstructed tower and walls at Xanten on the Rhine. This shows how towers under the Principate did not protrude and how the walls did not have deep moats in front, being designed merely to break the impact of attack.

PERMANENT FORTIFICATIONS

By AD150 Rome had surrounded its empire with permanent defences in stone, wood and turf, some still impressive today. But these walls and ramparts were not intended as impregnable defences. Instead, they were built as bases from which troops would march out to fight. Even the grandest wall, Hadrian's Wall across northern England, was intended not as an impermeable barrier but to control movements across the frontier.

The Servian Wall around Rome built in the 370s BC was massive – 10ft (3m) wide and 30ft (9m) high – enough to defy even Hannibal. But after this war, Rome no longer needed such domestic defences, as its frontiers became ever more distant. When the Rhine and Danube became Rome's *de facto* northern Continental frontiers after Augustus, Roman camps along them developed into permanent stone-built fortresses.

These fortresses were generally built on flat ground for convenience, rather than for defence. Each followed a rectilinear plan derived from marching camps. The fortress of the Sixteenth Legion at Neuss on the Lower Rhine is typical: a rectangle 500 by 700yd (450 by 650m) with walls 15ft (4.5m) high and a surrounding ditch. The walls were intended to protect only against surprise attacks. The *principia*, or legionary headquarters, where legionary records and standards were kept, faced the legate's house, the *praetorium*, an imposing edifice built around a courtyard, often with hypocaust underfloor heating in northern Europe. Barrack blocks, where the legionaries slept eight to a room, lined the perimeter, with a large gap between them and the walls to allow troops to form up. With workshops, baths, granaries and a hospital, the legionary camp was almost self-sufficient. The auxiliaries' cohorts had similar, if smaller, forts.

Although still committed to taking the offensive, the Romans came to build extensive lines to control their frontiers. The gap between the upper Rhine and the Danube was covered by the advance under the Flavians and Trajan to a line along the Taunus Mountains and River Neckar, then south-east to the Danube near Regensburg. Shortening the frontier, this was defended not by a stone wall but by timber, later stone, towers. These were connected by *limes*, patrolled frontiers,

Right: The ruins of Aquinicum, a legionary fortress near Budapest on the Danube, overlooked by a modern white building.

defined as much as defended by a narrow wooden palisade, with forts for auxiliary cohorts every few miles. There were almost 100 camps, connected by 1,500 towers, along this new 310-mile (500km) frontier. They signalled to each other using heliographs (sun signals), smoke or fires. Guarding the Rhine from Bonn to the North Sea, forts lined the west bank, with watchtowers between. A similar chain ran down the Danube to the Black Sea, the river serving instead of a palisade.

In North Africa, where the threat came from fast-moving Berber raiders, the long desert frontier was defended by other *limes*. Low, continuous walls, and a series of *fossata*, deep, flat-bottomed ditches or trenches, formed unmanned but continuous barriers inland from the wheat and olive lands of Rome's breadbasket. Although raiding Berbers could cross walls by breaking them down, they were slowed down and forced to return laden with booty through the same gap. There, waiting Roman patrols from nearby forts could cut them off. These barriers made it difficult for the Berbers to raid at will. Such crossing places corresponded to recognized transhumance routes (used by seasonally migrating flocks of sheep) and provided patrolled crossing points to collect customs dues.

HADRIAN'S WALL

The most imposing and monumental of Roman fortifications is Hadrian's Wall. Hadrian ordered its construction during his visit to Britain in AD122, although his original plan was not fully implemented. Running 76 miles (120km) between the Tyne and Solway, the wall was first built partly in turf and timber, only the eastern 45 miles (73km) being built of stone from the beginning. The wall was about 18ft (5.5m) high and 6–8ft (1.9–2.4m) wide, with a ditch that was about 25ft (7.6m) wide and about 10ft (3m) deep,

with another ditch, the *vallum*, behind. This second ditch was to keep civilians out of the military zone and to channel traffic to customs points. Every Roman mile there was a milecastle, with gates opening to the north flank and two turrets between. These were usually tiny – about 14sq ft (1.3sq m) inside – but the milecastles had garrisons of a century. About 15,000 auxiliaries were deployed along or around the wall. Most were not strung out along it but concentrated in camps for 500 or 1,000 men, such as Housesteads, from which they issued forth to deal with intruders. The wall was not a hermetic frontier but controlled traffic and impressed natives. Forts like High Rochester, 30 miles (48km) north, provided advance posts, while strong reinforcements could be summoned from the legionary fortress at York to the south.

Below: The fort at Vindolanda (Bardon Mill) lies south of Hadrian's Wall in Northumberland, with part of the actual wall reconstructed.

THE GREAT FORTS OF THE LATER EMPIRE

Above: Sited on the right (hostile) bank of the Rhine, the massive fortress of Deutz was built by Constantine I in AD310. Huge circular towers and walls 65ft (20m) high were designed to overawe the barbarians as well as repel their actual attacks.

Below: Pevensey Castle on the south coast of England was one of a string of the massive fortresses on what became known as the Saxon Shore, built to provide secure bases for the fleets patrolling against invading Saxon pirates.

Changes in the Roman army in the later 3rd and early 4th century AD turned it from a fundamentally offensive force to a predominantly defensive one. They also changed its approach to fortification. The Romans finally began to build fortresses that, with their huge towers and complex gatehouses, looked like real castles, rather than barracks surrounded by quite thin walls. Like real castles also, these forts came to control important passes and crossings and were built on easily defended sites. From the mid-4th century AD, they also grew increasingly cramped inside, in stark contrast to the spacious bases of the Principate. Such castles, cripplingly expensive to build, anticipate those of the Middle Ages.

In the AD260s, Gallienus had begun to reorganize the army and Aurelian had given Rome its new wall in AD272–5, but it was only under Diocletian (AD284–305) that the radical shift to a new type of fort-building fully emerged. It can be seen right across the empire – even in parts not controlled by Diocletian, such as Britain, where the admiral of the *classis britannica*, Carausius, had made himself independent in AD286 – so it clearly represented a widespread trend.

THE NEW FORTRESSES

Typically these new fortresses had several common features: they had fewer entrances (often only one) guarded by a complex gatehouse that sometimes had a portcullis. They had massive projecting towers that allowed the archers, or soldiers operating the catapults now sometimes mounted on them, to cover the approaches. Their walls were much thicker and higher than those of earlier forts, sometimes up to 65ft (18m) high and 15ft (4.6m) thick. Finally, their ditches were wider and deeper and their berms (the strip between ditch and wall) wider. Old military camps were often adapted to the new fortress style, typically with fewer buildings inside, suggesting that they housed less forces, and that civilians may have sheltered inside the walls in times of invasion. It is also likely that these empty spaces sometimes sheltered mobile forces, the *comitatenses*, *en route* through the empire.

Some of the finest surviving examples of these massive new fortresses can be found on the Saxon Shore, the south-east coast of Britain that was fortified from the mid-3rd century AD onwards against

Above: On Constantine I's death, Constantine II and his brothers divided the empire in three.

the new threat from Saxon raiders. Portchester near Portsmouth, the best preserved, dates from the AD280s. Within its giant walls, still rising some 30ft (9m) above the estuary, a medieval church and castle nestle comfortably in opposite corners, with open fields between them. Along the Rhine, similarly huge structures were built to confront the new barbarian threats. The fortress at Deutz on the east (German) bank of the Rhine is typically imposing. Built by Constantine I in AD310 to defend Cologne, its 65ft (20m) walls were punctuated by even taller circular towers. At the other end of the empire, forts such as that at Qasr Bsheir in Jordan, built under Diocletian, were constructed with projecting towers to provide enfilading fire. Like medieval castles, such fortresses must have been defensible for long periods even by very small garrisons and could counter barbarian superiority in the field.

PSYCHOLOGICAL WARFARE

All these massive walls might suggest that Rome's enemies had become markedly more proficient in siege warfare. This was certainly true of the Sassanid Persians, who were far more determined and skilled fighters than the rather shambolic Parthian Arsacid dynasty they replaced. On the eastern frontier, long and complex

sieges became common. Those at Dura-Europos and Amida, where the Persians were victorious, and at Nisibis, where they were not, were typical. But the Romans built equally massive fortresses all along their northern frontiers, and very few barbarian tribes, if any, were ever good at proper sieges. But they would have certainly been impressed by these towering walls. So, in a more positive way, would the Roman soldiers inside them, especially as they were normally poorly trained and ill-equipped *limitanei* (frontier guards). Few Germans would have even attempted a siege against such an overwhelming example of Roman military engineering as Deutz. If they could not rush the castle by surprise or capture it by treachery – Rome itself only fell to the Visigoths when someone opened a gate to them – barbarian invaders would bypass them. This gave the Romans time to recover, to bring up forces from the mobile reserves and to stage a counter-attack. If the Romans could no longer overwhelm the barbarians by their unfailingly aggressive spirit, they could attempt to do so by their monumental fortifications.

Below: On the east coast of Kent, Richborough (Rutupiae) was the original Roman chief port of entry for Britain. Its fortifications were massively augmented in the later empire with huge walls, of which large sections still remain.

CITY WALLS

Above: The double walls around Constantinople (Istanbul) built by the emperor Theodosius II in the 5th century AD *still stand and have even been reconstructed for a small section. They repulsed attackers for 1,000 years.*

Below: The Porta Nigra (black gate) was the entrance, both ceremonial and fortified, to Trier, the capital of Gaul in the later empire. Its towers rise more than 70ft (20m).

Since Augustus, Rome had been an open city, the Servian walls were allowed to decay as they were engulfed by the growing capital. This reflected well-founded Roman confidence in its military prowess, which kept enemies safely distant. Similarly, cities in the provinces seldom needed walls unless on or near frontiers.

There were exceptions to this pacific norm, for older cities often retained their walls. Pompeii, far from any frontier, kept its boundary walls for ceremonial rather than military purposes, until Vesuvius destroyed it in AD79. In Boudicca's revolt in Britain, unwalled Colchester, London and St Albans were all sacked in AD61. So the Romans then built walls for a few towns, mostly those close to barbarous areas. But these walls, like those of the military camps, remained modest perimeters, gateways being more ceremonial than functional. However, further walls were added to London and other British cities after alarming barbarian attacks in AD193.

All this changed radically in the mid-3rd century AD. In the face of massive and repeated barbarian incursions, cities in near panic rushed to surround themselves with walls, using any materials that came to hand, including columns, tombstones and statues. Often these enclosed a far smaller area than before. Autun, for example, an important city in central Gaul, gave itself walls that covered only a third of its original area. Milan, for a time the capital of the western empire, enclosed less than 300 acres (120ha) within its new walls. Cities in the east did not shrink so much. Their walls were often restored, while in Britain the walls of London and York received progressively more massive fortifications but still protected the same areas. In Trier, which became the capital of Gaul and at times of the whole westernmost empire, gigantic walls protected an area of nearly 600 acres (240ha), making the walled city as large as it had ever been. Noteworthy at Trier is the ceremonial but also functional Porta Nigra (black gate), which has survived almost intact. Its two grand semicircular projecting towers rise to four tall floors over 70ft (20m) high and incorporate a portcullis, a device that went back centuries but which had become far more common. Trier remained impregnable until the whole of the Rhine frontier collapsed in AD406.

The walls Aurelian erected around Rome in the AD270s dwarfed those of all other western cities. Built chiefly of brick-faced concrete in great haste, the Aurelianic walls incorporate numerous pre-existing monuments such as the Pyramid of Cestius (a tomb), the walls of the Praetorian camp, the Porta Maggiore, part of Claudius' aqueduct and the small Amphitheatrum Castrense. About 20ft (6m) high and 12ft (3.6m) thick, they had square towers at about every 60yd (55m) with a platform for a catapult on top, while the major gateways had arched entrances flanked by twin semicircular towers. The entire circuit, covering most of Rome as it then was, was nearly

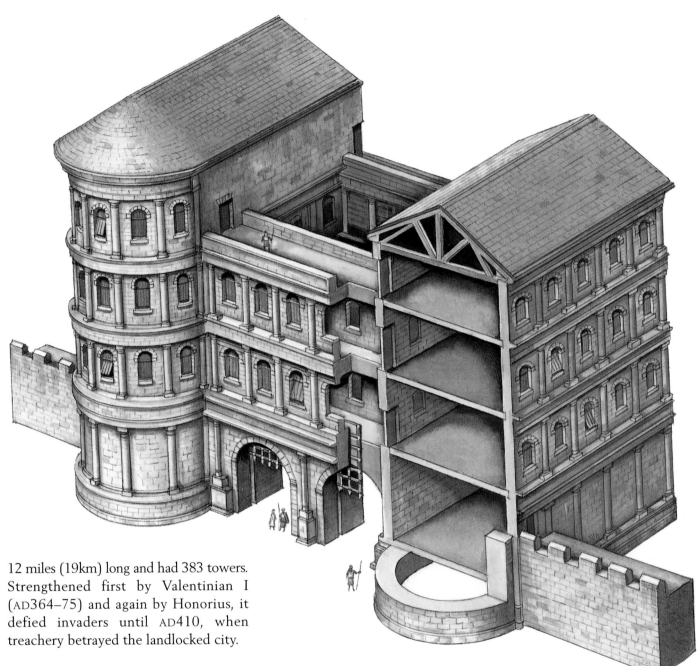

12 miles (19km) long and had 383 towers. Strengthened first by Valentinian I (AD364–75) and again by Honorius, it defied invaders until AD410, when treachery betrayed the landlocked city.

THE WALLS OF CONSTANTINOPLE

By far the grandest, most effective and best-preserved of late Roman city walls are the double (in some places triple) Theodosian walls of Constantinople, now Istanbul, the heart and head of the east Roman empire that metamorphosed into the Greek Byzantine empire. The walls were constructed between AD413 and AD437 in the reign of Theodosius II – a reaction to the sack of Rome. They replaced Constantine's shorter wall, which no longer contained the expanding city. The outer Theodosian walls were 20ft (6m) high with a deep moat in front of them. The inner walls were 40ft (12m) high, with 96 polygonal or square towers. The walls ran for almost 4 miles (6.4km) on the landward side of the peninsula and continued as a single wall right the way round the tip. On the other side of the Golden Horn, the small city of Pera was similarly defended, and a chain could be drawn across the harbour mouth to bar it to enemy ships. The walls defied all invaders – except for traitors – until 1453, when they finally fell to the Turkish besiegers' artillery. This probably makes them the most lastingly and consistently successful defences in history.

Above: The Porta Nigra (black gate) of Trier dates from the 4th century AD. Rising over 70ft (20m) the gate's twin towers incorporated a portcullis. It owes its remarkably good state of preservation to part of it being made into a chapel in the Middle Ages.

CHAPTER X

THE GREAT WARS

More than any other factor it was war that helped to mould Roman society and its empire. Certain wars in particular propelled Rome first to dominance and then to absolute rule of the Mediterranean world: the wars against Carthage, in which Rome almost foundered; the wars in the eastern Mediterranean, which made Rome amazingly rich; and finally, Caesar's conquest of Gaul, which led to the expansion of Roman influence into northern Europe. Caesar's dazzling success was balanced by the more mixed results of Claudius' and Agricola's campaigns in Britain, which helped to link Britain with the Continent. But the unsuccessful wars in Germany left most of that country permanently outside the Roman *imperium* (empire), with momentous long-term consequences both for Germany and for Rome.

Civil wars helped to determine the form of government that Rome would have when ruling its new empire. As the empire matured, Rome reached something like its natural boundaries. From now on, any war would be defensive or, increasingly and catastrophically, internecine. The earlier great wars tend to be well recorded and provided some of the best examples of human conflict for many later generals and rulers. But the instrument of Rome's victories was always its army, unequalled both at marching and at fighting, relentlessly aggressive and willing to suffer almost any level of casualties if it led to final victory.

Left: Of all Rome's opponents, the most formidable was Hannibal, the Carthaginian general who invaded Italy.

MARCHING AND FIGHTING

By the late 2nd century BC, the Roman army had become the world's first large-scale, semi-permanent professional army, a status it maintained with relatively few changes for almost 400 years. In so doing, it developed fixed routines that struck contemporaries as formidably impressive. Flavius Josephus, writing around AD70, repeats the admiring comments made by Polybius over two centuries earlier. The Romans organized their armies for their frequent marches, especially through hostile territory, in the same methodical way that they did everything else. When they engaged in actual combat, their relentless, controlled ferocity, coupled with a readiness to take high casualties if necessary, tended to overwhelm far larger numbers. This combination helped them to win their greatest wars.

When a full-sized Roman army was on the move, according to Josephus, it was preceded by light infantry and cavalry acting as scouts. Then came the vanguard, one legion plus cavalry, the legions drawing lots to decide which should be the vanguard – a prestigious if perilous position. Next came the camp surveyors, ten men detached from each century, followed by the pioneer corps, which had to remove obstacles in the army's path and build any necessary bridges. The general's and officers' baggage train came next, well protected by a strong mounted escort. Equally well protected behind it came the general himself, riding with his bodyguard of select cavalry and infantry. There followed the legionary cavalry, 120 for each legion, and then the mule trains carrying the numerous catapults and siege

Below: The sight of Roman legionaries marching in full armour towards them must have been intimidating to enemies, as these re-enactors demonstrate as they tramp along in formation.

engines. According to Vegetius writing in the 4th century AD each century had its own *carroballista* (a light, bolt-shooting catapult) and each cohort had its own *onager* (a heavy stone-slinging catapult), so this mule train must have been large. Finally came the main body of the legions, all carrying their rations, camp-making tools and armour, marching six abreast. They were preceded by their *aquilifer*, (eagle-bearer) and the trumpeters, and followed by their own baggage trains. A full legion of around 5,500 men must have spread for about a mile. Behind the legionaries marched the auxiliaries, with the rearguard composed of infantry and crack auxiliary cavalry. At the very end came the camp followers: wives, prostitutes, merchants and traders, including slave-dealers who could profit from Roman victory – slavery was the normal fate of any prisoners of war.

Roman armies were not as flamboyant or colourful as many Greek or Parthian forces, especially after Marius' reforms, when the richer soldiers stopped supplying their own armour. However, the well-drilled advance of up to 50,000 men – not such an uncommon number in the late Republic and Principate – must have been intimidatingly impressive.

BATTLE STATIONS

One of the advantages of the Roman *triplex acies* – the triple line of troops – was that troops did not have to fight to victory or to the death, but could be reinforced from the ranks behind. Unlike both the Greek *phalanx* and the Celtic-German mass, which relied on keeping the front ranks fighting until they triumphed by weight of numbers or else broke, this reduced the chances of panic. Iron discipline and rigorous drilling practice made complex manoeuvres second nature, even in the heat of battle. Their long, curved shields also helped to protect their comrades while moving backwards and forwards. But the *triplex acies* in no way softened the rigours of war. Centurions and the *optiones*, their

lieutenants, kept the men fighting, pushing them back into line and threatening cowardice with punishment.

In the Republic, legionaries had advanced shouting, banging their weapons against their shields. But by Caesar's time they kept silent until within almost 50ft (15m) of the enemy, when they yelled and threw their javelins in one broadside. Superb discipline allowed their dense formation to be maintained until the last minute. Then the soldiers fought close up, using the boss on their shields to punch the enemy in the face while they stabbed him with their *gladius*.

The centurions led their men aggressively, but even the generals stayed in close contact with their troops – to oversee fighting and to reward or punish individual soldiers. In close combat, when a gap was made in the enemy's line by killing several soldiers, a bravely determined legionary would fight his way into it. He was in extreme danger until joined by his comrades. But if enough managed to do so, the entire enemy line could start to buckle. Fighting at such close quarters was exhausting, both physically and psychologically, and the forces often used to break off at times, hurling abuse at each other from lines only a few yards apart, before re-engaging. Perseverance and stamina, more than spectacular individual exploits – coordinated so that the legion became one huge stabbing and thrusting machine – dominated and decided most battles. These were qualities Roman legionaries had in abundance.

Above: The Via Appia to the south of Rome. Good roads were a secret of Rome's success in conveying troops quickly to all parts of the empire.

Below: The Roman army marched along its empire's well-paved roads in sandals and boots. Army boots have been found in a number of places, including Vindolanda in Northumberland, England.

THE PUNIC WARS
264–146BC

Above: Cannae, site of Rome's worst military disaster in 216BC, when Hannibal annihilated a Roman army. But his victory did Hannibal little good in the longer term.

Below: At Cannae, Hannibal destroyed a numerically far superior army by thinning out his centre (blue) and letting it bend like a bow under Roman attack (red). Then his cavalry encircled the legions, driving them into a dense mass unable to wield their swords properly.

When Rome blundered into war with Carthage in 264BC, it began an epic contest that would test its foundations. Carthage was a richer, larger and more sophisticated state than Rome. Its string of fortified bases stretched from Cadiz in Spain to Tripoli in Libya, and it was in the process of extending its control of Sicily. Greek observers must have expected it to contain, if not crush, what was still a farmers' republic. But Rome surprised the Greeks by its final victory over Carthage, which made it the dominant power first in the west Mediterranean and soon in the whole inland sea.

WAR AT SEA

The First Punic (Latin for Carthaginian) War was unusual for Rome as it was decided mostly at sea. Recognizing the need to counter Punic naval supremacy, the Romans quickly built fleets and defeated the Carthaginians with the *corvus*, the iron boarding device that let Romans fight as if on land. The *corvus* was a double-edged invention, however, as it made a galley top-heavy and many

HANNIBAL CROSSES THE ALPS

Few feats have captured the popular imagination more than Hannibal's crossing of the Alps. He took the land route to Italy because the Romans controlled the sea and also because no one expected it.

After leaving Spain with an army 40,000 strong and 37 elephants, Hannibal found a Roman army awaiting him in the Rhône delta. To avoid it, he headed north of Avignon before crossing the Rhône. His elephants, however, lured on to rafts, panicked, some upsetting their rafts to wade across, using their trunks as snorkels. He then took a route further north but early snow added to the problems caused by hostile Celts. It took Hannibal 15 days to cross the Alps, and on the way he lost about a third of his army, more of his baggage train and almost all his elephants, but when he arrived in the Po Valley he posed a novel threat to Rome.

fleets sank. Rome's victory in 241BC was won by normal galleys. This was after Regulus had come to within a day's march of Carthage but was beaten by the Spartan general Xanthippus in 255BC. Regulus was taken prisoner and sacrificed his life for his city, a patriotic act not atypical of Romans at the time.

ROMAN DEFEAT

Regulus may have been no military genius but, in the next war, Cornelius Scipio (later Africanus) was. This was fortunate for Rome, for Hannibal was a fearsome enemy whose daring was shown by his unprecedented choice of route over the Alps, and by his defeats of Roman armies at Ticino and Trebbia in the Po Valley in

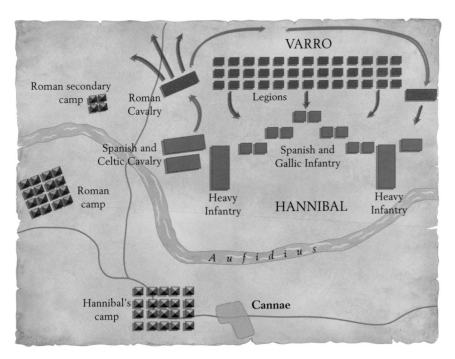

218BC. After being ambushed in a mist, 30,000 Romans died. Hannibal, entering Italy on his one surviving elephant, defeated Rome again at Lake Trasimene in 217BC. He ignored the undefended road to Rome, perhaps because he lacked a siege train, but a year later annihilated Rome's biggest army yet – 80,000 men – at Cannae. Here Roman military amateurism was shown at its most inept. Trusting in their numbers, they let their central infantry push back the thin Punic infantry line. As Hannibal intended, this bent rather than broke, enveloping the enemy, while the superior Carthaginian cavalry, routing the Roman horsemen, circled round to attack from the rear. Packed so tightly that they could not fight, some Romans then fled but many more were cut down. Roman losses reputedly approached 70,000 that day.

When Hannibal's peace offers were rejected, the war became one of attrition and, despite the defection of some major cities like Capua, Rome here had the advantage. Hannibal could train his disparate troops, who included Spaniards, Gauls, Numidians, Samnites and other disaffected Italians, into a unified force, but he needed reinforcements, which never came. Meanwhile, Roman reserves of manpower – sources say over 700,000 – were readily available. Provided the Romans followed the unpopular scorched-earth tactics of Fabius Cunctator, their (emergency) dictator, they would win, even if at great cost to Italian agriculture.

SCIPIO IN SPAIN AND AFRICA

In the event, Rome counter-attacked, striking at Hannibal's base in Spain to prevent reinforcements reaching him. Scipio captured Cartagena in 209BC and defeated Hasdrubal's army at Baecula. Scipio finished off Carthaginian power at Ilpica in 206BC. In these battles he emulated Hannibal's encircling tactics to great effect. Despite the Senate's denial of adequate troops, he invaded Africa in 204BC and won over Massinissa of Numidia. With this fine Numidian

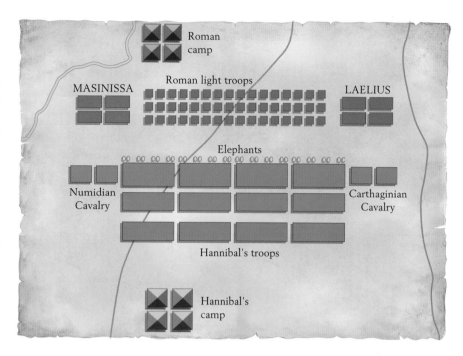

cavalry, Scipio finally defeated Hannibal at Zama in 202BC. The final battle between the two generals was a slogging match, Hannibal's many elephants being countered by Roman discipline, and was finally decided by Roman cavalry.

The Third Punic War of 149–146BC was an unequal and unnecessary contest. The Carthaginians, despite economic recovery, presented no military threat to a Rome still paranoid about Hannibal, but war was fomented by the Numidian king, encroaching on Carthaginian territory. It led to the final destruction of Carthage.

Above: The battle of Zama, which ended the Second Punic War, was won chiefly by the discipline of Roman legions after they had repelled Hannibal's elephants.

Below: Hannibal used elephants as tanks. But they were a two-edged weapon, easy for a coolly determined opponent to turn back or avoid, and liable to stampede in blind panic.

CONQUERING THE GREEKS
200–133BC

Above: Athens, though no longer important politically, also suffered in the wars that marked Rome's conquest of Greece. Later it became the empire's university town.

Below: The theatre on the Acropolis of Pergamum, the capital of the wealthy Attalid kingdom, Rome's chief ally in the Greek world.

The eastern Mediterranean world conquered after 200BC appeared to many Romans as wealthy, sophisticated and alluring, but also effete and even dissolute. In a long series of wars, Alexander's generals, the *diaodochi* (successors), had created three powerful Greek-ruled kingdoms: the Antigonids in Macedonia, the Seleucids in Asia Minor, Syria and Mesopotamia, and the Ptolemies in Egypt and Palestine. These dominated the ancient world from the Adriatic to central Asia, but the cities of Greece proper remained independent and feuding. The recurrent wars between the great Hellenistic powers (as the expanded Greek world after Alexander the Great is known) were conducted in a relatively civilized, limited fashion, like those of the 18th century. Their professional but expensive armies relied mainly on spearmen massed into *phalanxes* and armed with sarissas, pikes up to 20ft (6m) long, supplemented by dashing cavalry with plumed helmets, fierce-looking chariots and many elephants. Such military splendours, however, especially the rigid formation of the *phalanx*, could not compete with the flexible maniples of battle-hardened Roman legions led by generals who had learnt their trade in the rigours of the Punic Wars. The Romans' brutally realistic attitude to war shocked the Greeks, who preferred to resort to diplomacy and negotiations rather than needless battles.

Philip V of Macedonia, a successful if impetuous ruler, unwisely allied himself with Hannibal after Cannae, partly because Rome had annexed nearby south Illyria. This First Macedonian War fizzled out in 205BC but Rome did not forget Philip's action. Urged on by smaller Greek states anxious that Philip's alliance with the Seleucid Antiochus III threatened their independence, Rome sent Flaminius in 200BC to drive the Macedonians from Greece proper. At the battle of Cynoscephalae in 197BC, Flaminius displayed the flexibility pioneered by Scipio Africanus to defeat Philip, his maniples outflanking the clumsy *phalanx* on what was admittedly mountainous ground. Macedonian power in Greece was ended, though Macedonia itself was not destroyed, and Flaminius promised the delighted southern Greek cities liberty. It was to prove a hollow promise, for he meant self-rule as subordinate allies, not full freedom.

KING OF KINGS
Antiochus III was still undefeated, however. A capable and highly ambitious monarch, he appeared to Rome to be recreating Alexander's vast empire, for not only had he reconquered much of central Asia, but he menaced both Egypt and Europe, and was calling himself King of Kings. Even worse, Hannibal, exiled from Carthage, was now a guest at Antiochus' court. In 192BC Antiochus sent a small force into Greece proper to help the Aetolians, disgruntled by the

THE TANKS OF ANTIQUITY

When the Romans first encountered elephants in Pyrrhus' army in 280BC, they were panic-stricken. But they soon learnt to deal with these armoured giants by opening their ranks to let them through, or by repelling them by javelin volleys. In war elephant charges could inflict terrible damage upon infantry that panicked, while their smell drove horses unused to them mad with fear. But elephants were a double-edged weapon, for they in turn were easy to panic and could turn against their own armies. Because of this, mahouts, their riders, carried hammers and chisels to kill them if needed.

The Hellenistic monarchs used Indian elephants, who were more easily trained and came from the elephant stud farm the Seleucids had established in Syria. But Hannibal and other Carthaginians used the North African forest elephant (now extinct), which was ridden like a horse. The Romans occasionally also deployed elephants in their armies, impressing enemies unused to them. However, they chiefly used them for animal and hunting displays, slaughtering them in large numbers in games to amuse the Roman populace.

nominal Roman commander, but Scipio himself was ill on the day of the battle. The key role in the battle was taken by Eumenes of Pergamum, a Hellenistic ally of Rome, whose heavy cavalry routed the Seleucid *cataphracts* and then returned to attack the Seleucid infantry in the rear. The Seleucid chariot and elephant charges had been repulsed earlier by the Roman legions, but the Macedonian *phalanx*, 16,000 strong, stood firm against Roman attacks until their stampeding elephants, panicked by Roman javelins, broke up their ranks. Finally, the Pergamene cavalry was able to surround the remaining Seleucid forces.

This defeat proved decisive. Antiochus had to pay a huge indemnity, withdraw completely from Asia Minor and expel Hannibal. The Seleucids were never again a great Mediterranean power. The Romans, as was their custom at the time, made no new provinces but gave the western Seleucid territories mostly to Eumenes, whose last descendant bequeathed them to Rome in 133BC. However, the Romans were now incontestably masters of the eastern Mediterranean too. Later Roman wars in Greece merely confirmed Roman supremacy, and this was challenged seriously only when Rome itself was divided at the time of Mithradates.

Above: A Roman legionary with a long oval shield and plumed helmet.

Below: Hannibal and his elephants fighting a Roman legion in north Italy, after the school of Raphael.

recent settlement. This roused Roman wrath and they sent an army to defeat it the next year at Thermopylae. Rome followed this up with a naval victory and landed troops in Asia Minor for the final conflict at Magnesia in Asia Minor in 190BC.

For this deciding battle, Antiochus mobilized huge forces of over 70,000 men, including heavy Persian-style *cataphract* cavalry and large numbers of war elephants and chariots. However, the core of his army remained the *phalanx*. This formation, 32-men deep, bristled with spears and was almost invincible to frontal assault. Scipio Africanus was an unofficial adviser to his brother, the

CAESAR'S CONQUEST OF GAUL
58–50BC

Caesar's proconsular command in 58BC, for the exceptionally long term of five years, included Cisalpine Gaul (the Po valley) and Transalpine Gaul (southern France) with Greek cities at Marseilles and Antibes, a Roman colony at Narbonne and, lining the Rhône valley, various Celtic tribes. The vagueness of this northern frontier allowed Caesar, keen to rival Pompey's eastern conquests, to intervene far beyond his province. The Helvetii trying to migrate to the Atlantic, gave him an excuse. A series of bitter, genocidal wars resulted in all Gaul (France, Belgium, the Rhineland and western Switzerland) being conquered and Romanized. This conquest led to the extension of Roman power northwards and the enrichment of Caesar. In the long term it produced the civilization of France. This makes it among the most significant conquests in history.

The Celtic world Caesar destroyed was underestimated by classical writers because it lacked cities and literacy. But the Gauls were skilled metal workers, producing striking stylized artworks. They were great horsemen and had many types of carriage, while the Veneti in Brittany

were fine mariners. The Gauls were also pioneers of the wheeled plough. Above all, they had an acute poetic and religious sense. Most of what we know of Celtic life comes from biased writers such as Caesar; only echoes of Celtic legends survive in Welsh and Irish poetry. However, the Gauls were fatally disunited politically, with about 60 separate states in 58BC. Caesar easily recruited Gallic cavalry to fight their fellow countrymen.

Caesar swiftly crushed the Helvetii at Armecy in 58BC, killing tens of thousands, forcing the survivors back to Switzerland. The next year, he attacked Ariovistus, a German king who had crossed into Gaul. Caesar routed the Germans in Alsace and then turned on the Belgae, living north of the Seine. In 57BC he also crushed the Nervi in Artois before other Belgae had mobilized, a victory that made him arbiter of Gaul. With his command renewed at Lucca in 56BC, Caesar returned to find that the Veneti in Brittany, angered by his proposed invasion of Britain, had revolted. Building a fleet, he defeated them at Quiberon Bay. Early in 55BC he repelled another German invasion even more brutally, building a timber bridge across the Rhine, a feat that stunned opinion in Rome.

Caesar's two "invasions" of Britain in 55BC and 54BC were also intended as propaganda. The first attack was a near disaster: many ships were damaged by tides that Caesar had not anticipated and he himself returned home after only 18 days. The next year he returned with a far larger force of five legions and 2,000 cavalry and forced Cassivellaunus, ruler of the Catuvellauni, the most powerful southern British tribe, to submit after storming his capital. But the conquest proved illusory: the Britons rejected Roman suzerainty as soon as Caesar left. Meanwhile, there was rebellion in Gaul.

Above: The siege of Alesia in 52BC, where the Gallic leader Vercingetorix had retreated, was the final battle in Caesar's conquest of Gaul.

Below: Caesar built a double wooden wall around the fortress at the siege of Alesia, to keep the Gauls in and prevent their relief army of 80,000 men breaking through.

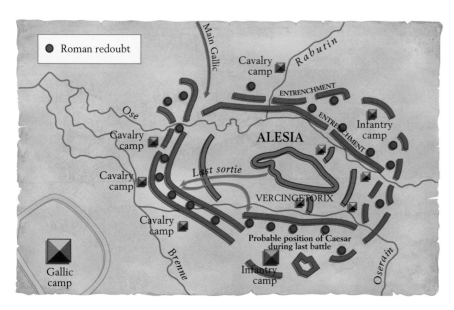

Left: Caesar's conquest of Gaul was marked by numerous campaigns of lightning rapidity that overwhelmed the far more numerous Gauls before they had time to mobilize. His legions marched from the Rhine – which they bridged – to the Atlantic, on which they sailed, and back with a speed that stunned Romans and Gauls alike. (Only the Britons were unimpressed.) But the conquest of Gaul was only settled by the drawn-out siege of Alesia.

Below: Vercingetorix, last and greatest war leader of the Gauls, shown heroically on horseback. His scorched-earth tactics were less heroic, but they nearly defeated Caesar, whose troops lived off the land and who could not capture Alesia by direct assault.

THE SIEGE OF ALESIA

In 52BC the Gauls united behind a single leader, Vercingetorix of the Arverni in central Gaul. He decided to defeat Caesar by a scorched-earth policy to deny him supplies – the Roman army lived off the land – refusing direct battle. He drew them into central Gaul where Caesar suffered a defeat attacking the fortress of Gerovia, which encouraged other tribes to join the revolt. But Vercingetorix mistakenly retreated behind the walls of Alesia with 90,000 men, thinking it was impregnable. Caesar recognized that it was "on the crown of a hill high enough for blockade to be the only means of capturing it". He built a huge double line of walls, an example of bi-circumvallation, about 14 miles (22km), to starve the Gauls – who included women and children – into surrender. The 80,000-strong Gallic relief army failed to break through Caesar's lines, fortified by iron-tipped spikes dug into the ground. In desperation, Vercingetorix tried three times to break out before surrendering in late 52BC. This ended the Gallic wars.

The Romans showed no mercy to the Gauls, killing about a third of the Gallic population in the wars. Caesar won by his lightning rapidity and the discipline of his legions. The conquered land was later divided into three provinces (Aquitainia in the south-west, Lugdunensis in the centre and Belgica in the north-east) and assessed for tribute. Ultimately, Gaul would prove the most receptive and fruitful of all Rome's conquests.

THE LAST CIVIL WARS: 49–30 BC

Above: A statue of Pompey, showing him posing rather improbably as a god or hero. He was, however, an excellent general and statesmanlike in foreign affairs. But in Roman politics he could never decide which faction to support, a fatal indecisiveness.

Below: Major battle sites of the last civil wars.

Fresh from his conquest of Gaul, in January 49BC Caesar had the best army: experienced, loyal, large – ten legions – and to hand. By contrast, his adversary Pompey's best troops were in Spain and out of practice. Caesar had no wish to start another civil war; memories of the conflict between Marius and Sulla were still fresh in the public mind. His enemies in the Senate tried to divest him of his Gallic command and refused to let him stand for consul *in absentia*. If he returned to Italy as a private citizen he faced immediate prosecution that would end his political career, if not his life. According to Suetonius, as he hesitated on the banks of the river Rubicon marking the borders of Italy, a ghostly figure appeared from the twilight and crossed over. Caesar then moved into Italy with his army – an act of treason – and triggered civil war.

With just one legion, Caesar raced down the east coast to Brindisi but failed to catch Pompey and his other opponents before they left for Greece, where Pompey had huge support. Before turning east, Caesar crushed the Pompeian forces in Spain at Lerida. In 48BC he crossed to Greece, eluding Pompey's numerous ships. Antony joined Caesar three months later with reinforcements, but attempts to blockade Pompey's base at Durrachium (Durazzo) failed disastrously. Pompey out-walled him and he withdrew.

The deciding battle took place in Thessaly on 6 June 48BC at Pharsalus. It was probably the largest battle ever fought between Romans; Pompey had 80,000 troops and was strong in cavalry, but most of his infantry were out of condition. Caesar had fewer men but all were skilled, hardened veterans. The brilliant discipline of Caesar's legionaries, who advanced with their *pila* (javelins) as pikes, countered Pompey's cavalry's initially successful charge. By attacking their flank, the legions drove Pompey's horsemen back. Pompey was killed soon after in Egypt.

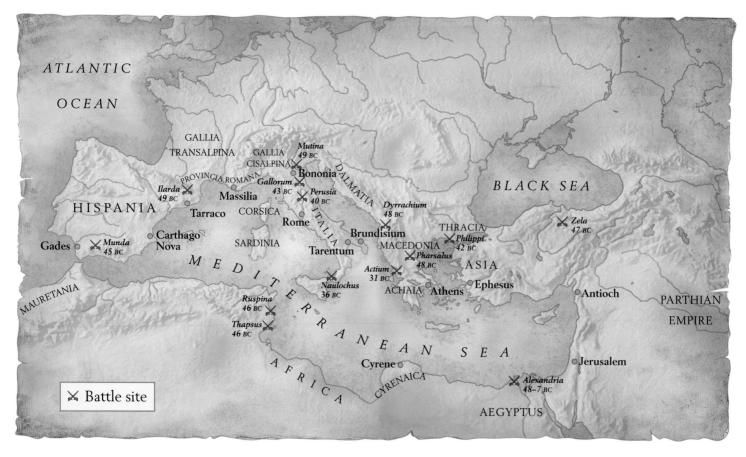

× Battle site

Right: Actium, last battle of the civil wars, was decided at sea when Antony's fleet, trying to escape the blockade, was defeated.

With great speed, Caesar won many other battles around the Mediterranean. But he was less good at establishing peace. After his assassination in 44BC, civil war flared up again between his assassins, led by Brutus and Cassius, and his supporters, Antony and Octavian. The two battles of Philippi in 42BC were won by Antony, who went on to rule the eastern half of the empire and pursue his relationship with Cleopatra. Inevitably, the two dynasts moved towards a renewal of war by 32BC.

ACTIUM: THE LAST BATTLE

Despite Octavian's lurid propaganda campaign, Antony was still popular with his own troops. He also had Cleopatra's wealth, which could give him a fleet, as well as promises of support from many eastern client kings, including Herod the Great. Octavian had the recruiting grounds of Italy, and a very good general in his friend Agrippa. Once again the rivals converged on Greece, Agrippa slipping across the Adriatic in the winter of 31BC, followed by Octavian in the spring. But Antony made a mistake when he took Cleopatra with him to western Greece. His own men began to believe Octavian's propaganda about their general and began to desert. The final battle took place on 2 September 31BC when Antony led his fleet in an attempted breakout Although he had many quinqueremes and more troops, Antony's fleet was defeated by Agrippa's, which used smaller, swifter Liburnian galleys. Antony broke off the battle, following Cleopatra's flight to Egypt. Many of his supporters then surrendered. The following year, Antony and Cleopatra committed suicide when the Caesarean troops entered Alexandria, so ending the last Roman civil war for a century.

Right: At Pharsalus, Caesar's more disciplined but outnumbered troops defeated Pompey's army by flank attacks.

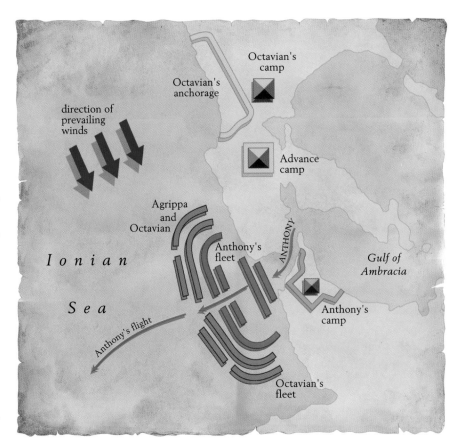

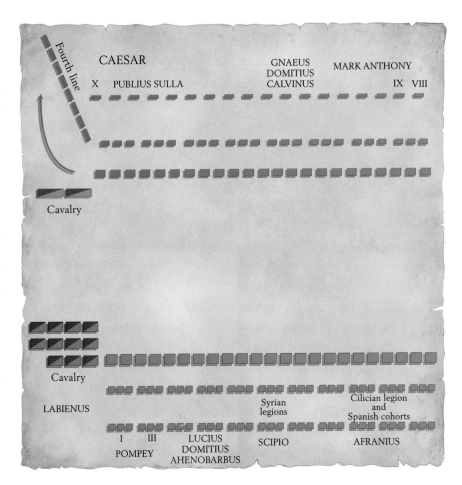

ALONG THE ELBE: 12BC–AD16

Although Caesar had proclaimed the Rhine as the natural, almost inevitable, north-west frontier of the empire, this was not so evident to his successor Augustus. Germanic tribes had already infiltrated west of the river into Gallia Belgica, the north-eastern Gallic province. Further, a German invasion in 17BC by the Sugambri and Isupetes tribes, which had defeated the Romans under Lollius, called for revenge. Augustus, confident after victories in northern Iberia (23BC), the Alpine provinces (16–15BC) and the Balkans (13–9BC), saw no reason to halt the expansion of the empire on this frontier.

Rome's geographical knowledge of northern Europe became more vague the further east it looked, but the tribes between the Elbe and the Rhine did not appear exceptionally formidable. It seemed that Germania could be conquered and pacified as easily as Gaul, a considerably larger, more populous area. A frontier along the Elbe to the Danube would eliminate the awkward upper Rhine–Danube junction, and shorten the whole frontier by almost 300 miles (480km).

There were differences between the two lands, however. If thought barbarous by Greeks and Romans, *Gallia comata* (long-haired Gaul), beyond Rome's old Mediterranean province, had been wealthy and dynamic in its rural way; its fertile land had supported advanced farming. Western Germany, by contrast, had thin soils with heavy, dark forests and many bogs and heaths. Partly because of this, the German tribes were less well developed and less settled than those of Gaul or Britain and their shifting settlements were less easily controlled. But such differences were not then apparent to the Romans.

Accordingly, Augustus ordered an advance to the Elbe, with troops commanded by his stepson Drusus in 12BC, while his other stepson, Tiberius, finally pacified the Pannonian plain. Although Drusus' fleet was wrecked by tides in the Zuyder Zee (his men were saved only by his Frisian allies), in three successive campaigning seasons his armies still advanced up the Main and Lippe valleys towards the Elbe.

Drusus' death in 9BC meant that Tiberius replaced him before retiring in 6BC from public life, in presumed disgust at Augustus' open preference for his grandsons. The German campaigns at first seem to have progressed slowly but steadily, even without Tiberius. Very soon traders and tax-collectors, in the normal pattern, entered the region, which began to be organized and taxed as a province. However, a reaction to the Roman advance led to the formation of a powerful Marcomanni kingdom in Bohemia. To deal with this threat, in AD6 a two-pronged invasion of the area was planned from the Rhine and the Danube. Tiberius, back from voluntary exile in Rhodes, was about to strike north from near Vienna with a huge force of 12 legions when news came of a massive revolt in Pannonia and he turned east. The gruelling war that followed, "the most serious

Above: The Elbe in north Germany proved a frontier too far for the Romans after the disaster that befell Varus and his legions in AD9.

Below: The "Gemma Augustea" shows Augustus and the goddess Roma receiving Tiberius, who, if charmless, was a very fine general.

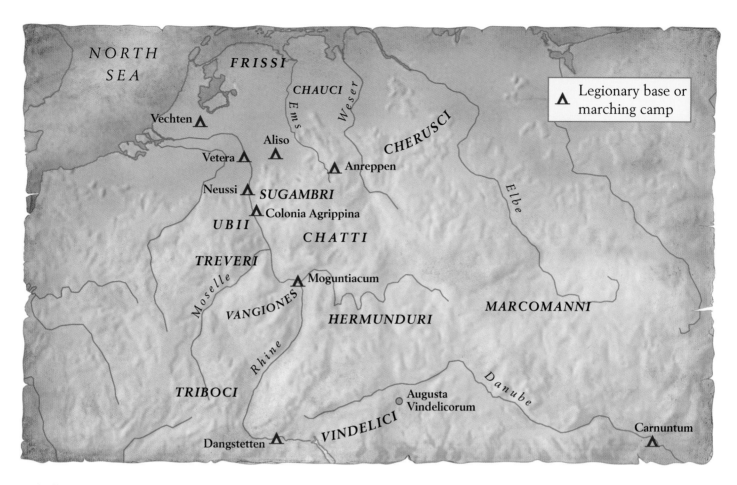

of all our foreign wars since the Punic wars", according to Suetonius, distracted him. Meanwhile, there was disaster in Germany proper.

THE VARUS DISASTER

Quinctilius Varus, who commanded three legions in north-west Germany, was less a soldier than an administrator, although he had suppressed a revolt in Judaea as governor of Syria in 4BC. Hastening in to deal with a revolt by the Cherusci, one of the German tribes, in AD9, his army was ambushed in the Teutoburg Forest near Osnabrück. Varus had been betrayed by the Cherusci king Arminius (Hermann), supposedly a Roman ally. Surrounded by Germans, Varus committed suicide and his three legions were lost. The whole Roman position east of the Rhine began to unravel rapidly. Back in Rome, the aged emperor Augustus was crushed by the news. He ordered special patrols around the city, reputedly banging his head against the wall and crying, "Quinctilius Varus, give me back my legions!"

In fact, the other German tribes did not join the Cherusci (the Marcomanni in particular quarrelled with them) and there was no general attack across the river Rhine. However, Tacitus was right when he referred to the Cherusci king Arminius as "the liberator of Germany", for his revolt marked the end of real Roman attempts to subjugate Germany. Drusus' son, Germanicus, led a series of major punitive raids over the Rhine, in AD15 finding and burying the bones of Varus' legions, and the following year sailing up the river Ems to defeat the Cherusci in a set battle.

However, Tiberius, the new emperor, then recalled Germanicus. Tiberius preferred to rely on diplomacy and bribes to control the German tribes. This was successful, for Arminius was soon killed in a conspiracy by his own people. The frontier then became established on the Rhine, and northern and central Germany remained permanently outside the Roman empire, although influenced by trade and other contacts with it.

Above: The attempted Roman conquest of Germany.

Below: The Rhine offered a convenient frontier for the Romans along much of its length but was not impassable.

THE CONQUEST OF LOWLAND BRITAIN: AD43–70

Above: The bookish emperor Claudius proved remarkably successful as a conqueror, adding lowland Britain to the empire in what appeared a relatively simple campaign. But the island was not at first a great asset to the empire.

Below: The hill fort at Badbury Rings, Dorset, was one of the many oppida, *or fortified British townships, that the Romans stormed in their initial conquest of Britain.*

Paradoxically, one of the most professional of Rome's military campaigns was carried out at the orders of one of its least military emperors, Claudius. This was no coincidence. Aware he lacked the soldiering experience of a Roman aristocrat, Claudius needed to conquer Britain. His predecessor, Caligula, had massed troops on the Channel as if for an invasion but ordered them to throw javelins at the sea, according to Suetonius. But Claudius was serious. The uncomfortable, marginally dangerous journey he made north for the surrender of Colchester (Camulodonum) shows the importance he attached to this campaign.

Ever since Julius Caesar had invaded and misleadingly claimed that he had conquered Britain in 55–54BC, the island had intrigued the Romans. It had a reputation – overrated, it turned out – of being rich in gold, and the south was inhabited by tribes like the Belgae related to those in Gaul. The Gallic connection was a reason for invasion, for the Druids reputedly helped keep alive Gallic hostility to Rome. Another excuse was

that Caratacus, an heir of King Cunobelin (Cymbeline), had attacked Verica, who appealed to Rome for help. Prestige was, however, the chief reason for the invasion. It was 40 years since Rome had gained a major new province.

Four legions were mustered under Aulus Plautius, 40,000 men including auxiliaries. Despite a mutiny by troops alarmed at embarking for an unknown land, they landed safely at Richborough, and after two days' bitter fighting defeated the Britons at the Medway. Another victory followed when the Romans crossed the Thames. Plautius, impressed by British resistance, halted the advance until the emperor could arrive with reinforcements, which included some elephants. Then Claudius watched his troops storm Colchester, the Catuvellaunian capital, and declared it the capital of the new province (and six years later, a Roman colony), before returning home to celebrate a triumph.

Plautius continued the swift conquest. Vespasian, commanding the Second Legion, struck south-west, capturing 20 *oppida* (tribal strongholds). Meanwhile, the Fourteenth Legion advanced north-west and the Ninth Legion moved north. Within four years a provisional line was established along the Fosse Way from Lincoln to Exeter. Tribes such as the Iceni and the Brigantes became client kings, shielding the new province. This began to fill with Roman merchants and adventurers. But Caratacus escaped to continue resistance in the Welsh hills.

Plautius' successor, Ostorius Scapula, tried to strengthen the new province by disarming all tribes south of the Fosse and pushing the frontier closer to Wales. Caratacus, defeated in battle, took refuge with Cartimandua, Queen of the Brigantes, who handed him over to the Romans in AD51. Caratacus was paraded through Rome but pardoned by Claudius.

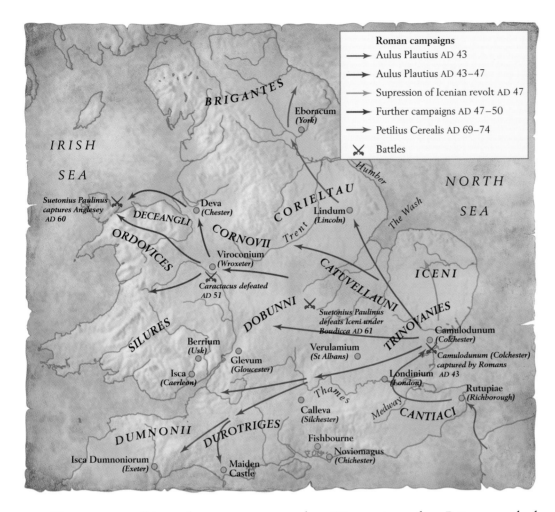

Left: Claudius' invasion of Britain at first restricted itself to the south-east of the island, with a possible provisional frontier along the Fosse Way and a capital at Colchester, although campaigns further west were needed to hunt down Caratacus. But the Romans soon found themselves drawn into Wales to suppress the Druids in AD60, and then Cerialis had to march north to control the large but troubled kingdom of the Brigantes.

The conquest did not, however, go so smoothly as it approached upland Britain. The Brigantes' kingdom was riven by disputes; Cartimandua was driven out by her consort after a disagreement and had to be reinstated by the Romans. Rome's real efforts, under the new governor Suetonius Paulinus, focused on subduing Anglesey, centre of political and religious resistance. The Romans crossed the Menai Straits and overran the island, cutting down the sacred Druidical groves. Then, suddenly, the whole province was endangered by a new revolt.

BOUDICCA'S REVOLT

The last Iceni king, Prasutagus, had made the emperor co-heir with his two daughters. But a venal procurator, Decianus Catus, and his loathed *publicani* seized land and goods. When Boudicca, the widowed queen, was flogged by Romans and her daughters raped, the Iceni rose in revolt. Joined by the Trinovantes, the Britons sacked Colchester and moved on London. Paulinus hurried with a few troops to London. Realizing he could not defend an unwalled city, he withdrew, "undeflected by the prayers and tears of those who begged for his help", in Tacitus' words. The Britons sacked London and St Albans, reportedly killing 70,000 people. Paulinus defeated them near Towcester – according to Tacitus, 80,000 Britons were killed and 400 Romans. Paulinus took a terrible vengeance, even on Britons who had stayed neutral. But before the whole province was devastated, Paulinus was checked by the intervention of Julius Classicianus, the new procurator. Of partly Gallic descent, Classicianus recognized the Britons' real problems and his report led to Paulinus being replaced by the more conciliatory Turpilianus. These two pacified the province so effectively the south never rose again.

Below: Queen Boudicca, who traditionally led her people, the Iceni, in a revolt that nearly ended Roman rule in all Britain.

AGRICOLA'S NORTHERN CAMPAIGNS: AD79–84

Above: Although Agricola marched far up the east coast of Scotland, the Romans did not penetrate the highlands proper, such as Glen Quoich.

Under Agricola, the Romans certainly came closer to conquering all Britain than at any other time. According to Tacitus, Agricola's completion of the conquest was prevented only by the jealousy of the emperor Domitian, who recalled him just as final victory was in sight. *"Perdomita Britannia et statim missa"* (Britain was completely conquered and at once let go), he commented sourly. But Tacitus was Agricola's son-in-law and shared the aristocracy's general hatred of Domitian. Just how feasible such a conquest was remains debatable, and Domitian did have valid reasons for recalling some legions.

When Agricola, who had just been a consul, arrived in Britain as governor, probably in late AD78, he was returning to a province he had fought in as a young man. Taking command of his old Twentieth Legion, then based at Viriconium (Wroxeter), he immediately went on the offensive against the Ordovices of mid-Wales and almost annihilated them. He built forts at Caernarvon and other places in north Wales, but also began "encouraging wild men who lived in scattered settlements… to live in a peaceful manner. Agricola … helped them officially to build temples, *fora* [market places] and private houses… and had the children of important Britons educated in civilized ways", recorded Tacitus. Many Britons now became Romanized, as the numerous buildings of this Flavian period show.

Right: Agricola's campaign, possibly intended to complete the conquest of Britain, started with a two-pronged attack on each flank of the Pennines. Once into what is now southern Scotland, his armies united to push up the east coast, establishing a line of forts centring on the new legionary camp at Inchtuthil. Roman victory in the supposedly decisive battle of Mons Graunpius – the site has yet to be determined – in fact did not conclude the conquest. The Caledonians vanished into the highland mists and soon after Agricola himself was recalled, his forts being abandoned a few years later.

Agricola's campaign in Scotland AD 78–84

Battle of Mons Graupius AD 83 (suggested locations)

CALEDONII

Tay

VENICONES

Fort at Inchtuthil abandoned AD 87   Inchtuthil

Forth

Agricola advances to the river Tay AD 79

NORTH SEA

Antonine Wall

DUMNONII

Clyde

VOTADINI

SELGOVAE

Romans control southwest Scotland AD 79

NOVANTAE

Tyne

Hadrian's Wall

In AD79 Agricola sent two large columns of troops up each side of the Pennines, overawing the Brigantes and reaching the Tyne–Solway line. The next year he pressed on to the Forth. Reuniting his armies, he then marched north again, building forts as he went. A provisional line across Scotland, from the Clyde to the Forth, was probably established and he campaigned in south-west Scotland. Looking across to Ireland, he estimated that its conquest would require only one legion – suggesting wild optimism or poor geography on his part. However, north-east Scotland drew him back. In summer AD82 or 83 he moved north with a supporting fleet through increasingly hostile territory with the permission of the new emperor, Domitian. The Ninth Legion was almost destroyed when it became detached from the main army. At Mons Graupius (probably near Inverness), Agricola's army finally met the main Caledonian forces mustered under King Calgacus. According to Tacitus, these northern Britons had about 30,000 men. This was far more than Agricola's forces, which included auxiliaries, among them some Britons. Although the Caledonians had the advantage of the slope and a prepared position, Roman discipline overcame Celtic courage. Reportedly, 10,000 Caledonians were killed for only 360 Romans, although 20,000 Caledonians escaped. These figures may exaggerate the extent of the victory, but Scotland did seem truly conquered.

Agricola ordered the construction of a full-scale legionary camp for the Twentieth Legion at Inchtuthil, the largest of a chain of forts that stretched almost from the Moray Firth to Loch Lomond. A fleet went north to circumnavigate Britain and confirm it really was an island. Agricola was presumably planning another campaign to the extreme north, but Domitian recalled him. Problems on the Danube meant reinforcements were needed. About AD86 Inchtuthil and other forts north of the Clyde–Forth line were dismantled and Rome's advance into Scotland abandoned.

The Highlands were left untamed, indeed untouched, despite Tacitus' claims to the contrary, and the southern uplands were still disputed. From unconquered Scotland would later come many of the tribes that would threaten Roman Britain.

BETWEEN TWO WALLS

The northern frontier remained unsettled until the famous visit of the emperor Hadrian in AD122. Hadrian generally favoured easily defensible frontiers, even if this entailed some withdrawal, and he now chose the line along the Tyne to the Solway for his great wall. At first built partly in turf and timber, it was soon wholly consolidated in stone, requiring the excavation in total of some 2 million tons of rock and soil. It was ultimately the most imposing fortification in the empire. However, this did not mean that the Romans rejected all interests or control north of the wall. Patrols and forts, such as Newstead on the Tweed, were maintained well to the north. In AD139 under Antoninus Pius, the frontier was advanced to the waist of Scotland again and a new turf wall some 37 miles (59km) long was built. This was the Antonine Wall, about 100 miles (160km) north of the existing line. Hadrian's Wall was not completely abandoned, but some of its gates were removed. However, an uprising led to the abandonment of the Antonine Wall in the early AD150s. It was reoccupied and finally abandoned again and dismantled in AD162. Hadrian's Wall again became the frontier, but due to Rome's civil wars it was overrun in the AD190s, with tribesmen raiding as far as York. To restore the situation, Septimius Severus visited Britain in person and twice invaded Scotland, perhaps reaching the Moray Firth. But when he died at York in AD211 his sons abandoned his planned conquests. Hadrian's Wall, substantially repaired, once again became the frontier of Roman Britain. Beyond it, the Caledonians began to organize themselves into threatening confederacies that would soon ravage the south.

Above: An emblem of the Twentieth Legion, once commanded by Agricola, which spear-headed his new campaign.

Below: Ruins of a granary at Housesteads on Hadrian's Wall.

TRAJAN AND THE CONQUEST OF DACIA

Above: Battle scene between the Dacians and the Romans from the Ludovisi Sarcophagus. The wars of AD101–6 , which removed a threatening enemy and gained much gold, proved to be Rome's last wholly profitable war of conquest.

Below: A river ferry passes the Iron Gates on the Danube, the great gorge that divides the river. The Romans built a road along the south cliff face.

Trajan (reigned AD98–117) was the last emperor to expand the empire significantly. If his wars in Asia proved a costly failure, his conquest of Dacia was a triumphant success. It led to the removal of a significant threat on the river Danube, a huge gain in booty for the Roman treasury and, despite Roman withdrawal 170 years later, to the enduring creation of the only Latin people in eastern Europe: the Romanians.

Dacia, a mountain-ringed, fertile and gold-rich land, had been a powerful, centralized kingdom under a ruler called Burebista in Caesar's time. Its people were renowned as fighters and skilled metallurgists and engineers, and had developed their own coinage. In AD85 Dacia acquired a brilliant new leader in Decebalus, who called himself High King. He may have had some experience of Roman military life, for he began organizing a powerful army on Roman lines. Twenty years of war followed – they proved among the fiercest Rome ever fought in Europe.

Domitian at once sent an army under Cornelius Fuscus to repel Dacian incursions, but it was humiliatingly defeated. Calling in legions from Britain and elsewhere, the Romans mounted a further campaign that won a victory at Tapae (near Turnu Severin) in AD88. However, the revolt of Antoninus Saturninus, the legate of upper Germany, in January AD89 meant that the troops had to deal with threatened civil war. The result was an uneasy truce. Domitian concentrated on containing the Dacian threat, quelling the tribes in Pannonia and building an earthwork across the Dobrudja, between the Danube and Tomis on the Black Sea, to prevent Dacian raids at this marshy extremity.

Trajan, who became emperor in AD98, was an experienced soldier. He boosted the Roman army's strength to perhaps 400,000 by recruiting two legions, besides doubling the size of the first cohort in each and adding new auxiliary forces. Seeing how Dacian power and pride were continuing to grow he decided to deal

with the Dacians. With other frontiers peaceful, he concentrated 13 legions plus auxiliaries (*c.*130,000 men) on the lower Danube. He crossed the river at the head of this force in AD101.

The wars, vividly recorded on Trajan's Column in Rome, lasted five years. The first led to an inconclusive victory, with Decebalus accepting humiliating terms. Trajan now prepared for a larger invasion by having Apollodorus build his bridge across the Danube and construct a road through the Iron Gates Gorge. Here the river narrowed between cliffs and the armies were able to march all the way along the Danube. The war resumed in AD105 and the final attack in AD106 overwhelmed the Dacian capital of Sarmizegetusa Regia. Decebalus committed suicide. His head later graced Trajan's triumph, along with a huge quantity of gold, the last really significant war spoils in Rome's history.

On the map, the new province – which lengthened the imperial frontiers by some 350 miles (560km) – looked vulnerable. However, on the ground the reality was rather different. By projecting Roman power to the edge of the Eurasian steppe, Trajan made it easier to control the Sarmatian, Carpi and Iazyges tribes on either side. A line of defences along the great mountain wall of the Carpathians, the *limes Porolissensis*, protected the new province with auxiliary-garrisoned forts. These were linked by watchtowers and backed by the Thirteenth Legion stationed at Apulum, reaching a total of 30–40,000 men (about the same as Britain). Dacia itself was settled by Romans, and the gold mines, an imperial monopoly, were profitably exploited.

THE PROVINCE ABANDONED

Hadrian is said to have contemplated abandoning the new province completely. This would have been in keeping with his general policy of retrenchment, although jealousy of Trajan's success could also have played a part; his destruction of the amazing Danubian bridge Apollodorus

had built seems pettily negative. But he was dissuaded by the pleas of the colonists themselves – the productive gold mines may have swayed him too – and he evacuated only the Banat plain to the west of the province, which was vulnerable to raids from Sarmatian tribesmen. Over the following century, the whole middle and lower Danubian area, from modern Budapest down to the Black Sea, prospered and became Romanized and increasingly urbanized. It was to provide vital reservoirs of troops – and emperors – in the 3rd century. One of these Illyrian emperors, Aurelian, accepting that Dacia was no longer defensible against new enemies such as the Goths and Gepids, finally evacuated it in AD270, settling its Latin-speaking inhabitants in a new province, Dacia, south of the Danube (approximately northern Serbia). However, some Latin-speaking Dacians must have survived the endless waves of invasion, probably sheltering in the Carpathians to re-emerge centuries later, still speaking their basically Romance language.

Above: The inauguration at Dobrela of the bridge over the Danube, which was built by Apollodorus for Trajan.

Below: Trajan's Column in Rome still proclaims his many victories.

TRAJAN AND THE EAST

Ever since Pompey had marched through Asia in the 60s BC, many Romans had dreamt of eastern conquests. There was widespread admiration for Alexander the Great, who had conquered the Persians *en route* to India. Parthia, the successor to the eastern Persian empire from the Euphrates to central Asia, was a ramshackle, semi-feudal monarchy, which was often unable to control its nobles and which evoked little loyalty from its varied subjects in Mesopotamia (Iraq).

There were more material reasons for invading Parthia and trying to annex at least its richest part, Mesopotamia. The great Hellenistic city of Seleucia-on-the-Tigris (opposite Baghdad) still flourished. In the 1st century AD the city had a population of *c.*600,000, almost as big as Alexandria's. Mesopotamia was very fertile, while its cities' trade with India reputedly surpassed Syria's. The ancient "Fertile Crescent", from the Gulf to the Mediterranean, had often been ruled by one monarch, most recently by the Hellenistic Seleucids. There was no good reason why it should not be again.

Augustus had prudently disappointed Roman expectations that he would revenge the Parthian defeats of Crassus (in 53BC) and Antony (in 36BC). Instead, by a peaceful agreement in 20BC Rome received back the legionary standards lost by Crassus, and Parthia (briefly) recognized Armenia as Rome's client, a diplomatic success that propagandists cried up as a great Roman victory. But the four legions Augustus stationed in Syria, to control that wealthy province and protect the eastern frontier, posed little threat to Parthia, as it realized. The kingdom of Armenia, a pivotal buffer or sometimes client state, caused more problems as it wavered between Rome and Parthia. Nero's fine general Corbulo, by mixed diplomacy and arms, arranged a Roman investiture (crowning) for an Arsacid (Parthian) king of Armenia in AD66, so appeasing both sides.

The Flavians had advanced the frontier east by annexing small client states. Trajan continued this policy, peacefully annexing Arabia Petraea (Jordan) in AD106 with its rich trading city of Petra, and building a military highway through the desert, so rounding off the eastern frontier. Although Antioch, the empire's third largest city, was only 100 miles (160km) from the frontier, the Parthians remained a minor threat. Trajan did not need to launch a war of conquest, but it seems he felt drawn east. Using Parthian interference in Armenia as an excuse, he launched a grand attack on the Parthians from the headquarters he set up at Antioch in late AD113.

Above: The Parthians relied heavily on horse archers such as this one, about to fire his recurved composite bow.

Below: Trajan's triumphal arch at Benevento, Italy.

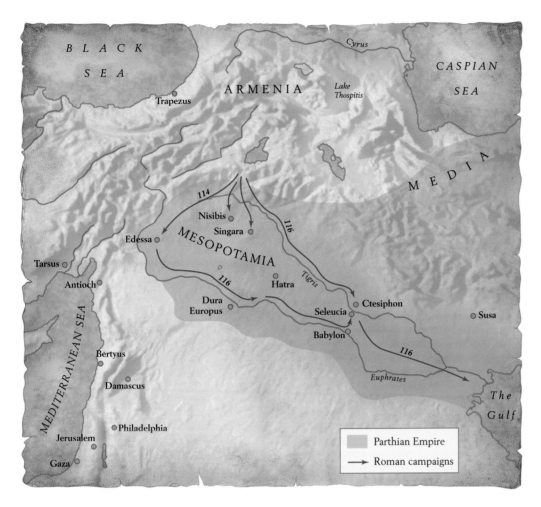

Left: Trajan's conquest of the east started with a successful attack on Armenia in AD114. A massive assault then over-ran all Mesopotamia down to the Gulf. But the Romans' rapid advance left their flanks exposed to counter-attacks while Jewish revolts in the rear threatened Rome's hold of the east. Finally, Trajan's failure to take the key city of Hatra led to the collapse of the invasion even before his death in AD117.

Below: Trajan shown triumphant in military uniform, a captive crouching at the feet of this most genial but expansionist of emperors.

RETREAT FROM THE GULF

Armenia was annexed in AD114 and at first the conquest of Mesopotamia seemed a huge success. Ctesiphon fell and Trajan sat on the Golden Throne of the Parthian kings, hailed by his army as *Parthicus* (conqueror of Parthia). East of the Tigris, a new province of Assyria (approximately Kurdistan) was created, completing the project of detaching what is now Iraq from Iran, and Trajan sailed south down the Tigris to the Gulf. According to Cassius Dio, on seeing the ocean and a ship setting out for India he said, "I would certainly have gone there too had I been younger." But he was 65 and in poor health. He returned via Babylon, already a ruin, to see the room where Alexander had died 400 years earlier. There he received news that all his new conquests were in peril. A wave of Jewish revolts had broken out, while the Parthians were harrying the eastern flanks of the new provinces. Failing to take the city of Hatra in central Mesopotamia, Trajan began recalling his troops. He died of a stroke in AD117 in Cilicia, but his eastern conquests had predeceased him. Hadrian completed the withdrawal and the return to the status quo, except that Armenia was once more in the Roman sphere.

Later campaigns in the reign of Marcus Aurelius between AD162 and 166 were scarcely more successful. Although Seleucia was captured and destroyed, a devastating plague sprang from its ruins. It was left to Septimius Severus to establish a defensible new frontier in AD198 along the lines of the Khabur river and Jebel Singara ridge, making northern Mesopotamia a defensible bulwark. But his victory also proved costly in the longer run, for it so weakened the Parthian empire that it was replaced 30 years later by the far more aggressive Sassanids.

CHAPTER XI

DEFENDING THE EMPIRE

After Trajan's death amid the ruins of his plans for conquering Asia, Hadrian reverted to a generally defensive policy. This was on the whole continued by his successors, despite later minor offensives. A few of these proved successful, like Septimius Severus' annexation of upper Mesopotamia, but most, like Marcus Aurelius' wars on the Danube or Septimius' own Caledonian campaign, failed with the death of their imperial instigator.

A total and official lack of aggressive wars, which had long kept soldiers busy and offered them chances of booty and promotion, posed its own problems. Hadrian addressed these by conducting vigorous exercises, which kept troops on their mettle, and by a huge fortifications programme, of which Hadrian's wall across northern England is only the most famous example. These walls were mostly built by legionaries themselves, so fulfilling the double function of adding to the empire's security while keeping its defenders occupied. But with some 6,000 miles (c.9,600 km) of land frontier, even Rome could not wall them all, and natural frontiers had to be exploited whenever possible. In the shorter term these proved adequate to protect the empire from its external foes, provided that no civil wars distracted the troops, especially when fortifications were supported by colonies of veterans. But certain corners of the empire always posed special problems, which drove even Hadrian to aggressive wars.

Left: Ruins of a milecastle on Hadrian's Wall, England, the most impressively surviving fortified frontier in the empire.

THE DILEMMAS OF DEFENCE

Above: Imperial policy moved decisively on to the defensive under Hadrian, but there was no change in military tactics.

Below: The cardo maximus (High Street) of ancient Gerasa (Jerash), Jordan, one of the many cities that thrived in the 2nd century AD.

For a long time, the Roman empire famously lacked a proper central reserve. The 25 legions Augustus left at his death in AD14 were deliberately dispersed on distant frontiers after inner provinces such as Spain were pacified. They were supplemented by equal numbers of cheaper auxiliaries. The only central force the *princeps* had at his command were the nine Praetorian cohorts, stationed in Italy and in Rome itself. These were crack troops but too few in number (*c.*4,500) to form more than a large bodyguard.

Some military historians have condemned Augustus' policy as a short-sighted economy that left the empire vulnerable to any invasion once the thin perimeter defences of legionary and auxiliary forts had been pierced. Others have condoned it as springing from the Principate's limited finances and the resultingly skimpy army, which had to defend nearly 4,000 miles (6,400km) of frontier with only 300,000 men. Both have argued over the dilemmas of defence: whether it should be preclusive, making invasion impossible by investing all manpower in a heavily fortified border, or whether it should be a defence in depth. This would rely on a massed central reserve swinging into action against intruders but would leave outer provinces exposed as "marcher" territories. The fate of the later empire, however, which had a strong central reserve and also many troops on the perimeter, yet which was finally overwhelmed, suggests that such arguments miss the point.

There was little purpose in having a strong central force stationed at Milan so long as the main power of the army was its heavy infantry, as it was until the late 3rd century AD. Legions with baggage trains could not march more than 15 miles (24km) a day even on Rome's fine roads. Cologne on the Rhine was 67 marching days from Rome, for example, while the journey from Rome to Antioch took 124 days hard marching.

Nor could Romans make much use of marine internal lines of communications. At the heart of the empire, the Mediterranean scarcely offered speedy alternative transport, and the Roman army avoided sea travel wherever possible as it was too risky. The sea could be too rough for travel even within the normal sailing season of April to October, as ancient navigation skills were limited. It could take 55 days to reach Syria by sea – faster than by land but still slow. Logistics argued against a large central reserve, which could not reach a threatened area in time. Instead, troops were withdrawn from one currently peaceful front to fight on another troubled one. This could cause problems – one reason Agricola could not complete his conquest of northern Britain was because Domitian had recalled some of his troops to fight the Dacians – but

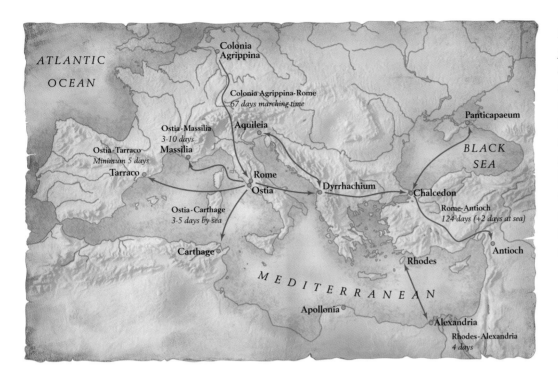

Left: Rome's almost central position in the Mediterranean did not help its military communications as much as might be expected. Moving troops from one frontier to another, whether by land or sea, was generally a slow business – one reason why emperors long dispensed with a central reserve that could not have reached threatened areas in time.

fortunately not more than one frontier was seriously threatened at any one time before the 3rd century AD.

However, the legions of the earlier Principate were *not* usually stationed to hold a fixed perimeter, although auxiliaries might patrol one. Legions were stationed in often indefensible spots so that they could pre-empt, or react to, any attacks before invaders had harmed unprotected lands behind the frontiers. One of Rome's boasts about the *Pax Romana* (Roman peace) was that its citizens had no more need of arms when only a few miles from the frontier than they did in Rome itself. There were, moreover, cogent political reasons for not having a large reserve force, especially one stationed in Italy. Armies were long commanded by legates of senatorial standing – potential rivals for the imperial throne as numerous revolts distracting emperors, from Saturninus in AD89 to Avidius Cassius in AD175, showed. Even without ambitious generals, after the Year of the Four Emperors in AD68–9 the armies grew conscious of their king-making potential. From the 3rd century AD onwards, the soldiers hailed their commanders as emperors with catastrophic frequency.

RESERVE OR BODYGUARD?

Septimius Severus, victor of the civil wars of AD193–7, purged the Praetorian guard, replacing them with his soldiers and stationing a newly created legion, the Second Parthica, near Rome. This created a force of 15,000 men, anticipating a central reserve. In the AD260s, Gallienus created a new reserve at Milan, using mostly cavalry *vexillationes* (detachments) from many legions. By the time this force was established, Gallienus had lost control of much of the empire, while the Danube frontier had collapsed and barbarians were threatening Italy. Milan therefore very nearly *was* the front line. It remained the main western capital after Roman recovery in the 4th century AD. By then, the Tetrarchy had begun a formal division between the *limitanei*, numerous frontier troops, and the *comitatenses*, superior mobile troops. Constantine took this further, concentrating the *comitatenses* and the new elite *palatini* in cities. The central reserve, 150,000 strong, had almost become a gigantic imperial bodyguard.

Below: Septimius Severus (AD193–211), under whom the empire reached its maximum permanent extent, began to create a central reserve by stationing a legion near Rome. But this, even when combined with the purged Praetorian guard, was still little more than a large imperial bodyguard.

NATURAL FRONTIERS
THE RHINE AND UPPER DANUBE

Above: If despotic and paranoid at home, Domitian (AD81–96) pursued a vigorous expansionist policy in south-west Germany.

The problems that faced all Roman imperial governments in the defences of the two key frontiers, the Rhine and Upper Danube, in the late 1st and 2nd centuries AD, derived from the geography of the region. Not long after it leaves Lake Constance, the river Rhine starts to make a reasonably good frontier. Fast-flowing, it soon enters a deep, almost gorge-like valley, navigable by the Roman patrol flotillas. By Mainz, it has become a formidable river and easily defended. But the Danube, most obviously in its early stretches before the Lech joins it, is not remotely such an effective water barrier.

Both rivers' upper reaches tended to freeze over in winter and shrink alarmingly in summer droughts, so making naval patrols often impossible and barbarian crossings all too easy. Even more worrying, the valley of the river Neckar offers enticing pathways up beyond the Danube's source for possible invaders. The land in the south-west corner of Germany is mountainous and well-wooded – the Black Forest still covers much of it today – and is therefore difficult to patrol. The obvious answer, which meant overturning Augustus' famous deathbed advice *"coercendi intra terminos imperii"* (keep within the frontiers of the empire), was to advance the frontier, to cut off the "re-entrant"

angle between the Rhine and Danube and also, incidentally, to shorten the overall frontier by about 170 miles (270km).

The Flavian emperors Vespasian, Titus and Domitian were the first to have the time, energy and perhaps the vision to attempt this. After the serious revolt by Civilis in AD69–70 in the lower Rhine, when many troops went over to the Gallic separatists, the entire Rhine frontier was systematically reorganized. Vespasian began splitting up the legionary camps to avoid concentrating too many soldiers under one general and rebuilding turf and timber fortifications in stone. He also ordered the annexation of the Black Forest, but left this frontier unsecured at its northern end. It was left to Domitian, the least loved of emperors to date (except perhaps by the army), to advance the frontier permanently and effectively.

Domitian's war of AD83–5 against the Chatti tribes, which was much ridiculed by Tacitus, led to the slow but systematic advancing of the frontier across the river Rhine to a line that exploited natural features, the steep rather than high Taunus Mountains and the river Main. This line linked up with Vespasian's Black Forest forts further south, pushing along the Neckar almost to the headwaters of the Danube, so cutting off half the re-entrant and projecting Roman power into central Germany. The land along the lower Main valley was very fertile, useful for feeding garrisons. Later, the Antonine emperors extended the *limes* – a term that had, by the 2nd century AD, come to mean a fortified line of defence, though originally it meant only a path or a boundary – to the Danube near Regensburg (Castra Regina), which was a legionary fortress. The road connecting the two rivers from Mainz to Regensburg became a major imperial highway, shortening the journey to the Danube by 11 vital days. By finally

Below: Hilly and thickly wooded, the Black Forest area remained impenetrable for the Romans until it was finally absorbed into the empire.

closing off this axis of potential invasion, this permitted the romanization of the areas far behind it. Although no real towns grew up within the new province, others lining the Rhine and Danube could now flourish in its shelter.

THE *AGRI DECUMATES*

This territory was known as the *Agri Decumates*, or lands that paid taxes, in contrast to "free Germany" beyond. A part of Upper Germany, the territory remained a militarized zone, but an increasingly prosperous one, defended by the longest and, in some ways, most imposing of all Roman fortifications. These were built mainly – initially entirely – of timber and turf, and included wooden watchtowers – probably with two men in them – every third of a mile (530m). These towers were easily visible to each other down lines cleared of woodland and linked by ditches. Palisades and even

hedges were added under Hadrian. The aim was not to interdict movement across the frontier completely – any more than with Hadrian's Wall – but to slow down and hamper any raiders and smugglers.

Auxiliary cohorts stationed every 5 miles (8km) or so backed them up, some of their forts being built in stone. In total, following the bends of rivers or the lines of hills in a way that makes sense on the ground if not on the map, the line covered some 300 miles (480km) with more than 60 forts and 900 signal towers. In fact this created a larger fortification than Hadrian's Wall, but, due to its mainly timber construction, it has left far fewer visible traces. (One or two forts, such as Zugmantel, have been reconstructed.) In the turmoil of the 3rd century AD, the line became increasingly difficult to hold and it was finally abandoned by AD260. The frontier then returned to its former limits under Augustus.

Above: South-west German reconstruction of a watchtower, typical of the hundreds that guarded the Agri Decumates.

Below: The Agri Decumates reduced the length of the frontier and speeded communications.

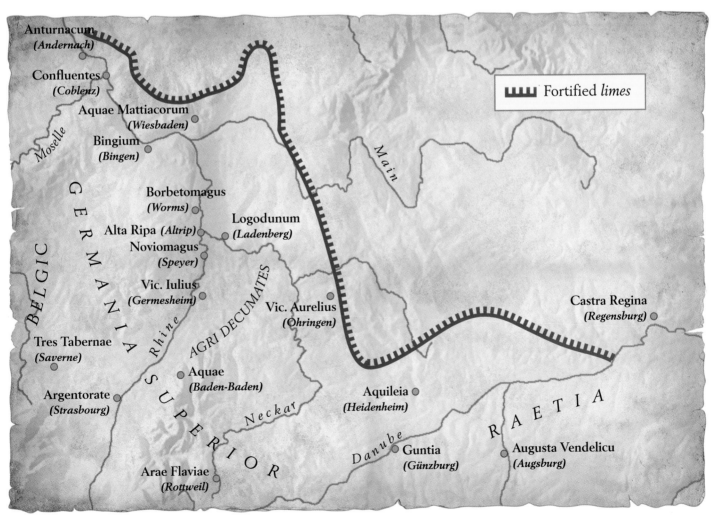

NATURAL FRONTIERS
THE MIDDLE AND LOWER DANUBE

Above: This scene from Trajan's Column in Rome shows Roman soldiers cutting down trees to build fortifications or war machines during the Dacian wars. At times, the army's demands could deforest whole regions.

Augustus had given Rome its longest land frontier – along Europe's longest river – when he occupied all the Danubian lands from the Alps down to the Black Sea. This was for a long time the empire's least developed region. It lacked any real towns or even the rich, if still predominantly agricultural, culture of pre-Roman Gaul and Britain. It was strategically important, however, because it dominated Italy's most accessible passes through the Julian Alps and provided a land route from the eastern empire to the west.

Slowly, the area was organized into provinces. These ran behind the river from Alpine Raetia and Noricum (Switzerland, southern Bavaria/north Austria), through the plains of Pannonia with its large rivers – the Save and Drave as well as the Danube – to Moesia (Bulgaria and northern Serbia). Ultimately, the whole region was to become Rome's prime recruiting ground, providing many great later emperors including Aurelian and Constantine. It was a vital defence against invaders, as

they moved from deepest *barbaricum*, the barbarian world, to the empire. Its final loss foreshadowed the western empire's.

As on the Rhine, Augustus had not originally intended to halt his sweeping conquests on the south or west bank of the river. However, all plans to occupy part of Bohemia (so creating a new line along the Elbe down to the North Sea) had to be aborted after a major revolt in Pannonia and Dalmatia that started in AD6. Coupled with Varus' German disaster in AD9, this marked the end of Augustan expansionism, although the huge Danubian basin remained relatively lightly garrisoned. In the 1st century AD it had only six legions – two of them initially in Dalmatia rather than on the river – compared to the eight on the much shorter Rhine frontier.

Diplomacy (always a major part of Rome's defence), coupled with bribes, kept the various nomadic tribes and peoples of the Pannonian plain divided and harmless; the Iazyges were often paid to keep the menacing Dacians in check.

Right: Rome's long and potentially most dangerous frontier was the Danube, beyond which lay the immensity of the Eurasian steppes, source of endless new invasions. From the early 2nd century AD, this frontier required ever-larger garrisons. Once across its perimeter defences, barbarians could easily penetrate into Italy, as happened in AD166 and on many subsequent occasions.

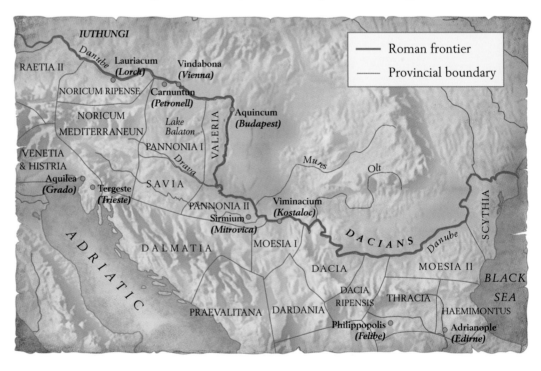

Right: Marcus Aurelius (AD161–80) whose trans-Danbian plans expired with him.

However, when Decebalus, a formidable ruler, became High King of Dacia in *c.*AD85, his country's potential was quickly mobilized. Heavy raids across the Danube into Pannonia generated a quick, if initially unsuccessful, Roman reaction. Domitian's wars with Dacia led to a truce that was more in Dacia's favour than Rome's, due to Saturninus' revolt in AD89. Domitian not only paid Decebalus a subsidy, which was common enough practice, but also lent him engineers to fortify his capital of Sarmizagetusa Regia, which was nothing of the sort. In the following years the Iazyges, a nomadic people, became a problem too, raiding across the Danube and requiring Rome's finally successful attentions. Trajan's great conquest of Dacia in AD101–6 needs, therefore, to be seen in the light of a breakdown of the whole earlier system. Its success can be gauged by the 60 years of prosperous peace that followed. Flotillas – one on either side of the Iron Gates Gorge, which divided the Danube – helped keep the river free of intruders, turning it into a useful waterway as much as an effective barrier.

MARCUS AURELIUS'S CAMPAIGNS

The plague that devastated the empire from AD166 after the triumphant Parthian campaign (which itself had drawn off whole legions from the Rhine and Danube), gave the barbarians their chance. The Germanic Marcomanni and Quadi and the Iazyges crossed the lightly defended river and pushed on, bypassing forts, into Italy, attacking Aquileia (near Trieste) in AD167. For the first time in 260 years, barbarians were in Italy. Other barbarians opportunistically pushed through the Balkans to sack Eleusis, on the doorstep of Athens.

Marcus Aurelius, despite the plague and acute financial problems, raised two fresh legions (from gladiators among others), sold even the palace ornaments to pay for them and went north to repel the invaders. His long and hard campaigns along the Danube drove them back over the river. He now decided to copy Trajan, not out of vainglory – he was after all a philosopher – but from necessity. He probably intended to create new provinces of Marcomannia (the Czech Republic) and Sarmatia (Slovakia/Galicia). By advancing the frontiers, Rome would be able to meet the barbarian tide on the far side of the Carpathian and the Sudeten mountains. Whether his great project would have succeeded if the revolt of Avidius Cassius in Syria in AD175 had not distracted him and he himself had not died in AD180 is unclear. What is certain is that the Danube basin in the 3rd century became a key area for barbarian attacks. However, it had also become so deeply Romanized that it was a source of strength as well as weakness, right down to the fall of the western empire in the 5th century.

Below: A model of the key Dacian fortress of Bildaru in the mountains of Transylvania captured by Trajan's men.

NATURAL FRONTIERS
AFRICA, ARABIA, MESOPOTAMIA

Rome had desert frontiers in Arabia, Mesopotamia and North Africa. In Asia, Rome faced sporadic Arab raiders and its one equal, the Parthian, later Sassanid Persian, empire. In Africa, Rome often faced little – often no – opposition, for the deserts of Libya harboured only nugatory populations of Berber nomads. Egypt was almost impregnable behind its deserts, except from Asia, for upstream the Nubians – as Rome called the Sudanese – were no threat.

Cyrenaica and Tripolitania (Libya) may have needed almost no defence, but Roman Africa, that thin slice of the great continent seldom more than 100 miles (160km) deep, was an increasingly important province. Dry-farming employed a cunning combination of olive

trees and wheat fields. It used every drop of moisture through irrigation and, by so holding back the desert, beneficially modified the climate. Africa satisfied much of Rome's demand for olive oil. Josephus described it as "that third part of the world, which feeds the city of Rome for eight months of the year and happily accepts taxation, although only one legion is stationed there".

For the Berbers it was worth raiding. To protect against their attacks, which generally followed the Atlas valleys as they ran down towards Carthage and its intensely fertile hinterland, a series of walls called *clausurae* (closures) were built. Some 15ft (4.5m) high, they closed off the valleys or at least made it extremely difficult for such invaders to return with

Below: The ruins of the triple arch at Lambaesis (Tazoult, Algeria), built by Septimius Severus (AD193–211). The Libyan-born emperor was particularly interested in North Africa, embellishing its cities and advancing the frontiers.

much booty. A joint letter from eastern and western emperors (Theodosius II and Honorius), written in AD409, indicates that Africa mattered to both parts of the empire. It also shows that there were *fossata* (ditch works) and *limites* (fortified lines) further south, where fertile land gives way to desert, with watchtowers.

Archaeology has tentatively confirmed this skeletal defence system, which exploited the *chotts* (sand seas, at times full of salt water) and mountains of the Haut Plateaux. Running from east to west, these were the *limes* of Tripoli, the *limes* of Numidia, inland from Carthage, and the *limes* of Mauretania, inland from the Algerian coast. None of these was a solid continuous defence like Hadrian's Wall, because the distances were too immense. Hadrian had ordered the construction of such a line on his visit to Africa in AD128. He realized that nomads and farmers were interdependent: nomads supplied useful extra seasonal labour, farmers repaid them with food-stuffs. The one legion was stationed at Lambaesis, just behind the central *limes*. Later, under Septimius Severus, forts were built much further inland. In Tripolitania Ghadames, some 300 miles (480km) inland, was the most advanced of four forts, built in AD200 and abandoned around AD263. Such forts were intended to control desert routes.

THE EASTERN FRONTIERS

Until Vespasian began annexing them, a screen of client states shielded the Roman provinces from the Arabian desert. But when Trajan took over Arabia Petraea (Jordan) in AD106, the problem of patrolling the edges of the Arabian desert confronted the Romans directly. Trajan built the Via Nova (new road), a military highway from the Gulf of Aqaba north-east past Bostra and Damascus. This was a patrolled *limes* in the old sense of a dividing line with forts built along it, from which cavalry patrolled. The Arabs were more numerous raiders than the Berbers – and in the 7th century AD became

invaders – but did not at this time pose a major threat to the blooming wheat fields of Transjordania. Later, Septimius pushed the frontier 50 miles (80km) east from the Via Nova, but it was further north that he made his major contribution, almost solving the perennial frontier problem with Parthia.

He did this by annexing upper Mesopotamia. Here his new frontier ran along the Khabur river, a small tributary joining the Euphrates 50 miles (80km) north of the key fortress of Dura-Europus, then running along the hills of Jebel Sinjar. These rise to 4,800ft (1,460m) above the desert – high enough to receive 8in (20cm) of rain a year, vital for supplying garrisons. Septimius probably stationed a legion at Singara on this line, and he certainly fortified Nisibis to its rear. His military road ran on to the Tigris at Eski Mosul (old Mosul). Here a walled city 3 miles (4.8km) in circumference was built, the easternmost limit of Rome's might. It would need a change of dynasty in Ctesiphon before such a powerful line would be challenged, and it lasted as long as the empire itself.

Above: The ruins of Dura-Europus on the Euphrates in Syria, once a vital fortress on Rome's eastern frontier. Captured by the Persians c.AD256 after a long siege, it was so badly damaged that it has never been reoccupied.

Below: These laws about the development of Roman lands in Africa are dated AD209.

COLONIES AND SETTLEMENTS FOR VETERANS

Below: Colonies, originally planned chiefly for legionary veterans, were established right across the empire from the time of Julius Caesar onwards. They acted as a backup to regular legions and, more crucially if less intentionally, helped Romanize the empire. Colonies like York and Cologne later became important cities.

From the mid-Republic, Rome had expanded its power by the planting of colonies in strategically important places, first in peninsular Italy, then in Cisalpine Gaul. Originally, these *coloniae* were always settlements of Roman citizens with a standard Roman city constitution, but later some had only Latin rights, a halfway house to full citizenship that proved very useful in the Principate. All helped knit the empire together.

Gaius Gracchus had first proposed planting a colony for landless Romans outside Italy at Carthage, an idea revived by Saturninus in 102BC for the veterans of Marius' armies for North Africa, southern Gaul and Greece. However, it was Julius Caesar who started founding colonies for his veterans on a massive

scale: in Spain, where the charter of Urso (Colonia Genetiva Julia) survives and where older cities such as Cartagena and Tarragona became full Roman colonies; in Gaul, at Fréjus (Forum Julii) and Arles (Arelate); at Carthage and Corinth (both ruins since 146BC) and in Greece, Syria and even on the Black Sea coast. Many of these had strategic value.

Augustus, who reputedly had 300,000 veterans to find land for after Actium in 31BC, founded about 75 settlements. Twenty-eight were in Italy, such as Turin (Augusta Taurinorum), whose fine gate survives, and Aosta (Augusta Praetoria), facing the Alps. He stressed in the *Res Gestae*, his memoirs, that he paid fair prices for the land. More were scattered across the empire: Mérida and Zaragossa

(Caesar-Augusta) in Spain; Nîmes and Avignon in Gaul; Patras and Nicopolis (near Actium, "city of victory") in Greece; and on round the empire, in Africa, Macedonia, Syria, Galatia (north central Turkey) and Pisidia (central/south-west Turkey). Some were built for defence, such as those in Galatia and Pisidia, while others became thriving cities. Tarragona claimed to have a population of 400,000 in the 2nd century AD – which is probably an exaggeration, although it was the capital of the whole Iberian peninsula and a centre of the imperial cult.

All these generally small settlements – usually a couple of thousand veterans, growing perhaps into a city of between 10–15,000 – helped the urbanization and Romanization of the whole empire. Their elderly soldier-citizens could theoretically provide reinforcements to legionary forts and more certainly provided potential recruits for the next generation's legions. As they became permanent, some of the great military bases around the frontiers developed into towns with their outlying *canabae* (settlements). Sometimes, as at Cologne (Colonia Agrippina) in AD51, a colony was founded on the Rhine's west bank to incorporate these. In eastern Algeria, a Trajanic veterans' colony at Timgad (Thamugadi), has remained almost perfectly preserved, its porticoes and arches looking out over a now desiccated but once very fertile landscape.

PROUD TO BE ROMAN

As the colonies became established, they developed a competitive pride in being Roman. Local aristocracies, especially in the west – the long-Hellenized east was rather different – vied to become Roman in clothes, deed and name. Men whose fathers had been Gaulish chieftains began taking Roman triple names and their sons began to think of themselves as Romans. In Vienne (Vienna) on the banks of the Rhône, for example, Strabo reported early in the 1st century AD that "the Allobroges used to be always at war but now they

farm the plains and valleys, living in villages except for their nobles who live in Vienne. That was once a village... but now they have made it into a city." Italians began settling there as early as 70BC, and a century later Claudius could praise it as *ornatissima et valentissima colonia* (an excellent, flourishing colony). Up river on the other side, its rival Lyons (Lugdunum, the "dun" recalling a Celtic origin) had a theatre for 11,000 spectators, an odeon for more select audiences seating 5,000 and a large, centrally heated basilica. Lyons prospered at the centre of Gaul's Roman road network.

Further north, the city of Trier (Augusta Treverorum) became a centre of industry and commerce where the tribe of the Treveri settled and became fully Romanized. A school of sculpture also developed there. The city later became the capital of Gaul, at times of all the west, with a basilica, baths and palaces. In Britain, the tiny but fully self-governing *colonia* of Gloucester (Glevum) was founded under emperor Nerva (AD96–8), joining Lincoln and Colchester in this prized status. More populous was nearby Cirencester (Corinium), which boasted the full range of civic amenities although it was not a *colonia*. Hadrian gave Latin rights to many settlements, whereby all members of their councils as well as their decurions (officials) received Roman citizenship. In this way, Roman civilization and citizenship were spread.

Above: The ruins of the theatre at Bostra, now in Syria, which thrived after Trajan annexed Arabia Petraea, making it the capital.

Below: An evening view of Timgad, Algeria, in what was then a very fertile province.

THE JEWISH REVOLT

Above: Perhaps the most holy of the religious treasures that the Romans brought back from their sack of the Temple in Jerusalem was the seven-branched candlestick, here shown on the Arch of Titus in Rome being paraded in triumph by soldiers.

Below: The bitter siege and total destruction of Jerusalem by Titus in AD70 led to the permanent ruin of the Temple restored by Herod, and so to the last stage in the Jewish Diaspora that had begun centuries earlier.

Uniquely among the disparate peoples of the empire, the Jews refused to accept the Graeco-Roman culture all around them, proudly aware that they had a tradition to rival it. The Romans, despite initial good intentions and a total lack of racist feeling, could not understand a people so different, in their exclusive monotheism, from any of their other subjects. Set between the wealthy provinces of Syria and Egypt, Judaea was too strategically important to be ignored, however. The Jewish Diaspora, which had started some three centuries before following the conquests of Alexander the Great, meant that Jews were already spread across the eastern part of the empire, and there was a Jewish community in Rome by Julius Caesar's time.

Herod the Great, who died in 4BC, had pursued a pro-Roman and Hellenizing policy. His kingdom came under direct Roman rule as a procuratorial province in AD6 because his less than competent successors quarrelled among themselves. Many of their Jewish subjects (Jews were not the only inhabitants of the kingdom, Hellenized Syrians being numerous) objected strongly to the house of Herod but did little, being divided: Samaritans versus Judaeans, reformist Pharisees against Sadducees, with the Zealots as politically active extremists. However, when Rome gradually found itself ruling almost the whole area after the death of Herod Agrippa II in AD44, Jewish resentment was unified against the hated occupier. The troubled province of Judaea, one of the least popular posts for an equestrian governor, does seem to have been unusually badly administered.

A revolt finally broke out in AD66. It was centred on south Judaea and Jerusalem. The governor of Syria, Cestius Gallus, hastening south from Antioch with inadequate forces, was heavily defeated and beat a retreat. Encouraged by his defeat, other Jews now joined the revolt. The emperor Nero, who had become deeply suspicious of military rivals, entrusted the suppression of the revolt to Vespasian, an officer long out of favour but one who had had a good record of storming forts 20 years before in Britain. Vespasian proved a brilliant choice, methodically putting down the rebels, in particular reducing the fortress of Jotapata in Galilee under its Jewish commander, Josephus. By building a huge mound to approach its walls, the three legions involved were able to overwhelm the defenders, especially after Josephus changed sides. At this stage, however, Vespasian was distracted by the Civil War of AD68–9 and went to Alexandria to organize his empire-winning campaign. He left his son Titus to finish suppressing the Jews.

THE SIEGE OF JERUSALEM

By AD70, Titus had closed in on Jerusalem. Heavily fortified and ornamented by Herod the Great, the city was divided into five separately walled parts. It had been well provisioned, but fighting between rival groups of fanatics

led to much of their food being burnt. Only at the very last minute did the Jewish factions cease fighting each other. The Old Upper City had Herod's huge palace on its west flank and just north-east of it lay the massively walled Temple Enclosure, with the Second Quarter and the larger New City to its north. Titus had four legions at his disposal, enough men to surround the whole city with a siege wall.

Although the defenders made aggressive sorties to attack the Romans, the final outcome was never in doubt. But at first the Romans' earthworks were undermined by the energetic defenders and collapsed. After rebuilding these and a further 13 days' fierce fighting, the Romans entered the less heavily defended New City and pushed on, breaking through the wall of the Second Quarter to attack the great fortress of Antonia (named after Mark Antony), which immediately adjoined the Temple. This required two new ramps. It fell only when the defenders' tunnels, meant to cause the collapse of these Roman works, actually

Below: The Arch of Titus, emperor AD79–81, was built to commemorate his victory in the Jewish war of ten years earlier.

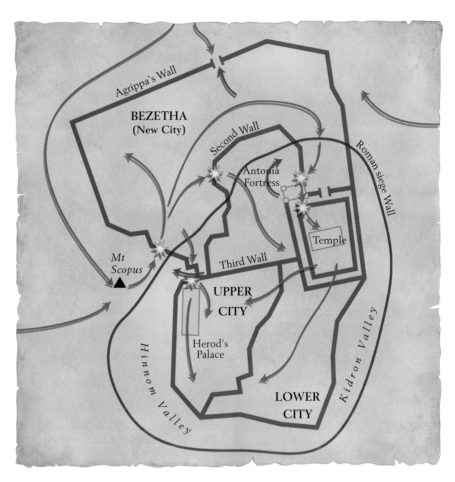

undermined their own walls. A small group of legionaries then scaled the walls and killed the sentries, before sounding their trumpets to tell Titus to start the attack on the fort's inner walls. Weeks of heavy fighting were required to capture the Temple itself, which was burnt to the ground (perhaps accidentally). The loss of this great building, so central to Judaism, disheartened the defenders, but they fought on heroically. The Upper City was the very last to fall. After 18 days of preparation, during which legionaries and auxiliaries raised mounds on the west and east sides respectively, the Romans renewed their assault and finally stormed the area around the palace. The whole city was then pillaged before being systematically set on fire. During the five-month siege, the defenders had become so famished that, according to Josephus, mothers had eaten their own children. Titus ordered that just three towers and part of the wall be left, as poignant reminders of the ruined city.

Above: The siege and capture of Jerusalem in AD70 by the Romans under Titus was the crucial engagement of the Jewish revolt. The five-month siege saw the Romans circumvallating the city as usual. They attacked the less well-defended New Town first, before moving upwards and inwards, firing the Temple and finally taking the Upper City, sparing no one in the city.

THE SIEGE OF MASADA

Above: An aerial view of one of the camps in the circumvallation at Masada, Israel, where several hundred Jewish zealots defied the Romans under Falvius Silva until AD73. Today, the desert site remains almost perfectly preserved due to its remoteness and aridity.

The last chapter in the bloody Jewish revolt of AD66–73 was the siege of Masada, which required one legion and 4,000 auxiliaries to suppress it. Famous because of its site, Masada is a rock rising some 1,300ft (396m) above a high, arid plateau, surrounded by precipitous cliffs that make it seem impregnable above the great valley of the Dead Sea. Herod the Great had converted it into a fortified palace and place of refuge, but by AD70 it was occupied by just a few hundred extremists, called the Sicarii. The fort was equipped with deep water cisterns and storerooms containing such vast amounts of food that it could not easily be starved out. Flavius Silva, legate of the Tenth Legion, therefore decided on a direct assault. This would make a dramatic statement about Rome's power and the perils of challenging it. It has left the most graphic and complete evidence of Roman siege warfare of any site.

The legionaries built a wall of local stone some 4,700yd (4,300m) long with towers every 30yd (27m) or so to circumvallate the rock, plus eight forts for themselves, inside which they built low-walled cabins. Across the tops of these they put their leather tents, for protection against the blazing midday sun and the bitterly cold night winds of the three-year siege. They then built a huge ramp up the west side of the hill and winched their siege engines up it. Realizing that they could not escape, the Sicarii men committed mass suicide, after killing all their women and children. This finally ended the revolt – at least according to Josephus, the rebel leader turned Roman, who was, however, not an impartial observer.

BAR KOCHBA'S REBELLION

The fall of Masada did not, however, end simmering Jewish discontent with Roman rule across the eastern Mediterranean. Even before Trajan's grand attack on the Parthian empire faltered in AD117, a huge Jewish revolt in Cyrenaica, Cyprus and Egypt had flared up in AD115. More than 200,000 Greek-speaking neighbours of the Jews in these countries were reportedly

Right: The fortress–palace built by Herod the Great on the northern side of Masada as a place of refuge in case his subjects ever turned against him. Herod never needed it, but his fortifications helped the Sicarii defy Rome until the very end of the Jewish revolt.

ROME AND THE JEWS

Looking at Rome's repeated suppression of Jewish revolts, we might imagine that the Romans were deeply anti-Semitic. Nothing could be less true. As the cases of Herod Agrippa, a close friend of the emperor Claudius, St Paul – a Jewish Roman citizen – and especially of Flavius Josephus demonstrate, the Romans were not racist in any modern sense. Nor were they religiously intolerant like many later Christian persecutors of Jews. In general, the Romans were indifferent to racial and religious differences, despite having a certain distaste for unwashed, drunken Germans. Their crushings of Jewish rebellions were always politically motivated, carried out with their usual brutality so as to discourage others.

The Romans first encountered the Jews in the mid-2nd century BC. They had just revolted against the Seleucid Hellenistic monarchs of Syria, who had tried to enforce the cult of Zeus (Jupiter) at Jerusalem. Out of distrust for the Seleucids, Rome supported this Maccabean revolt and Judaea became independent with Roman approval. The Romans were at first impressed, if puzzled, by the conservatism of Jewish religious beliefs and social customs, and they tried to accommodate them. Jews were generally exempted from emperor worship – such worship was a political rather than religious act – and military service was seldom forced on Jews for the same reason. A few Romans, attracted by its highly ethical message, converted to Judaism in the 1st century AD before the spread of Christianity. However, Jews were by then scattered so widely across the empire – in Syria, Egypt, Asia Minor (Turkey), Cyrenaica (Libya), Cyprus and even Rome itself – that Rome was inevitably drawn into many local Jewish–Gentile quarrels.

killed before the Romans managed to repress it. Yet this was still not quite the end of the Jewish–Roman wars.

Hadrian was among Rome's wisest and most humane emperors. He probably envisaged the empire becoming an equal commonwealth of all its provinces rather than being ruled just for Rome's sake. However, as a passionate philhellene (lover of Greece), he did not understand why any people should not want to participate in the splendours of Graeco-Roman culture. He therefore established a Roman colony at Jerusalem, which he renamed Aelia Capitolina, building a temple to Zeus/Jupiter on the very site of the ruined Temple. This so enraged the Jews still living in Palestine that in AD133 they rose again under Bar Kochba, a talented general, and proclaimed their own state. It took the Romans years of bitter, small-scale fighting to suppress this revolt, after which Jews were banned from Jerusalem. Later, Antoninus Pius (reigned AD138–61) quietly revoked his predecessor's decree and allowed any Jews, who wished to, to return to the now utterly desolate site of Jerusalem.

Above: Storehouses and deep wells inside the fort of Masada. It was so well supplied that the Romans could not hope to starve it quickly into surrender.

Below: Remains of the Jewish fortification at Masada. Behind its walls, Zealots called the Sicarii retreated, thinking they had made themselves impregnable to all attacks.

CHAPTER XII

DECLINE AND FALL

Few historical topics are more fascinating than the decline and fall of world-conquering powers. In Rome's case this took centuries rather than years. The empire had survived a near-total collapse in the 3rd century AD and even the 5th century AD saw only the fall of the western half of the empire – and half of that was recovered by the eastern empire in the 6th century AD. The story is much more complicated than one of inexorable decay.

Although there were a handful of brilliant or exceptional barbarian leaders, notably Attila the Hun and Gaiseric the Vandal, most of the barbarians who overran the empire in the 5th century AD were not especially formidable. Similar tribes had already tried to invade the empire in the preceding centuries and been repulsed, albeit at an often huge cost. This suggests that the fall of the western half of the empire might have been averted by intelligent, consistent and, above all, unified strong government. But the imperial rulers' record in the 5th century AD is one of indecision, feebleness and above all of suicidal disputes, as internecine fighting squandered Rome's remaining strength in civil wars. It was hardly surprising that some, although never all, of the brightest and the best citizens of the western half of the Roman world finally lost faith and hope in their government, turning instead to the City of God to be found only in heaven.

Left: Sacrificing to the pagan gods – a political as well as religious gesture that vexed an increasingly Christian empire.

THE 3RD-CENTURY CRISIS

Above: The reign of the perverted emperor Elagabalus drew Rome further into her 3rd-century AD crisis.

Below: The Emperor Decius addresses his troops. He became the first Roman emperor to be killed (by the Goths) in battle in AD251, setting an ominous precedent.

In some ways it is remarkable that the Roman Empire survived the 3rd century AD at all. The civil wars, foreign invasions, plagues and other calamities it suffered for more than half a century after 235AD would have been enough to cause the terminal disintegration of most empires. But centripetal patriotism, a loyalty to the idea as much as to the reality of Rome, proved in the end just strong enough to ensure the empire's survival, for a while. It survived, however, in a different form and at a price that grew steadily more crushing, financially, socially and politically.

Cracks in the golden surface of the *Pax Romana*, the Roman peace, had appeared as early as the reign of Marcus Aurelius (AD161–80). The plague – possibly smallpox – which the victorious legions brought back with them from Parthia in AD165, devastated the empire and kept recurring for years. Combined with a series of invasions, primarily but not exclusively along the Danubian frontier – even Egypt suffered a brief

attack – followed by the long debauchery of Commodus' reign, this epidemic hit an already somewhat sclerotic empire. The empire's economy had almost certainly started to stagnate by the mid-2nd century AD; by the century's end it was probably contracting.

Far worse, however, were the civil wars that followed Commodus' assassination in AD192. Septimius Severus finally won the civil wars in AD197 but at a terrible cost, both military and economic. Both Severus' and his enemy Albinus' armies had huge casualties in the last campaign. In these wars, trained Roman soldiers were killed fighting each other, a loss the empire could no longer easily make up. Severus, a brutally vindictive man, sacked Lugdunum (Lyons) so thoroughly it never recovered its wealth or status as Gaul's prime city. By comparison with his thuggish son Caracalla, he was an ideal ruler, but the latter's murder brought no improvement for there followed the reign of the manic pervert Elagabalus.

The murder of the last Severan, the ineffectual Alexander, in AD235, is usually taken to mark the end of the Principate and its replacement by mere anarchy. The year AD238 saw the coinage of seven distinct emperors and there were at least 50 claimants to the imperial throne in the half century after AD235. Some of these formed wholly separate states, such as the Gallic, British and Spanish empire of Postumus.

The problem of the succession, always tricky in the crypto-monarchy that was the Principate, became crucial in the ensuing chaos. Of the 27 or so "regular" emperors, 17 were killed by their own troops or officers, two were forced to commit suicide, one died a natural death and the rest were killed in battle. Even outstandingly successful and popular emperors such as Aurelian (AD270–75) were murdered. The custom by which the Senate had sanctioned (even if it did

not always control) the choice of the next emperor became an outmoded farce. Elevation to the imperial purple became effectively a deferred death sentence.

The barbarian peoples outside the empire had long been waiting for an opportunity to renew their raids. Now, with the Romans at each other's throats, they saw and seized it. Tarragona and Athens, both many hundreds of miles from a frontier, were sacked in the AD260s. Once barbarians had penetrated the outer frontier defences, Rome's good roads facilitated their raids, now that there were no longer forces waiting to repel them. The interior cities, with their long-disarmed citizens and no tradition of self-defence, were easy prey. Soldiers had to be called in to build many of the walls for the cities in Gaul, for example.

ECONOMIC CRISIS
This damage to life across the provinces far beyond the traditional frontier zones proved hard to repair. At the same time the increase in the size and cost of the army meant a steep rise in taxes. Septimius Severus had increased Rome's military strength to 400,000 men and raised the army's pay by 50 per cent – perhaps an overdue rise, but Caracalla raised their pay again by another 50 per cent. To pay

for this and subsequent increases, Caracalla debased the coinage, a custom followed by so many of his successors that money became almost worthless. By the mid-3rd century AD, many traders and bankers were refusing to accept Roman coins. The armies resorted to exacting goods and services from the unfortunate civilians they were supposedly protecting.

The economic results were grim but are unquantifiable, for it was an economically ignorant age. It is estimated that at least 15 per cent of all arable land went out of production in the mid-3rd century AD. (Egypt, however, was probably thriving, and archaeological evidence from North Africa also suggests a period of economic prosperity.) But city life, especially in the west, also suffered terribly. The walls Aurelian gave Rome covered most of its existing urban area, but other cities shrank drastically. Within them, the old decurion class of local officials, who had been in many ways the backbone of the empire, began to collapse beneath an increasing burden of taxes. Those rich enough to do so withdrew to self-sufficient country estates; the less wealthy sank back into the urban poor. No matter what the tetrarchs and their heirs attempted, the blow to civic life, especially in the west, was to prove irreparable.

Above: Relatively unharmed by the 3rd-century crisis, North Africa still prospered, building amphitheatres such as this at El Djem, Tunisia.

Below: Philip the Arab (AD244–9) was the emperor who celebrated Rome's millennium in AD248, but it was not a timely celebration. The empire appeared to be collapsing. Barbarians had broken through on almost every frontier, while anarchy spread inside the empire.

THE EASTERN PROBLEM
THE POWER OF THE SASSANIDS

Above: The power of the Sassanids of Persia lay in their cavalry. This cataphract *(armoured horseman) charging with his lance formed the backbone of the army, although their lack of stirrups limited their impact.*

Below: This citadel, called the Redoubt, overlooks the river Euphrates in Syria at Dura-Europus on the two empires' much-disputed frontier. Both the Romans and the Persians appear to have occupied this citadel at different times.

For nearly two and a half centuries after the battle of Actium, Rome could regard the defence of its eastern frontier along the mid-Euphrates as something of an optional extra. The Arsacid Parthian empire facing it across the upper Euphrates may have been very large (it covered modern Iraq, Iran and parts of south Afghanistan), but it was seldom formidable, except when on the defensive. The Parthian empire's loose semi-feudal structure meant that its sub-kings did not always rally to help their nominal overlord.

Despite this, the Parthians had repelled Roman invaders from Crassus to Trajan, but they never seriously threatened Syria, the Roman province closest to them. Septimius Severus' campaigns in the AD190s again showed up Parthian weakness – he sacked Ctesiphon and annexed upper Mesopotamia, establishing a very defensible frontier province. However, he also unwittingly damaged the prestige of the Arsacid dynasty so badly that it succumbed to Ardashir, a Sassanid prince, in AD224.

The Sassanids came from the province of Persis (Fars). Guardians of Persepolis, Iran's ancient royal city, they were determined to revive the glories of the Achaemenid Persian empire of Darius and Xerxes. This had once extended west as far as the Aegean, so major conflict with Rome seemed inevitable. Early clashes were inconclusive, however. Neither Alexander Severus nor Gordian III were good generals, but their armies, ably officered, managed to avoid defeat, at least according to Roman sources.

The Sassanid army consisted of heavy cavalry – cataphracts, mainly noblemen and their supporters, who charged using lances – supplemented by numerous mounted archers. The Romans commented admiringly on the disciplined skill of these archers, which rivalled that of the legionaries' and was well suited to desert terrain. Persian infantry was of little use, but the Sassanids at times employed Indian elephants to great psychological, if not military, effect. Above all, the Sassanids developed a professional siege corps, something the Parthians had lacked but which was essential for attacking the walled cities of Mesopotamia and Syria. The Sassanids also revived the old Zoroastrian religion, a form of monotheism that stressed martial values and gave their empire a strong ideological basis.

In AD241 Shapur I succeeded to the throne (the Sassanids generally followed the hereditary principle) and began calling himself "King of Kings of Iran and non-Iran", a universalist title to challenge that of Rome. His reign of 32 years outlasted those of 16 Roman emperors. His western offensives began with forcing the new emperor, Philip the Arab, to make a humiliating peace in AD244. His second offensive in AD256 ended with the capture of 37 Roman cities,

Above: The "Arch of Chosroes" stands in the ruins of the audience hall of the Sassanian palace of Ctesiphon, near Baghdad, Iraq.

including Dura-Europus (which fell after an epic siege *c*.AD256) and Antioch, capital of the Roman east. All survivors were carried off into captivity. The emperor Valerian took a huge army of 70,000 men east to repel Shapur but it was hit by plague and cornered in Edessa. Valerian was captured and spent the rest of his life as a prisoner of the Persians, used as a human footstool by Shapur when the Persian king mounted his horse. After his death, Valerian's stuffed body was hung on the walls of a temple. The capture alive of a Roman emperor was an unprecedented humiliation for the empire but one that Gallienus, Valerian's son, was powerless to avenge.

The whole Roman east then seemed about to fall into Shapur's hands, as his forces overran Asia Minor and threatened Egypt. Fortunately for Rome, Shapur snubbed Odenathus, king of Palmyra, while returning to Persia in AD261. This proved a huge mistake. Odenathus accepted a Roman command. Palmyrene cavalry, perhaps the best in the east, now turned against Persia and Persian forces had to retreat for a time.

It would be a mistake to suppose that the Persians were always invincible. They had difficulty maintaining their conquests beyond the Euphrates so far from their Iranian power base. They could also be defeated in open battle, as Galerius, the Caesar of Diocletian, showed. After an initial defeat, Galerius triumphed over the Persian monarch, Narses, in AD298, annexing a useful slice of land beyond the Tigris. The subsequent peace lasted for 40 years.

JULIAN'S DEFEAT

Under Constantine and his successors, the peace unravelled. Constantius II spent much time in the AD340s fighting the Persians before turning west to deal with Roman rivals. The Persians then renewed the offensive, capturing the well-fortified city of Amida in AD359; they had been intending to bypass it until a catapult bolt killed the son of a client king and so forced them to attack. Julian, on becoming sole emperor in AD361, decided to avenge this defeat and crush Persia. After his defeat and death, half of Rome's territories east of the Euphrates were ceded to Persia by the new emperor Jovian in return for safe passage home. Oddly, the peace that followed lasted, with only minor disruptions, for 140 years.

Below: When the Sassanid Persian empire replaced the Parthians in c. *AD226, Rome faced far greater pressure on its eastern frontier. The Persians penetrated deep into Roman territory in the 3rd century AD, but the Romans counter-attacked later, pushing across the upper Tigris. Julian's invasion of AD363, intended to finish off the Persians, ended in defeat with Rome having to cede half Roman (upper) Mesopotamia. From then on the frontier remained relatively stable.*

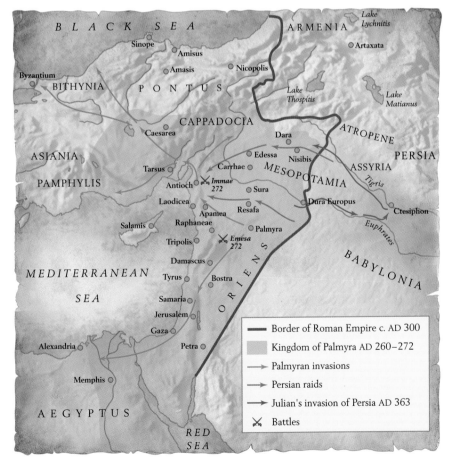

FOREIGN INVASIONS
FRANKS, GOTHS, ALAMANNI, HUNS

Above: A Visigoth chieftain on horseback leading his men. Not all Visigoths were mounted, but their cavalry was more formidable than that of earlier German tribes.

Below: This sarcophagus from the 3rd century AD shows Romans and Germans fighting hand to hand. By this time, Rome's earlier superb military discipline could no longer automatically be relied upon to win the day.

For more than two centuries the Romans under the Principate had faced generally quite small barbarian tribes who, if at times fierce and tough fighters, were seldom any real match for Roman arms or diplomacy. The latter, along with judicious subsidies or bribes, generally kept most tribes divided against each other or within themselves.

However, centuries of living so close to a far more united and powerful state began to have an effect on the tribes inside Germany. By the 3rd century AD, the older, smaller tribes such as the Chatti and Cherusci had coalesced into two far more potentially threatening groups: the Alamanni in southern Germany, whose name means "all men", and the Franks on the lower Rhine, whose name means "free men". These were loose confederations of similar tribes, rather than unitary kingdoms, but they would combine for the specific purpose of attacking the Roman empire.

THE GOTHS

More formidable were other new peoples who emerged in the 3rd and 4th centuries AD, most notably the Goths. Probably originating in southern Sweden, they migrated slowly south-east (too far east for Rome's knowledge) into the southern Ukraine. The Goths finally burst upon the Roman world in AD245 when they crossed the Danube delta and raided Moesia. Soon they were pushing further south into Thrace (European Turkey and north-east Greece), and in AD251 the emperor Decius went to repel them. He was unsuccessful and became the first emperor to be killed in battle. Emboldened, the Goths renewed their raids over the next 17 years, at times even taking to the sea and ravaging the Mediterranean.

At this stage, most barbarians were after loot and plunder, not lands to occupy. The Goths were crushingly defeated by the emperor Gallienus, at the head of his new cavalry corps, at Nish in Serbia in AD268, losing 50,000 men. Subsequently, the Ostrogoth half of the federation – their name probably means east Goths – retreated to the Ukrainian steppes. There they became formidable horsemen, creating a kingdom stretching from the Don to the Vistula, while their Visigothic cousins established a smaller adjacent kingdom north of the Carpathians. Although it is now known that the Goths did not have stirrups, so useful for heavy horsemen, they were far more effective cavalry than any the Romans had hitherto faced in Europe and posed a threat of a new order. However, for the time being they seemed settled along the north of the Black Sea. The Vandals were a Germanic tribe similar to the Goths, fewer in number but, it later turned out, even more opportunistic under the right leader.

Left: From the mid-3rd century AD on, Rome found itself facing new, much more formidable, groups of barbarian invaders than earlier. Some, such as the Franks and Alamanni in Germany, were coalitions of older tribes, but others, such as the Goths, were totally new peoples. These invaders penetrated frontier defences depleted by Roman civil wars to reach and sack cities as far afield as Tarragona in the west or Athens in the east. The emperor Gallienus' seemingly crushing defeat of the Goths at Nish in AD268 merely checked the invasions.

CHRISTIAN BARBARIANS

A new factor by the late 4th century was that some German peoples – the Visigoths, Ostrogoths and Vandals – had converted to Christianity. Unfortunately for them, it was not orthodox Catholic Christianity but Arianism, a heretical school that denied the divinity of Christ and followed the teachings of Arius, a Libyan cleric. Far from creating a tie with an increasingly Christian Roman empire, their Arianism served to separate Germans, as the one thing worse than a pagan to the Roman Church was a heretic.

One reason why the Franks became the ultimate victors in Gaul, giving their name to the new country, was that Clovis, their first great king, converted to Catholicism in AD496, so making his people acceptable to his Gallo-Roman subjects. Clovis married Clotilda, a Burgundian princess. The Burgundians, too, chose Catholicism and so became permanently embedded in their corner of Gaul, while the Visigoths, Ostrogoths and Vandals, despite conquering Spain, Italy and North Africa respectively in the 5th century, have vanished like smoke.

All the Teutonic invaders, no matter how uncouth and evil-smelling to the Romans, were nothing in comparison to a totally new threat from Asia that emerged in the late 4th century AD. The Huns, originally known to the Chinese – who had built their Great Wall against precisely such terrors – as the Hsiung-nu, entered the outer orbit of the Roman world in about AD370. Ammianus, the great 4th-century historian, described them as, "the most savage and hideous of all races. They have short bull-like necks and their bodies are short and deformed … They are stuck to their saddles, eating, drinking, bartering, even sleeping wrapped round their horse's neck. In fighting they excel by the great speed of their attacks… They are brave in war, faithless at keeping truces, deceitful, quick to anger and insatiably greedy for gold." Directly and indirectly, these savage nomads played a crucial part in the destruction of the western empire, before they vanished from European history, leaving nothing but evil memories, and their name on the Hungarian plains, where they had briefly settled in the 5th century AD.

THE LOSS AND RECAPTURE OF THE EAST: AD260-72

Above: A triad of gods from Palmyra, the great trading city in the Syrian desert that came to Rome's help in the 3rd century AD and then tried to create its own empire before being crushed.

Below: The wealth and polyglot sophistication of Palmyra were reflected in its flamboyant architecture. Classically Graeco-Roman in form, this was often baroque in spirit, as this ruined monumental arch suggests.

Superbly sited in a large oasis between the great cities of Mesopotamia and the ports of Roman Syria, Palmyra had grown wealthy from the most lucrative trade in the ancient world: transporting silks, spices, precious stones and similar luxuries from India and China to Rome. Since the reign of Vespasian, or possibly even earlier, Palmyra had been a Roman dependency. Its exact status was uncertain but it clearly enjoyed enough autonomy to contribute separate cavalry forces to the Roman armies that Trajan and Septimius Severus led against Parthia.

The excellence of Palmyrene cavalry – which included heavy armoured cataphracts and light mounted archers, as well as some camels – seems to have originated from their long-established roles guarding the camel trains that crossed the desert against Arab raiders. The city had a Semitic, mostly Aramaic-speaking population, but its culture was a luxuriant mixture of Roman, Greek and Semitic. Palmyra's exuberantly decorated "baroque" temples and colonnades testify to its great wealth.

Such cultural links, as well as its geographical location on the west side of the Syrian desert, automatically inclined Palmyra to the Roman side in wars with Parthia or Persia. However, the catastrophic defeat and capture of the emperor Valerian in AD260, when all Rome's Asian provinces seemed about to fall into Persian hands, encouraged Septimius Odenathus, leader of the most powerful tribe of Palmyra, to consider changing sides. In AD261 he approached the Persian king Shapor and offered to join him. Shapor, flushed with victory after three successful wars against Rome, rejected the Palmyrene prince. This proved a colossal mistake. Impressive though the Persians' gains were, they were operating in hostile country and their supply lines were perilously extended across northern Mesopotamia and Syria, being particularly vulnerable to any attacks from the south. These attacks Odenathus now delivered.

Within a couple of years, Palmyrene cavalry had driven the Persians out of Syria and the Roman part of Mesopotamia. The emperor Gallienus, distracted by troubles far closer home, made Odenathus *Dux Orientis* (Governor of the East). Under this title, Odenathus became the effective ruler of almost all Syria. In AD266 he even advanced deep into the Persian empire and defeated the Persians outside Ctesiphon. In the following year he turned north and marched into northern Asia Minor to repel a Gothic attack. His domestic position was insecure, however, and he was murdered on his return from this campaign, possibly at the instigation of

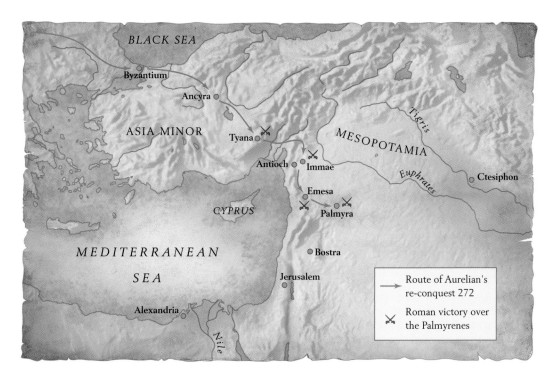

Left: The essential frailty of Palmyrene power was revealed when the emperor Aurelian marched east and crushed the Palmyrene army in a series of battles, culminating in the capture of Palmyra itself. Queen Zenobia was also taken and her rich city sank into ruined obscurity.

Gallienus, who had grown alarmed at the extent of his victories. This was by no means, however, the end of Palmyrene power, for Odenathus' widow, Zenobia, at once took control of the new "empire".

CLEOPATRA'S DESCENDANT

Zenobia claimed descent from Cleopatra, the last Ptolemaic queen of Egypt and Mark Antony's doomed lover. She was certainly as beautiful (she was famed for her long black hair), and as ambitious, although she seems to have been a better military and diplomatic leader, winning over many Arab chieftains and princes to her cause. Palmyra, although a wealthy trading city, did not compare with the huge kingdom of Egypt, so Zenobia needed all the support she could find to continue her city's fine balancing act between the Roman and Persian giants.

Proclaiming herself regent to her young son Vaballathus, Zenobia reasserted Palmyrene control over Syria and Roman Mesopotamia, again winning the acquiescence of Gallienus and then of his successor Claudius II in AD268. However, when she invaded Egypt and Asia Minor in AD270, she openly broke with Rome. Alexandria held out against her and her forces were too thinly spread to control most of the territories they had conquered. In AD272 she had Vaballathus crowned as *imperator* and Augustus, and she herself took the title of Augusta. Aurelian, the new emperor in Rome, would not accept this outright challenge and, after defeating the Goths again on the Danube, he marched east.

Although the Palmyrenes were still superior in cavalry, Aurelian managed to defeat them outside Antioch at Immae. In a second battle at Emesa, Zenobia was again defeated and retreated to Palmyra, hoping that Aurelian's army would be unable to supply itself in the desert. But it was Palmyra that ran short of food and Zenobia decided to escape and seek help from the Persians. Captured just as she was about to cross the Euphrates, she was taken back to Rome where she was paraded in gold chains in Aurelian's triumph the following year, before being allowed to retire to Tivoli. Aurelian spared Palmyra itself, possibly aware of its potential value as an ally, but news of a second revolt reached him in AD273. Quickly returning, he retook the city and punished its massacre of the small Roman garrison left there by sacking it so thoroughly that it soon passed almost completely out of history.

Above: Palmyra was typical in the way it absorbed the Hellenistic culture that had spread across Asia after Alexander and which Rome further encouraged.

THE SPLINTERING EMPIRE

Above: Gallienus, whose reign (253–68AD) saw the empire almost disintegrate.

Rome might have expected to find its conquests ever ready to revolt the moment that central power weakened. In AD68–9, the Year of the Four Emperors, there was indeed a serious rebellion. Civilis, a Batavian (from modern Holland) who was also a Roman citizen and commander of an auxiliary unit of Batavians, roused a revolt along the lower Rhine. He even persuaded some legions to join him before he was suppressed. Yet this was in fact almost the only significant revolt of its kind in Europe. From the time of the reign of Hadrian (AD117–38), the provinces were treated as equal partners in a commonwealth, a trend confirmed when Caracalla (chiefly for financial reasons) granted almost all free men Roman citizenship in AD212. When the empire nearly broke up in the 3rd century AD, it did so because Rome was not providing the protection the provinces expected and needed.

Gaul, the largest and probably most populous of the western provinces, was the leader in this revolt. There had long been a tendency by Rome to downgrade the importance of the Rhine frontier compared to the Danube. By the AD240s there were only four legions along the Rhine, as opposed to 12 on the, admittedly longer, Danube. The legions were also constantly weakened by calls for *vexillationes* (detachments), leaving too few troops to deal with the threat from the new confederacies: the Franks on the Lower Rhine and the Alamanni in southern Germany. Raids across the Rhine began in the AD230s, intensified in the AD250s and led to major invasions. The Franks penetrated through Gaul to sack Tarragona in north-east Spain in AD260, while the Alammani crossed the *Agri Decumates* and the Alps before being defeated near Milan in AD259. Then, in AD260, news of the emperor Valerian's humiliating defeat and capture by the Persians shook the Roman world to its very foundations.

In the circumstances, separatism appeared desirable. Marcus Postumus, a nobleman of Gallic descent and the governor of Lower Germany, was proclaimed emperor by his troops in AD260 after defeating some invaders. Marching on Cologne, he then captured and killed the emperor Gallienus' young son Saloninus, who had recently been made Augustus. Expelling barbarians and re-establishing the Rhine frontier, he won

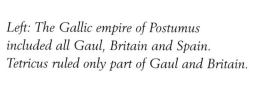
Gallic Empire of Postumus 261
Gallic Empire of Tetricus 271

Left: The Gallic empire of Postumus included all Gaul, Britain and Spain. Tetricus ruled only part of Gaul and Britain.

Left: The imperial baths of Trier, which probably date from the early 4th century AD. In the late 3rd century AD, the city became the proud capital of the separatist Gallic empire. Later it was the capital of the western Caesars under the Tetrarchy and throughout the 4th century.

recognition by the legions in Britain, Spain and even Raetia, so that the whole western quarter of the empire had seceded. Postumus made it clear that he did not intend to march on Rome, and was left in peace for five years. He then established a separate Senate at Trier, his capital, which he began fortifying and embellishing with an amphitheatre and palaces, while restoring the ravages made by barbarians. The Gallic empire seemed set to survive.

Gallienus recovered Raetia in AD263, but his attack on Postumus two years later in AD265 failed. Surviving Gallienus' murder by a year, Postumus was killed by his own troops in AD269 when he refused to let them sack Mainz after they had defeated another usurper. In the ensuing anarchy, Spain abandoned its Gallic allegiance, as did the south-east of Gaul, but the rest of that province and Britain remained independent until Aurelian led an army against them in AD274. The last Gallic emperor, Tetricus, seems to have reached some kind of understanding with Aurelian. Tetricus's life was spared and he even became governor of Lucania in southern Italy.

A BRITISH EMPIRE

Saxon raids along the coasts of Britain and northern Gaul had led to the expansion of the powerful *classis britannica*, the British fleet, which was based in large fortresses on each side of the Channel. Its admiral, Carausius, quarrelled with the western Augustus, Maximian, in AD286 – he was accused of pocketing Roman goods recovered from Saxon raiders – and declared himself independent. He was a skilful admiral and general, for he got the backing of his troops and maintained his hold on the Channel ports, defeating Maximian in AD289. Carausius then assumed the full panoply of titles, including Caesar, Augustus and *pontifex maximus* (chief priest), and on his coinage presented himself joint ruler with Diocletian and Maximian. Unimpressed, they sent Constantius Chlorus, the western Caesar, to defeat him. Constantius regained the Gallic ports, including Boulogne, in AD293. This led to Carausius' murder by his chamberlain Allectus, who took his place. Four years later, Constantius' invasion forces overwhelmed Allectus with a two-pronged attack and Britain was restored to the empire after ten years' independence.

Below: Roman soldiers from a Gallo-Roman carving. Gaul became so deeply Romanized that the separatist empire of Postumus copied Rome's, complete with Senate and baths. But Gaul returned to the empire by AD274.

THE FIRST RECOVERY
AD260–76

Above: The Porto San Sebastiano, one of the heavily fortified gates in the Aurelianic walls around Rome, was extended by Valentinian I and Honorius.

Below: The largest and most imposing walls in the 3rd century AD very suitably encircled the capital. Built by the emperor Aurelian, they proved effective against direct assault but not blockades.

By AD260, in the wake of the capture of the emperor Valerian by the Persians and the loss of his huge army, the empire seemed doomed to disintegration. Decades of civil wars had alerted the barbarians to its weaknesses, and invasion followed invasion: the Alamanni had finally overrun the *Agri Decumates* by AD260 and threatened southern Gaul and northern Italy; the Franks crossed the Lower Rhine and soon reached Spain; the Goths, Heruli and Gepids poured through Dacia and into Moesia, sacking cities as far apart as Trebizond in AD255 (north-east Turkey) and Athens in AD267, while Saxons raided the coasts of Britain and a German tribe, the Juthungi, ravaged central Italy. On top of all this, the empire had been suffering from plague intermittently for years. The economy, already stagnant if not in decline earlier in the century, now declined still faster, although some untouched areas such as Egypt and North Africa seemed to have remained quietly prosperous. Everywhere rapid inflation continued, fuelled by successive tamperings with the coinage that gave the government a short-term boost at a crippling long-term cost.

For the first time in centuries, men began openly to despair of the power of the Romans, looking around for alternatives, be they manifestly separatist emperors in Gaul or effectively independent Palmyrene rulers in the east. Yet amazingly, at this darkest hour, a recovery began that within two decades had stabilized most of the frontiers, expelled most of the barbarians and even begun to reform the army, currency and administration. The credit for beginning this turnaround must go to the emperor under whom the empire had seemed lost and who has long been maligned for it: Gallienus.

Gallienus had been co-emperor with his father since AD253, being left in command of the west while Valerian went east in AD254. He had a major success in turning back the Juthungi in

AD259 from their first Italian attack, but the news of his father's defeat triggered a rash of usurpers; traditionally, 20 pretenders arose in his reign. They forced him to spend as much time fighting rivals as barbarians, although he temporarily acknowledged the independence of the Gallic empire under Postumus in AD260. He did so to concentrate on the defence of Italy, where he made Milan his effective capital. Here he assembled a strike force, composed of crack troops, mainly cavalry, recruited from armies on the Danube, in Asia and Africa. He minted a new gold coinage, the *multipla*, to pay this force. This special army seems not to have had a separate base and was probably stationed in cities, themselves now increasingly fortified. An extensive programme of qualitatively different fortifications had already begun, with huge towers and much thicker walls, all intended to endure long sieges. It was to continue throughout the following decades.

Gallienus' chief innovation seems to have been a policy of elastic defence. Replacing the earlier preclusive policy, this essentially meant giving up trying to hold the frontier at every point but instead waiting until the invading enemy could be advantageously attacked with superior forces. The policy bore fruit when Gallienus cornered an army of Goths at Nis in AD268. Unfortunately, although he had tried to secure the throne by forbidding senators from holding command, Gallienus failed to prevent the real threat from his own officers. Aureolus, his cavalry commander, declared himself emperor in AD268 and Gallienus abandoned his Gothic campaign to hurry back. In the subsequent siege of Milan, he was assassinated.

THE ILLYRIAN EMPERORS

Gallienus had come from the Roman nobility, but from now on a new breed of soldier-emperor was to dominate the succession: the Illyrian or Balkan emperors. First of these was Claudius II

"Gothicus", so-called because he defeated the Goths in AD269. His death from plague the next year led to the succession of Aurelian. Aurelian was indisputably a great soldier: he repelled the Vandals, Marcomanni and Juthungi, crushed the Palmyrene revolt and reconquered Gaul, although he had to abandon Dacia. But he had other attributes: he showed unusual clemency to rebels such as Zenobia, queen of Palmyra, and Tetricus, the emperor of Gaul; he built the walls around Rome, which, still standing, perpetuate his name; he was severe towards extortionate officials, one of the banes of every administration, and he built a huge Temple of the Sun in Rome. His death – he was murdered by his private secretary for reasons that are unclear – was much mourned. A series of short-lived Illyrian emperors followed; all were murdered by their troops. Only one, Probus, reigned long enough, from AD276 to 282, to have much impact, again defeating various German invaders before being murdered. Two years after his death, Diocletian found himself emperor and inaugurated what would become a very different regime.

Above: The walls hastily constructed by the emperor Aurelian around Rome in the AD270s were the first walls Rome had needed for 300 years, and they have survived for 1,700 years.

Below: Greatest of the Illyrian emperors was Diocletian who reformed the empire.

THE TETRARCHS' ACHIEVEMENTS: AD284–305

The empire that the Illyrian-born soldier Diocletian gained in AD284 was less immediately imperilled than it had been 20 years earlier, but it was still in a highly precarious state. The military had been expanded but new ways of paying for it had not been found. Inflation continued, with the result that the armies were still being paid – when paid at all – either in kind, by exactions, or in almost worthless coinage. The cost of both bore crushingly on the taxpayers, who were faced with huge, unpredictable demands.

Above all, the problem of the succession, the cause of incessant, empire-wrecking civil war, remained unsolved. Only one emperor had died a natural death in the preceding 70 years. All the rest had been murdered, often by their own armies. Diocletian, however, managed to retire and die in bed, and two subsequent emperors (Constantius Chlorus and Galerius) also died a natural death. Diocletian might have assumed this was due to the Tetrarchy, that system he had devised with four rulers – two senior Augusti and two junior Caesars, the latter the Augusti's designated heirs. In fact, it was almost entirely due to Diocletian's own *auctoritas*, the respect in which he was held, that led the other emperors to ask him to reassume the throne at their last meeting in November AD308, three years after his retirement. The almost farcical chaos that overtook the rigid tetrarchical system – with numerous emperors emerging or re-emerging – exposed its shortcomings. Chief among these was its total disregard for hereditary sentiment. As Constantine demonstrated when acclaimed by his father's army on the latter's death in York in AD306, this remained very powerful.

In another sphere, the Tetrarchy proved more successful. Diocletian saw that the empire needed more than one *imperator*, or supreme commander. In the almost constant wars, often fought on several fronts, the long absence of the emperor on one front could too easily provoke discontent, even rebellion, on another. This was probably why he made another Illyrian soldier, Maximian, a fellow Augustus – a policy pioneered by Marcus Aurelius – and then appointed junior Caesars. Diocletian also developed the policy (which had originated with Domitian 200 years earlier) of making the emperor appear truly imperial, even divine. This led to elaborate court ceremonies and palace hierarchies. Although a further strain on the taxpayer, these should not be over-stated. Compared to the army, the tetrarchical bureaucracy was still quite small.

Diocletian had mixed success with his financial and economic reforms. He issued his famous Edict of Maximum Prices in AD301, fixing maximum prices for a wide range of goods and services to counter inflation. The attempt failed.

Below: The north wall of Diocletian's Palace at Spalato (Split), Croatia, showing the ornate but massively built Porta Aurea (Golden Gate) built c.AD300. Diocletian's palace-fortress epitomized the spirit of the age, grandiose and yet defensive.

Left: Galerius (Augustus AD305–11) sacrificing to the pagan gods. Galerius instigated the last and worst persecution of the Christians in AD303–11. He thought them both sacrilegious and unpatriotic, but he failed to exterminate Christianity.

However, he had more success with taxation. He based taxes on a hypothetical unit that varied according to the quality of land held. Taxes were now assessed annually by the Praetorian prefect of each province. The *decurions* (officials) of the cities were made responsible for collecting taxes in their province. These were in kind and overwhelmingly agricultural. To ensure that tenant farmers paid them, they were increasingly tied to their land by imperial edicts; other trades were also declared hereditarily binding. Although oppressive, this system was superior to the naked exactions and chaos of the previous century.

MILITARY SUCCESSES

In one sphere, the Tetrarchy was undoubtedly successful: the military. The army was again expanded – to perhaps 500,000 men – with a formal separation of the frontier troops, the *limitanei*, commanded by a *dux* (leader), from the *comitatenses*, the mobile forces under the commands of *comites*, counts, not tied to specific frontiers. These battle troops were no longer under the control of the local governors, whose provinces were much reduced in size if they were increased in number, for a dual system of civilian and military government had by now been established. The aim, successful but superfluous as it turned out, was to prevent provincial governors from revolting.

But army commanders continued to rebel. With these armies, often stationed in camps so heavily fortified that they begin to deserve the name of castles, Diocletian and his colleagues won a series of major campaigns, most notably that of Galerius against the Persians in AD297–8, which gained a new province. At the same time, Constantius was regaining Britain from a usurper. His victory was more typical of the generally defensive victories of a defensive age. It epitomizes the real but limited achievements of the Tetrarchy, principally the sharing of power between several emperors, which led Gibbon to call Diocletian the second founder of the Roman empire. They allowed the empire to continue, in a controlled, rigid but viable manner, for further generations.

Below: This column shows Diocletian embracing his colleague Maximian.

CONSTANTINE
THE LAST GREAT EMPEROR?

Above: One of the new solidi, gold coins issued by Constantine, showing him in idealized perpetual youth – he was noted for his vanity, in his later years wearing a wig. His new coinage proved enduringly successful, however.

Below: A relief from the Arch of Constantine in Rome illustrating his victory at the Battle of the Milvian Bridge in AD312 over his rival Maxentius. He attributed his victory later to a religious dream, but Maxentius was already an unpopular ruler.

The giant head and hands, sole surviving fragments of the titanic figure of Constantine that once dominated the Basilica Nova in Rome, seem to proclaim him one of the greatest emperors. His massive building programmes – at Trier, Rome and especially at Constantinople – reinforce this claim. Certainly, he changed the empire. He left it on the way to becoming Christian; gave it a new capital that became the centre of a new civilization (although he cannot have foreseen this); reformed the army again, if in ways that even contemporaries criticized; and defeated all his enemies, mainly Roman but also foreign – Franks, Sarmatians and Goths – before dying in bed, leaving the empire to his sons. How far he was a truly great ruler remains debatable.

Son of Constantius Chlorus, the Augustus of the west approved by Diocletian, Constantine was acclaimed by his troops at York in AD306. His rise to sole lordship of the empire was by typical rather than glorious means. His attack on Maxentius, ruler of Italy, in AD312 was standard action for an emperor controlling only the western provinces. His subsequent unprovoked attacks on his co-Augustus in the east, Licinius, had little justification except that of final success in AD324. If Constantine was more openly Christian than Licinius, the latter did not persecute Christians as a sect.

Constantine fought effectively against invading barbarians, from the Franks on the Rhine to the Goths on the Danube in his later years. These, along with success in more frequent civil wars, demonstrate military competence. But his military reforms – employing Germans in his crack *palatini* regiments, keeping large forces around him almost as a bodyguard – struck some contemporaries as more concerned to safeguard his power than his people. Quartering troops in towns also caused problems with military discipline. His military record was therefore mixed.

In founding Constantinople as his new capital – intending it less as a replacement for Rome than as a complementary eastern capital – Constantine showed great foresight. The best-defended site in Europe, at the crossroads of several major trade and military routes, Constantinople prospered, the one city in the empire that grew throughout the 4th century AD. According to legend, Constantine traced out its walls guided by a vision. In fact, his wall needed replacing by the Theodosian walls within a century, as the city's population approached three-quarters of a million people.

Constantine enduringly, if unwittingly, reformed the currency. This had been debased many times, so he issued a new coinage, the gold *solidus*, literally solid gold. It became widely accepted for many centuries after his death, a sign of Byzantine economic strength. This high-quality coinage was made possible by his pillaging of pagan temples. Treasures that generations had donated to their gods over the centuries were seized and often

Left: Constantine built his new city of Constantinople (formerly Byzantium, today Istanbul) at a strategic position overlooking the Bosphorus. He would deserve to be remembered as a ruler touched by greatness simply for choosing this superb site for his new capital.

melted down. This was despoliation on a scale comparable with Henry VIII's dissolution of England's monasteries in the 1530s. But the *solidus* was a high-value coin, no good in daily use where inflation continued. Constantine's tax reforms were mixed; his taxes were so onerous that fathers reputedly sold their daughters into prostitution to pay them.

THE FIRST CHRISTIAN EMPEROR?

Constantine's greatest fame is as the first Christian emperor. Certainly, he forged the linkage of empire and Church – in the east until 1453, in the west until the 11th century Investiture Conflict – and ensured that the empire ultimately became Christian. This took time, however. Mass conversions of peasants in Asia Minor were still being carried out 200 years later. Constantine's own religious beliefs remain uncertain. Like his father, he initially worshipped *Sol Invictus*, the Unconquered Sun. After victory at the Milvian Bridge in AD312, he began sporting Christian as well as pagan insignia on his standards, but the Edict of Milan in AD313 granted toleration to *all* faiths, not just

Christianity. Constantine seems to have developed an interest in theological speculation – it was the golden age for it – chatting in bad Greek to bishops at the Council of Nicaea in AD325, although he was thought not to understand abstruse doctrinal points. He favoured the Church by financial measures but did not discriminate against non-Christians – more than 90 per cent of the population – in the army or administration. He continued to use the pagan title *pontifex maximus* (chief priest), did not object to the renovation of temples in old Byzantium and was baptized only on his deathbed. Admittedly this was common at the time, baptism being thought to wash away all existing sins.

Constantine was the last emperor to rule the whole Roman world for a lengthy time (AD324–37). There would be other valiant emperors after him, but none who could be considered great. The empire that he left his successors still looked brilliant, powerful and wealthy. But the extravagances of his court and capital and the rapacity of his tax-collectors, along with his reliance on Germans, augured ill for its longer-term health.

Above: This aqueduct supplying Constantinople with water was begun by Constantine but completed in AD378 by the emperor Valens, whose name it bears. The city had from the start excellent water supplies, as well as huge cisterns to enable it to withstand long sieges.

CONSTANTINE'S HEIRS

It would be fair to say that Constantine's heirs had most of his vices and few of his virtues. The one exception, Julian, ended his reign in military disaster. On Constantine's death in AD337, the army mutinied and murdered many of his family. Constantine II, Constans I and Constantius II, the three surviving sons, divided the empire between them. Constantine was killed in AD340 attacking Constans, who became sole ruler of the European provinces, before being murdered in AD350. Constantius II refused to accept Magnentius, the new western ruler, and finally defeated him in AD353. The empire was now reunited, if exhausted by renewed civil strife.

Constantius was judged stupid and vain by contemporaries. He was certainly fond of showy display: on his triumphant entry into Rome in AD354, he posed immobile in his chariot as though made of ivory and gold. A fanatical Christian, he enforced Arianism (a belief later declared heretical) upon the empire and surrounded himself with sycophantic eunuchs. But he still needed a co-emperor and first chose his half-cousin Gallus in AD354. However, Gallus' highly erratic behaviour, which recalled Caligula's, led to his downfall. Constantius then turned to the sole surviving member of his family, Julian, the son of Constantine's half-brother Julius Constantius, one of the victims of the murders of AD337.

JULIAN

Until then, Julian had led the life of a philosophy student. Unwillingly called from Athens to become Caesar in Gaul in AD355, he astonished everybody by displaying military genius. Julian made

Above: Julian, sole emperor AD361–3, was the last pagan emperor. He was also almost the only later emperor to realize how high taxation was crushing the poorer people in the empire. His tax reforms, like his pagan restoration, however, proved short-lived.

Right: In AD363, Julian's army reached the walls of the Persian capital Ctesiphon, behind which stood its royal palace with its huge arch, but he failed to take it. In the subsequent retreat, Julian lost his life and Rome many of its best troops and half of upper Mesopotamia.

the small city of Paris (Lutetia) his base and recreated a proper army, repelling the barbarians. His greatest victory was at Strasbourg (Argentoratum) in AD357. Against an army of 35,000 Germans, he fielded some 13,000 men. After a long and hard-fought battle, the Romans won, with only 243 losses. Julian then crossed the river Rhine to campaign in Germany and re-established most of the Rhine frontier. He also tried to make the tax-collection system more efficient by stamping out corruption. He sacked some particularly extortionate officials, which boosted his popularity with the populace.

Constantius, now paranoid about his cousin's successes, ordered him to dispatch most of his best troops east in AD360. However, they revolted and acclaimed Julian Augustus: the empire seemed destined for yet another round of civil wars. Constantius turned his armies in the east to the west, but Julian struck first. The city of Aquileia in northeast Italy held out against his troops, but he marched east along the Danube and had reached Sirmium in the Balkans when news came of Constantius' death in late AD361. The empire was united again.

Julian's sole reign lasted only 18 months, but he filled it with activity. He sacked many of the well-paid imperial courtiers and officials. He then revealed his long-standing pagan beliefs, reopening pagan temples while banning Christians from teaching Greek and Roman classics – a major cultural blow. He even tried to encourage the Jews to rebuild the Temple in Jerusalem, as this would confound Christian prophecy. His gaze, however, was focused on the east.

PERSIAN NEMESIS

Julian decided to invade Persia for the usual Roman reasons: popular opinion expected the emperor to emulate Alexander the Great, and Persia appeared an enemy that could finally and profitably be defeated, unlike the drifting swarms of barbarians. An element of official revenge undoubtedly also played its part.

"We must destroy a dangerous nation whose swords are still wet with our brothers' blood!" Julian proclaimed, according to Ammianus. He gathered an army of 65,000 men, supplied by 1,000 boats and 100 galleys. He then sailed and marched down the Euphrates. Although he captured forts and defeated part of the Persian army, the main Persian forces avoided battle, instead adopting a scorched-earth policy to deny the Romans supplies. Julian decided to strike north-east across the Tigris into fresh lands, perhaps aiming to meet reinforcements from Mesopotamia, and the army began its retreat harassed by Persian mounted archers. Hurrying to help part of the army under attack, he left off his armour and received a fatal arrow wound, dying that night. Julian was the last significant non-Christian emperor, the last emperor with a real interest in Graeco-Roman culture, a writer of note and the only later Roman emperor to begin to comprehend the problems of the crushing weight of taxation upon the ordinary taxpayer. His death was a loss in more ways than might be expected.

Above: A coin of Constantine II, the oldest surviving son of Constantine I, whose reign of three years ended in AD340 when he was killed attacking his co-emperor and brother, Constans.

Above: The Romans continued to maintain and even expand their chain of fortresses and watchtowers, often on a large scale, all around the coasts of Britain until the very end of Roman rule in c.AD400. This suggests that they valued the province highly.

BRITAIN REGAINED AND ABANDONED

A realist in military matters, the emperor Septimius Severus nevertheless thought it was worth making the long journey north to Britain and campaigning for two years into Scotland. Britain mattered to Rome. The traditional view that the province required a military garrison disproportionate to its tiny population and wealth has been modified in recent years by archaeological finds. These suggest a far larger population than once thought – perhaps around four million. London, a great trading centre, was certainly the second biggest and richest city north of the Alps, with a population of around 40–50,000 at its 2nd-century AD peak. Whatever the exact figures, defending the island was clearly not just a matter of military prestige but also one of retaining a valuable province.

In the mid-3rd century AD, Britain was almost untouched by the waves of invasion that ravaged much of the empire, becoming part of Postumus' Gallic empire. Some Gallo-Romans may have migrated at this time to the relative security Britain offered, bringing their skills and wealth with them. Around this time, Saxon raiders along the shores of the Channel demanded the expansion of the existing *classis britannica*, the British fleet, and the construction of a chain of typically huge forts along the south-east coast. This fleet and the coastal forts formed the basis of the rebellion by the admiral Carausius and his successor Allectus in AD286–96, which for a moment made Britain a separate empire. But Allectus seems to have been an unpopular tyrant and by AD296 the Caesar Constantius Chlorus was poised to regain the province. His invasion met with little opposition; the citizens of London were particularly pleased that his troops reached the city before Allectus' unpaid Frankish mercenaries, who wanted to sack it. On his coins Constantius was hailed as the "restorer of eternal light".

Right: Foundations of a Roman watchtower survive high on the cliffs above Scarborough, Yorkshire, and formed part of the chain of forts and signalling stations constructed along the Saxon Shore of eastern Britain during the 3rd and 4th centuries AD.

Constantius' time in Britain seems to have been fruitful. He recruited British *artifices* (skilled men) to restore the fortifications of Autun, one of Gaul's chief cities. He himself went north, again restored Hadrian's Wall, campaigned far into Scotland and finally died at York in AD306, a city whose walls were much strengthened during his reign.

The 50 years following Constantius' death have been called the golden age of villa life in Roman Britain. Again, recent archaeological evidence suggests that the villas built then were not the provincial half-timbered structures once thought. Some were large, complex and luxurious country houses, almost comparable in scale with those of 18th-century country houses, such as North Leigh in Oxfordshire. Cities now had their defences strengthened, but villas seem to have been unprotected, presumably because they were mostly in the safer, southern half of the province. This British wealth clearly persisted into the AD350s, despite the problems of Magnentius' unsuccessful bid for power, for the emperor Julian sent to Britain for 600 shiploads of wheat to feed his army on the Rhine in AD359.

THE FINAL COLLAPSE

Around AD367 all the barbarians around Roman Britain reputedly conspired to attack it in the same year: Caledonians from the north, Irish raiders from the west and Saxons from the east. Many Roman troops seem to have abandoned their posts, some even joining the barbarian looters who ravaged the whole island. The emperor Valentinian sent Count Theodosius, father of the future emperor, to Britain with some crack troops in AD368. Reaching London, Theodosius was greeted ecstatically by its citizens. From there, he issued proclamations offering amnesties to all troops who had deserted. Reforming the Roman armies in Britain, he systematically cleared the province, rebuilt the walls of many cities and

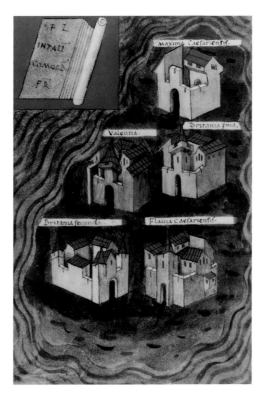

increased the number of coastal watch towers in the north and in Wales. Traditionally, he even marched north into Scotland again, naming the area between the two walls Valentia after the emperor.

However, Theodosius' restoration was Rome's last really effective intervention in Britain. Troops were withdrawn to support usurpers such as Maximus Magnus, who took many soldiers with him in his bid for the throne in AD383. Only 20 years later, many of the remaining troops were withdrawn by Stilicho, the west's effective ruler, and the remainder probably followed the usurper Constantine when he crossed to Gaul in AD407. Left to themselves, the British may have organized some defence, but by the AD430s the province had slipped out of the decaying Roman empire. In AD446 the Romanized Britons allegedly made a last appeal for help to Aetius, the west's great general, but in vain. He was too preoccupied with the Huns. The Saxons may have started settling in large groups along the east coast soon after, while the western areas were ruled by Romano-Celtic princes. This marked Rome's final abandonment of Britain.

Left: The Notitia Dignitatum *listed in great detail Roman troop positions and fortresses in Britain and across the whole empire in* AD395. *This illustration actually dates from 1436 and so shows fortresses in Britain more imaginatively than literally.*

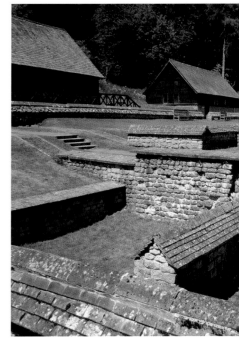

Above: The remains of the Roman villa at Chedworth near Cirencester. Romano-British villas flourished up to the mid-4th century AD, *often becoming large, even luxurious complexes of buildings, complete with baths and hypocaust central heating.*

Above: An aureus *(gold coin) showing the emperor Valens (*AD*364–75) who led the army of the east to disastrous defeat by the Goths at Adrianople in 378*AD*. He was an Arian Christian and persecuted orthodox Christians, pagans and Jews.*

THE GOTHIC PROBLEM

By *c.*AD350, the Ostrogoths had established a huge realm from the Vistula to the Don, centred on the grasslands of the Ukraine well suited to their cavalry. Although not averse to raiding the Roman empire, here they posed little threat. Their Visigothic cousins meanwhile occupied the Dacian region. Both had converted to Christianity. The type that they learnt through a missionary, Ulfilas, was Arianism, which denied the divinity of Christ. However, it was not religion that led to the Goths' next clash with Rome.

Moving west across the steppes of Eurasia, the Huns burst into the world of Germans and Romans around AD373. The Ostrogoths, routed by them, fled west, driving their Visigothic cousins before them. "News spread through the Gothic peoples of a race of men, never before known, risen as if from under the earth and destroying all in their path," recorded Ammianus. The Visigoths,

panicking at tales of Hunnish ferocity, approached the Danube frontier and requested *receptio*, official permission to settle inside the empire. This had been granted to many Germans, often with success. The emperor Valens, senior emperor at the time, agreed provided the Goths surrendered their arms. He hoped that they would supply recruits for the army and farm deserted lands in Thrace. Ammianus described Valens as "overjoyed at the prospect". His joy was short-lived.

The Visigoths began crossing the Danube in late AD376. The river was swollen with rain and many drowned. The survivors were abused by corrupt Roman officials, who sold them dead dogs as food at inflated prices and raped their women. To pay for food, many Visigoths had to sell their children into slavery; the going rate was reputedly one dead dog per child. Meanwhile, Ostrogoths had also crossed the river. Fighting broke out and the Goths turned to pillaging the

Right: The battle of Adrianople in AD*378 was a disaster from which the Roman empire never fully recovered, for it let the Goths into the empire* en masse. *The army of the emperor Valens, hurrying from Constantinople, blundered upon the Gothic forces led by Fritigern, who had formed a defensive circular* laager *with their wagons in its centre. The battle was decided by the return of the foraging Gothic cavalry who encircled the Romans. Valens himself died in the battle.*

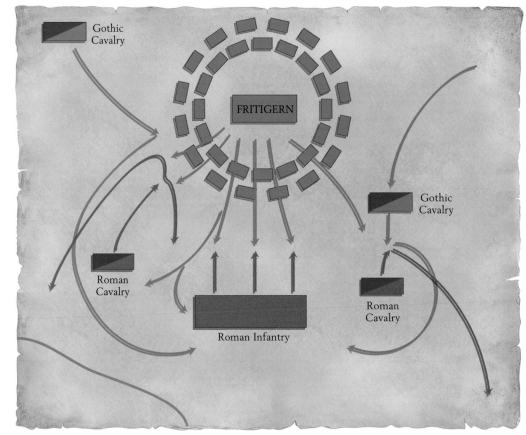

lands. They attempted to take Adrianople but its walls, as usual, defied them. The emperor Valens, deciding to deal with the invasion in person, assembled his armies at Constantinople in summer AD378 and rode north to meet the Goths.

THE BATTLE OF ADRIANOPLE

On a scorching hot day in August AD378 the army of the east, with 60,000 men, approached Adrianople. The Romans, who had been marching all day, were tired and thirsty, but when they saw the Goths ahead, Valens decided to attack at once. He was misled by reports that there were only 10,000 armed Goths ahead and wanted the glory of victory before his co-emperor Gratian joined him.

The Visigoths had formed their wagons into a *laager* (circle). Fritigern, the Visigothic leader, sent out for his cavalry, which was foraging, and for his Ostrogoth allies and their cavalry. Roman skirmishers seem to have begun the battle before Valens intended, for the Roman lines were not fully formed when the Visigoths counter-attacked, driving the skirmishers back into the Romans' main troops. The Gothic cavalry returned and, catching the Roman cavalry in the flank, drove it

from the field. Despite this, the Roman infantry in the centre rallied and, until sunset, the battle raged outside the *laager* like "the waves of the sea", according to Ammianus. However, the Gothic cavalry so tightened its grip on the encircled Romans that the soldiers could no longer wield their weapons effectively. Valens himself fell in the battle and his army fell with him.

Two-thirds of this great army was destroyed, but the Goths were unable to capitalize on their victory. They could not even capture Adrianople, with Valens' treasure and huge supplies within it, and their attack on Constantinople was a complete failure. Even so, two large Roman armies commanded by emperors had been defeated in 15 years. The new emperor Theodosius was forced into a wholesale policy of appeasement. He let the Visigoths settle *en masse* inside the empire in Pannonia and the Ostrogoths in Moesia. Further, he recruited Goths into the army, not just as individuals or small groups, but in whole tribes commanded by their chieftains. While earlier Germans had been Romanized by service in the imperial army, the Roman army now rapidly became barbarized.

Above: Nothing remains of the original walls around Constantinople (Istanbul) built by Constantine I in AD324. Later superseded by the Theodosian walls, they repulsed the Goths.

Below: Theodosius I (AD379–95), presents laurel crowns to the winners of a chariot race in Constantinople. The city shared Rome's urban amusements and also her imperial aspirations.

THE FATAL WINTER

Above: Theodosius I was the last emperor to rule the whole Roman empire.

Below: The interior of the Porta Nigra (Black Gate) at Trier.

In the later 4th century AD, the Rhine frontier looked relatively secure. It had been restored first by Julian and then by Valentinian (AD364–75), who had built or rebuilt many forts along it. He had even crossed the river once more to campaign in Germany, more than 400 years after Julius Caesar first crossed it. Valentinian was the last Roman general ever to do so.

Central to the defence of the frontier was the great fortified capital of Trier (Augusta Trevorum). Trier had replaced Lyons as the first city of Gaul in the 3rd century AD and was progressively fortified and adorned under the emperors Postumus, Constantius Chlorus and Constantine, whose capital it was for six years (AD306–12). A huge basilica, baths, palace and gates – the still-surviving Porta Nigra – and the large area enclosed by its massive walls testify to its

wealth. Set about three days' march back from the Rhine frontier in the fertile Moselle valley, the city of Trier had good communications with the Rhine front to the east and with the rest of Gaul behind it. From it, one road ran due west to Reims, another north-east to Coblenz on the Rhine, another south-west.

The lower Rhine below Cologne, where the river often overflowed its banks and so was hard to patrol, was abandoned as a frontier, probably early in the 4th century AD. However, a new *limes* stretched west from Cologne along the line Maastricht–Tongre–Bavay–Tournai–Boulogne. Roman outposts remained as far north as the Rhine's mouth, but this *limes* linked the Rhineland with the Channel and so with Britain. South along the Rhine's banks ran a line of much-strengthened frontier forts, manned with *limitanei*. However, all fortifications were useless without enough soldiers. In AD383 a rebel general in Britain, Magnus Maximus, was proclaimed emperor by his troops. He crossed to Gaul and held court at Trier from where he ruled the westernmost three provinces and was recognized (reluctantly) by Theodosius I. When Magnus marched south into Italy in AD388 to be defeated by Theodosius, he must have taken troops from Gaul and Britain – mobile *comitatenses* rather than stationary *limitanei*. Both were needed in the north.

By AD395, after another round of civil wars, the empire was divided between the sons of Theodosius: the ineffectual Arcadius in the east and the even more incompetent Honorius in the west. Stilicho, a Vandal by birth but deeply Romanized, was to govern the western empire until his murder in AD408, in some ways very effectively, but his attention was focused on the Danube and Italy, to the fatal neglect of the Rhine.

Around AD400, Germany was in turmoil. Suebians, Burgundians, Gepids and Vandals (cousins of the Goths) were

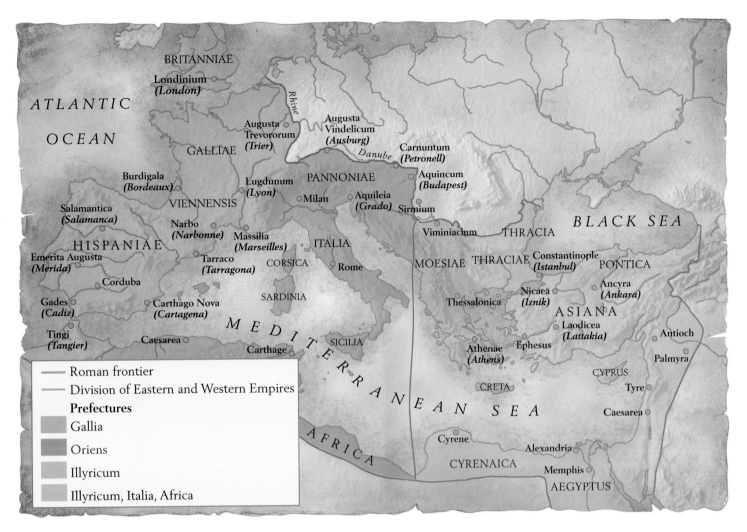

Roman frontier
Division of Eastern and Western Empires
Prefectures
Gallia
Oriens
Illyricum
Illyricum, Italia, Africa

pressing on older-established groupings such as the Franks and Alamanni, all of them alarmed by the advance of the Huns to the east. The winter of AD406–7 was unusually severe and the Rhine froze all the way down to the sea. On the very last day of AD406, a horde, perhaps 300,000 strong, led by the Vandals crossed the river. Trier was sacked so thoroughly it never recovered. (The fact that its great walls could not repulse the barbarians suggests that the city was hardly defended.) Other garrisons cowered uselessly behind their walls, deprived of the *comitatenses* essential to strike back. The barbarians pushed on through the frozen countryside, the Vandals finally crossing the Pyrenees into an almost undefended Spain. With them went the Suebians and the Alans, an Iranian people. The Burgundians turned due south, settling at first around Lake Geneva before expanding to occupy the

land that still bears their name. The Alammani took Alsace, annexing that area for the Germanic world. Meanwhile, further north, in a less rapid but more enduring conquest, the Franks were pushing slowly but irreversibly forward, first to the Somme, then to the Loire. By AD496 they had conquered most of Gaul, giving it a new name: France.

In AD416 the Visigoths, acting now as *foederati* for Rome, temporarily drove the invaders of Spain into the far north-west, but the Vandals were not defeated. By AD429 they had overrun southern Spain (whose name Andalucia recalls their stay) and soon after began their conquest of North Africa, Rome's vital granary. By AD439, they had captured its capital Carthage, the western empire's second city. They had completed a long and profitable journey from their crossing of the frozen Rhine. As a result, the western empire was now doomed.

Above: The Roman empire c.AD400.

Above: An ivory diptych (double panel) dated AD406 shows the consul Probus and Honorius, the disastrously ineffectual emperor of the west (AD395–423), in whose reign Rome was sacked by the Goths in AD410.

THE SACK OF ROME

Above: An ivory panel of Stilicho (c.AD365–408), the regent of the west for the child-emperor Honorius. Though a competent general, Stilicho's devious negotiations with the Goths finally led to his death and left Rome at their mercy.

Right: Alaric's Visigoths ride into Rome. In fact, Rome's capture and sack was less dramatic but still epochal.

The sack of Rome by the Visigoths in AD410, although a crucial moment in world history, was not as dramatic as many might expect. Pictures of wing-helmeted barbarians brandishing bloody axes over weeping maidens, while palaces, libraries and temples burn in the background, exaggerate. The actual sack, although damaging materially as well as psychologically, was, by the age's standards, restrained, partly because the Visigoths were Christians. In any case, Rome's fall was caused more by the imperial government's miscalculations and vacillations than by Gothic desire to ravage the city. What the Visigoths wanted – and finally got – were titles, land and money for serving as Rome's ultimately surprisingly faithful *foederati* in Gaul. The cause of the sack of Rome lies as much with incompetent Roman government as with rapacious invaders.

Stilicho, who became regent of the western empire for the child-emperor Honorius in AD395, seemed to spend as much time intriguing against his rivals in Constantinople, where he aspired to become regent, as in repelling invaders. However, he was good at the latter. On two occasions he had the Visigoths, led by Alaric, at his mercy after defeating them: in western Greece in AD395 and in northern Italy in AD402. Both times he let them escape, perhaps because his troops were incapable of pursuit or maybe for less honourable motives. Yet although he may have played the Goths off against the eastern government at times, he was no traitor; he was merely trying to use them as Theodosius I had done. This appeasement led to his death, when public opinion turned against him for the loss of Gaul to Vandal, Suebian and other invaders in AD408. His murder was followed by the slaughter of many German mercenaries in the Roman army and the exodus of 30,000 others to join Alaric, gravely weakening the field army.

After extracting titles and money from the eastern empire and pillaging the Balkans, Alaric decided that the west offered richer pickings. The news of the death of Stilicho, which left the empire without a protector, led to three further

Visigothic invasions of Italy, the first in October, AD408. Bypassing the fortified cities and moving south, the Goths reached Rome and marched on to the port of Ostia. The Aurelianic walls around Rome, which had recently been strengthened and repaired, presented formidable barriers that should have repelled almost any barbarian. However, Rome was a populous inland city: it could be starved into surrender.

The Visigoths themselves also faced starvation, for they had no supply train. The first siege ended inconclusively when Alaric accepted a huge bribe of 5,000lb (2,268kg) of gold, 30,000lb (13,600kg) of silver and 3,000lb (1,360kg) of pepper. The second siege ended when Alaric installed a puppet emperor, Attalus, in Rome, who made him Field Marshal of the West (*magister utriusque militum*). When Attalus failed to please Alaric, the latter marched for a third time on Rome. The Ravenna government may have been pursuing a policy of attrition, hoping that the Goths would starve faster than the citizens of Rome and so be forced to retreat. If so, the strategy failed lamentably. On the night of 24 August AD410, someone – a Roman concerned at the sufferings of starving citizens, a disaffected slave – opened the Salarian Gate and the Goths entered the Eternal City. The unthinkable had happened.

THE AFTERMATH OF THE SACK

The Goths spent a mere three days in Rome, which had no food for their hungry army. Although they did not destroy the great city, they ransacked it and when they rode south they took with them Galla Placidia, the 16-year-old half-sister of the emperor Honorius. The shock of the sack meanwhile travelled round the Roman world. In Bethlehem, St Jerome was stunned, and in Africa St Augustine was moved to write his masterpiece, *The City of God*, to rebut pagan allegations that Rome's fall was due to its desertion of its ancestral deities in favour of Christianity.

The Visigoths reached the Straits of Messina, as Alaric wanted to conquer Africa. However, storms dispersed his fleet and he himself died on the way back through Italy. (Legend says that he was buried under a river briefly diverted for the purpose.) His successor Ataulf led the Visigoths out of Italy into south-west Gaul, where he married Placidia, showering her with Roman booty. Constantius III, who now became co-emperor, refused to accept this situation. Using Rome's monopoly of naval forces, he drove the Goths into Spain, where Ataulf was killed. The next Visigothic king, Vallia, agreed to return Placidia to the Romans and become a *foederatus*, in exchange for receiving lands around Toulouse. In Spain, Vallia campaigned against barbarian invaders while Constantius, capturing the city of Arles, re-established partial Roman control over southern and central Gaul. By AD421, when Constantius died, the Roman empire in the west seemed to have survived the ultimate disaster. However, unnoticed by the court in Ravenna, the Vandals, escaping the Visigoths, had occupied Andalucia by AD422 and were casting their eyes on Africa.

Left: The Mausoleum of Galla Placidia (lived AD388–450) at Ravenna. She was the sister of the emperor Honorius, mother of Valentinian II and effective empress of the west in her later years. Though strong-willed, her rule was nearly as disastrous as her brother's due to her personal vendetta with Aetius, Rome's last great general.

Below: An early 5th-century AD ivory showing Serena, niece of the emperor Theodosius I, who married Stilicho. Although of Vandal ancestry, Stilicho was very much part of the Roman imperial establishment and not remotely "barbarous".

THE FALL OF ROME
HUNS, VANDALS AND AETIUS

Above: Alaric, king of the Huns (AD434–54), was Rome's most ferocious enemy, but he actually harmed the empire less than the cunning Vandal king Gaiseric, who seized Africa and sacked Rome itself in AD455.

As long as the western empire ruled the seas and could control Africa, the coasts of Spain, southern Gaul and Italy itself, it could hope to survive. However, the growing threat from the Huns, excessive preoccupation with Gaul at the expense of Africa and endless palace conspiracies combined to wreck the empire's last hopes of survival. When it finally collapsed, it did so almost unnoticed, having become irrelevant to most people.

The deaths of Constantius III in AD421 and Honorius two years later left Rome leaderless. Galla Placidia, Constantius' widow, managed, with east Roman help, to get her son Valentinian III on to the throne in Ravenna by AD425. Placidia was regent for her son at first. Unfortunately, she loathed Aetius, the Danubian-born soldier who now emerged as Rome's last effective general. Aetius had been a hostage of both the Visigoths and Huns. He got on well with the latter, understanding barbarians better than most Romans, but he was soon caught up in palace intrigues. Boniface, governor of Africa, first quarrelled with Placidia and then was reconciled, receiving the lofty title of *patricius*. Aetius, realizing that Placidia meant to destroy him, raised an army. With it, he fought Boniface in a great battle near Rimini. Although Boniface won, he died of his wounds and Aetius regained control of the government with Hunnish help by AD433. Meanwhile, Africa was being lost.

In AD429, Gaiseric, the Vandal king, led his 80,000 people across the Straits of Gibraltar into Africa. By AD431 he controlled the western African provinces. The recall of Boniface to Italy to fight Aetius allowed the Vandals to consolidate their conquests and they were accepted as *foederati* by Aetius. However, they soon resumed their attacks. By AD439, Gaiseric had captured Carthage, the second city in the western empire, giving him a fleet and control of the vital grain supply to Rome. The loss of Carthage was disastrous to the empire, but Ravenna agreed by a treaty of AD442 to accept the Vandals. Valentinian even promised to let his 5-year-old daughter marry Gaiseric's son, Huneric. Soon Gaiseric began extending his realm, capturing Sardinia, Corsica and Sicily, while his pirates raided as far as Greece. However, Aetius had his attention focused elsewhere.

In the AD430s Aetius had emerged as the clear arbiter of affairs in Gaul. In AD436 he called in the Huns to control the restless Burgundians – they killed 20,000 of them in battle – while his own troops drove the Visigoths back from Narbonne. In AD446, the despairing Britons even appealed to him for help, without success. By then, other even worse problems were emerging.

Below: This ivory shows Aetius, the last Roman general worthy of the name, presiding as consul over the games in Rome.

THE LAST VICTORY

In AD434 Attila became co-king of the Huns, whose empire stretched from Germany to the Volga. He soon killed his brother and terrorized the eastern empire into paying him tribute. In AD450 a new eastern emperor, Marcian (AD450–57), refused to pay any more. Attila turned for compensation to the weaker west where he had a strange excuse. Valentinian III's sister Honoria had had an affair with her steward. When this was discovered, she was kept in seclusion but smuggled a ring to Attila, asking for help. Seizing this excuse, and demanding half the empire as his dowry, Attila invaded Gaul. Only Paris resisted his 300,000 strong hordes and Attila sacked city after city with horrifying brutality. The Visigoths joined Aetius and, at Châlons sur Marne, their combined forces met Attila. The battle raged all day and left *cadavera vero innumera* (truly numberless corpses). The Romans threatened the Hunnish flank, but it was the Visigoths who bore the brunt and Theodoric, their king, was killed, which makes him an unsung saviour of western civilization. At the day's end, Attila decided to retreat for the only time in his life.

Next year, Attila invaded Italy. Aetius had no troops this time, but Pope Leo I rode north and somehow persuaded Attila to withdraw. Within two years he was dead, his empire disintegrating with him. Aetius, the architect of his defeat, did not live to enjoy it, however, for Valentinian III, in a jealous rage at the general who had outshone him, personally killed him. Early in AD455, two of Aetius' former soldiers killed Valentinian in turn, and the empire began its final decline. Gaiseric now appeared with a huge fleet, taking a leisurely 14 days to sack Rome, removing even the gilded roof tiles from the temples.

Various emperors, mostly puppets of German generals, followed over the next 20 years. Only Marjorian (AD457–61) deserves the title. He made a brave, if unsuccessful, attempt to defeat Gaiseric, before being murdered by Ricimer, the German power behind the throne. Finally, in AD476, the boy emperor mockingly called Romulus Augustulus – in reference to Rome's first king and first emperor – was deposed by another German, Odovacer. The imperial insignia were sent to Constantinople, the fiction being that the empire had been reunited. Few people outside Italy noticed.

Above: The Battle of Châlons sur Marne in AD451, when Aetius repulsed the Huns and their allies under Attila, was the last Roman victory, albeit one gained with Visigothic aid and resulting in little more than a draw. But Gaul was saved from the Huns.

WHY ROME FELL AND BYZANTIUM SURVIVED

Above: Theodora was allegedly a prostitute before she married the emperor Justinian. She then became one of the greatest empresses, rallying her despairing husband during the "Nike" riots and helping him rule the resurgent empire.

Right: The Mediterranean world c.AD526 after the final fall of Rome. Of the many barbarian successor states, Theodoric's Ostrogothic kingdom in Italy seemed far the strongest and richest, but it was soon reconquered by the Byzantines (east Romans), who had never accepted the loss of the west. Only the Franks and the still pagan Saxons formed enduring kingdoms.

Edward Gibbon, author of *The Decline and Fall of the Roman Empire* (1776), summarized the causes of Rome's fall as the "triumph of barbarism and religion". Gibbon meant that, while barbarians threatened the empire from outside, Christianity undermined it from within, encouraging men to neglect their duties as soldiers to become monks or priests. But his explanation ignores the survival of the more Christianized east Roman (Byzantine) empire for 1,000 years.

Some moralists once saw in the fall of the Rome the "wages of sin" – meaning sexual excesses. Debauchery, according to this theory, so rotted the moral fibre of once upright Romans that they could hardly crawl from their marble baths. They perhaps read Gibbon's description of the teenaged emperor Gordian III whose "22 acknowledged concubines and... 62,000 volumes attested the variety of his inclinations... it appears that both the one and the other were designed for use rather than ostentation". Gordian (reigned AD238–44) was an ineffectual emperor, but no historian today attributes his failure to his sex life or bibliophilia.

Most later Roman emperors were neither nerveless nor effete. The great soldier–emperors of the 3rd and 4th centuries AD, such as Aurelian, Constantine I or Valentinian I, were energetic, brave generals. Their military efforts were ultimately in vain, however. This has led historians to seek social and economic causes for Rome's fall.

A plausible culprit is malaria. This may have spread as deforestation of mountains led to the formation of more marshes ideal for malaria-bearing mosquitoes. Malaria reduced the overall population,

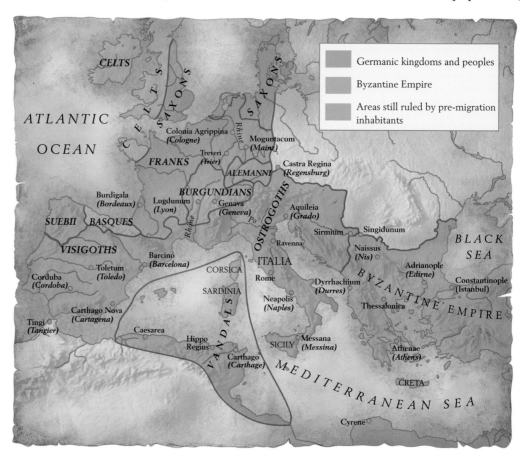

undermining the health of survivors. Similarly, plague, which hit the empire from AD165 on, must have played a part. But recent studies show that climate change did not affect the empire.

Each theory may explain an aspect of Rome's decline but cannot account for the survival of the similarly afflicted eastern empire. This rode out the 5th-century AD cataclysm relatively unharmed, to enjoy a golden age in the 6th century AD. Some historians have given up trying to explain the fall of Rome. Others have minimized the importance of imperial collapse, stressing the continuity of life in western Europe after AD476. Certainly, the German invaders had little new to offer, often perpetuating Roman customs. In Italy under the Ostrogoths c.AD500, the Senate still sat in Rome, aqueducts flowed and races were still run in the circus. Meanwhile, the Catholic Church expanded across western Europe and Latin survived, if mutating into varied forms. The one exception was Britain, where Anglo-Saxons deleted Romano-British culture. The Belgian historian Henri Pirenne argued that the real break between ancient and medieval worlds came in the 7th century AD with the Arab conquest. This divided the Mediterranean world, turning North Africa, Syria and Egypt away from Europe and towards the Islamic east.

For many people the question of why Rome fell remains as intriguing as ever. It is possible to discern major causes. Some were social and economic, a few were psychological and religious (shown by the growth in monasticism). However, political and military factors played an enormous and ultimately fatal part.

THE RICH–POOR DIVIDE
Essentially, Rome's civilization was urban, "a confederacy of cities". Although most of the empire's cities had 10–30,000 inhabitants, and only a handful were much bigger, most cities (outside Egypt) were self-governing. This was partly

because many had old and proud civic traditions, but more because the Principate lacked the governmental machinery for direct rule. Instead, it relied on unpaid officials, the decurions.

These men formed a middle group or class beneath the aristocracy of senators and equestrians. They included former centurions, local officials and landowners. From the 3rd century AD, this group was burdened with onerous tax demands by central governments. Faced with rebellions if they tried to collect the taxes and personal ruin if they did not – for the government made them personally liable – some decurions abandoned urban life altogether and withdrew to the country. Urban life, once so vigorous, decayed.

The plight of the peasants was worse. Most land was cultivated by labourers working as tenants for large landowners. After AD200, facing increasingly heavy taxation, some peasants became outlaws – central Gaul was ruled by the Bagaudae robber league – but most sought the protection of landowners to defend them from rapacious officials. This hurt both imperial revenues and farming. By AD400, up to a third of agricultural land in Africa, the west's most productive region, had gone out of cultivation.

Above: Justinian I (AD527–65), here shown in mosaics at Ravenna flanked by his courtiers, was the greatest east Roman, or Byzantine, emperor. He reconquered half the western empire and ordered the final and permanent codification of Roman law.

Below: The Cathedral of Hagia Sophia (Holy Wisdom) was Justinian's supreme monument in Constantinople (Istanbul), marking a radical development in late Roman architecture. Later a mosque, it is today a museum.

Above: Constantine I (AD306-37) was the effective if unwitting founder of the Byzantine empire by choosing Byzantium, so superbly sited, as his new capital, and also by converting to Christianity.

MILITARIZATION, BARBARIZATION

Under the Republic, civilians had usually controlled the military. Citizens were expected to fight for the city but were forbidden to bear arms within the city's sacred *pomerium* (boundary). Augustus upheld this tradition. In Rome he was merely *princeps*, first citizen. The Praetorian guard, although really part of the regular army, was always seen as different. This noble fiction, fraying as early as Domitian, survived until the reign of Septimius Severus (AD193–211). Under the Severans, who posted a legion near Rome, the reality of military power became brutally apparent.

After Gallienus (AD253–68) banned senators from army commands, most civilians lost all experience of – and taste for – military life. The military became a caste apart, recruited no longer from the cities but from less Romanized border peoples such as the Illyrians. Increasingly, these were supplemented by non-Roman auxiliaries. Earlier emperors had employed auxiliaries, but these had been under Roman command. From the time of Constantine, however, Germans came to dominate the best regiments, the *Palatini*. After the disaster at Adrianople in AD378, whole peoples of dubious loyalty, like the Visigoths, were enrolled in the Roman armies. If barbarians never accepted Rome's draconian discipline, soon Roman troops also rejected it. Vegetius, writing *c.*AD400, lamented the decline of the old discipline, which had once made the Roman soldier so effective. Even worse, Roman armies too often fought each other.

CIVIL WARS WITHOUT END

"The Roman world is collapsing… Fighting among ourselves costs us more than fighting our enemies." The lament of St Jerome from Bethlehem in Palestine comes from AD396, just as the western empire began to collapse. Jerome was primarily worried about the Huns then threatening the eastern provinces, but his diagnosis was accurate. Even when the empire was being overrun, pretenders still denuded frontiers of their garrisons.

A crucial weakness of the Roman empire was its lack of an accepted system of succession. Monarchies are normally hereditary. In theory, the empire was not a monarchy, but emperors exploited dynastic feeling where they could, even if they had catastrophic heirs. Diocletian devised an elaborate succession for the Tetrarchy. Unfortunately, he ignored hereditary sentiment among the army and imperial contestants themselves, so that his system, too, failed. Armies continued to proclaim emperors to the end. In AD407, troops in Britain followed the pretender Constantine to Gaul, thereby stripping Britain of its last troops.

The main imperial government behaved no better. The two most capable west Roman generals of the 5th century, Stilicho and Aetius, both fell victim to palace coups. Personal feuds between generals, encouraged by the empress Galla Placidia, led to the loss of Africa to the Vandals. Such court conspiracies were far worse in the west than the east.

Left: The double walls of Constantinople, built by the emperor Theodosisus II in the 5th century AD, made a vital contribution to the Byzantine empire's long survival.

Byzantine Empire 527

Justinian's reconquests

BYZANTIUM'S STRENGTHS

The most obvious strength of the eastern empire was Constantinople's superb site. Its brilliantly fortified peninsula, coupled with a control of the sea that the Byzantines retained for centuries, made it impregnable to direct attack until the advent of gunpowder. (It fell to the crusaders in 1204 only through treachery.) Any enemy coming from the Danube would find his way blocked by its double walls. Persian and Arab invaders could not reach the European provinces. Its double walls protected not only palaces, libraries and churches, but also warehouses and workshops, for Constantinople became a great manufacturing and trading city, unlike Rome. Its many inhabitants considered themselves Christian Romans – "*Romaoi*" in Greek, the language they soon came to speak exclusively.

The eastern empire was also far richer than the west. Cities such as Antioch, Alexandria and Smyrna remained great trading centres. With their deep-rooted urban traditions, they survived to profit from the general economic recovery by AD500. The east was fortunate in that the Persian front was quiet at this time. Persia had problems of its own. This let eastern emperors concentrate on their short European frontiers. If Goths and Huns ravaged the Balkans in the 5th century, the rest of the eastern empire avoided direct attack.

In the early 6th century, the emperor Anastasius I (AD491–518), a financial genius, reorganized the army and left a full treasury. Under the rule of Justinian I (AD527–65) a splendid Byzantine culture emerged, embodied in the cathedral of Hagia Sophia (Holy Wisdom), with its radical new design and gold-crusted two-dimensional art. East Roman power reached westward, reconquering Africa and Italy. Byzantium retained outposts in southern Italy until 1071. By shielding Europe from Arab attack for so long, Byzantium helped the survival of western Christian civilization as well as its own.

Above: The Byzantine Empire in the 5th and 6th centuries AD, showing Justinian's reconquest of the richer parts of the west.

Below: St Irene Church in Constantinople (Istanbul).

INDEX

ACKNOWLEDGEMENTS

Ancient Art and Architecture Collection: 36, 97t, 103, 140b, 162t, 164t, 165b, 168t, 174b, 181b, 185t, 198t, 212t.
The Art Archive: 5b, 10c, 12l, 12r, 33b, 44t, 45, 49t, 51b, 52t, 55, 58-59, 66t, 70t, 72b, 73t, 75b, 76t, 78, 79, 82, 85, 87b, 175b, 254t, /The Bodleian Library 166, 169b, 237t, /Dagli Orti 18t, 20t, 30b, 41b, 42b, 94t, 95b, 96t, 100t, 101b, 102, 104t, 105t, 107t, 112b, 113, 114t, 115t, 116t, 123, 128-9, 130-1, 137t, 138, 139b, 141b, 145, 151t, 159b, 167t, 168b, 182t, 184t, 187b, 195t, 196t, 197, 207b, 208, 209b, 216-17, 220, 224b, 225, 227, 229, 231t, 233b, 238, 239b, 240t, 241, 243t, 244t, 248t, 256b, /Museo Prenestino Palestrina 19t, 148b, 150, /National Achaeological Museum Chieti 137b, /National Museum Bucharest 142-143.
Bridgeman Art Library: 12c, 29b, 33t, 46b, 53t, 57, 62t, 69, 75t, 120b, 122b, 126b, 127b, 175t, 183b, 192t, 230, 242t, 243b, /Index 203, /Lauros Giraudon 186, 224t.
Colchester Museums: 153.
Corbis: 8t, 73b, 83, 84b, 88t, /Paul Almasy 4, 71t, 190t, 252, /Archivo Iconografico 13c, 24b, 50b, 67b, 108t, 109t, 114b, 117, 120t, 125b, 144b, 146, 151b, 164b, 199, 206, 235, 245, 255t, /Arte & Imagini srl, 109b, /Nathan Benn 214b, /Yann Arthus-Bertrand 115b, /Dave Bartruff 25t, /Bettmann 49b, 53b, 125t, 171b, 190b, 222t, /James P Blair 8b, /Jonathan Blair 88b, /Burstein Collection 46t, /Michael Busselle 204b, /Christie's Images 5t, 10r, 14-15, /Dean Conger 119, 209t, /Robert Estall 65b, 155, 156t, 251t, /Macduff Everton 112t, /Shai Ginott 215t, /Jason Hawkes 127t, 192b, /John & Dallas Heaton 29t, /Lindsay Hebberd 202b, /John Heseltine 22b, /Chris Hellier 249, /Historical Picture Archive 212b, /John Howard Cordaiy Photo Library Ltd 236t, /Hulton – Deutsch 43b, /Hanan

Isachar 121, 156b, /Mimmo Jodice 106t, /Bob Krist 191, /Paul H Kuiper 176t, /Charles & Josette Lenars 144t, 148t, 149, 167b, 180, 214t, 215b, /Araldo de Luca 16-17, 68t, 70b, 122t, 133, 139t, 140t, 152, 160-1, 174t, 178-9, 185b, 188, 255b, /Franz-Marc Frei 44b, /Francis G Mayer 10l, 13l, 63t, 218, /Michael Nicholson 54t, 157t, /North Carolina Museum of Art 27t, /Richard T Nowitz 54b, 184b, /Dagli Orti 11l, 52b, /Polypix Eye Ubiquitous 237b, /Vittoriano Rastelli 157b, /Carmen Redondo 35t, /Scheufler Collection 20b, /Grant Smith 141t, /Roman Soumar 173t, /Stapleton Collection 74, /Vince Streano 236b, /Liba Taylor 47t, /Gustavo Tomsich 1, 23b, 250t, /Ruggero Vanni 35b, 72t, 98-9, 135t, 172b, 226, 240b, 248b, /Vanni Archive 97b, 106b, 172t, 232b, 234t, /Sandro Vannini 48t, 195b, /Patrick Ward 116b, 126t, 173b, 200-1,

/K M Westermann 211t, /Nik Wheeler 110-11, 165t, /Wild Country 194, /Peter M Wilson 247b, /Roger Wood 7, 9b, 89, 91t, 94b, 132, 171t, 211b, 219t, 221, 234b, 250b, 256t, /Adam Woolfitt 101t, 158, 176b, 196b, 233t, 239t.
Dr Jon Coulston: 135b.
Dr Hazel Dodge: 24t, 181t.
Mary Evans Picture Library: 11c, 13r, 23t, 37, 136, 193b, 242b.
Getty Images /Bridgeman: 25b.
Robert Harding Picture Library: 19b.
www.miniatures.de<http://www.miniatures.de>: 154, 205.
Scala, Florence: 2-3, 6, 9t, 11r, 18b, 21, 22t, 26, 28, 30t, 31, 32, 34, 38-9, 40, 41t, 42t, 43t, 47b, 48b, 50t, 51t, 56, 63, 64, 65t, 66b, 67t, 68b, 71b, 76b, 77, 80-1, 84t, 86, 87t, 90, 91b, 92, 93, 95t, 96b, 100b, 104b, 105b, 107b, 108b, 118, 124, 134, 159t, 162b, 163, 169t, 170, 198b, 202t, 204t, 207t, 213, 219b, 222b, 228, 231b, 244b, 246, 247t, 251b, 253, 254b.